■ *MANAGING INDUSTRIAL CONFLICT:*
SEVEN MAJOR DISPUTES

Sander Meredeen

*Senior Lecturer, Department of Industrial Relations,
University of Strathclyde, Glasgow, Scotland*

D1337404

Hutchinson
London Melbourne Auckland Johannesburg

Hutchinson Education

An imprint of Century Hutchinson Ltd
62–65 Chandos Place, London WC2N 4NW

Century Hutchinson Australia Pty Ltd
PO Box 496, 16–22 Church Street, Hawthorn, Melbourne,
Victoria 3122, Australia

Century Hutchinson New Zealand Limited
PO Box 40–086, Glenfield, Auckland 10.
New Zealand

Century Hutchinson South Africa (Pty) Ltd
PO Box 337, Bergvlei, 2012 South Africa

First published in 1988

© Sander Meredeen 1988

Set in 10/11 Linotron Sabon
by Input Typesetting Ltd., London
Printed and bound in Great Britain by
Anchor Brendon, Tiptree, Essex

British Library Cataloguing in Publication Data
Meredeen, Sander
  Managing Industrial Conflict.
  1. Great Britain. Industrial relations Disputes. Management aspects
  I. Title
  658.3'15'0941

ISBN 0–09–173226–3

For Bruce and Clive
■ *in admiration and with abiding love* ■

Hi-nay mah tov u-mah na'im
Shevet achim gum yachad

What could be better or more heart-warming
Than brothers who live together in harmony?

Psalm cxxxiii

WAR *consisteth not in battle only, or the act of fighting; but in a*
tract of time, wherein the will to contend by battle is sufficiently
known; and therefore the notion of time is to be considered in the
nature of war; as it is in the nature of weather. For as the nature
of foul weather, lieth not in a shower or two of rain; but in an
inclination thereto of many days together: so the nature of war
consisteth not in actual fighting; but in the known disposition
thereto, during all the time there is not assurance to the contrary.
All other time is PEACE.

Thomas Hobbes: *Leviathan* I, 13

A wise prince must observe these rules: he must never take things
easy in times of peace, but rather use the latter assiduously, in order
to be able to reap the profit in times of adversity. Then, when his
fortunes change, he will be found ready to resist adversity . . .

As for intellectual training, the prince must read history, studying
the actions of eminent men to see how they conducted themselves
during war and to discover the reasons for their victories or their
defeats, so that he can avoid the latter and imitate the former.

Niccolo Machiavelli: *The Prince* Ch. XIV
(Translated by George Bull)

CONTENTS

ABBREVIATIONS USED IN THE TEXT

ACAS	Advisory Conciliation and Arbitration Service
AEU	Amalgamated Engineering Union
AUEW	Amalgamated Union of Engineering Workers
BACM	British Association of Colliery Managers
BSC	British Steel Corporation
CBI	Confederation of British Industry
CEGB	Central Electricity Generating Board
CRP	Colliery Review Procedure
CSEU	Confederation of Shipbuilding and Engineering Unions
EEF	Engineering Employers' Federation
EEPTU	Electrical, Electronic, Plumbing and Telecommunications Union
EIS	Educational Institute of Scotland
GMBATU	General Municipal Boilermakers and Allied Trades Union
GMWU	General and Municipal Workers Union
HTA	Head Teachers Association
ILO	International Labour Organization
ISTC	Iron and Steel Trades Confederation
ITO	International Thomson Organization
NACODS	National Association of Colliery Overmen, Deputies and Shotfirers
NAS/UWT	National Association of Schoolmasters/Union of Women Teachers
NATSOPA	National Society of Operative Printers and Assistants (now SOGAT)
NCB	National Coal Board
NEC	National Executive Committee
NGA	National Graphical Association
NUB	National Union of Blastfurnacemen
NUJ	National Union of Journalists
NUM	National Union of Mineworkers
NUT	National Union of Teachers
NUVB	National Union of Vehicle Builders
PAT	Professional Association of Teachers
SOGAT	Society of Graphical and Allied Trades
TGWU	Transport and General Workers Union
TUC	Trades Union Congress
UDM	Union of Democratic Mineworkers

PART /

■ TOOLS OF ANALYSIS

CHAPTER 1

■ Why study conflict management?

The strike is amongst the most highly publicized and least studied social phenomena of our time.

Joel Seidman, Professor of Industrial Relations, University of Chicago in *Foreword* to Bernard Karsh: *Diary of a Strike* (1958)

In embarking on this study of conflict management, the author makes one fundamental assumption: namely, that industrial conflict is here to stay. In recent years, the number of officially reported industrial disputes in Britain has fallen dramatically — from an average of around 3500 separate disputes in the mid-1960s — to an all-time low of 900 in 1987. With certain noteworthy exceptions, which constitute the basic material for this study, the vast majority of these disputes continue to be small in scale, involve relatively few workers and are soon over. Such dry statistics have emboldened some commentators to conclude that Britain has passed its historical high watermark of industrial conflict. The strike is said to have gone 'out of fashion' as a means of resolving industrial disputes, having been displaced by 'the new realism'. Similar optimistic claims have been made in the past — not always supported by later history.

Other commentators, of less sanguine or more radical persuasion, have responded by observing that since the primary causes of industrial conflict remain largely unaltered — injustice, exploitation, the inequalities of power, income and status — whether under capitalist, socialist or so-called 'social-market' economies, conflict has not been removed but has simply gone 'underground'. Conflict is still very much present, they argue, but it exists below our viewing horizon from whence it will shortly spring with renewed vigour. At that point, it is asserted, industrial conflict will re-emerge with increased ferocity, because the stakes will then be even higher than they are today.

We do not propose to enter the lists of that argument, for we are not concerned here with explaining *why* there is industrial conflict or whether the level of such conflict in Britain or elsewhere is likely to increase or decrease in future years. We do not address those specific problems, important though they are. Instead of setting out from the usual assumption of social harmony and industrial cooperation in order to explain the emergence of conflict, we set out from the opposite assumption: namely, that conflict between individuals and groups in their working relationships is an inevitable — some indeed would say a necessary and even a desirable — feature of *all* human societies.

We are, therefore, less concerned with *why* conflict exists than with *how* that conflict is managed. We seek to explore the motives and to understand the behaviour of those who engage in industrial conflict; to examine their objectives; to discover why they choose particular strategies and tactics to help them achieve their objectives; to find out whether or not those strategies and tactics succeed, and why.

The principal focus of attention here lies less in *individual* conflict — though that certainly provides the staple content of most contemporary novels, stage, film and television drama — and more in the character and outcome of the peculiar form of conflict that seems to be woven into the texture of contemporary society — namely, the *collective* conflict that arises between the competing interest groups that make up the working life of all liberal democratic (i.e. capitalist) societies.

Such conflict takes place amongst many diverse groups:

(i)   between the capitalist owners of property and the propertyless working class;

(ii)   between managers and supervisors of enterprises in both the private and public sectors and those whom they manage and supervise;

(iii)   between skilled workers who have completed a lengthy training or apprenticeship and those who are deemed to be 'unskilled' or 'semi-skilled';

(iv)   between production and maintenance workers; young workers and older workers; men and women workers; black and white workers; night-shift and day-shift workers; and so on.

In short, the possibility of industrial conflict exists amongst the members of the widest variety of potentially cooperative but frequently antagonistic interest groups working in contemporary organizations. Each episode of conflict may be described as a limited trial of strength intended to preserve or, more usually, to modify the industrial status quo — that is, to bring about some change in the rules that regulate the relationships of individuals and groups in employment.

In the second half of the twentieth century, intermittent conflict between management and unions has become a hallmark of all the advanced industrial societies. Such conflict disrupts the normal rhythm of wealth creation and the steady distribution of goods, services and incomes of all kinds. The more technologically advanced and interdependent the economy, the greater the disruption caused by so-called 'industrial action' — a late twentieth century euphemism for industrial *inaction* of all kinds.

The inconvenience, discomfort, distress and deprivation suffered by many citizens as a result of a particular episode of conflict has been reflected in the widespread and growing demand that governments should introduce stronger labour laws to regulate employment relationships more closely and to restrict the scope for industrial conflict. Yet, despite some bold and imaginative attempts by successive British governments to introduce such laws to prevent or to curb the level of industrial conflict, management and unions continue to resort periodically to strikes and lock-outs, together with a variety of lesser forms of economic sanctions, to achieve some desired change in the industrial status quo.

The disruption caused to the economy and the suffering inflicted on the general public by industrial disputes are seen by strikers as a regrettable but largely unavoidable consequence of the failure of their employer to grant some concession in the course of collective bargaining that would render industrial action unnecessary. It may be noted in passing that in the majority of strikes that affect the general public, strikers normally take steps to alleviate any severe hardship to those least able to defend themselves against such disruption — for example, by seeking to maintain power and other supplies to hospitals and similar essential services. That said, the rest of the community is expected to suffer in silence, or, better still, to understand the causes of the dispute, to accept the legitimacy of the strikers' action and, wherever possible, to mobilize itself into some form of mass pressure group or lobby to help bring the dispute to a speedy conclusion, by the application of public opinion and political pressure-group action.

In some cases, such strategy on the part of the strikers pays off, as when the government intervenes to help end the dispute. In other cases, public opinion swings against the strikers and in favour of government non-intervention. In either case, public opinion constitutes an increasingly significant constituency to which the three principal parties — employers, workers and the State — must have continuous regard throughout any major industrial dispute. The Deputy Leader of Britain's Opposition Labour Party, reviewing the role of the media in the protracted miners' strike of 1984–85, assessed the importance of public opinion in these terms:

> *In democracies, strikes are determined by public opinion. It may be that the people would never have backed the miners. But winning them over is what the media battle ought to have been about. That should have been the strategy.* [1]

Yet, despite their obvious undesirable consequences, we should not assume that the outcomes of every major industrial dispute are wholly detrimental or destructive of advanced industrial societies. Collective bargaining between management and unions is one part of the sophisticated mechanisms developed by most advanced industrial societies for the anticipation, prevention and resolution of such protracted conflict. It is the widespread, almost universal acceptance and practice of collective bargaining which helps to convert potentially *destructive* conflict into *constructive* conflict — that is, conflict which aims at the resolution of long-held and legitimate claims and grievances that inevitably emerge amongst the diverse and competing interest groups of every liberal democratic society.

Collective bargaining does not, of course, remove the sources of such conflict, but it does help to resolve it in many cases. In other words, collective bargaining diverts conflict by institutional means into channels where it can do least harm to the social fabric. 'For us', wrote the distinguished German sociologist, Ralf Dahrendorf, 'the essential fact is that by collective bargaining the frozen fronts of industrial conflict are thawed'. [2]

Before condemning all such episodes of conflict as disruptive to the workings of modern interdependent economies, we should perhaps reflect on the issues that give rise to such conflict, the ways in which specific episodes of conflict are managed, and the costs and benefits of their final outcomes. If our society appears threatened by too much conflict, we should pause to consider the kind of society in which such conflict is suppressed. Is it the existence of industrial conflict itself that we find so disturbing? Or the widespread extent and the increasing ferocity of such conflict? Are we not most concerned with how such conflict is handled? In other words, how well or how badly do we manage that inevitable industrial conflict?

In attempting to describe, to analyse, to understand and to explain how industrial conflict is managed, we shall be drawn into the discussion of human behaviour in one of its most complex settings, for the collectivity — the workgroup, the strike meeting, the top management policy review — is an amorphous entity whose behaviour rarely conforms to any consistent internal logic. In employment relations, the apparent rationality that leads workers and managers to behave in a particular way at the outset of an industrial dispute may be transformed into quite different and less comprehensible rationalities during the course of that dispute. The role of the irrational should never be underestimated in the conduct of human affairs — least of all, perhaps, in labour disputes that touch upon such fundamental issues as human dignity, pride in craft, the threat to self-respect and status, as well as the potential loss of jobs and incomes. A dispute that appears to an outsider to be susceptible to cool analysis and speedy resolution will often prove intractable because the living experience of that dispute is felt quite differently by those who are directly and immediately involved.

The present study will develop and apply a form of reconstructive analysis to seven major British disputes that have taken place over the last twenty years. Such an analysis seeks not merely to explain the origins of such disputes but also to trace the consistent configuration through which every major dispute passes, from its origin to its resolution. For, if conflict is inevitable, we need to understand something more than its immediate and underlying causes, its incidence and its manifestations. We also need to understand how employers and employees, management and unions come to define their policy objectives; how they seek to mobilize their resources and increase pressure on their bargaining partners (opponents or adversaries), thereby helping to overcome resistance and so achieve their policy objectives in industrial conflict.

Following this introductory chapter, Chapter 2 deals with the analysis of conflict management. It examines briefly the problem of bias in reporting and interpreting the 'facts' of an industrial dispute — the motives of the principal protagonists as well as the strategies and tactics employed by both sides. Chapter 2 ends by introducing a seven-stage analytical model of industrial disputes, together with a set of seven critical questions in dispute analysis.

Part II is devoted to the reconstructive analysis of seven major British disputes. A brief introduction answers the question: Why these disputes? This is followed by seven self-contained chapters, each devoted to one particular dispute and the central underlying issues.

Part III examines the lessons to be drawn from the experience of conflict, described and analysed in Part II. Chapter 10 summarizes those lessons before going on to propose four sets of practical guidelines for the better management of industrial conflict by those primarily involved — policy-makers, employers and managers, employees and trade unions, and third parties. Chapter 11 offers a summary and conclusions, which draw together the main argument of the book.

In this study the author has concentrated on the more immediate practical issues of managing major episodes of conflict in Britain over the past 20 years. He has deliberately refrained from ambitious sociological theorizing or the attempt to draw useful comparisons and contrasts between the management of industrial conflict in different contemporary societies. Such theoretical and comparative studies are certainly required if we are to advance the study of conflict management and contribute to its improvement. Readers who seek new academic and theoretical insights into conflict processes and resolution are referred to the companion volume *Managing Industrial Conflict: Theory, Practice and Policy*, in which the author sets out to integrate the conclusions of this study into a wider conceptual and theoretical framework. For a comparative dimension, readers are referred to a third volume by the same author — *Managing Industrial Conflict: Seven Major North American Disputes*.

REFERENCES

1 Roy Hattersley: 'There was no strategy — just day after day of cleverly executed tactics', The Listener Review of Books, *The Listener*, 8 May 1986, p. 22.
2 Ralf Dahrendorf: *Class and Class Conflict in Industrial Societies*, Routledge & Kegan Paul, London, 1959, p. 260.

CHAPTER 2

■ The analysis of conflict management

A labour Clausewitz, able to treat the subject and analyse in sufficient detail the strategic and tactical conditions of successful striking, is still unpublished.

Nachum Barou, quoted by K. G. J. C. Knowles: *Strikes: A Study in Industrial Conflict* (1952)

RECONSTRUCTIVE ANALYSIS OF INDUSTRIAL DISPUTES

In setting out to analyse the management of an industrial dispute, it is first necessary to reconstruct the events that compose the dispute. Despite the rich variety of their contexts, their diverse subject matter, their distinctive origins and initially inscrutable outcomes, all industrial disputes are susceptible to reconstructive analysis, which renders them more intelligible to those who are not directly involved.

This reconstructive analysis will need to take into account the subjective meaning and significance of the dispute to those directly involved. However, the subjective version of events given by the principal protagonists in an industrial dispute must obviously be treated with caution, for we need to guard against the selective interpretation of events in which we ourselves have been closely involved.

All human perception is inevitably selective in scope, limited in range and subjective in character. We observe events from a particular geographical, historical and ideological standpoint — our personal 'window on the world'. The particular disputes that we choose to study, the 'facts' that we elicit about those disputes, and the value that we place on those 'facts' pose similar problems for professional historians, for seasoned journalists and for students of industrial relations, all of whom struggle to reconstruct and make sense of a sequence of historical events. The solution to these problems must lie in a soundly-based social science training, more specifically in historical analysis, followed by years of practice in trying to make sense of 'what happened in history'. Above all, perhaps, we need to honour the complexities of our subject matter and to be aware of our own bias.

Expressing concern at the threat posed by the Government's education cuts to scholarship, science and society, Peter Slee recently focused attention on the particular intellectual value of such training in historical analysis.

> ... *the student should be aware that history is made by historians, that every historian is directed to the past by things which interest him in the present. He cannot escape the inbuilt bias that determines not only what he considers as 'relevant' to his investigation but also how he interprets that evidence. Historical problems generate historiographical controversies and at the heart of every disagreement lies a different approach. It is a skill indeed to uncover the basis of a man's thought and to understand how it affects his approach to a pressing problem. It is a skill sadly lacking in the handling of industrial disputes and in man-management generally but one which can, with care, be developed systematically by problem-solving exercises.* [1]

When the veteran Labour Editor of a leading British newspaper set out to provide an 'objective' account of a major industrial dispute within his own publishing house, he soon found himself confronted with some typical problems of historical analysis:

> *Few events in the dispute were unambiguous. If I talked to two people straight out of the same meeting, I got two different versions of what happened.* [2]

When reconstructing and analysing the events in an industrial dispute, therefore, it is essential to distinguish between facts as we experience them and our own subjective interpretation of those facts. But which facts? Or, rather, whose facts? For, as students of social history, we must recognize from the outset that, in reconstructing an industrial dispute, we are not merely 'fact-gatherers' or 'fact-analysts'. The particular facts that we choose to gather and the way we approach their analysis will reflect our existing ideas of what is and what is not significant:

> *The idea that one can trace the causal connections of any events without employing a theory, or that such a theory will emerge automatically from the accumulation of a sufficient amount of facts, is of course sheer illusion. The complexity of social events in particular is such that, without the tools of analysis which a systematic theory provides, one is almost bound to misinterpret them.* [3]

In other words, we already impart some degree of personal bias and exercise some value-judgements when selecting the material that we choose to analyse. Whilst we may never entirely free ourselves from that bias or arrive at 'value-free' judgements of social events, we need to be conscious of and, as far as possible, to discount our own ideological preferences. For we always operate under a prior set of theoretical assumptions about our world and the way in which it works. Such theoretical assumptions define our ideological position and, in turn, lead us to select one or more sets of 'facts' for the initial analysis.

Marxists have laid particular stress on the need for theory in the writing of history. In the words of the historian, Werner Sombart:

> *Facts are like beads; they require a string to hold them together . . . No theory — no history.* [4]

The British sociologist, Vic Allen, has written in much the same vein:

> *There is no such phenomenon as an objective social fact; that is, a fact which retains its meaning and significance to all users and in all circumstances. Data derives its meaning from the manner in which it is used and this, in turn, depends on the conceptual orientation of the user.* [5]

Some twenty years earlier, an American sociologist, Bernard Karsh, reflected on the same issue from a non-marxist standpoint. More specifically, he questioned the meaning and value of the 'facts' that we select for analysis in an industrial dispute:

> *Facts do not speak for themselves: they have no intrinsic meaning or value. They take their meaning and their value from the way they are bound together by theory. That is, facts become meaningful as they are lifted from the level of the fortuitous and related to the more abstract . . .*
>
> *Facts are empirically verifiable observations, but they are never gathered at random. They may be gathered in accordance with an unconscious preference, or they may be gathered in terms of some systematic scheme. For the scientist, facts are meaningful products of efforts to relate them to a point of view. Science seeks to structure facts in some consistent fashion so that an orderly relationship is established between and among the facts. This logical structure or systematic scheme we call 'theory'.* [6]

In the pages that follow, we hope to be consciously aware of our own bias but shall not devote much time to the vain pursuit of objectivity. Instead, we shall follow Karsh's advice, seeking to maintain a clear distinction between facts as 'empirically verifiable observations' and facts as 'meaningful products', related to a particular point of view. Following Karsh, we believe that 'what happened in history' depends on which 'history' — *whose* story — we choose to believe. More simply, what happens in an industrial dispute depends very much on *who you are* and *where you stand* in relation to that particular dispute. The answers given to those questions will largely determine *which* reports of the dispute you regard as being significant, as subsequently interpreted after considerable reflection, with the benefit of the only *perfect* science — hindsight.

TYPICAL CONFIGURATION OF INDUSTRIAL DISPUTES

Despite superficial differences in their timing, their subject matter, their duration and their outcomes, all industrial disputes may be viewed as short-term episodes of (generally) disruptive conflict between two or more collective interest groups within a continuing employment relationship. Such disruptive episodes frequently comprise emotionally-charged, dramatic events because each side seeks to advance its own interests and to maximize its own advantage by threatening or imposing economic sanctions against the other side.

In theory, each side purports to be acting rationally in pursuit of its own 'legitimate' objectives. In practice, both sides act from a mixture of motives, seeking to achieve all or most of their own objectives and/or to frustrate the other side from achieving theirs. Each side seeks to exploit a favourable conjuncture of circumstances (e.g. a shift in the existing balance of power) to achieve some immediate, intermediate or ultimate benefit under the existing rules or agreements between the parties, or to change those rules or agreements in its own favour.

Inherent in every such episode of conflict is the actual use or implied threat of graduated sanctions by one side against the other. Sanctions applied by organized labour may take a wide variety of forms, ranging from a token stoppage of work, through the imposition of a limited or open-ended overtime ban, work-to-rule, withholding of cooperation, to the ultimate resort: an open-ended all-out strike. On the side of management, sanctions may range from a reduction in overtime working, through the lay-off of some proportion of the total workforce, to the ultimate use of the collective lock-out of all employees — the exact equivalent on the employers' side to an open-ended all-out strike on the part of employees.

The *occasion* of an industrial dispute (i.e. the timing and circumstances of its origin) must be distinguished carefully from its underlying *cause(s)*. First impressions of the cause of a dispute cannot be accepted at face value, for the root causes of an industrial dispute are frequently complex and rarely immediately visible. They are often deeply buried within the context of a specific organization at a particular stage of its economic development, within a much wider social, economic and political setting. Industrial disputes do not simply 'happen'. They usually have a well-defined pattern of causation, even though the weighting attached to different causal factors will vary with the standpoint and ideological preferences of the conflict analyst.

In one of the earliest-known attempts to discover an analytical model, applicable to all kinds of labour disputes, Hiller (1928) drew a distinction between four stages of a strike: (i) mobilization, (ii) preparation, (iii) maintenance and (iv) demobilization. [7] Such a model may be useful in *strike analysis* but less useful for *industrial dispute analysis*, where terms like *mobilization* and *demobilization* seem less appropriate.

Over thirty years ago, a group of American sociologists (Gouldner, 1954; Kornhauser, 1954; Merton, 1957) progressively sharpened the distinction between 'manifest' issues (i.e. issues that express immediately apparent or overt discontent) and 'latent' issues (i.e. issues that express more hidden or submerged discontent). In their valuable case study on the national steel strike of 1980, Hartley, Kelly and Nicholson (1983) note that 'some authors have attempted to circumvent potentially hazardous philosophical disputes on the meaning of causation,'[8] in industrial disputes by adopting this distinction between manifest and latent issues. Whilst acknowledging the utility of the distinction, Hartley, Kelly and Nicholson consider that 'the emergence, instigation and progress of a strike is better captured by using a threefold distinction between underlying *issues*, strike *triggers*, and strike *demands*'.

Once again, that threefold distinction may prove useful for the analysis of union-initiated strike causation but appears less relevant for the equivalent analysis of management-initiated disputes.

In seeking to interpret and understand the significance of any major industrial dispute, we must attempt to reconstruct the sequence of events that made up the dispute, focusing first on the historical and organizational environment in which the dispute has taken place. Having located the dispute in its wider economic and political context, we may then seek to trace the course of the dispute from its earliest origins to its final settlement, not neglecting the important aftermath, in which the dust settles on the dispute as the parties adapt themselves to a new or modified relationship. Such an approach should enable us to develop a reconstructive analysis of the dispute, based on our own subjective observation and interpretation of events, together with those of the protagonists themselves and of other well-informed commentators. Given patience, it should be possible, by this means, to arrive at a set of reasoned and balanced judgements on the dispute — in particular, to discover how far the outcomes of the dispute reflect each side's declared or implicit objectives — and how far each side's conduct or management of the dispute helped to bring about those outcomes.

To provide a convincing reconstructive analysis of a major industrial dispute, the conflict analyst must show what transpired at *seven crucial chronological stages* in the typical configuration of every industrial dispute:

(1) **The pre-dispute context** or unique historical setting in which the root causes of the dispute are to be found.

(2) **The challenge** thrown down by one side, which 'initiates' the dispute.

(3) **The initial responses** made to that challenge by the other side in the dispute (which often 'triggers' the conflict).

(4) **The consequences**, which flow directly and indirectly from the interaction of the challenge and the initial responses.

(5) **The climax** or point of greatest pressure, which immediately precedes the resolution of the conflict.

(6) **The settlement**, which determines the substantive outcomes of the dispute.

(7) **The aftermath**, in which the parties count the cost, assess the gains and losses, seek to learn the lessons and resume some new or modified relationship.

Setting aside short-duration disputes, almost over before they have begun, most major disputes involving the threat or use of sanctions by one side against the other, pass through the seven analytical stages outlined above. Regardless of the type of industry, the subject matter of the dispute, whether of relatively long or short duration, and of whatever outcome, nearly all significant industrial disputes conform to this typical seven-stage configuration, which will now be examined in greater detail.

The seven-stage analysis of an industrial dispute

Every industrial dispute is a unique episode of social conflict within a continuing employment relationship. Whether it occurs in the primary, the secondary or the tertiary sector of an industrial economy, whether in a growth area or a declining area, whether it is union-initiated or management-initiated, every industrial dispute acquires a distinctive character that derives from a unique conjuncture of historical circumstances. This includes the type of organization in which the dispute takes place, the nature of the specific issues in dispute, the character of the parties in the dispute, as well as the personality of the principal protagonists involved on both sides. By analysing the very rich and diverse materials that go to make up such major industrial disputes, we may hope to develop some useful theory to explain the origins, evolutionary development and eventual outcomes of such disputes. [9]

An industrial dispute is neither a completely 'random happening' nor a fully-controlled experiment in social engineering. It is probably best described as a 'semi-autonomous' event, arising out of the ever-present possibility of conflict that is structured into all employment relationships. At various times in the course of a protracted dispute, one side may appear to be in the ascendancy, with the outcome of the dispute well within its control. At other times, a dispute will appear to slip out of the control of both the principal protagonists and to take on a life of its own.

Every dispute nevertheless has a beginning, a middle and an end — no industrial dispute, even the most protracted, goes on for ever. Every major industrial dispute goes through a distinctive life-cycle of seven analytical stages, as shown in Table 2.1.

Table 2.1. Typical configuration of an industrial dispute

			Seven stages			
1	2	3	4	5	6	7
Pre-dispute context	Challenge	Responses	Consequences	Climax	Settlement	Aftermath

These seven stages comprise the following:

Stage 1: The pre-dispute context which is crucial to the origins of the dispute and which often exerts a powerful influence on its subsequent development and eventual outcomes. The context of the dispute enriches our understanding of the dispute's deeper causation, as distinct from its more immediate origins. It comprises a unique combination of economic, social, and organizational factors, which together make up the dispute's special historical setting. The weighting attached to these factors will vary from one dispute to another; but without some consideration of these contextual factors, the dispute will be virtually meaningless. The context sets the scene, provides the prologue and introduces the principal protagonists in the drama that is about to unfold.

Stage 2: The challenge in which one (or more) of the protagonists initiates the dispute by presenting some grievance — a claim or a set of demands — in order to secure a concession or some positive response from one (or more) of the other protagonists. The challenge encapsulates the initiator's strategic objectives and usually identifies the more explicit and immediate causes of the dispute. Since it is intended to be taken seriously, the challenge is nearly always accompanied by the tactical threat or use of economic sanctions, which, in the case of a union-initiated dispute, may range from a brief stoppage of work or some other token action (e.g. the imposition of a local overtime ban), through various intermediate stages, to open-ended, all-out strike action (e.g. a total, national, industry, company or plant-wide collective withdrawal of labour).

Although these examples are taken from a typical union-initiated dispute, it is important to note that the original challenge may equally be thrown down by management when it seeks, for example, to introduce some significant change in working methods, employment levels or machine utilization. Whether management or union-initiated, no dispute begins without an explicit challenge — a gauntlet thrown down by one side (the initiator) and picked up by the other side (the respondent).

Stage 3: The initial responses in which the challenge is either deflected (i.e. the demands are conceded by the respondent) or, more usually, accepted (i.e. the demands are rejected by the respondent). The initial responses offered to the challenge by the respondent represent a countervailing strategy. This strategy is translated into defensive, evasive or counter-offensive tactics, which aim to side-step, reduce or neutralize the threat presented by the initiator or to minimize the cost to the respondent of the implied or actual sanctions contained in the challenge.

Initial responses are generally of three basic types:

(i)   placatory — if the respondent's intention is to satisfy the initiator's demands or at least to signify a willingness to concede all or part of the claim or to redress the alleged grievance to some degree;

(ii)   hostile — if the respondent's intention is to reject the demands outright or to dismiss the alleged grievance without further consideration of its merits, and so to risk the application of further, tougher or wider sanctions by the initiator;

(iii) ambiguous — if the respondent's intentions are unclear but appear neither to concede nor to reject the demands or the alleged grievance but to prevaricate or play for time — for example, by issuing a statement that the respondent refuses to act under the duress of industrial action (or the threat of a lock-out or shut-down) but is willing to consider the claim on its merits when full normal working is resumed.

Stage 4: The consequences which may range widely in scope and content from the more predictable appeals to reason, through the mobilization of public support, to the organization of sympathetic or solidaristic industrial action by workers (or employers) not immediately involved in the dispute. Consequences may extend further to the most unexpected or unintended repercussions — such as the total or partial lay-off of personnel not immediately involved in the dispute, the disclosure of information previously withheld — or to invocation of the State either in the form of an action in law to head off the actual or threatened sanction, where this can be shown to be unlawful (e.g. by means of an injunction or court order against unlawful industrial action without a prior ballot), or in the form of some State (or private) conciliation, mediation or arbitration of the issues involved.

Because the consequences that flow from the outbreak of an industrial dispute are both intended and unintended (i.e. anticipated and unanticipated), their content, variety and timing are nearly always unpredictable. This is the stage of attack and counter-attack, of thrust and parry, bluff and double-bluff, advance and retreat — culminating in a decisive move by one side or the other to sue for peace or to initiate the search for some form of compromise resolution of the dispute. In such a compromise, neither side secures *all* of its objectives but each side achieves *sufficient* gains to permit the final outcome to be seen as 'an honourable peace', secured without the humiliation, 'loss of face' or bitter recrimination so often produced by total victory or total defeat.

The alternative to a compromise resolution of the dispute is a sudden 'knock-out' blow, whereby one side attempts to exploit its superior bargaining power by forcing the other side to make some major concessions which, it is hoped, will bring the dispute to a climax and eventual resolution on terms that come close to its original strategic objectives.

Stage 5: The climax which represents the point of greatest pressure exerted by one side to overcome the resistance of the other, to break the negotiating deadlock or dispute stalemate and so to influence the outcome of the dispute directly or indirectly in one's own favour. In private sector disputes, the climax is often brought about by the sudden stepping up of economic or social sanctions by one side against the other (e.g. by a union decision to extend the dispute by bringing additional workers out on strike; or by an employer's decision to close down the dispute-affected plant or to dismiss the strikers). A well-engineered and timely initiative of this sort may quickly build up the climax of the dispute — for example, by forcing a recalcitrant bargaining partner to return to the bargaining table to negotiate a compromise solution to the dispute.

In public sector disputes, particularly those affecting essential services such as food, water or power supplies, public health, safety, transport or communications the climactic point of the dispute may often result from direct or indirect government intervention in the form of conciliation or the setting up of an independent Court of Inquiry to look into the causes and circumstances of the dispute and to make recommendations that may help to bring the dispute to a speedy conclusion.

The precise timing, form and substance of this climax-building initiative is of the utmost importance to students of industrial conflict management. It is often a major factor in determining the terms of the dispute settlement and frequently exerts a profound psychological influence on the aftermath of the dispute.

Stage 6: The settlement at which the substantive terms are agreed for ending the dispute, and any new agreements or understandings are reached either to restore the *status quo ante bellum* (the conditions prevailing in the pre-dispute context) or to amend the pre-existing agreements or understandings on terms acceptable to both parties. Depending on the relative bargaining power of the parties, the settlement may allow one side to insist on some variation in the *status quo* *ante bellum*, thereby signifying the achievement, in whole or in part, of its original strategic objectives at the expense of the other side.

The settlement may also provide the parties with an opportunity to assert or to reaffirm one or more of the basic procedural rules or principles that have hitherto governed their relationship (e.g. the observance of an agreed disputes procedure or the stricter enforcement of some cherished but frequently neglected principle, such as a 'peace obligation' or a 'No strike – No lock-out' clause, more honoured in the breach than the observance). The overenthusiastic insistence by one side on extracting such concessions from the other may well delay or frustrate the peace process and so prevent the settlement from taking place. The reason why the 'winning side' hesitates to impose harsh conditions on the 'losing side' at the end of a protracted dispute was supplied with admirable clarity by Allan Flanders:

> *Professional negotiators know the dangers of pressing a temporary bargaining advantage to the full, regardless of whether it can be sustained. They are, as it were, in the business for a long time to come . . .* [10]

Stage 7: The aftermath which represents 'the beginning of the end' of the dispute. It may be characterized as a period of heart-searching and recuperation, in which both sides take stock of their respective gains and losses immediately following the settlement. Each side normally conducts its own separate inquest into what happened during the course of the dispute, and why. This is a time when old scores may be settled as intra-organizational differences within each side, which remained submerged during the dispute, begin to break the surface. In the immediate aftermath of most disputes, the parties settle down to make the best of the new or modified relationship, seeking to preserve, as best they can, the precarious peace of the delicate aftermath stage. There may be some attempt by one side or the other to insist on the *more* rigorous application of the agreements or understandings reached at the settlement, or, paradoxically enough, a *less* rigorous application in order to allow some 'healing of wounds' to take place. During the aftermath, the lessons of the conflict are learned and internalized by mature protagonists, for after a major industrial dispute, nothing is ever quite the same again.

Now is the time when those outside the dispute produce and publish their own independent and more considered assessments of the longer-term effects and repercussions of the dispute on the wider society. Professional commentators provide their own interpretations of what transpired during the dispute by piecing together their own and other people's perceptions of what *really* took place. Informed students of industrial relations may now attempt to place the dispute within some broader framework of industrial relationships within the organization, the industry, the sector or the national system, and to calculate the overall cost of the dispute and its implications for the community and for the political economy.

CRITICAL QUESTIONS IN DISPUTE ANALYSIS

Before embarking on any serious investigation in the social sciences, we need to develop and apply a consistent set of questions that serve as the framework for our initial analysis and subsequent interpretation. To explain this need, we draw upon an analogy from a totally different field of human activity.

In the critical appreciation of a work of art — a book, play, film, sculpture, or painting — we seek to arrive at some considered judgement of its overall worth. If we are to transcend our immediate, purely intuitive and emotional responses, we require an analytical framework for structuring our thoughts. We might, therefore, begin by posing a first question along the following lines: *(Question 1): What is the artist trying to achieve?* Until we have answered that question, we cannot usefully proceed to the second question: *(Question 2): Has the artist succeeded in achieving those objectives?* Unless we have answered both those questions, to our own satisfaction, we cannot proceed to the final and crucial question: *(Question 3): Was the artist's effort, in our judgement, worthwhile?*

By posing such questions in a consistent sequence, we approach aesthetic appreciation and analysis with some measure of objectivity — that is, we reduce the risk of judging the artist's work by some false criteria, thereby underrating (or overrating) its significance, or indeed of completely missing its point.

By analogy — and after allowing for real differences between aesthetic appreciation and critical social analysis — we propose asking seven critical questions to elicit the relevant information that will serve as the framework for our reconstructive analysis:

(1) **What was the dispute about?**
     (i.e. What were the central issues in the dispute? What were the objectives of the parties engaged in the dispute?)

(2) **How significant was the pre-dispute context?**
     (i.e. What were the most important environmental pressures, or constraints, immediately prior to the dispute, that contributed to its origins, influenced its development and determined its eventual outcomes?)

(3) **What were the dominant strategies and tactics of the parties?**
     (i.e. What main lines of action or means did the parties decide to pursue in order to achieve their objectives?)

(4) **How far were those strategies and tactics successful?**
     (i.e. Were the lines of action or means chosen by the parties relevant and effective in the achievement of their objectives?)

(5) **Who won?**
    (i.e. Did the outcomes of the dispute predominantly favour one side or the other?).

(6) **What were the costs and benefits of the dispute to the parties?**
    (i.e. Which of the parties, if any, appeared to emerge from the dispute with higher settlement gains than losses?)

(7) **What were the lessons of the dispute?**
    (i.e. What can we learn about the management of industrial conflict from a study of this particular dispute?)

Our reconstructive analysis of an industrial dispute begins by attempting to identify the central issues involved in the dispute by asking (*Question 1*): *What was the dispute about?* To this apparently innocuous question we are unlikely to receive a simple or straightforward answer, for two reasons:

(i) We are trying to establish the perceived aims and objectives of the principal protagonists in the dispute on initiating, or responding to, the original challenge that triggered the dispute. But we can never be sure that we have correctly established or understood those perceptions.

(ii) We are trying to disentangle and make sense of human motivation and behaviour, which are not always susceptible to rational analysis: motives are invariably complex, generally mixed and frequently confused. Reason and passion both play their part. Individuals are not always consistent in what they say or in what they do.

So we must expect more than one unequivocal answer to our first question. Indeed, we should expect, and therefore look for, a *range of issues* underlying every significant industrial dispute before we can identify the *central issues*, which maintain their salience throughout all or most of the dispute. Unless we succeed in pinpointing these central issues over which the dispute was ostensibly fought, our dispute analysis is likely to be fatally flawed from the outset.

Having established the respective aims and objectives of the parties, we need to familiarize ourselves with the unique environmental context in which the dispute occurred — (*Question 2*): *How important was the context?* The answers to this question are crucially important to our understanding of the conduct of the dispute because they indicate the scope for action, the opportunities and the constraints facing the parties within the historical context immediately preceding the dispute.

Having identified the objectives of the parties (Question 1) and achieved a better understanding of the pre-dispute context (Question 2), we turn next to strategic choice — that is, the main lines of action selected by the parties to help them to achieve those objectives. (*Question 3*): *What were the dominant strategies and tactics adopted by the parties?* Here, we need to identify any significant strategic shifts, as well as the more frequent tactical manoeuvres that occur during the course of every protracted dispute.

This is followed logically by *(Question 4): How far were those strategies and tactics successful?* In other words, were they of practical value in helping the parties to achieve their respective objectives? This question calls for an overall judgement as to the relevance or appropriateness of the instrumental means chosen for the attainment of a predetermined set of policy objectives.

With motive, opportunity and means accounted for and assessed in Questions 1 – 4, we may proceed to the controversial, indeed vexed, question *(Question 5): Who won?* Here, again, an analogy may be helpful. The theory behind games of skill allows us to ask a series of legitimate questions about the outcome of a particular sequence of games (e.g. a tennis match): Who won? By what score? After how long? We may expect an unequivocal answer to each of those questions because tennis, by its own internal rules, is a 'win/lose' game, i.e. there can be only one winner and one loser, determined by calculating the number of games and sets won by each player. We may note in passing that the International Lawn Tennis Association adopted its now familiar 'tie-break' rule to ensure that protracted and evenly-balanced final set matches are brought to a speedy conclusion. In other forms of interpersonal or intergroup games of skill (e.g. a horse race or a football match), the outcome may be more ambiguous: in a football match there may be a final draw-score (unless the match is to be decided by penalty goals), even after extra time has been played; and two horses may pass the winning post in a nose-to-nose photo-finish. In neither case is there an immediately obvious, outright winner.

In other sports (e.g. a boxing match or ice-skating contest), the players themselves may not always know the winner of the contest until after the umpire or judges have given their considered verdict. Even then, there is still scope for dispute as to the 'real' winner. For, wherever subjective assessments of technical content and artistic merit have to be reconciled, there is always the possibility of 'political' or other pressures to contend with. It is not unknown for some commentators to argue that the 'loser' was in reality the 'winner'.

Similar possibilities exist in evaluating the outcome of most industrial disputes. The judgement as to who won depends on the subjective views of the respondent, on the respondent's pre-dispute perspective of the issues involved, on the timing of the question, and so on. Our judgement on which side has emerged as the 'winner' in an industrial dispute may well change with the passage of time. At the moment of settlement, one side may appear to be the outright winner. From the standpoint of history — and with the benefits of hindsight — events may take on an altogether different perspective. At the end of the Second World War, Britain was amongst the victors whilst Germany and Japan were amongst the vanquished powers.

Forty years on, with the wisdom of hindsight and in the light of their subsequent economic standing in the league table of world powers, a sceptical historian might question which nations were the 'winners' and which the 'losers'.

As in international conflict, so in industrial conflict our perception of the outcome of a dispute on the day of settlement may be highly misleading. What appeared on that day to be an outstanding victory may seem more like defeat — or at best a pyrrhic victory — when viewed from a distance, with the longer-term costs and benefits counted on both sides.

This leads us logically to an evaluation of the price of winning and losing *(Question 6): What were the costs and benefits of the dispute?* Here, again, we inhabit a twilight world of misinformation and disinformation, partly fact but mostly speculation. All social costs are notoriously difficult to assess; but to attempt any reliable estimate of the cost of particular industrial dispute is a hazardous, even foolhardy, undertaking. As Jean-Daniel Reynaud, a distinguished French scholar, has observed on this point:

> *Il est, certes, difficile de mesurer le cout d'un conflit du travail, plus encore de l'ensemble des conflits. Le cout immediat apparent, c'est a dire la production perdue fait de l'arret, est en effet trompeur (The costs of an industrial dispute are certainly difficult to assess — those of industrial conflict in general are even more hazardous. The immediately obvious cost — that of production directly lost as a result of a work stoppage — is in itself quite misleading.)* [11]

Not only is it unwise to rely on the immediate and more obvious costs of lost production. Even the best available estimates may have to be discounted. Accountants are reluctant to admit the 'real' cost of an industrial dispute to the enterprise because it might seem:

(i) to *understate* the extent of the damage inflicted by the dispute and so appear to play down its significance for both management and workers;

(ii) to *overstate* the damage inflicted by the dispute and so reduce public confidence in management's competence which, in turn, might reduce the value of the company's shares on the stock market.

For both reasons, accountants are generally equivocal in their estimate of strike losses to their own organizations.

In recent years, especially in more protracted public-sector disputes, management has developed the practice of releasing estimates of both the known and the projected losses caused by the dispute as one means of bringing direct pressure to bear on the strikers or, more indirectly, of bringing home the likely cost of the strike to consumers as taxpayers, to the government as managers of the economy, and to the public at large.

Managerial estimates of 'the cost of the strike to the nation' are, however, often wildly inaccurate or intentionally misleading. They must be regarded in the first place as 'disinformation' i.e. false information deliberately put out by one side to confuse, mislead or intimidate the other side. Amongst sophisticated practitioners of the art of conflict management, this resort to deliberately misleading information is a well-understood part of the psychological warfare that characterizes much industrial conflict in the last quarter of the twentieth century.

What has been said so far relates only to the *economic* cost of an industrial dispute — tangible costs that can be quantified or assessed with some reasonable degree of accuracy. But there are the less tangible, non-quantifiable, but no less significant costs of another kind — the psychological damage caused to a strife-torn enterprise; the demoralization of company managers and supervisors who may well feel betrayed by their own workers or by more senior management; the distress caused by rifts in an otherwise united workforce by factional disputes between different groups of workers, quite apart from the loss of self-respect that results when harsh settlement terms, dictated by the 'winners', are imposed on the 'losers'.

Set against these economic and psychological losses, there are, of course, corresponding economic and psychological gains or benefits. For it would be foolish, as well as misleading, to believe that all sides lose from an industrial dispute. From time to time, it is asserted by those who should know better, that an industrial dispute represents nothing but losses all round. In the words of one leading British industrialist, at the end of a protracted dispute that had not ended well for the employers:

> *There are no winners, only losers.* [12]

That pessimistic pronouncement seems to miss one of the crucial aspects of any industrial dispute — namely, the all-important sense of psychological satisfaction that comes from pursuing or defending what one knows to be true, the rightness of one's cause, the feeling of pride in having taken a stand on some issue of principle and in having seen the struggle through to the end, win or lose. Asked how he felt on the morning of 4 March 1985, at the end of the year-long miners' strike and in the very moment of defeat, NUM President Arthur Scargill is reported to have said:

> *The strike is over; but the struggle goes on until we have won the battle for pits, for jobs and for our communities.* [13]

The costs and benefits of industrial action are clearly not to be measured simply in arithmetical terms.

Finally, in any worthwhile dispute analysis, it is important to ask *(Question 7): What are the lessons of the dispute?* — that is, what lessons do the parties to the dispute appear to have learned from the dispute? And, what general lessons may be drawn from our own analysis?

From time to time, sceptical commentators may deny that any learning has taken place because they perceive no significant change in the attitudes or behaviour of their subjects. Maréchal Dumouriez, commenting on the restored Bourbon monarchy after 1815, denied that the monarchists had learned anything from the cataclysmic events of the French Revolution when he wrote in *L'Examen*:

> *Les courtisans qui l'entourent [Louis XVIII] n'ont rien oublié et n'ont rien appris (The courtiers who surround King Louis have forgotten nothing and learned nothing.)* [14]

Such a statement is merely polemical. It reflects the ideological preferences of the writer but tells us nothing reliable about the restored Bourbon monarchists. In Dumouriez's view, the Bourbons continued to behave, after their restoration, *as if* they had learned nothing and forgotten nothing. But that behaviour provides no definitive answer to the question:

> *What lessons, if any, do you derive from your experience of recent events?*

The answers given to such a question would obviously reflect the respondents' subjective evaluation of their own learning. But that evidence, by itself, in no way denies, disproves or diminishes the theory that there is a 'learning process' at work in society or that the lessons learned are 'real' for the learners.

Applying these notions to the specific case of an industrial dispute, we may note that whilst the parties to a dispute will often emerge bruised and battered from the contest, occasionally 'punch-drunk' and sometimes incoherent, they are rarely at a loss to say what they feel they have learned from the experience. One frequently-heard comment amongst strikers who feel they have been forced back to work against their will, echoes the cry of the defeated pugilist down the ages: *We was robbed!* This is usually followed by some pungent and derogatory remarks directed towards national or local union officials who are alleged to have 'done a deal' over the heads of the strikers who feel that they have been 'sold down the river', presumably into some form of industrial slavery. Such comments inevitably reflect the emotional state of the strikers at the time of the settlement. At some later stage, however, when emotions have cooled, strikers and union leaders will often reflect with profound insight on the lessons they have learned from their experience of the conflict, as the following anecdote clearly illustrates:

Some time after the end of the 1984–85 miners' strike, the TUC General Secretary chanced to meet the NUM President in the lobby of Congress House:

Norman Willis: *Hello, Arthur. Haven't seen you up here since your recent fracas. Tell me, what do you feel about it, now it's all over?*

Arthur Scargill: *Norman, if I had to go through the whole strike, all over again, I wouldn't change a single thing!*

There was a markedly different response from Scargill's Vice-President, Mick McGahey. Throughout the dispute, McGahey had argued that the miners were not going to be 'constitutionalized out of a strike'. Two years after the strike ended — and on the eve of his retirement from active union affairs — McGahey's reflections were much more critical on his own union's handling of the dispute and its failure to ballot its members:

> *To say that you can go through a year's strike with all the traumatic events we went through from March 1984 to March 1985 and say we'd do all the same things again — No! . . . Did we sufficiently recognize the plans of the government — their organizational ability, their use of the police? Was mass picketing the answer? Because even at Orgreave, where we had the most famous and biggest picket, the police outmatched us . . . Did we in the course of that year, going through the British coalfield, see mass meetings as mass movements — when they were just mass meetings? Did we underestimate the ability of the media to isolate many miners on the question of violence on the picket line?*

> *The miners never demanded a ballot vote, and the constitutional process allowed the miners to have a ballot vote had they demanded it . . . [But] I'm not sure . . . the ballot vote question did not enter people's minds — because of the traditional democracy of the British people. They asked — why not a ballot vote? And did that not isolate us? [15]*

REFERENCES

1   Peter Slee: 'Concern for skills', *Universities Quarterly: Culture, Education and Society*, Vol. 40, No. 2, 1986, p. 169.
2   Eric Jacobs: *Stop Press*, Routledge & Kegan Paul, London, 1981.
3   F. A. Hayek: *Capitalism and the Historians*, Routledge & Kegan Paul, London, 1954, pp. 23–4.
4   Werner Sombart, quoted by Hayek: *Capitalism and the Historians*, Routledge & Kegan Paul, London, 1954, p. 57.
5   Vic Allen: *The Sociology of Industrial Relations: Studies in Method*, Longman, London, 1971, p. 121.
6   Bernard Karsh: *Diary of a Strike*, University of Illinois Press, Urbana, 1958, p. 167.
7   E. T. Hiller: *The Strike: A Study in Collective Action*, Arno Press, New York, 1928.

8 J. Hartley, J. Kelly and N. Nicholson: *Steel Strike*, Batsford, London, 1983.

9 For the author's attempt to distill a plausible theory of conflict management, see *Managing Industrial Conflict: Theory, Practice and Policy*, Hutchinson, London, 1988.

10 Allan Flanders: *Management and Unions*, Faber & Faber, London, 1970, p. 22.

11 Jean-Daniel Reynaud and Gerard Adam: *Conflits du travail et changement social*, Editions du Seuil, Paris, 1978, p. 69.

12 Sir Geoffrey Hawkings, President, Engineering Employers' Federation, commenting on the end of the 1979 engineering dispute. See Part Two, Chapter 4, Introduction.

13 Arthur Scargill, President, National Union of Mineworkers, commenting on the end of the 1984–85 miners' dispute, quoted in *The Guardian*, 4 March 1985. See Part Two, Chapter 8, Introduction.

14 Maréchal Dumouriez: *L'Examen*, cited by Cohen: *Dictionary of Quotations*, Penguin, Harmondsworth, 1975.

15 Mick McGahey, cited by John Lloyd and John Sweeney: 'Anger is not enough', *New Statesman*, 3 April 1987, pp. 18–9.

PART II

■ SEVEN MAJOR DISPUTES

WHY THESE DISPUTES?

The seven disputes selected for reconstructive analysis in Part II are in one sense 'unrepresentative' of industrial conflict in Britain in the period 1968–88. Why then have they been chosen? The vast majority of British industrial disputes over the past twenty years have comprised small-scale, short-duration work stoppages of an unofficial and unconstitutional character, involving relatively few workers. Whilst such disputes might in one sense be 'representative' of British disputes over the past twenty or so years, they would hardly furnish relevant data for the reconstructive analysis of major industrial disputes or the study of industrial conflict management. Attention has been focused instead on seven *major* disputes, i.e. disputes of outstanding importance or of exceptional interest to students of recent British history, because of the interplay of two or more of the following significant features:

(i)   their large scale;
(ii) their protracted duration;
(iii) their unusual pattern;
(iv) their peculiar subject matter;
(v)   their distinctive character;
(vi) their significant outcomes.

A *major* dispute is defined here as one that makes a significant impact on the organization, the industry or the sector in which it occurs, or even on the wider society and political economy as a whole. All seven of the disputes considered in Part II may lay claim to that distinction. But there are several other ways in which these seven major disputes, individually and collectively, may certainly be said to be representative of recent British industrial disputes:

(i)   They involve many *important organizations in both the declining and the growth sectors of British manufacturing and service industries, both private and public* (e.g. motor manufacture; iron and steel; coal mining; engineering; school teaching);

(ii) They cover *an important range of issues that are central to an informed understanding of contemporary British industrial relations* (e.g. employment and unemployment; shorter working time; new technology; sex discrimination; pay and payment systems; power, ideology and the right to manage);

(iii) They deal with *medium and large-scale organizations in both the private and public sectors* (e.g. Electrolux, Ford and Times Newspapers in the private sector; British Coal, British Steel and school teaching in the public sector);

(iv) They involve *some of Britain's largest and most powerful trade unions* represented on the General Council of the TUC (e.g. TGWU, AEU, EETPU, GMBATU, NUM, NUT, NGA, etc.);

(v) *They cover union-initiated disputes*, aimed at securing improved
pay and conditions of work, equal pay for women workers,
shorter working time, the defence of jobs and related issues of
central concern to the labour movement; *but they also cover
management-initiated disputes*, aimed at securing increased
labour productivity, reduced manning and more flexible
working arrangements, the introduction of new technology, the
closure of uneconomic plant and the reassertion of the right to
manage — all matters close to the managerial heart;

(vi) They cover *disputes whose outcomes were predominantly in
favour of management* (e.g. coal and steel) as well as those
whose outcomes were *predominantly in favour of unions* (e.g.
Times Newspapers, engineering) and *those favouring both sides
about equally* (e.g. Ford, Electrolux and the teachers).

The following table attempts to summarize the 'representative'
character of these seven disputes and shows that, between them, they
cover all or most of the central industrial relations issues that have
preoccupied practitioners, policy-makers and the informed public in
Britain over the past two decades.

It will be noted that five of the seven disputes are shown as
having been initiated by trade unions — three in the private manufacturing sector and two in the public sector. This should not be taken
to imply either that most recent major British industrial disputes were
in the private sector or that trade unions, rather than management,
carry the *moral responsibility* or blame for these disputes, i.e. we
should not confuse the *occasion* of a dispute with its *cause*. The
dispute, in these particular cases, was 'initiated' by a union challenge
to management, even though the industrial action was 'triggered' in
each case by management's rejection of a union claim. Nor is it
implied that there have been comparatively few recent major disputes
in the public sector. An attempt has been made to strike some kind
of balance between a number of independently important criteria, so
as to provide a representative selection of recent major British
disputes. The final selection of the disputes inevitably reflects the
author's interests, tastes and prejudices as well as his desire to cover
as many different types of disputes and issues as possible. Some
important major disputes have regrettably been omitted — for
example, the dramatic union recognition dispute at Grunwick in 1976
or the crucial disputes involving print unions at Mr Eddie Shah's
Stockport Messenger in 1984 or at Mr Rupert Murdoch's News
International, centred on Wapping in 1985–86 — mainly for reasons
of space, or because the disputes happened too long ago, or were not
fully resolved at the time of planning and writing this study.

In addition to providing a reconstructive analysis of a specific
dispute, each of the seven chapters that follow also addresses a
particular theme or issue, central to the subject matter of the dispute
featured in that chapter. Between them, these seven chapters span

Principal employer involved	Principal unions involved	Sector	Initiated by	Central issues	Outcome predominantly favouring
1 Ford Motor Co. Ltd	AUEW TGWU	Private Manuf.	Unions	Job grading Equal pay Observance of procedures	Both sides
2 Electrolux Ltd	AUEW GMWU	Private Manuf.	Unions	Pay differentials Job grading Incentive pay Bargaining structures	Both sides
3 Times Newspapers Ltd	NGA SOGAT NATSOPA	Private Manuf.	Management	New techonology Right to manage	Unions
4 Federated engineering employers	CSEU	Private Manuf.	Unions	Shorter working time Pay levels	Unions
5 British Steel	ISTC	Public Manuf.	Unions	Pay levels Manpower levels Right to manage	Management
6 National Coal Board	NUM	Public Service	Management	Manpower levels Right to manage Role of State	Management
7 Local Education Authorities	NUT NAS/UWT	Public Service	Unions	Pay levels Conditions of employment White-collar militancy	Both sides

most of the central issues that represent the substantive content of British industrial relations over the past two decades.

In order to bring out the distinctive theme of each chapter and the central issues underlying each dispute, the structure of all seven chapters adheres closely to a standard format of an Introduction and nine sections:

Introduction: **A brief introductory section**, which identifies the dispute and sets the scene for what follows.

Section 1: **A thematic section**, which outlines the background to the central issues or subject matter of the dispute.

Section 2: **A narrative section**, which provides a descriptive account of the dispute, following the seven-stage configuration outlined in Part I, Chapter 2, pp. 15–18.

Section 3: **A central section**, which presents a reconstructive analysis of the dispute, covering the seven critical questions outlined in Part I, Chapter 2, pp. 19–20.

Section 4: **A final section**, which offers some conclusions on the dispute together with a 1987 Postscript that reports significant events following the dispute.

Section 5: **A chronology of the dispute** by key dates and events.

Section 6: **A listing of Who's who** in the dispute.

Section 7: **References.**

Section 8: **Six study questions** on the chapter, some of which can be tackled only after further reading.

Section 9: **Suggestions for further reading.**

Since each chapter is self-contained and follows a standard format, the seven chapters may be read in any preferred order, rather than in the chronological order in which they are presented. To assist the reader, chapter lengths in Part II have been kept to a consistent length, despite variations in the duration and complexity of the disputes under discussion.

CHAPTER 3

■ The long road to equality —
THE FORD EQUAL PAY STRIKE, 1968

*The cry for equal pay has been repeated loud and clear for
so long that it has almost ceased to register in the minds of
politicians and public alike.*

Baroness Edith Summerskill
The Times (10 May 1968)

*The dilemma which faces the Company and, we believe, the
whole of British industry is that, having taken a stand on
the side of law and order in industrial relationships, what
can be done to prevent the disruption of its operation by
the irresponsibility of people who choose to ignore
Agreements entered into in good faith?*

Leslie Blakeman
Director of Industrial Relations
Ford Motor Company Limited

INTRODUCTION: A PROFITABLE DAY AT THE RACES

On the afternoon of Tuesday 28 May 1968, all 187 women employed
as Sewing Machinists at the Ford Motor Company's River Plant at
Dagenham, Essex, stopped work in protest against their job grading
and pay. On the following morning they failed to report for work
and instead spent the day — Derby Day — at the races. History does
not record whether they placed any bets or won any money on Epsom
Downs that afternoon, but one thing is certain: by their simple protest
strike on 29 May 1968 and their determined action over the weeks
that followed, this handful of women won themselves an honoured
place in labour history by securing equal pay for the women of
Britain. More than that — they helped shape the future course of
British industrial relations.

The Ford Sewing Machinists' strike was a landmark in the
evolution of industrial relations at Ford and in the history of industrial
conflict in Britain. From small beginnings, it became the biggest and
most important strike by any group of British women since the
Bryant & May Matchgirls' strike in 1888.

The *internal* consequences of the dispute for management and
unions at Ford were both immediate and long-lasting: after a decade
of set-backs and defeats, the rank-and-file leadership drew inspiration

and renewed strength from a successful campaign, waged against the combined forces of Ford management and most of the Ford unions. Within ten years of the dispute, many of those rank-and-file leaders were sitting as full members of the Ford National Joint Negotiating Committee (NJNC) — the body whose decisions they fought throughout the dispute. Management, in turn, was forced to take steps to meet a powerful threat: a novel combination of shopfloor militants and the newly-elected left-wing leadership of two major unions. The dispute compelled management to come to terms with the shopfloor.

The *external* consequences of the dispute were no less far-reaching:

(i)   the strike led directly to the Equal Pay Act 1970 and indirectly to the Sex Discrimination Act 1975

(ii)   the strike coincided exactly with the publication of the Report of the Donovan Commission, set up to inquire into the state of British industrial relations in the 1960s. It thus focused public attention on the need for the Government to 'do something' to reduce the incidence of strikes in Britain. Within twelve months of the Sewing Machinists' dispute, Harold Wilson's Labour Government introduced a Labour Relations Bill 1969 — which was never enacted — that sealed the fate of the first Wilson Government and prepared the way for Edward Heath's Conservative Government of 1970–74 and the notorious Industrial Relations Act 1971

(iii) the strike exerted a major influence on the development of the women's movement in Britain, an influence whose full effects were probably not felt until the 1980s.

SECTION 1: THE CHANGING ROLE OF WOMEN IN THE BRITISH ECONOMY

Women have always played a significant role in the British economy. In pre-industrial Britain, women worked alongside men on the land, helping with the harvest, taking care of livestock, milking cows, sheep and goats, churning cream into butter, preparing meat for the table and wool for the weaver's loom. In effect, women were engaged in dual employment: outside the home, they shared most, if not all, of the most physically demanding work undertaken by men; inside the home, they were responsible for such domestic duties as cleaning, cooking and caring for children, the aged and the sick. [1]

Women were the mainstay of the 'domestic' system of production, which prevailed until well into the 19th century in many parts of Britain. For example, women sorted, cleaned and carded raw wool, spun it into yarn and helped with domestic weaving, although the operation of the handloom itself was traditionally regarded as 'man's work'. Under the 'domestic' system of manufacture, the employer's agent delivered raw materials or semi-finished goods, which were made up by women at home into gloves, stockings, lace or other finished goods to be collected and paid for by the agent at incentive piece-work prices, which varied with the season and the state of local trade.

With industrialization, women were amongst the first workers to be 'gathered in' to the new system of factory production, notably in the northern textile and clothing industries. Whilst coal-mines had their share of women workers, the heaviest, most uncongenial but better-paid jobs in iron foundries, steelworks, shipyards and railway workshops were reserved for men. There thus evolved a system of 'dual labour markets' — a form of industrial apartheid under which women were excluded from certain jobs, which became the traditional preserve of men, leaving a restricted range of jobs open to women. Only rarely (e.g. in time of war or of extreme shortage of manpower) were women considered for such jobs.

By the end of the last century, women were significantly over-represented in the food, drink and tobacco industries, in the textile and clothing trades and in the emerging ranks of routine clerical and secretarial workers. They were significantly under-represented in more demanding and better-paid posts. The ancient professions — law, medicine and the church — were closed to women, as was access to higher education for the vast majority of women. By the turn of the century, only a handful of middle-class women had succeeded in obtaining a university degree.

The First World War (1914–18) transformed traditional thinking on women's employment. This was reflected in a vast upsurge in women's participation rates in the economy. The mass mobilization of women into coal-mining, iron and steel, shipbuilding and repairing, engineering and munitions industries was stimulated in part by patriotic sentiment and in part by the Government's promise of equal pay for equal work. Women were seen to be capable of undertaking most, if not all, of the jobs traditionally reserved for men. [2]

The end of the war brought a sharp reversal in that trend. Women factory workers almost everywhere were paid off and sent home to make way for 'returning warriors'. Throughout the interwar period, conventional social pressures plus heavy male unemployment forced many 'career women' to revert to their more traditional roles of mother, housekeeper and home-maker. Although a small number of exceptional women succeeded in entering Parliament, business and the professions, the vast majority of intelligent women settled for the drudgery of traditional housework. Thousands of unmarried women and war widows were forced to accept 'sweated' employment outside their own homes. More women entered 'domestic service' (i.e. became servants in middle-class homes) than all other forms of paid employment taken together. Women shop assistants soon outnumbered men in retail outlets of all kinds. The 'needle-trades', other than men's bespoke tailoring, were dominated by low-paid women workers, many of whom worked very long hours in their own homes for scandalously exploitative rates of pay. New factories (e.g. in light engineering and food processing) attracted large numbers of women but very few rose above the ranks of assembly-line workers to become supervisors or managers.

The outbreak of the Second World War in 1939 once again transformed that position. Women were not only recalled from domestic labour to undertake essential war work, but were actively encouraged to join the uniformed armed forces to release men for more active front-line duties. During the next five years, women were found to be the equals of men in carrying out the widest range of jobs previously undertaken exclusively by men for more than a century. Women not only dug coal, built ships, made steel and operated engineering lathes, they also drove trains and lorries, flew planes and generally took charge in thousands of workshops, canteens, hospitals and offices on the home-front as well as on the battle-front.

Unlike their counterparts of 1914–18, however, the women who came into paid employment during the Second World War represented a new generation: better educated, more self-confident, more articulate and with a greater consciousness of their own worth, they determined never again to revert to second-class citizenship. In the immediate post-war decades, many women — and particularly married women — were encouraged by their employers (and some by their husbands) to remain at work, undertaking many of the newly-created jobs that derived from the application of new technology and reinvestment for the expanding world markets of the post-war decades of economic growth. [3]

Prevalent attitudes to women and work were nevertheless slow to change. In the primary sector of the economy, all the better-paid jobs in fishing, agriculture, mining and quarrying were still the preserve of men; in manufacturing, women were employed in increasing numbers and in a wider variety of jobs than ever before; in the fast-growing service sector, women began to emerge for the first time in significant numbers in posts of seniority and responsibility. In the civil service and the teaching profession, amongst doctors and lawyers, in sales offices and department stores, more women were promoted to senior and better-paid jobs. But the change was gradual and its extent should not be exaggerated. Key jobs in industry, commerce and the public service — from the shopfloor to the boardroom — were still the exclusive preserve of men. It was commonly said at the time that it was easier for a woman to become Prime Minister of Britain than to become a skilled electrician or plumber — a point demonstrated by Margaret Thatcher in 1979. Britain still has virtually no women electricians or plumbers, only a small number of qualified women engineers and a mere handful of women MPs.

The reasons for the persistence of discrimination against women in the British economy need first to be identified before ways of overcoming that discrimination can be discussed. Beginning with the demographic data, we may note that, whilst the number of girls and boys are roughly equal at birth, women outnumber men in every age-group beyond middle age. Education statistics and examination results show that whilst girls perform at least as well as boys at school, they opt for predominantly 'arts' subjects and are consequently under-represented in the physical sciences (e.g. chemistry, physics, engineering) and other traditionally 'male' subjects (e.g. metalwork, technical drawing). Over 80% of boys and 70% of girls in Britain do not go on to any form of post-school education. Amongst those who do, men outnumber women at every significant level of further and higher education, with the single exception of continuing education (i.e. evening classes). In higher education, where men take first and second degree courses, more women settle for non-degree (e.g. diploma and other) courses. [4]

The very different educational experience of men and women is reflected in later job choices and career paths. In proportion to population, men outnumber women in the professions, in the higher level of management, in business, commerce, the civil service, public administration, Parliament, political parties and trade unions. Despite the fact that Britain has been ruled for almost 40 years by a female monarch and has elected a government headed by a female Prime Minister since 1979, women are still sharply segregated into distinct areas of employment by the operation of 'dual labour markets'. More specifically, there is employment discrimination 'before the market' (i.e. when women seek employment but fail to be selected); 'after the market' (i.e. when women are hired into certain kinds of jobs but not others) and 'after employment' (i.e. when women are denied equal opportunities with men for training and promotion to more responsible and better-paid posts).

A 1984 study by Martin and Roberts provides comprehensive findings on a range of issues of central concern for an understanding of both women's position in the labour market and the place employment has in women's lives:

> *There has been a period of sustained growth in women's labour force participation, such that by 1980 women constituted about 40% of the total labour force and about 10 million women were economically active . . .*
>
> *It is clear that while women's relationship to paid work is different from men's, it has also been changing as economic and social changes have increasingly brought women into the labour market . . . Because most married women have the primary responsibility for childbearing and domestic work, their husbands are the primary wage earners. In one sense, women do not participate in the labour market on the same terms as men over their lifetime and the conditions in which they offer themselves, for example, as part-time workers, may*

> *go some way to explaining the segregated and secondary value of much of the work they do.* [5]

The clearest evidence of both direct and indirect discrimination is to be found in the census data on occupational distribution in Britain. Although women now constitute more than two-fifths — and married women about one-third — of the country's total labour force, they are concentrated into a very limited range of jobs:

> *However women's occupations are currently classified, the nature of their occupational distribution, the extent of occupational concentration, and the degree of occupational segregation at the workplace is crucial to any understanding of women's position in the labour market . . . Women are concentrated predominantly in a few occupations, mostly in the service sector. This distribution has remained relatively stable over the last 15 years. Women working in part-time jobs are more likely to be in the service sector and in low-level jobs; in fact 70% of women working in service jobs are working part-time.* [6]

Explanations of this occupational segregation tend to cluster around two key points:

(i)   the fact that women are socialized from infancy into gender roles that society has chosen for them;
(ii) the operation of dual labour markets, which channel women into certain traditional jobs and prevent them from gaining access to others. [7]

From early childhood, through schooldays and into early adult life, girls are generally found to have fewer career aspirations and lower material expectations from employment than men. This initial psychological handicap is later reinforced by the operation of dual labour markets at both the macro- and the micro-economic levels of analysis, where men occupy most key decision-making positions.

New patterns in female employment, rates of pay and earnings began to emerge after the mid-1970s with the passage of new labour laws (Equal Pay Act 1970; Sex Discrimination Act 1975; Equal Value Amendment 1984), aimed at eliminating employment discrimination and promoting equal opportunities. Although the gap between men's and women's pay rates (and to a much lesser extent their earnings) for the same or broadly similar work began to narrow from around 60% to nearer 75% between 1976 and 1979, they diverged again in the 1980s as the recession drove many women out of full-time employment and significantly retarded progress towards more equal opportunity for women into higher-paid jobs.

One of the indirect effects of the economic recession in Britain in the 1980s has been to encourage employers to secure lower unit labour costs by developing more flexible, non-traditional patterns of working time. As men were progressively laid off and then made redundant, many employers began to restructure their workforces to ensure the availability of a central 'core' group of employees — permanent, skilled, relatively well-paid, mostly male — and a much larger reserve or 'peripheral' group of temporary, less-skilled, relatively low-paid, mostly female employees. [8] In many sectors, full-time working has given way to short-time and part-time working; permanent employment to temporary employment; regular working to casual working. Although women may appear to have been the principal beneficiaries of these changed working patterns, they frequently work shorter hours, for lower rates of pay, with significantly lower earnings and with fewer fringe benefits than the men whom they replace.

One of the most striking features of the post-war British economy has been the rapid decline of manufacturing, matched by an equally rapid growth in the service sector. Over the 25 years from 1951–76, women's employment in manufacturing reduced by some 30% (three times faster than for men) but increased in the service sector by 68% (nearly three times faster than for men). [9] Whilst the decline in manufacturing was by no means uniform across the entire range of traditional 'women's jobs', it was most severe in textiles, clothing and footwear, food, drink and tobacco — the very industries in which women's employment was most densely concentrated. Amongst white-collar workers in both the private and public sectors, women's jobs have tended to be harder hit than those of men, as traditional secretarial and clerical skills have been displaced gradually by the computer and the word-processor.

To summarize: over the past two decades, women's employment has been marked by three related trends:

(i) women's economic participation rates have continued to represent the biggest single factor in the growth of the country's workforce;

(ii) economic recession has reduced women's employment faster than men's in traditional manufacturing industries but has increased women's employment in the service sector, a trend which has been reinforced by the impact of new technology;

(iii) in restructuring their workforces to meet the demands of economic recession and the impact of new technology, many employers have replaced jobs traditionally filled by full-time, permanent male employees with jobs to be filled by part-time, temporary female employees.

Although the combined effect of these trends may have been to disperse women into a wider range of occupations, it has not been without adverse implications for their earnings and conditions of employment:

Overall, part-time workers are less likely to have access to or to have good provision of conditions of employment like paid holidays, sick pay or an occupational pension scheme. They are also less likely to have promotion and training opportunities in their jobs and less likely either to be a member of, or to have the opportunity to belong to, a union. In general, women's employment status as a full or part-time worker had a stronger effect on her access to good pay and job benefits than her occupational level and whether she works with men as well as only with women. [10]

If these trends persist, as seems likely, there is every reason to believe that women will come to occupy a dominant, but segregated, position in many sectors of Britain's employed workforce by the end of the century. For, as history shows, progress is slow along the long road to equality. During the transition period, women have been forced to fight for the modest advances that they have won. Current evidence suggests that women will continue to face massive discrimination over the entire range of their employment experience — from pre-employment recruitment screening and selection, through pay and conditions of employment, to pension and post-employment benefits. They still have many battles to fight before they begin to approach equal pay and equal employment opportunities with men.

SECTION 2: THE FORD EQUAL PAY STRIKE, 1968

(1) The pre-dispute context

In December 1965, following a series of disruptive disputes on pay differentials, the Ford Motor Company Limited (Ford) invited the unions to take part in a comprehensive joint review of the company's hourly-paid wage structure. [11] Their reaction was predictably cool: with all its faults, the Ford wage structure had many advantages over others in the motor industry. It was simple to understand, easy to administer and free from internal wage drift. It comprised four grades of labour — skilled, semi-skilled, unskilled and women — each with its own hourly rate, negotiated at the Ford National Joint Negotiating Committee (NJNC). Some 80% of all workers at Ford were classified as 'semi-skilled', which allowed easy mobility between different production jobs in the same pay grade without loss of pay. Since there were no incentive payments, the only variations in weekly earnings were due to the number of hours worked, plus the premium additions for overtime, shift and weekend working. Non-negotiable merit money helped to 'lubricate' an otherwise tight and inflexible grading structure.

But advancing technology had eroded many of the traditional job gradings; there was little relationship between effort and reward; merit money had simply become another means of paying enhanced rates to workers who might otherwise withhold cooperation or strike for higher pay. A new job-evaluated wage structure was long overdue and the unions eventually agreed to participate in a comprehensive wage structure review.

The problems of conducting such a review were formidable: over 42 000 hourly-paid workers, spread across 24 separate plants, occupying over 700 job titles — all needing to be identified, described and evaluated before any attempt could be made by management to negotiate with the unions at NJNC the number of new grades needed, the jobs in those grades and their appropriate pay differentials.

The review was divided into three distinct stages:

(i) *The fact-finding stage* — in which trained Assessors prepared job profiles (i.e. Job Descriptions and Job Analyses) after shop-floor observation and discussion of the job with the employee, the Supervisor and the Shop Steward. Each profile was then double-checked for completeness, internal consistency and value against representative benchmark jobs, first by one of eight Divisional Review Committees, representing management and shop stewards in that Division, and then by a Central Review Committee, composed of senior managers and a full-time union official.

(ii) *The proposal stage* — in which the company examined the facts revealed by job evaluation, and formulated its proposals on the changes it wished to introduce into the old structure.

(iii) *The negotiation stage* — in which the company and the trade unions at NJNC attempted to reach agreement on the company's proposals.

Using the results of the job evaluation, Ford proposed a Two-Year Pay and Productivity Deal for reforming the old wage structure:

(i) The old four-grade structure should be replaced by five new grades.

(ii) Women's jobs should fall into appropriate grades, as determined by evaluation, without sex discrimination.

(iii) Conditions allowances should be discontinued because working conditions would be covered by job evaluation.

(iv) Merit money should be replaced by a more equitable scale of service increments.

In April 1967, the company proposed these radical changes to the unions at NJNC, setting in train a complex set of pay and productivity negotiations at each of the company's 24 separate UK plants, required to ensure formal government approval under the terms of the existing prices and incomes policy. These separate productivity bargains were eventually brought together at the NJNC for ratification and inclusion in a Two-Year Agreement, containing a crucially important and explicit clause providing for 'no economic claims' during the life of the contract. The complete package deal was finally agreed by the Unions, vetted and approved by the Department of Employment and Productivity and put into effect in September 1967.

(2) The challenge

By the middle of 1968, Ford's Director of Labour Relations, Leslie Blakeman, seemed confident that Ford's new wage structure and productivity deal was beginning to pay off. Within one year, the number of man-hours lost through work stoppages had been halved. Grievances over the new wage structure were still flooding into the company's Industrial Relations Department but the prospects for industrial peace at Ford seemed bright.

In 1968, Ford's total hourly-paid workforce exceeded 42 000, amongst whom were some 900 women workers (about 2% of the total). Roughly half of those women were employed as Sewing Machinists in the Dagenham (Essex) and the Halewood (Liverpool) Trim Shops, making up backs and cushions of car seats, door and facia pads and headlinings. This work was divided into three, separate, linked operations: (i) a preparatory stage, in which bolts of leather-cloth or fabric are unrolled and cut into shapes by the male Bench Hands and Leathercutters; (ii) an intermediate stage, in which the shaped pieces are rough-stitched by a first group of Intermediate Sewing Machinists; and (iii) a final stage, in which the pieces are finished off by a second group of Final Sewing Machinists.

Of the 380 Sewing Machinists employed by Ford in 1968, 187 worked in the Trim Shop of the Dagenham River Plant, and about the same number in the Assembly Plant at Halewood on Merseyside — all engaged in broadly similar work. Since the women were prevented by the protective clauses of the Factory Act from working shifts, three male Sewing Machinists covered the night shift at the River Plant, mainly doing sewing repair work that could not conveniently be done during the day shift. At the Ford Research and Development Centre at Dunton, not far from Dagenham, there were two women Sewing Machinists employed in making up new prototype seats and cushions for use on new car models.

In April 1967, when the company put forward its pay and grading proposals, the new job title of *Production Sewing Machinist* was introduced to cover both the Intermediate and Finishing Operations. In accordance with the job evaluation evidence, this *Production Sewing Machinist* job was placed in Grade B, whereas the *Prototype Sewing Machinist* was placed in Grade C of the new wage structure. Although no objections were initially raised to these proposed gradings, the Production Machinists eventually complained to their union that their job ought to have been allocated to Grade C, like that of their sisters, the Prototype Machinists.

In October 1967, after detailed inquiries and checks, the company confirmed that both gradings were correct: the Prototype job carried a significantly greater responsibility than the Production job and this justified its higher grading. A majority of the Dagenham Sewing Machinists were members of the National Union of Vehicle Builders (NUVB), whose General Secretary, Charlie Gallagher, appeared to accept the company's explanation. So far as management was concerned, the grievance had been dealt with and disposed of. The engineering and transport unions (AEU and TGWU) had registered no formal complaint about the grading of their Sewing Machinist members.

But the disgruntled Sewing Machinists refused to let the matter rest. They formally recorded their protest that the grading of their job (Grade B) did not reflect the substance of their job descriptions. The matter was repeatedly raised with local management in the early months of 1968, but the Plant Convener, Henry Friedman, refused to put the matter through the Grading Grievance Procedure.

On 22 May, the Sewing Machinists voted to impose an unlimited overtime ban, followed by a one-day strike on 29 May if their job was not upgraded to Grade C by that date. The Convener implied that there must have been some 'manipulation' of the Intermediate Sewing Machinist job description because the assessment levels clearly justified Grade C.

Despite repeated management efforts to persuade the Sewing Machinists to remain at work, to allow their grievance to be examined under the jointly-agreed Grading Grievance Procedure, the Convener made clear that, unless the company agreed to upgrade the women's job from Grade B to Grade C by Tuesday 28 May, they would take strike action on the following day. The company and the joint Grading Grievance Committee refused to respond to this threat of industrial action. When a meeting with the Convener broke up in disorder without agreement, all 187 Sewing Machinists in the Dagenham River Plant stopped work and walked off the job. The strike had begun.

(3) Initial responses

From the company's viewpoint, there was only one possible response to the strike threat: to stand firm, to take the one-day strike and the overtime ban, if necessary; and to make clear beyond any possible doubt that, so far as the company was concerned, the women's jobs were correctly graded. If the women felt that they had a genuine grievance, they must submit it through the agreed Grading Grievance Procedure.

On their return to work on Thursday 30 May, the strikers were each given a letter, warning them that, by taking unconstitutional action, they were in breach of their individual contracts of employment; that such action would do nothing to help their case, but might have serious consequences for their continued employment if it were repeated. The women refused to accept the letters and handed them back to their Supervisor. They then held a meeting, at which they resolved not only to continue their overtime ban but to

take further strike action on Monday 10 June if their upgrading claim
had not been met by then.

The company now recognized that a protracted and potentially
damaging dispute was in prospect. Throughout the following week,
senior members of Blakeman's staff held meetings with the River
Plant Shop Stewards and then with Union District Officials in an
attempt to get the overtime ban lifted, to clarify the issue and to direct
the women's grievance into constitutional channels. But the women
were determined and there was no holding them back. On Friday 7
June the women voted unanimously for an all-out strike, saying that
they would not return until their jobs had been upgraded to Grade
C.

(4) Consequences

The Dagenham strike was widely reported by the media on Monday
10 June. Press reports suggested, for the first time, that the women
were taking industrial action not simply on account of their grading
grievance but on the grounds that the company had deliberately
discriminated against women in the new wage structure. As far as
Ford was concerned, there was no foundation for that allegation.
Management concluded that the Convener was exploiting a genuine
grievance amongst the women by converting it into a much wider
claim for equal pay.

It is an axiom amongst negotiators that management will not
meet strikers or discuss the merits of their case without first securing
a full return to normal working. A meeting was therefore held on
Tuesday 11 June between the company and National Officers of the
two principal unions concerned, Charlie Gallagher (NUVB) and Les
Kealey (TGWU), to discuss ways of securing a return to work. The
company suggested alternative ways of dealing with the women's
grading grievance once the strike was called off. Kealey promised to
do his best but Gallagher said that he would recommend his Executive
to make the strike official.

On the same morning, the Sewing Machinists, led by their
Convener, lobbied members of the Executive Council of the engineering union (then the AEF, later the AUEW, now the AEU) and
persuaded them to make the strike official on behalf of their small
number of Sewing Machinist members. Within two working days of
an unconstitutional walk-out, this small and previously obscure group
of women workers had gained official strike support from the two
principal unions involved.

Ford management reacted by calling an emergency meeting of
the NJNC in an attempt to isolate the AEF and the NUVB, bringing
pressure to bear on them to end the strike. Blakeman pointed out
that, whatever the strength of the women's case might be, the NJNC
represented the final stage of the agreed Disputes Procedure and that
every attempt must be made by members of the NJNC to end the

dispute. Gallagher simply confirmed that the NUVB had made the strike official on the grounds of discrimination. Speaking for the AEF, Birch said that the principal issue was not grading, but equal pay for women. It was simply unfortunate that Ford happened to be selected as the first target of a national equal pay campaign.

In view of this impasse at NJNC, Ford took immediate steps to deal with stoppage in its own way:

(i)   it called another emergency meeting of the full NJNC for the following Monday 17 June;

(ii) it contacted the Department of Employment, and began to apply pressure on the Secretary of State, asking her to intervene directly in the dispute;

(iii) it issued a Press Statement saying that the women's strike action now threatened continuity of production throughout the company and that, unless there was an immediate return to work, massive lay-offs would follow, with the complete closure of Dagenham Body and Assembly Plants by the following Tuesday.

These steps were speedily implemented. The London evening papers carried the late news that Barbara Castle had decided to intervene and had called the parties to meet her at St James's Square, the Headquarters of the Department of Employment, on the following morning.

On arriving at St James's Square on Saturday 15 June, Gallagher was besieged by a delegation of women strikers. They had heard about the meeting and suspected a sell-out by Gallagher and Mark Young, the Trade Union Side Chairman of the NJNC. Joint discussions went on all morning. Eventually, Blakeman and Young informed the Department that they both favoured the NJNC as the best means of settling the issue.

On Monday 17 June, the NJNC decided to appoint a Joint NJNC Committee of Inquiry into the strike. Blakeman agreed that the Inquiry could go ahead on one clear condition:

> *Nothing we do is going to undermine the Agreement we made last year and our New Wage Structure because we have got 40 000 people's wages depending on it. Destroy that and you destroy the whole thing, and we shall be in chaos again.* [12]

But on Tuesday 18 June, management's worst fears were confirmed. The women not only failed to report for work, but picketed the River Plant, carrying placards which proclaimed that the struggle would continue. Not one of the Sewing Machinists attempted to cross the line. The strike was 100% solid.

On Wednesday 19 June, both sides were called to St James's Square to be informed that the Secretary of State, Mrs Barbara Castle, intended to set up an immediate Court of Inquiry under the chairmanship of Sir Jack Scamp. She therefore appealed to the strikers to end their stoppage. But the women refused. Mrs Castle then called on senior representatives of the four principal unions to meet her at St James's Square on Saturday morning. She told them of the damaging effect of the strike, not simply on Ford's export performance but on the country's balance of payments, and urged them to bring their influence to bear on the women to get them back to work. Without their return, the Court of Inquiry could not go ahead. They assured Mrs Castle that they would do their best but held out no prospects of an early return to work.

On Thursday 27 June, the Sewing Machinists announced that they had decided not to return to work or to meet again until the following Thursday. Sir Jack Scamp deplored their decision and urged Gallagher to do his best to secure a return to work. But Gallagher declined: his union had made the strike official and he could do no more than report back to his Executive. Blakeman expressed his extreme disappointment at this outcome. Ford was losing £1 million of sales revenue each day that the strike continued. The matter was, therefore, of the greatest significance, not just for Ford but for the nation. He again urged that everything possible should be done to end the strike.

That afternoon, Ford management reviewed its options for ending the dispute. For Blakeman, this was the most serious dispute in his 15 years with the company, yet management had failed to end it. Blakeman had already hinted to the unions that, to get the women back to work, the company was willing to reduce the differential between men's and women's rates. But he was not prepared to surrender to strike pressure. Furthermore, there was a Two-Year Agreement, which the company refused to break unilaterally. But something must be done to end the strike. The Dagenham car compounds were congested with unfinished vehicles. Since the company had got no outside help, it must act alone.

That evening, Blakeman outlined his interpretation of events to the Board and secured their approval for a new plan of action:

(i)   By Monday, the NUVB would probably seek to widen the strike and the trade union side of the NJNC would probably support the union.

(ii) The Department of Employment was trying to persuade National Officials to call off the strike to allow the Scamp Inquiry to begin work, but it was unlikely that they would succeed.

(iii) This meant an imminent shut-down of Ford's Halewood and Dagenham Plants, with subsequent lay-off at all other plants in the company.

(iv) Joint Works Committees should therefore be called at all plants on Friday, to inform shop stewards of the critical position regarding lay-off.

(v)   Further lay-offs should begin in the Dagenham Press Shop on Monday.

(vi)   Personal letters should be delivered to the women strikers on Friday, urging them to think again about continuing the strike and inviting them to an urgent meeting to work out some solution.

(vii) Telegrams should be sent at once, seeking a meeting with the Minister of Technology, Tony Benn; with Barbara Castle; and with the Prime Minister, Harold Wilson, if possible.

(5) The climax

By 10 o'clock on Friday 28 June, the tide had turned in management's favour. The company's telegram to the Prime Minister appeared to have broken the negotiating deadlock. Mrs Castle had invited the women strikers to come and see her in St. James's Square and asked management to stand by. At 3.45 pm on Friday 28 June, Barbara Castle adjourned her meeting with the Sewing Machinists and invited Blakeman and others into her suite at St James's Square. She told them that the women felt 'cheated' over their grading and would not go back to work unless they got something out of their strike. The company somehow had to convince the women that the grading system worked. At General Motors' Vauxhall Plant, women employees got 93% of the men's rates. Was Ford willing to match that? Blakeman reminded Mrs Castle that he had already offered to discuss with the unions the question of the women's pay differential — but not under the duress of a strike. He tried once more to explain the differences between the work of the Intermediate Machinists and the Final Machinists. But the women rejected his job evaluation arguments. They insisted that they had all been 'trade-tested' and had therefore all been treated by the company as skilled workers and they ought to be in Grade C. Mrs Castle could see they were getting nowhere and decided on a different approach. Kicking off her shoes and tucking her legs up under her on the settee, she addressed the Sewing Machinists, woman to women. She pointed out that both Ford and their unions were 'prisoners' of the job evaluation and grading scheme, which could not simply be set aside. Job evaluation by itself wouldn't solve the problem. But she knew the company was willing to seriously re-examine the women's pay differentials. She trusted the company and the women must trust her. But the company would not talk under the duress of the strike. So, first, they must go back to work and then allow the unions to present their claim for a change in pay differentials. Finally, they must use the grading grievance procedure and the Court of Inquiry to solve their grading claim. In return, the Government had already promised to legislate on equal pay, as quickly as possible.

After an hour's adjournment, the women agreed to recommend a return to work on Monday. Mrs Castle was delighted. Drinks were produced with Mrs Castle proposing a toast: 'To the victory of common sense'. She had already announced in the Commons on Wednesday that she was going to introduce an Equal Pay Bill and now gave the women an assurance that it would be phased in as quickly as possible.

(6) The settlement

At NJNC on Monday 1 July 1968, Blakeman gave a brief account of events since the last meeting. He noted that the women had refused to return to work, despite the setting up of a Court of Inquiry to examine the issue of grading and alleged sex discrimination. However, now that the women had returned to work, the company was willing to discuss the differential between men's and women's pay rates through Procedure. Ford was prepared to increase the women's existing rate from 85% to 90% of the men's equivalent rate for each grade. The Trade Union Side eventually agreed to recommend acceptance of this offer if the company would increase the figure to 92%. The company agreed, urging the trade unions to signify their formal consent as quickly as possible. The strike was as good as over.

(7) Aftermath

The women returned to work in a mood of jubilation tinged with disappointment. They had secured a far more generous pay settlement than they had ever imagined possible, but had failed to secure their upgrading. Reports from the River Plant indicated some local bitterness, after the strike, amongst members of supervision who felt that the company should have stood firm and not given way to strike pressure.

In the immediate aftermath of the strike, the most important effect was the boost given to the morale of Dagenham shop stewards by the women's strike. After several years of setbacks and 'defeats', they felt psychologically renewed and refreshed by the women's 'victory', which they originally failed to support.

SECTION 3: ANALYSIS OF THE DISPUTE

(1) What was the dispute about?

The fierceness and duration of the Ford dispute centred largely on confusion amongst the parties on the central issues underlying the strike. Ford's Sewing Machinists had long nursed a grievance about their pay and grading under the old wage structure. This derived from the nineteenth century engineering industry, comprising four distinct pay grades, each with its own basic hourly pay rate:

Grade I: Skilled time-served craftsmen
Grade II: Semi-skilled male workers

Grade III: Unskilled male workers
Grade IV: All women workers

This pay structure was inherently discriminatory in that the women's basic hourly pay rate was always less than that of the unskilled males. But at Ford, women workers suffered a five-fold discrimination:

(i)   they were all recruited into a limited range of low-paid jobs, mainly in the Trim Shop;

(ii)   their jobs were all in the same pay grade, regardless of the tasks that they carried out;

(iii) their rate of pay in Grade IV was always lower than that of the three male grades;

(iv) their weekly earnings — as distinct from their pay rates — were always lower than those of men because they were prevented by the Factory Acts from working shifts, nightwork or weekend overtime;

(v)   they received less merit money than their male counterparts because their basic rates at Ford were already higher than those paid in any other industrial employment close to their homes and domestic responsibilities.

The new 1967 wage structure, based on job evaluation, promised to change all that. Since the purpose of job evaluation was to establish the level of job demand in different work tasks, it had no more regard to the worker's gender than her age, nationality, colour or creed. It was the jobs themselves that were assessed under job evaluation, not the men or women doing them.

When the new job grading and pay proposals were published in April 1967, the jobs of Intermediate and Final Sewing Machinists were both placed in Grade B, whereas the jobs of the Prototype Sewing Machinists were placed in Grade C. This shattered the Dagenham women's heightened expectations and they refused to accept that job evaluation had done justice to their work. The River Plant Convener, Henry Friedman, who had been a member of the Divisional Review Committee during the job evaluation programme, was convinced that the Sewing Machinists' jobs should have been placed in Grade C. He therefore concluded that, since the Sewing Machinists were all women, the company had deliberately manipulated the Sewing Machinists' job profiles in order to keep their jobs in Grade B. He was, therefore, not prepared to accept the new gradings or to progress the women's claim for up-grading through the normal Grading Grievance Procedure.

From the outset, therefore, the women saw the dispute as being concerned with two related issues (i) alleged incorrect grading of their jobs; and (ii) alleged sex discrimination by Ford to keep their jobs in Grade B. That was the company's understanding of what the dispute was initially about. However, within 24 hours of the women's walk-out, the media were reporting that they were not only on strike over their grading or alleged discrimination but were also demanding equal pay. In short, Friedman had converted a bread-and-butter dispute over pay and grading into a much wider-ranging political issue: equal pay for equal work.

For Ford management, the heart of the dispute was the fact that, in backing the women's strike, the unions had broken four separate agreements:

(i)   they had refused to put the women's grievance through the jointly-agreed special Grading Grievance Procedure;
(ii) they had ignored the jointly-agreed and long-established disputes procedures for resolving issues that arose between the company and the unions;
(iii) they had taken unconstitutional strike action in support of a claim for equal pay that had never been presented at NJNC;
(iv) they had broken the Two-Year Pay and Productivity Agreement, which provided for no further economic claims against the company.

For rank-and-file activists and the two principal unions concerned, the broken agreements were regrettable but relatively trivial compared with their members' genuine and legitimate grievance over grading, sex discrimination and equal pay:

(i)   *The Sewing Machinists* clearly believed that their grading was wrong but were easily persuaded by the Convener to accept that they were the victims of sex discrimination. They nevertheless saw the dispute as a straightforward grading issue.
(ii) *The Convener* was convinced that the Sewing Machinists' job should have emerged in Grade C of the new wage structure. He could find no explanation other than deliberate manipulation by the company. For the Convener, the central issue in the dispute was sex discrimination by Ford.
(iii) *The unions* were initially reluctant to support the women but were persuaded that the issue was not simply one of grading but sex discrimination. For the unions the dispute was an opportunity to secure equal pay for their women members, even though they had never formally lodged a claim for equal pay at the Ford NJNC.
(iv) *The company* acknowledged that there might be errors in the original job evaluation and had therefore proposed a grading grievance procedure to deal with any grievances. But it denied any manipulation of the job evaluation results or any deliberate sex discrimination. For the company, the dispute arose from the unions' failure to abide by jointly-agreed procedures for resolving disputes.

(2) How important was the context?

The year 1968 served as a watershed in the history of British industrial relations. It was the year of the publication of the Donovan Commission Report on Britain's industrial relations, which was to fix the eyes of public policy-makers on the key issue of how best to reform Britain's system of industrial relations — more especially, whether the law should play a bigger part in securing effective reform. The Ford Sewing Machinists' strike must therefore be seen in that historical context.

Like many other British manufacturing companies, Ford had suffered for years from intermittent work stoppages in protest against perceived injustices in the pay and earnings differentials of its large and heterogeneous workforce. Competitive sectional wage and grading claims were a regular feature of its industrial relations. The new wage structure was a radical attempt by Ford to deal with the root causes of that disruption. The cost of carrying out the job evaluation programme and of implementing the new wage structure had been high but Ford had seen it as an investment in good labour relations. The Two-Year Pay and Productivity Agreement offered Ford workers substantial improvements in pay and conditions in return for a period of industrial peace and predictable labour costs, without further economic demands.

Ford received wide publicity for its success in reforming its wage structure, by securing the unions' cooperation and subsequent agreement to a new, job-evaluated wage structure, tied to a comprehensive productivity package that restored the link between effort and rewards in Britain's troubled motor industry. Like the Fawley Productivity Bargaining Agreements secured by Esso in 1965 [13], Ford's 1967 Pay and Productivity Agreement was held up by the Labour Government as a model of voluntary reform in pay and bargaining structures without the need for legislation to compel that much-needed reform.

The long-awaited Donovan Report [14], published in May 1968, had strongly favoured a voluntary rather than a legalistic approach to the reform of Britain's industrial relations. Coming in the very month of that Report, the Sewing Machinists' strike was therefore seen as threatening the very basis of patiently-negotiated, voluntary reform. As Blakeman told the Scamp Court of Inquiry:

> *With due respect, I would ask the Court to keep in mind, throughout this hearing, two fundamental points. First, the Ford Motor Company has a collective bargaining system such as had been advocated by the Donovan Commission on the general premise that a system of company bargaining is to be preferred to industry-wide bargaining, and that a move in this direction would lead to greater harmony in our national industrial relations. My company shares that view provided there is some integrity on both sides. Secondly, the contentious*

point of this issue would never have arisen if we, as a company, had not embarked two years ago upon an exercise to change our wages structure so that it would meet the demands of modern, progressive and competitive industry. The need for just such modernizing plans, resulting in up-to-date wages structures, is evident throughout industry in this country today and is one of the root causes behind the malaise in the present British economy. [15]

But there was another sense in which the historical context was important to the conduct and outcome of the dispute. For decades, British women had found no opportunity to achieve equal pay in industry. By 1968, there was a change in the social climate.

(3) Why did the women declare an all-out strike?

The choice of an appropriate strategy by workers engaged in an industrial dispute is never easy, even amongst hard-bitten, rank-and-file activists. The choice is more difficult when the workers concerned have never before taken strike action. The Ford Sewing Machinists had no previous experience of fighting a battle of their own, let alone one of this nature. In the words of the Convener, Henry Friedman:

They were quite unprepared for the task ahead, which entailed taking on the might of Ford — a multinational Company — with an annual global budget which in 1968 exceeded that of India. [16]

The odds stacked against them appeared to be overwhelming. If the strike were to succeed, it needed official support from at least two of the unions whose members were directly involved. The women were convinced that Ford had denied them their rightful grading but this factor alone was unlikely to win them either local or official union suport. The question of the women's grading had somehow to be stepped up and converted into an issue on which unions would find it difficult to deny official support. The alleged sex discrimination provided the answer. In the Convener's words:

There was virtually no prospect of obtaining support from any of the major unions on the narrow issue of a grading grievance. Attracting support from other departments or plants on economic issues that are craft-based or sectional in character is always difficult. Interunion, interplant rivalries, as well as personality clashes, are additional factors that make solidarity action a rare event. [17]

The one-day token strike on Wednesday 29 May 1968 brought home to the company that the women were in earnest, but Ford refused to be moved by such pressure. During the following week, urgent talks were held between senior management, the women's shop stewards, the Convener and District Officials, but they came to nothing. By Thursday 6 June, they realized that something more than a token stoppage would be needed to force the company's hand.

When the strike committee met that weekend to reappraise the situation, two points clearly emerged:

(i)   Since no support could be expected on grading, the grievance would have to be linked to the sex discrimination and equal pay issue, and be subordinated to them.

(ii) It was essential to gain time to mobilize outside support for the equal pay cause, not only from the unions at national level, but from women's organizations, Members of Parliament and other civil rights campaigners.

On the following Monday, the women rejected their District Official's recommendation to return to work to allow their grievance to be investigated. Since the women were determined not to return to work empty-handed, they endorsed the proposed strategy: to fight the issue to a finish in an all-out, open-ended strike.

(4) Why did management not concede the claim?

Although the financial cost of conceding the women's claim for upgrading was relatively small, Ford felt bound to resist it because of its possible repercussions:

(i)   To give way to strike pressure would have opened the floodgates to similar claims for upgrading from many other groups of workers.

(ii) To act unilaterally in reducing the differential between men's and women's pay was tantamount to breaching the Two-Year Pay and Productivity Agreement which, in turn, risked another pay claim by male employees.

(iii) To concede the union demand for equal pay when no such claim had been presented at NJNC would have brought the jointly-agreed collective bargaining machinery into disrepute.

(iv) To concede the claim for equal pay might have been miscon-strued as an admission by Ford that it had discriminated against women under its new wage structure. Ford felt bound to deny such a claim for four reasons:

(a)   Discrimination of any kind was in direct conflict with company policy, although Ford *had* been notorious for its discriminatory employment policies in the 1930s.

(b)   The new wage structure was based on the systematic evaluation of work, not workers, which set out to preclude the possibility of inherent sex discrimination.

(c)   The company had made it clear that it was not opposed to equal pay in principle and that, as soon as women carried out jobs in the higher grades, they would receive the appropriate grade rate for the job.

(d)   The company had also agreed that if and when the protec-

> tive provisions of the Factory Act were removed, and women agreed to work shifts, accepting all the obligations that men accepted, their rates of pay would be raised to full equality with those of the men.

But Ford was unable to use such sophisticated arguments against a group of women strikers whose emotions were running predictably high in the early days of their first-ever strike. Instead, the company told the unions quite bluntly that it was not prepared to negotiate under duress but that, if the women returned to full normal working, it was prepared to consider their claim for upgrading on its merits. By this time, however, the two principal unions (AUEW and NUVB) had made the strike official, so there was no turning back. It was the breach of faith on the part of those unions, their disregard of jointly-agreed procedures, and their failure to respect the NJNC bargaining machinery, which persuaded Ford that it must not yield to strike pressure. As Blakeman told the Scamp Inquiry:

> *The complexity of the details and technicalities that make up the whole sorry story of this dispute must not be allowed to cloud this simple issue. If the company had to concede to pressure by groups resorting to unconstitutional action, it would make it impossible to apply a fair and consistent wages structure and would destroy the whole fabric of collective bargaining.*
>
> *The dilemma which faces the company and, we believe, the whole of British industry is that, having taken a stand on the side of the law and order in industrial relationships, what can be done to prevent the disruption of its operation by the irresponsibility of people who choose to ignore Agreements entered into in good faith?* [18]

(5) Who won?

Although the outcomes of an industrial dispute are often difficult to assess, they are frequently discussed by both sides in terms of victory and defeat. For the Ford Sewing Machinists, there was no doubt who had won. In the words of the Convenor:

> *... when you've made a claim on behalf of 300 women, and [somebody] offers you half as much again for three or four times that number of women; plus the promise of equal pay; and you've negotiated the settlement at rank-and-file level with the assistance of one or two unions against the orchestrated disapproval of all the other unions, of the company and even of the government, because of incomes policy; and despite the kind of male cultural prejudice against women which prevailed at the time — if, in the face of all these odds, you've broken through, then everybody — even the people who were hostile*

and who are still hostile today — said clearly: The company was defeated.

In other words, although Ford refused to concede on the grading issue, it was forced directly to pay more money to more workers and indirectly to concede the issue of equal pay, a principle for which the trade unions had been working without success for over one hundred years. According to the Convener:

> *On the trade union side, such an outcome was seen by friend and foe alike as an outright victory for the workers and an outright defeat for the company. It's judged at that level, on those simple criteria . . .* [19]

From the company's viewpoint, the outcome was naturally seen somewhat differently. In seeking an acceptable formula for ending the dispute, management was constrained by four major factors:

(i)   it could *not* compromise the job-evaluated grading because that risked the disintegration of the whole of the new wage structure;

(ii) it could *not* reopen the Two-Year Agreement unilaterally without risking a major claim by the men for the restoration of their differentials;

(iii) it could *not* act outside the limits of incomes policy and needed the blessing of the Secretary of State for Employment to any changes in the Agreement;

(iv) it could *not* drop the principles that guided its new industrial relations strategy, which included reasserting control by the NJNC as the joint body through which negotiated solutions must be found for all major industrial relations disputes.

The company therefore devised a three-point peace formula to overcome these four constraints:

(i)   The Court of Inquiry would deal with the allegation of sex discrimination and report after hearing the evidence submitted by both sides.

(ii) Once the women had returned to work, the NJNC would be convened to receive the company's proposal to increase the women's rate from 86% to 92% of the equivalent male grade rate.

(iii) The Secretary of State would introduce an Equal Pay Bill in Parliament, as soon as possible, which would progressively remove sex discrimination by making it unlawful to pay different rates of pay to men and women engaged in the same or broadly similar work.

This was the formula that got the strikers back to work. It enabled the Court of Inquiry to dismiss the allegation of sex discrimination in the new wage structure, and it allowed the NJNC to agree to reduce differentials between men and women's pay, without provoking a further wage claim on behalf of male employees. Despite the heavy financial losses caused by the strike, the company could reasonably argue that it had not made concessions under duress, that it had preserved the new wage structure, and that it had restored credibility to the Ford NJNC. For Ford, the necessary price had been paid to achieve these objectives.

(6) Costs and benefits of the dispute

The most immediate and obvious cost of the strike to the company was the loss of three weeks production and sales revenue. This was quantified by Ford at around £1 million per day, but the real cost was not so much economic as psychological: the loss of faith in established disputes procedures and the fact that the NJNC was unable to resolve the Sewing Machinists' issue through those procedures. The company's attempt to set up an internal NJNC Inquiry was frustrated by the decision of two unions — the AEF and the NUVB — to make the strike retrospectively official. What the company feared more than anything else was the loss of confidence in the NJNC as a viable negotiating body.

By the end of the dispute, the company could point to several significant gains that helped to offset the cost of the strike. First, the Court of Inquiry cleared the job evaluation scheme of any taint of sex discrimination and a subcommittee subsequently vindicated the company's decision to place the women's jobs in Grade B. Those findings helped to consolidate the job-evaluated wage structure on which the company relied to control competitive grading claims over the following twenty years. Second, the outcome of the dispute restored faith in the NJNC by the joint decision to reopen the Two-Year Agreement for the sole purpose of adjusting the differentials between men's and women's grade rates. Third, the company had focused the Secretary of State and the country's attention on the outdated provisions of the Factory Acts, which prevented women from working shifts and from earning the same as men.

But the principal benefits were clearly on the side of the unions. Although the women failed to establish their claim for upgrading, they soon recovered their strike losses through much higher grade rates. The dispute boosted the morale of the Ford shop stewards by showing that it was possible to win a dispute despite the initial opposition of both company and unions. By mounting an effective campaign against pay discrimination, the women brought sufficient pressure on government to compel it to introduce legislation to make such discrimination unlawful. Finally, the outcome of the dispute provided an enormous stimulus to the women's movement in Britain at a crucial point in its development. The Equal Pay Act 1970 (plus the Equal Value Amendment Regulations 1984), and the Sex Discrimination Act 1975, which established the Equal Opportunities

Commission, all stemmed directly or indirectly from the Ford Sewing Machinists' strike. In this sense, it was the working women of Britain as a whole who were the principal beneficiaries of the dispute and its outcomes.

(7) Lessons of the dispute

In his own analysis of the dispute, the Convener pointed to some of the lessons learned by rank-and-file activists in deciding the strategy and tactics for running a major dispute:

(i) By confining the strike to those workers directly involved, it was possible to avoid diluting the strength of the women's grievance, thereby insulating the strike from any undermining influence:

> *One of the lessons we'd learned by 1968 was that you either have a mass strike, with everybody involved, or you have a restricted strike, in a key section, with nobody involved. The worst situation is one in which other workers, who are not concerned with the issue, become involved, or, as a result of being laid off, feel entitled to a voice in determining what should happen next. So, you avoid that situation like the plague.* [20]

(ii) By refusing to return to work in exchange for the promise of a Court of Inquiry, the strikers kept the issue alive and so helped to influence the outcome in the women's favour*.

(iii) In complex multi-plant, multi-union situations, the rank-and-file leadership must secure the official support of at least one or two unions, in order to prevent collusion between other unions and the company in their joint attempt to crush the dispute in its early days:

> *Company plus union officials versus rank-and-file leadership you lose; national officials plus rank-and-file leadership you win. That's why the women went . . . to lobby their officials before the NJNC: there must be no collusion with the company.* [21]

But Ford also learned lessons from its own handling of the dispute:

(i) Management grossly underestimated the strength of grievance amongst the Sewing Machinists and failed to respond positively to their grievance.

(ii) Management never expected a group of women employees to

---

* According to Friedman, this later became known as 'Scargill's Law', following the adoption of the precedent by Arthur Scargill during disputes in the coal-mining industry.

take all-out strike action in support of their own grievance, or to stay out on strike for so long.

(iii) Management failed to anticipate that the women strikers and the unions would win such immediate and widespread support for their equal pay campaign.

(iv) Management failed to anticipate a powerful new alliance, which was to be forged between Ford rank-and-file activists and some of the newly-elected left-wing members of union Executives.

(v) The trade union side of the NJNC could no longer be relied upon to repudiate unofficial and unconstitutional strike action, or to uphold long-established disputes procedures enshrined in freely-negotiated collective agreements.

The most important lesson of all, perhaps, was that Ford could no longer rely on the views expressed by trade union officials at NJNC as accurately reflecting those of the shopfloor. The Sewing Machinists had expressed a genuine and legitimate grievance to their unions but this had not been represented properly by union officials to the company. Ford recognized that the company would have to come to terms and deal more directly with shop stewards instead of relying primarily on union intermediaries. As Ford's Director of Industrial Relations later told a House of Commons Committee:

> *We are trying to make sure that all the things we bargain, all the new procedures we set up are with the willing concurrence of our employees ... We are absolutely convinced that the only solution to the problem is to get complete involvement.* [22]

Ford's Managing Director, Sir Terence Beckett, later Director-General of the Confederation of British Industry, expressed the same idea in much broader terms:

> *Over the years, a whole set of panaceas have been advanced on this, and we joined in the national feeling that such-and-such would solve the problem. But in the end we have come down to the basic situation that we, the unions and our own workforce together have got to sort the thing out. Government will not do it for us and it was probably unreasonable to expect that they ever would. We have really got to sort the thing out for ourselves.* [23]

SECTION 4: CONCLUSIONS AND 1987 POSTSCRIPT

Although the Ford Sewing Machinists felt that they had won a significant victory at the end of their 1968 strike, they had failed to win their claim for upgrading and this continued to rankle over the years. The Equal Pay Act 1970, which their strike inspired, made it unlawful for employers to discriminate between the pay of men and women engaged in the same or broadly similar work. But this was of no direct or immediate benefit to the Ford Sewing Machinists, for two reasons:

(i) There was no evidence to show that the Ford job evaluation scheme was inherently discriminatory.

(ii) The Equal Pay Act could only be applied where a woman could show an Industrial Tribunal that she was paid less than a man engaged in a comparable job, i.e. doing the same or broadly similar work.

That was the state of the law on pay discrimination in Britain from 1975 to 1984. In that year, a ruling of the European Court of Justice compelled the British Government to introduce an amendment to the Equal Pay Act, bringing it into line with the law of other member countries of the European Economic Community. The effect of this Equal Value Amendment was to allow women to bring cases of alleged pay discrimination to an Industrial Tribunal where they could show that their work was *of equal value to that of a male employee*, even though the male employee was not engaged in the same or broadly similar work.

In the spring of 1983, an application was submitted by three Ford Sewing Machinists to the London North Industrial Tribunal, alleging that the Ford job evaluation scheme was inherently discriminatory. These grounds were later changed to allow the application to deal with the women's complaint under the Equal Pay (Amendment) Regulations, which came into operation on 1 January 1984.

After hearing six days of evidence from the women and the company in April 1984, the Tribunal's majority decision, published 11 June 1984, said that:

> *There are no reasonable grounds for determining that the work of the applicants is of equal value to that of the male comparators specified in the originating applications and their applications are therefore dismissed.* [24]

Following this decision, and after an interval of seventeen years, the 240 Ford Sewing Machinists renewed their claim for upgrading at the NJNC, as part of the Ford unions' 1985 pay claim. This time, the TGWU (which now represented all the women) argued that the company should help to resolve the issue by:

(i) allowing independent assessors to examine the women's claim for upgrading;

(ii) expanding the women's job content to allow their jobs to be regraded.

When the company rejected both suggestions as impractical, the women began their second strike against the company's refusal to upgrade their jobs to Grade C. As in 1968, the strike again stopped all vehicle production at Ford, with some 8500 other Ford workers laid off without pay. Moreover, union negotiators refused to sign a draft agreement on the 1984 pay deal, unless the issue was resolved. Finally, after seven weeks of strike action, the women returned to work after accepting an NJNC proposal on 28 December 1984 to set up a specially-constituted arbitration panel to examine their grievance. Both sides agreed in advance to accept the panel's findings as binding. The panel's report, published in April 1985, concluded that the job should be upgraded from Grade B to Grade C and the company immediately implemented that recommendation with retrospective effect to January 1984.

Despite press speculation that the arbitration panel's decision had undermined the Ford wage structure, it remained intact and virtually unchanged in 1987, after an interval of twenty years. The Sewing Machinists' grading claim had been finally laid to rest.

CHRONOLOGY OF THE DISPUTE

21 May 1968	Sewing Machinists impose overtime ban and threaten strike on 29 May
29 May	Sewing Machinists one-day token strike
30 May	Strikers vote for further action on 7 June
7 June	Sewing Machinists begin all-out strike
11 June	AEF declare strike official
17 June	NJNC agree to conduct own Inquiry into dispute
19 June	Secretary of State appoints Court of Inquiry
22 June	Secretary of State urges ending of strike
27 June	Court of Inquiry begins
28 June	Secretary of State calls parties to talks
1 July	Strikers return to work
4 July	Court of Inquiry ends
21 August	Court of Inquiry Report published
4 September	Special Grading Committee confirms grading

WHO'S WHO IN THE DISPUTE

Beckett, Terence (later Sir)	Managing Director (later Chairman), Ford Motor Co. Ltd, 1974–80
Birch, Reg	Executive Councilman, Amalgamated Engineering Union
Blakeman, Leslie	Director of Labour Relations, Ford Motor Co. Ltd, 1966–69
Castle, Barbara	Secretary of State for Employment, 1968–70
Friedman, Henry	Convener, Dagenham River Plant, 1962–72
Gallagher, Charlie	Assistant General Secretary, National Union of Vehicle Builders, 1965–70
Kealey, Les	National Officer, TGWU (Automotive), 1956–69
Ramsey, Robert	Industrial Relations Manager, 1958–69

	Director of Industrial Relations, Ford Motor Co. Ltd, 1969–73
Scamp, Jack (Sir)	Director of Industrial Relations, GEC Ltd, 1960–70 Chairman, Ford Sewing Machinists' Dispute Court of Inquiry, 1968
Young, Mark	National Officer, EEPTU Chairman, Trade Union Side, Ford NJNC, 1966–69

REFERENCES

1 For a traditional interpretation of women's role in the 'domestic' economy, see Ivy Pinchbeck: *Women Workers in the Industrial Revolution, 1650–1850* (1930). For a more recent interpretation, see Linda Charles and Loran Duffin (eds): *Women and Work in Pre-industrial England*, Croom Helm, London, 1985.

2 See *Report of the War Cabinet Committee on Women in Industry*, Cmd. 135, HMSO, London, 1919.

3 See Sheila Rowbotham: *Hidden from History*, Pluto Press, London, 1977.

4 See Equal Opportunities Commission: Second Annual Report, 1977.

5 Jean Martin and Ceridwen Roberts: *Women and Employment: A Lifetime Perspective*, Department of Employment/Office of Population Censuses and Surveys, London, 1984, pp. 185–92.

6 Jean Martin and Ceridwen Roberts: *Women and Employment: A Lifetime Perspective*, Department of Employment/Office of Population Censuses and Surveys, London, 1984, p. 32.

7 For further details, see T. Mallier and M. Rosser: 'The Changing Role of Women in the British Economy', Natwest Quarterly Review, November 1979; Brian Chiplin and Peter J. Sloane: *Tackling Discrimination in the Workplace*, Cambridge University Press, Cambridge, 1982.

8 For an exposition of the 'core and periphery' model of employment, see John Atkinson: *Work Organization and Working Time*, Institute of Manpower Studies London, 1985.

9 For recent changes in the distribution of women's employment, see Equal Opportunity Commission: Annual Reports.

10 Jean Martin and Ceridwen Roberts: *Women and Employment: A Lifetime Perspective*, Department of Employment/Office of Population Censuses and Surveys, London, 1984, p. 189.

11 This section has been freely adapted from a more detailed account of the strike in Henry Friedman and Sander Meredeen: *The Dynamics of Industrial Conflict: Lessons from Ford*, Croom Helm, London, 1980.

12 Ford National Joint Negotiating Committee: Transcript of Proceedings, 17 June 1968, p. 7.

13 See Allan Flanders: *The Fawley Productivity Agreements: a Case Study of Management and Collective Bargaining*, Faber, London, 1964.

14 See *Report of Royal Commission on Trade Unions and Employers Associations (The Donovan Report)*, Cmd. 6362, HMSO, London, 1968.

15 Leslie Blakeman, *Record of Proceedings (Scamp Inquiry)*, Second Day, 3 July 1968, p. 78.

16 Henry Friedman in Friedman and Meredeen: *The Dynamics of Industrial Conflict: Lessons from Ford*, Croom Helm, London, 1980, p. 138.

17 Henry Friedman in Friedman and Meredeen: *The Dynamics of Industrial Conflict: Lessons from Ford*, Croom Helm, London, 1980, p. 139.

18 Leslie Blakeman, cited in Friedman and Meredeen; *The Dynamics of Industrial Conflict: Lessons from Ford*, Croom Helm, London, 1980, p. 121.

19 Henry Friedman in Friedman and Meredeen: *The Dynamics of Industrial Conflict: Lessons from Ford*, Croom Helm, London, 1980, p. 213.

20 Henry Friedman in Friedman and Meredeen: *The Dynamics of Industrial Conflict: Lessons from Ford*, Croom Helm, London, 1980, pp. 198–9.

21 Henry Friedman in Friedman and Meredeen: *The Dynamics of Industrial Conflict: Lessons from Ford*, Croom Helm, London, 1980, p. 201.

22 Robert J. Ramsey, cited by Meredeen in Friedman and Meredeen: *The Dynamics of Industrial Conflict: Lessons from Ford*, Croom Helm, London, 1980, p. 234.

23 Terence Beckett, cited by Meredeen in Friedman and Meredeen: *The Dynamics of Industrial Conflict: Lessons from Ford*, Croom Helm, London, 1980, p. 234.

24 See *Report of Reserved Decision of an Industrial Tribunal Hearing*, Held at North London on 3 & 4, 5, 6, 13 & 18 April 1984.

STUDY QUESTIONS

1. Why did the Ford Sewing Machinists take all-out strike action in pursuit of their grading grievance?
2. What is job evaluation? How far can it help to produce a payment system that is both efficient and equitable?
3. Examine the role of the Union Convener as a leading rank-and-file activist throughout the Ford Sewing Machinists' strike.
4. Is it possible for *all* sides to win an industrial dispute?
5. Trace the development of statutory non-discrimination provisions in Britain from the Ford Sewing Machinists' strike of 1968, through the Equal Pay Act 1970, the Sex Discrimination Act 1975, to the 1984 Equal Value Amendment to the Equal Pay Act.
6. How would you explain the changing role of women in the British economy?

SUGGESTIONS FOR FURTHER READING

Sir Cyril Asquith: *Report of the Royal Commission on Equal Pay, 1944–46*, Cmd. 6937, HMSO, London, 1946.
Huw Beynon: *Working for Ford*, Penguin, Harmondsworth, 1973.
Barbara Castle: *Diaries*, Weidenfeld and Nicolson, London, 1980.
Equal Opportunity Commission: Annual Reports.

Henry Friedman and Sander Meredeen: *The Dynamics of Industrial Conflict: Lessons from Ford*, Croom Helm, London, 1980.

Jean Martin and Ceridwen Roberts: *Women and Employment: a Lifetime Perspective*, Department of Employment/Office of Population Censuses and Surveys, London, 1984.

Sheila Rowbotham: *Hidden from History*, Pluto Press, London, 1977.

Sir Jack Scamp: *Report of a Court of Inquiry*, Cmnd. 3749, HMSO, London, 1968 and *Record of Proceedings (Scamp Inquiry)*.

H. A. Turner, G. Clack and G. Roberts: *Labour Relations in the Motor Industry*, Allen and Unwin, London, 1967.

Report of the War Cabinet Committee on Women in Industry, Cmd. 135, HMSO, London, 1919.

CHAPTER 4

■ The degeneration and reform of workplace relations —

THE ELECTROLUX PAY DISPUTE, 1975–78

The primary responsibility for the conduct of industrial relations within a concern, and the framework of collective agreements within which those relations are conducted, lies with the Board.

Donovan Commission (1968)

Although litigation in each individual case may produce a theoretically correct answer ... it is unlikely that the individual answers put together can produce a coherent wage structure capable of general application in other cases. That can only be done by negotiation.

Mr Justice Philips
President
Employment Appeal Tribunal

INTRODUCTION: WHICH WAY TO REFORM INDUSTRIAL RELATIONS?

In October 1976, the Employment Appeal Tribunal (EAT) met in London to hear an appeal by Electrolux Limited against a decision by the Bedford Industrial Tribunal that one of the company's employees, Mrs Ann Hutchinson, an AUEW shop steward, and six fellow women workers, were entitled to equal pay under Section 1(4) of the Equal Pay Act 1970.

When Mr Justice Philips, President of the EAT, enquired whether there were any similar claims from other Electrolux employees, he was plainly appalled to learn that there were no fewer than 700 cases waiting to be heard. Dismissing the company's appeal, Mr Justice Philips acknowledged the practical difficulties that might arise from the EAT's decision — but he then added some remarks of great significance to students of British industrial relations about what the law can and cannot achieve:

> In a complicated situation such as that confronting Electrolux Limited, where there are several hundreds of claims and the

circumstances of the appellants are not identical, a process of litigation under the Equal Pay Act 1970 can never produce a satisfactory result. Although the litigation in each individual case may produce a theoretically correct answer in accordance with the terms of the Equal Pay Act 1970, it is unlikely that the individual answers put together can produce a coherent wage structure capable of general application in other cases. That can only be done by negotiation, applying the current views, and statutory prescriptions on equal pay and equal opportunities. It may be that the Equal Opportunities Commission could be of assistance in such an exercise. Certainly, it lies beyond our competence and jurisdiction. [1]

In other words, although the Act was designed to remove pay discrimination, and although some 700 women employees at Electrolux were legally entitled to bring their cases to an Industrial Tribunal, the law per se could not remove that discrimination. According to Mr Justice Philips, the only way to achieve and maintain 'a coherent wage structure' — a fundamental feature of good industrial relations — was for the parties to sit down and negotiate some form of compromise resolution of their differences, perhaps with the help of an independent change agent.

The Electrolux pay dispute raises key questions for social policy: What is the role of the law in the reform of degenerate systems of industrial relations? How far can the law help to change industrial attitudes and behaviour unless those concerned are already committed to such changes? To what extent should management and unions rely on the law rather than on their own voluntary actions to achieve their objectives? Is it true to say that Britain has moved away from an essentially voluntary system of industrial relations towards a system of legal regulation? This chapter examines these questions.

SECTION 1: VOLUNTARISM AND THE LIMITS OF THE LAW

The 1970s were marked by a massive increase in the volume of British labour law. Before 1970, few industrial relations practitioners were trained lawyers or especially knowledgeable about the law because they did not need to be. Since 1980 they can no longer afford to ignore the major provisions of British labour law: for it now exerts a profound influence on British industrial relations. Most of this new legislation defines the mutual rights and obligations of employers and individual workers: the right to protection against unhealthy or unsafe working conditions and practices (HASAWA 1975); the right to seek employment, training and promotion without discrimination on grounds of race (Race Relations Act 1976) or sex (Sex Discrimination Act 1975); the rights of shop stewards to engage in legitimate trade union activities at the workplace without fear of victimization or dismissal (Employment Protection Act 1975, amended 1978); the right of women to maternity leave (Employment Protection Act 1975); and so on.

Taken together, these provisions introduced a new legal charter of industrial rights to British workers — a set of minimum employment standards with which employers must lawfully comply and which trade unions may seek to improve upon in the course of collective bargaining. It should be noted that none of these Acts impinges significantly upon collective industrial relations, i.e. the terms and conditions of employment which trade unions have achieved by collective bargaining and which are enshrined in the collective agreements that have formed the backbone of the British system of industrial relations. The distinction is of vital importance: for reasons of history, tradition and public policy, the British system of industrial relations evolved as an essentially voluntary system. This was based on the philosophical assumption, which both management and unions traditionally accepted, that the most effective way to regulate the complex relationships over the marketing of labour in a free society is by voluntary agreement between the parties. Such agreement followed more or less free collective bargaining, normally without recourse to the courts or to Parliament. In the words of Sir Otto Kahn-Freund, a distinguished authority on British labour law, writing in the 1960s:

> *There is, perhaps, no major country in the world in which the law has played a less significant role in the shaping of industrial relations than in Great Britain and in which today the law and the legal profession have less to do with labour relations.* [2]

In many other countries, the law has given trade unions positive collective rights — the right to exist, to organize workers into trade unions and to bargain collectively. In some countries, the law goes further, prescribing certain minimum collective rights over terms and conditions of employment, e.g. the right to a national minimum wage or a minimum number of paid annual holidays. By contrast, the British Parliament has traditionally kept out of collective relations between labour and capital. A limited number of Acts were passed in the nineteenth century to protect individual workers from the worst excesses of the new factory system: the Truck Acts, which required employers to pay their workers in coin of the realm and not in company tokens, intended to be redeemed at company stores; and the important series of Factory Acts, which prohibited the employment of women and young persons in certain particularly hazardous industrial processes and which restricted their employment on shift work, weekend overtime or for excessively long periods of time. The new legislation of the 1960s and 1970s remained very much within the voluntary tradition by addressing itself to individual employment rights, with individual remedies against alleged infringements either through the ordinary courts or, more usually, through special Industrial Tribunals (ITs), set up in the 1960s.

Insofar as collective industrial relationships are concerned, Parliament has traditionally preferred to build upon the pragmatic philosophy that pervaded Britain's first industrial revolution — namely, that the most enduring and workable solutions to the inevitable conflicts that arise between management and unions are those arrived at by the parties themselves when they sit round the bargaining table and attempt to reach voluntary agreements.

To assist the early unions in their attempts to achieve recognition and collective bargaining rights, and to redress in some measure the gross imbalance of bargaining power between employers and workers, Parliament conferred on trade unions certain legal immunities (or statutory exemptions), the effect of which were to enable trade unions to pursue their legitimate interest without fear of criminal prosecution or civil action for financial damages. From the last quarter of the nineteenth century, British trade unions have been free to organize workers, to bargain freely with employers or to take direct industrial action, including strikes, peaceful picketing at the place of work, and other actions intended to enforce their claims, *provided* (and only provided) such actions were taken 'in contemplation or furtherance of a trade dispute'. This so-called 'golden formula', which historically identified the legitimate areas of lawful trade union activity, emerged from the experience of Victorian employment relations and laid the foundations of the so-called *voluntary tradition* of British industrial relations in the first half of this century.

According to Allan Flanders, the voluntary tradition probably reached its high-point during the Second World War when Winston Churchill's wartime coalition government insisted on exhausting every possible means of reaching voluntary agreement with employers and trade unions *before* resorting to legislative controls over wartime labour. The voluntary tradition continued to flourish throughout the post-war reconstruction period. Yet, within ten years, it had come under severe criticism. Conservative lawyers, in particular, argued that the voluntary tradition had outlived its usefulness and the government was strongly urged to introduce much stronger, new, collective laws to regulate British industrial relations, notably to curb the alleged abuse of power by trade unions.

The two principal virtues claimed for the voluntary system were that it encouraged the development of:

(i)   flexibility — by allowing the bargaining parties to make, interpret and apply their collective agreements as changing circumstances required, without recourse to the courts;

(ii)   responsibility — by requiring the parties to act prudently and to reach sensible agreements to which they would be morally, though not legally, committed and would therefore do their best to honour.

The critics of voluntarism pointed to precisely opposite deficiencies:

(i)   a lack of flexibility — illustrated by union resistance to change and by management's failure to introduce new technology and to make better use of skilled manpower by tackling gross labour inefficiencies;

(ii)   a lack of responsibility — illustrated by the growth of unregulated plant bargaining, which encouraged leap-frogging (inflationary) wage demands enforced by unofficial and unconstitutional strikes, thus pressurizing managers to make concessions that eroded established differentials and undermined traditional, industry-wide bargaining.

Critics of voluntarism were especially alarmed by the increased number and spread of unofficial, unconstitutional strikes that disrupted the rhythm of production, adversely affected the quality of goods, endangered key delivery dates, added to the inflationary spiral of wage costs and so threatened Britain's ability to compete in international markets. In short, the voluntary system was said to be incapable of responding swiftly enough to the changing needs of a dynamic and modernizing economy. According to such critics, Britain was suffering from an insidious new disease: stagflation — the combination of stagnating productivity and inflationary price rises, which eroded the competitiveness of British goods and services. The whole economy threatened to drift rapidly into a state of 'industrial anarchy'. Trade unions were alleged to exercise a stranglehold on economic development — 'over-mighty subjects' whose abuse of power must be curtailed in the national interest. This theme, avidly taken up by the mass media, helped to produce an irresistible demand that the government should intervene and 'do something' to reform British industrial relations.

Harold Wilson's Labour Government, elected in 1964, swiftly responded to this pressure by appointing a Royal Commission, under the chairmanship of a distinguished lawyer, Lord Donovan:

> to consider relations between managements and employees and the role of the trade unions and employers' associations in promoting the interests of their members and in accelerating the social and economic advance of the nation, with particular reference to the Law affecting the activities of these bodies; and to report. [3]

The Donovan Report (1968) provided an authoritative analysis of industrial relations in post-war Britain. According to Donovan, its central defect was 'the disorder in factory and workshop relations and pay structures promoted by the conflict between the formal and informal systems' of bargaining. In theory, most, if not all, major issues were supposed to be settled by the formal system of national industry-wide bargaining conducted by powerful bodies of employers and trade unions. In practice, said Donovan, the formal system had been undermined and superceded by an informal system of workplace bargaining, conducted by shop stewards and managers, which was now more important than formal bargaining because it regulated the actual number of hours worked and paid, and the concessions achieved under local bargaining pressures. The assumptions of the formal system nevertheless continued to exert a powerful influence and so prevented the informal system from developing an effective and orderly method of regulation. 'The root of the evil' said Donovan, was to be found:

> *in our present method of collective bargaining and especially our methods of workshop bargaining and it is in the absence of speedy, clear and effective disputes procedures.* [4]

Donovan's description of 'two systems in conflict' helped to explain the dramatic increase in the number of unofficial (i.e. not union-sanctioned) and unconstitutional strikes (i.e. strikes in defiance of jointly-agreed procedural rules), the overwhelming majority of which arose, and were settled, within the workplace. Despite the emergence of decentralized workplace bargaining, most companies had failed to develop comprehensive and well-ordered domestic agreements. Companies had neglected their responsibilities for their own industrial relations. Many had no effective personnel policy, and perhaps no conception of one. According to Donovan's evidence, many practitioners expressed satisfaction with the existing system because it was familiar, comfortable and flexible. But for Donovan, these benefits were far outweighed by their disadvantages: namely, the tendency for extreme decentralization of bargaining and union self-government to degenerate into indecision and potential anarchy; the propensity to breed inefficiency; and the reluctance to change.

The most influential evidence to the Donovan Commission was provided by Allan Flanders, who characterized the system as being 'largely informal, largely fragmented and largely autonomous', i.e. bargaining was frequently beyond the control of national unions or employers organizations ('largely autonomous'); it comprised a series of generally uncoordinated claims and settlements, which destroyed any possibility of effective bargaining structures, coherent wage structures or equitable differentials ('largely fragmented'); and the settlements reached were rarely reduced to writing or adhered to because the parties wished to remain free to interpret those agreements as it suited them ('largely informal').

The Donovan Commissioners entirely accepted Flanders' evidence and incorporated it into their own thinking and prescription for reform. In effect, said Donovan, British management and unions were unaware that they were undermining their own economic future. Because bargaining was *largely informal*, it was impossible to know what rights and duties the parties owed one another in any conflict that arose between them; because it was *largely autonomous*, there was no effective control over wage levels and no linkage between effort and reward, so that unit labour costs were under continuous upward inflationary pressure; and because it was *largely fragmented*, different groups of workers secured different concessions from their employers on different issues at different times. All three elements combined to disrupt production schedules and the continuous creation of social wealth, with the result that delivery dates were missed, orders lost, management frustrated and the economy progressively and insidiously undermined.

Having identified the central defect in the system as 'institutional lag', i.e. the failure of the bargaining partners to develop and maintain up-to-date institutions for domestic bargaining and for the prevention and resolution of disputes, Donovan examined the alternative routes to reform. There were three principal schools of thought:

(i)   The radical school, represented by the Conservative lawyers and the main employer organizations, who wanted major revisions in the law to restrict the legal immunities of trade unions in order, as they saw it, to restore a better balance of bargaining power.

(ii) The traditional school, represented by Flanders and the so-called 'Oxford school' of academics, who wished to preserve the essentially voluntary character of British industrial relations by restricting the role of the law to a minimum framework and who advocated a Commission on Industrial Relations to assist the parties to reform their institutions voluntarily.

(iii) A compromise school, represented by Andrew Schonfield, a distinguished economist and Donovan Commissioner, who wished to retain the advantages of the voluntary system but who felt that voluntarism per se would not achieve the radical changes required quickly enough. Members of this school advocated some form of legal compulsion to force the pace of reform, particularly in such crucial areas as removing restrictive labour practices and of stimulating much-needed investment in new technology.

Donovan's 'judgement of Solomon' came down on the side of voluntary reform with the implied threat that, if the parties did *not* undertake the necessary reforms and put their own house in order, the government might eventually need to introduce legislation to bring about the changes required in the national interest. For Donovan, the remedy for Britain's disordered industrial relations was not to be found in industry-wide bargaining because the essential issues were domestic in character. What was required was 'effective and orderly collective bargaining' on such issues as the control of incentive schemes, hours worked, the linking of pay and performance, work practices, shop steward facilities, discipline, and so on. Industry-wide agreements could settle minimum rates of pay but only a factory agreement could regulate *actual* pay levels, produce an effective and coherent pay structure or provide an effective procedure for settling legitimate grievances within a factory. Such reform must therefore be sought in factory agreements or, in multi-plant organizations, in company agreements. Donovan placed the responsibility for achieving these reforms squarely upon the Boards of companies since they alone were in a position to bring them about. Board members should therefore begin an immediate review of industrial relations in their undertakings with six priority objectives in mind:

(i)   to develop comprehensive and authoritative collective bargaining machinery;
(ii)   to develop joint procedures for the rapid and equitable settlement of grievances;
(iii) to conclude agreements regulating the position of shop stewards;
(iv)   to adopt effective rules and procedures governing disciplinary matters;
(v)   to conclude agreements covering the handling of redundancy;
(vi)   to ensure regular joint consultation on measures to promote safety at work.

Finally, Donovan repeatedly sought to impress upon Boards of companies and upon the public that:

> *the primary responsibility for the conduct of industrial relations within a concern, and the framework of collective agreements within which those relations are conducted, lies with the Board.* [4]

With some important reservations, Donovan had vindicated the voluntary tradition. Yet there were many whose cynical verdict on Donovan echoed Dr Johnson's view of second marriage as 'The triumph of hope over experience'. For whilst the Commissioners — and subsequently the Wilson Government — stressed the value of voluntary reform, they appear to have grossly underestimated the massive investments in time, money and effort required to achieve significant voluntary reform in practice. The remainder of this chapter seeks to illustrate and analyse some of the processes and problems involved in attempting to reform workplace industrial relations in a single engineering factory between 1960 and 1980. Although these attempts culminated in a major industrial dispute in 1975, the chapter illustrates the much more important consequences of the dispute in the aftermath of 1975–78.

SECTION 2: THE ELECTROLUX PAY DISPUTE, 1975–78

(1) The pre-strike context

Electrolux Limited is the wholly-owned subsidiary of the Swedish manufacturing and marketing multinational, Electrolux AB of Stockholm. Founded in 1910, the company is now a household name, with major market shares in a wide range of domestic and commercial electrical applicances ranging from refrigerators, freezers, dishwashers, and vacuum cleaners (Electrolux), to washing machines (Zanussi), lawnmowers and powered garden tools (Flymo), sewing machines (Husqvarna), office equipment, calculators and typewriters (Facit) and commercial cleaning equipment (Columbus Dixon). The company's reputation as a leading supplier of high-quality domestic electrical appliances rests on the technical design and performance of its products, combined with an aggressive and responsive sales and service organization established in all five continents.

In 1975, Electrolux employed more than 75 000 people worldwide, of whom some 30 000 were in Sweden and about 7000 in Britain. The main Electrolux production site comprised two adjacent factories — one making refrigerators, the other vacuum cleaners — at Luton, Bedfordshire, an important industrial centre some 30 miles north of London.

Of Electrolux's 7000 British employees, less than half were engaged in the sales and service organization, spread across the entire country. Of the remaining 4000 employed at Luton, less than half were salaried staff and just over half were hourly-paid manual workers whose composition is shown in Table 4.1

Table 4.1. Composition of total manual workforce by sex and function, 1975

	Direct (Production workers)	Indirect (Non production workers)	Total
Men	1020	520	1540
Women	670	40	710
Total	1690	560	2250

Before the Second World War, Electrolux production was modest. Vacuum cleaners were already becoming popular amongst middle-class housewives in the 1930s but the domestic refrigerator was still regarded as an expensive luxury. During the Second World War, Electrolux developed a small, lightweight fridge, suitable for field-hospital units. It exploited this technical advance in the post-war period by winning a national contract to supply cheap, small refrigerators for the mass housing construction programme. In the 1960s, Electrolux captured the world market in small fridges for boats and caravans. In the 1970s, Electrolux again led the way in popularizing the cheap domestic freezer.

These changes in the design, construction, range and size of its products — together with the chronic shortage of skilled male labour — led Electrolux to recruit large numbers of women into its factories. Men continued to occupy all skilled jobs (e.g. toolroom and electrical and mechanical maintenance work) as well as the more physically arduous jobs — such as the fabrication and welding of refrigerator units, cabinet assembly and paint-spraying. Woman were almost exclusively employed on the lighter, more repetitive jobs, like the stamping and assembly of the rotors and stators of electric motors, vacuum cleaner and refrigerator assembly, inspection, packing, and despatch of products.

Over thirty post-war years, Electrolux achieved an almost perfect segregation of its hourly-paid workforce into two distinct internal labour markets. Of the total 1975 manual workforce of 2250, some 700 women — but no men — were employed in pay grades 01 – 09, carrying lower rates of pay than those of the lowest-paid men. Conversely, some 1750 men — but no women — were employed in pay grades 10 and above, carrying higher rates of pay than those of the highest-paid women. Despite this overtly discriminatory pay policy, the company was never short of female labour to meet its peak production schedules. Relatively high pay at Electrolux, coupled with the convenience of short work journeys, compensated women for the better pay and fringe benefits available at some of Luton's other major employers.

Electrolux's post-war record of rising production, successful innovation and sustained profitability is all the more remarkable when viewed against its abysmal industrial relations record. Like most other mass production companies, Electrolux exploited the economies of its growing scale of production by progressively applying a very high division of labour policy. This contributed to low-discretion work roles and low-trust dynamics on the shopfloor. Workers adopted a keenly instrumental attitude to their work, joining trade unions for reasons of self-protection and economic advancement rather than for ideological or political reasons. At Electrolux, as elsewhere in the British engineering industry, many disputes arose over the application of an incentive payment system, introduced by the company after the war to help motivate workers and so meet rising production schedules.

Throughout the 1960s and well into the 1970s, Electrolux displayed many of the worst features of British industrial relations portrayed by the Donovan Report. Although not 'representative' of British manufacturing industry, Electrolux was probably typical of many medium-size, federated engineering firms, producing consumer durables in the more affluent, full-employment areas of south-east England in that period. The Electrolux case therefore serves to illustrate many aspects of the critical degeneration of industrial relations in engineering — then Britain's largest and most important manufacturing and exporting industry:

(i) a fragmented and uncoordinated bargaining structure;
(ii) a distorted and inflationary wage structure;
(iii) an underutilized and obsolescent stock of capital assets;
(iv) poor labour productivity; high scrap rates; highly variable product quality;
(v) an apparently endless succession of small-scale, short-duration,

unofficial and unconstitutional strikes, mostly concerned with pay and incentive bonus earnings, with strong inter-union and inter-workgroup rivalries, interspersed with many protest strikes against company disciplinary and redundancy procedures.

Like many other companies, Electrolux had sought for years to improve its industrial relations but without much success. To understand the reasons for that failure, it is necessary to trace briefly the history of industrial relations at Electrolux, which provides the context of the 1975 strike.

The pre-war system of payment by time rates, under the national engineering agreements for federated establishments, was carried over into the post-war period of rapidly rising production, technical innovation and product differentiation. To elicit the additional effort required from its employees to sustain this greatly expanded output, Electrolux introduced a 'straight piecework incentive system' in 1949, with piecework prices that allowed a worker of average ability to earn up to 30% above basic (i.e. time) earnings. Management's incentive pay and performance strategy worked: production soared, company profits rose and its workers prospered by virtue of high, if variable, incentive earnings.

But no payment system, least of all an incentive system, is self-regulating. It requires regular adjustment to accommodate changes in raw materials, products, technology and new methods of working introduced from time to time. By 1959, the Electrolux incentive payment system was already plagued with problems; by 1969, it was clearly in decay, with unacceptable fluctuations in weekly earnings and growing friction between individuals and groups over bonus earnings. Many strikes took place over differentials in basic pay and the loss of any defensible relationship between effort and reward.

In 1960, to help achieve a standard work performance amongst all its production workers, the company adopted the British Standards Institute's 'work rating system'. A pricing factor was introduced, department by department, which enabled an average worker who maintained a 'standard performance' to achieve average departmental bonus earnings, thereby overcoming much of the dissatisfaction over intradepartmental bonus earnings. The results were initially encouraging: fluctuations in bonus earnings reduced to a point where they were no longer a primary source of employee discontent. Dissatisfaction now focused on differentials in basic time rates of pay.

In 1961, after many work stoppages over these pay differentials, the company attempted a comprehensive overhaul of its payment system but failed to secure the necessary joint union cooperation, mainly because the unions were acutely divided amongst themselves. The AEU was established at Electrolux as early as 1930 but its pre-war membership was never significant. By 1960, it had succeeded in organizing well over half of the Electrolux workforce. Of the remainder, several hundred were in membership of the GMWU (now

GMBATU), with a small group of electricians in the ETU (now the EEPTU). Competition for members had led to poor relationships between the two principal unions, with no agreed 'spheres of influence' and mutual allegations of 'poaching' of members. Shop stewards were elected annually from single-representative departmental constituencies to a Joint Shop Stewards Committee (JSSC), later to assume great importance in the company's industrial relations.

By the mid-1960s, the Swedish parent company had become seriously concerned about the rising number of disruptive work stoppages, with their damaging effect on product quality and reliability; about escalating unit labour costs; and about stagnating productivity levels at Luton. In 1968, the year of the Donovan Report, the Stanford Research Institute (Connecticut), headed by the distinguished Swedish–American organization analyst, Rensis Likert, was called in to investigate and report on the Luton factory. A number of important organization changes were introduced, intended to strengthen the management function, but no significant progress was made in improving industrial relations.

In 1969, Electrolux Limited invited its own employers' organization — the Engineering Employers' Federation — to prepare a confidential report on the steps needed to reform collective bargaining, to restore control over runaway bonus earnings and to heal the disastrous rifts in the company's industrial relations. The Federation recommended a Joint Management–Union Working Party to examine a number of specific proposals for reform, but nothing came of these proposals.

In 1969, the Labour Government, following the recommendations of the Donovan Report, set up a Commission on Industrial Relations (CIR) to assist companies and unions in promoting the voluntary reform of their industrial relations. In 1970, Electrolux requested the CIR to undertake a wide-ranging examination of its industrial relations and to recommend measures to promote improvements. The CIR Report attributed poor industrial relations in the company to seven principal sources:

(i) the failure in communications between (a) management and unions; and (b) the three unions on the Electrolux site;

(ii) the repeated attempts by the company to impose tighter controls over production costs, labour discipline and labour utilization;

(iii) the intolerable management delay in responding to a growing volume of legitimate shopfloor grievances;

(iv) the low status and ill-defined authority of the industrial relations department;

(v) major defects in the domestic grievance procedure, which was said to be slow and cumbersome in operation;

(vi) the lack of a clear, effective and coordinated industrial relations policy;

(vii)   the fact that many industrial relations decisions were taken by the Directors over the head of senior line management.

The CIR Report on Electrolux [5] recommended, inter alia:

(i)   the strengthening and upgrading of the industrial relations function with the appointment of a Board-level Industrial Relations Director;
(ii)   improved inter-union relations through increased contact between rank-and-file leaders at Electrolux who were operating without the benefit of their guidance or support;
(iii)   a 'fundamental reconstruction of the whole manual wages system'.

The third of these recommendations was described by the CIR as being 'essential to the establishment of a proper system of industrial relations at Electrolux'. According to the CIR, the company's piece-work incentive system was not merely anomalous but inherently unstable, producing gross fluctuations in the weekly earnings of particular groups and indefensible differences in the earnings potential between workgroups engaged in broadly similar work. According to the CIR, there was massive discontent amongst indirect workers in stores, transport and inspection functions who did not enjoy the benefit of incentive bonus earnings. Not only was the piecework system increasingly irrelevant to the new, machine-paced production technology being slowly introduced, the very existence of the system inhibited management from introducing new machines, lay-outs and products or from securing the much-needed increase in capital and labour productivity that the company needed to maintain profitability.

In 1971, having appointed its first Industrial Relations Director, the company commissioned a firm of British management consultants to assist it in 'devising and implementing a more orderly, effective and equitable wage payment system'. A Joint Management–Shop Stewards Working Group was set up to consider the consultants' proposals. The Group concluded that:

> although there was agreement on the benefits of a simple, logical, rational grade structure rewarding individuals according to the worth of their job [6]

there was no agreement on the means of achieving this mutually desired end.

In October 1972, the company came forward with its own unilateral proposals for a radically new *Comprehensive Pay and Productivity Agreement*. The company considered the heavy financial cost of its proposals to be fully justified by the desperate need to secure an effective and enduring solution to its many, aggravated labour problems. Finally, in November 1972, when the parties were poised to sign the new Agreement, the Conservative Government, under Edward Heath, executed its historic U-turn in economic policy by introducing — almost overnight — a statutory prices and incomes freeze. The Electrolux Agreement, trapped by this totally unexpected and unpredictable event, remained unsigned and was subsequently abandoned.

By 1973, Electrolux management had devoted thirteen frustrating years to unsuccessful attempts to reform its industrial relations by voluntary means. Not surprisingly, some members of Electrolux management had virtually abandoned hope of ever achieving the desired reforms. It was at precisely this point that the implementation of the Equal Pay Act presented the company with an important opportunity for a fresh initiative.

The Equal Pay Act, placed on the Statute Book in December 1970 [7], was considered so complex and costly to implement that managers and unions were given five years to prepare for its coming into force on 31 December 1975. At Electrolux, the company made use of this interval to set up a Management Equal Pay Committee to consider the implications of the legislation and to recommend steps to ensure company compliance. The Committee recommended the adoption of job evaluation, indirectly suggested by the Act, as the most effective means of arriving at equitable differentials between *salaried staff* jobs. But it did not recommend this solution for *hourly-paid* jobs because job evaluation had already been rejected by shop stewards during earlier pay reform talks and because the AEU, the majority union, was known to be opposed to the concept in principle. The company therefore developed its own unilateral proposals for solving what came to be known as 'the equal pay problem' in a Draft Equal Pay Agreement, which declared:

> *Job evaluation of all hourly-paid jobs is the only practicable way of giving effect to the Equal Pay Act at Electrolux.* [8]

The company then set out to persuade shop stewards that, although the major changes needed to implement the Equal Pay Act would inevitably disturb traditional wage differentials, these could be controlled by means of a jointly-devised and jointly-administered job evaluation programme, covering all jobs held by both men and women at Electrolux. But shop stewards totally rejected the idea that job evaluation was the only effective solution to 'the equal pay problem'. They were quite prepared to allow evaluation on 'women's jobs' but insisted that 'no male jobs are to be altered by change of work content, reclassification or method of payment'. Negotiations continued throughout 1974 with repeated company attempts to secure acceptance of its Equal Pay Proposals, based on its own unilateral evaluation of all hourly-paid jobs. Once again, the two sides failed to reach a negotiated agreement.

In January 1975, the unions came forward with their own solution to 'the equal pay problem' by asking the company to pay all its women workers 95% of the male semi-skilled rate — on the assumption that no women were employed on 'skilled' work. The company rejected this proposal outright, on the grounds that 'there are significant differences between the work that men do and the work that women do' — an indirect reference to the 'genuine material difference' clause that excluded equal pay under Section 1(4) of the Equal Pay Act 1970.

Having consulted its Head Office, the Luton District Committee of the AEU acknowledged that the Electrolux wage structure was 'antiquated and unwieldy'; recommended that the company should conduct a ballot of all women employees on its draft Equal Pay Agreement; but insisted that the company should abandon any ideas of carrying out a comprehensive job evaluation programme to establish the 'significant differences' between jobs.

The company responded by issuing a Statement on Equal Pay in May 1975. This Statement emphasized:

(i)   that a unisex grade/rate structure would in future apply to all manual workers;
(ii)   that women would then enjoy equal opportunities with men in selection, training and promotion to higher-graded jobs on exactly the same terms and conditions of employment;
(iii) that in the changeover to equal pay, no employee would suffer a reduction in earnings.

Despite the company's efforts to reassure the workforce, rumours soon swept through the plant to the effect that, if the company was allowed to implement its equal pay proposals:

(i)   men would lose their jobs to women employees;
(ii)   women would lose out in any job evaluation programme;
(iii) women would be forced to work night shifts, overtime and weekends before qualifying for equal pay with men.

Inspired by such rumours, several work stoppages occurred during the first week of May.

(2) The challenge

On the morning of Friday 9 May 1975, after several weeks of skirmishing, all 700 members of the female workforce at Electrolux walked out on strike in protest against the company's equal pay proposals — the first and only significant industrial action ever undertaken by these women acting on their initiative and on their own behalf. At first, hourly-paid male workers refused to support their women colleagues and continued to work normally, especially when the dominant union, the AEU, refused to make the strike official. The company clearly hoped that by this means they would isolate the women and bring their strike to a speedy end. However, the men soon changed their minds and, when the AEU made the strike retrospectively official, the GMWU (now GMBATU) soon followed suit. Electrolux management and workers had stumbled into their longest and most bitter dispute.

(3) Initial responses

Over the previous ten years, Electrolux management had become thoroughly familiar with petty industrial disputes of the short, small-scale, unofficial and unconstitutional variety. But it was certainly not prepared for an all-out stoppage of work by its 700 shopfloor women workers in support of their alleged pay inequality. When the women stopped work, the company initially hoped to maintain production without them but when the men came out in sympathy, management was compelled to close both its factories on the Luton site. Members of non-manual unions, non-union employees, members of supervision and management encountered mild but mostly good-humoured abuse as they made their way to work, through the picket lines established outside the main gates.

The company's senior policy-making body — the Management Committee — met daily to take stock and consider how best to end the stoppage and to respond to the women's demands for equal pay. Management was generally united by the knowledge that any concession to the women would be likely to produce a 'male backlash', notwithstanding the fact that the men had decided to support the women in their claim. The company therefore made clear to the strikers that it stood by its draft Equal Pay Agreement. If the strikers returned to work and wished to raise pay or grading grievances, as provided for in the draft Agreement, the company would give them speedy consideration. But there would be no concessions to strike pressure. The strikers were left to 'sweat it out'.

(4) Consequences

Almost immediately, as in the earlier case of the Ford Sewing Machinists, the attention of the British media was focused once more on a small group of 'petticoat strikers'. Women gave interviews to newspaper reporters and posed for press photographs whilst on picket duty outside the factory gates. Local and national television reporters, who seldom displayed any interest in the pay and conditions of women workers on assembly lines, suddenly developed an apparently insatiable appetite for news and gossip about the Electrolux women strikers. The usual visits were paid to the strikers by union activists, by radical socialists, by North American feminists and by Scandinavian TV crews keen to report to their fellow countrymen on a strike at the subsidiary of a Swedish multinational corporation.

By the second week of the strike, local officers of the Advisory, Conciliation and Arbitration Service (ACAS) had joined District Officers of the AEU and the GMWU, together with officers of the Engineering Employers Mid-Anglian Association, and senior members of company management, to seek ways of bringing the dispute to a speedy conclusion. Little common ground could be found and their efforts went unrewarded.

(5) The climax

By the third week of the dispute, the novelty of being on strike had begun to wear thin with most of the strikers, despite a continuous spell of unusually fine May weather. The strikers had now been paid all their outstanding earnings and were beginning to feel the pinch. With machines standing idle for three weeks and strike losses mounting, the company made one final effort to persuade the women to return to work. The Convenor was encouraged by senior Electrolux management to believe that some formula could be worked out jointly for meeting the women's legitimate demands and for complying with the new Equal Pay Act. By the end of the third week there was little enthusiasm for continuing the strike. The women had clearly dramatized their discontent and were ready to return to work and to await developments.

(6) The settlement

After three weeks of lost earnings, the entire workforce returned to work, having nominally accepted the company's draft Equal Pay Agreement. The strike was over but the underlying dispute was far from being settled. For the Agreement made clear that, if any woman felt that she was engaged in 'the same or broadly similar work' as a man alongside whom she worked, she was free to pursue her grading grievance under the domestic Procedure Agreement. If the outcome was shown to be in her favour, she would be paid retrospectively at the higher grade rate *provided* she agreed in return to undertake any of the work in jobs covered by that job classification, including, where necessary, the obligation to work night shifts, overtime or weekends, as required by the Agreement. It had thus taken the company the full five transitional years allowed by the Equal Pay Act to reach even this limited and precarious agreement with its workforce and the unions. In seeking to comply with the Act, the company had found itself embroiled in the longest, most bitter and most costly strike in its history and there were widespread fears that the dispute had opened up still further divisions in an already deeply-divided and sectionalized workforce.

The new Equal Pay Agreement took effect at the beginning of 1976 in an atmosphere of smouldering discontent and distrust amongst all the company's employees, each workgroup watching closely to see how their own earnings and job security would be affected by the coming of equal pay and equal opportunity to Electrolux.

(7) Aftermath

In May 1976, Mrs Ann Hutchinson, an AEU shop steward from the refrigerator assembly department, submitted a claim for equal pay on behalf of herself and six fellow women workers to the Bedford Industrial Tribunal (IT), on the grounds that they were entitled to equal pay under Section 1(4) of the Equal Pay Act 1970, as amended by the Sex Discrimination Act 1975. The company set out to refute Mrs Hutchinson's case by showing that there were 'significant differences between the things she does and the things they do' in accordance with Section 1(5) of the Act. The Tribunal found that the company was in breach of the Act and declared that the appellants were therefore entitled to the same time and piecework rates of pay for the work they did as the men directly alongside whom they worked.

The outcome of the Hutchinson case took the company by complete surprise. Faced with the prospect that other women employees, encouraged by Ann Hutchinson's victory, would bring similar complaints to the Tribunal, as well as the prospect of adverse reactions amongst men employees, the company decided to appeal to the Employment Appeal Tribunal (EAT) against the Hutchinson decision. Meanwhile, in July 1976, the Bedford Tribunal considered a similar complaint brought by another Electrolux woman employee on precisely the same grounds of 'the same or broadly similar work'. This time, however, the company briefed counsel who offered a much more detailed and coherent defence. As a result, the complaint against the company was dismissed.

In November 1976, the EAT gave its decision on the Hutchinson appeal, dismissing the company's case. Mr Justice Philips' words, quoted in the Introduction to this chapter, faced the company with an extraordinary set of dilemmas, which arose from the EAT's failure to clarify precisely how its decision was to be applied. For example:

(i) Did the award apply only to the seven named women employees — or to others engaged in 'the same or broadly similar work'?

(ii) Did the equal rates of pay apply to the jobs that the women employees were currently doing rather than to the seven named women?

(iii) If the rates applied to the women, did they carry their entitlement to equal pay with them, regardless of the jobs that they might subsequently be called upon to carry out?

(iv) If it applied to the jobs, what was to happen when the content of those jobs changed through time?

(v) Did the award of equal pay carry with it the corresponding obligations that were then attached to the higher rate of pay? If so, must the women be offered and accept new contracts of employment?

(vi) How was the company to resolve the conflicting decisions arising from different Tribunal hearings and still maintain the integrity of its wage structure?

Instead of pursuing such questions through the Court of Appeal, the company decided:

(i)   to pay the seven women the appropriate higher grade rate;

(ii)   to make clear that they would be expected, in return, to undertake all the conditions that went with the higher rate of pay, including the obligation to work shifts, if and when required;

(iii) to call on the District Officials of the unions concerned to help to resolve the questions thrown up by the Hutchinson decision;

(iv) to invite the Equal Opportunities Commission (EOC) to assist the company and the unions to achieve a more far-reaching and more durable solution to all these perplexing problems.

In the closing days of December 1976, the Electrolux JSSC issued its own Statement in reply to the company's decisions, to the effect that the seven women should receive equal pay but should 'remain on their own Contracts of Employment and not be subject to the same treatment as the men'. It was against this background of conflicting views on what needed to be done next that the company formally invited the EOC to undertake an investigation at Electrolux. It encapsulated its own view of the situation as follows:

> *For over ten years now, the company has laboured patiently with shop stewards and union officials to develop more productive and harmonious relationships, in particular, to work out a more rational, more equitable and more stable wage payment structure ... we have tried separately and jointly to identify the main problems and sources of dissatisfaction on both sides with the existing wage structure and to come up with constructive ideas for its reform. So far we have failed ... We have now become somewhat battle-weary (and) frustrated in our joint attempts to achieve a lasting solution ... Given an atmosphere of mutual respect and cooperation, we believe your investigation can help the parties to thrash out a wage structure which, in turn, will lead to new relationships. In such a situation, the removal of discriminatory practices which may exist becomes possible, further integration of management strengths and employee skills and experience can occur leading, in its turn, to greater success and security for all.* [9]

The company freely acknowledged that its employment policies were overtly discriminatory against women, particularly in its wage payment system. It welcomed the EOC Investigation in the hope that it would help to generate a climate of trust in which effective and lasting solutions might be found to the many intractable problems that afflicted the company and its employees.

In February 1977, having recognized the exceptional complexity of the problems of Electrolux, the EOC enrolled Lord McCarthy (formerly Research Director of the Donovan Commission, and one of Britain's leading academic industrial relations specialists) as Special Commissioner in charge of the Electrolux Investigation.

During the early months of 1977, the company supplied the unions with a complete set of its proposals for a *New Wage Structure based on Job Evaluated Grading*. In March 1977, these proposals were totally rejected by the unions, after consultation with their membership. Undeterred, the company called on ACAS to help to break the bargaining stalemate, but to no avail. It now seemed clear to the company that it had reached the limits of voluntary reform. For, despite the help of the independent but State-sponsored agency, ACAS, it had failed to reach a freely-negotiated Agreement with its workforce and unions and must therefore now await the results of the EOC Investigation and the eventual application of the law.

In a final bid to retain control over its own destiny, the company called on the services of an independent industrial relations consultant who had previously helped the company to improve its training programmes. Having taken stock of the situation, the consultant presented his own analysis of the company's position, with proposals for a radical new strategy for overcoming the bargaining stalemate. He argued as follows:

(i)   The immediate tactical problems facing the company and its workforce were concerned with equal pay and equal opportunity. The more significant strategic task was to help the company, the unions and the workforce to break out of the vicious circles of degenerate industrial relations in which they were trapped, into the virtuous circles of constructive, voluntary industrial relations reform.

(ii) The Equal Pay and Sex Discrimination Acts — and the EOC Investigation — should not be regarded as legal burdens but welcomed as catalytic agents for transforming the company's industrial relations. The Acts themselves appeared to raise more problems than they solved; but they might nevertheless help the company to resolve the bargaining stalemate by involving shop stewards in a genuinely participative experiment in job evaluation, thereby helping to change attitudes and behaviour in the workplace.

(iii) The key objectives for management in seeking to achieve this transformation were:

(a)   to end the disastrous fragmentation and sectionalism within the company's workforce;

(b)   to end the totally uncoordinated and leap-frogging system of pay bargaining that continued throughout the year, with piecemeal concessions made to strategic workgroups, simply to keep production going;

(c)   to completely restructure the runaway incentive bonus scheme with its inflationary effect on unit labour costs;

(d)   to put an end to the already high and rapidly-escalating level of disruptive disputes, undertaken with almost complete disregard for the agreed disputes procedure.

The company accepted the consultant's recommendation to press ahead with a joint job evaluation programme as the best means of solving both the immediate equal pay problem and the longer-term wage structure problem. The consultant convinced shop stewards that a jointly-designed and administered job evaluation programme would not only help to deal with the legal requirements of the Philips judgement, to the satisfaction of the women employees and the EOC, but would also provide detailed technical information about jobs and working conditions at Electrolux, which would assist their long-term bargaining objectives. The company provided assurances that there would be no unilateral management moves to change the existing wage structure until proposals had been negotiated and agreed with the workforce.

Throughout 1977 and 1978, the consultant steered a joint Job Evaluation Committee (JEC) through the design stages of the programme; supervised the evaluation of some 500 job profiles, arranged in a final overall rank order according to their total job value, and completed this programme in twelve months. The mutual trust and cooperation developed at the fact-finding stage were carried over into the proposal and negotiating stages, thus helping to bring about an early agreement on a New Wage Structure that took effect on 1 January 1979.

Whilst the job evaluation programme was in progress, proposals were simultaneously developed for reforming the uncontrolled incentive payment scheme. Having examined and rejected various alternative solutions, the company decided not to abandon incentives, as earlier recommended by the CIR, but to reform the existing scheme in two distinct stages:

Stage 1:   In 1978, the company took steps to compress the wide fluctuations in bonus earnings amongst different piecework groups. A notional factory average incentive bonus was established, to be renegotiated annually, with the progressive removal of anomalies over and above this average.

Stage 2:   In 1979, a set of newly-measured piecework prices was introduced to deliver 25 – 30% incentive effect of the British Standards (BS) 100 work standard. With a gross average earnings target of £180 per week in 1979, a production worker of average ability, who maintained an output performance of between BS 125 and BS 130, could expect to earn £120 per week in basic (time) earnings for a 40-hour week, plus £60 per week in bonus pay. Overtime or output performance above the BS 130 level would attract further premia or bonus earnings.

Despite the very complicated, delicate and time-consuming work involved in calculating, explaining and winning acceptance for these changes, both stages of reform were carried through without a single disruptive stoppage of work.

By 1980, pay bargaining at Electrolux was fully coordinated, within a single, common set of negotiations with a common settlement date. After 1979, all hourly-paid grades (i.e. basic pay rates) were reviewed annually in a joint, comprehensive bargaining round, producing a 12-month agreement, including a clause on 'No further economic claims' during the life of the agreement. As a result, the gross pay distortions, formerly caused by piecemeal, leap-frogging wage claims and concessions, were eliminated. The fact that all three unions took part in joint negotiations helped to produce a more representative pay bargaining system, thereby reducing the risk of shopfloor workers repudiating or dishonouring an agreement made in their name.

SECTION 3: ANALYSIS OF THE DISPUTE

(1) What was the dispute about?

Women employed by Electrolux were never militant trade unionists, but they had a keen sense of injustice. For years they had been excluded from higher-paid jobs and were disgruntled over the amount of effort that they were required to put into their work, as compared with some of the less-demanding but higher-paid jobs occupied by men. But it is difficult to imagine Electrolux women taking collective industrial action on their own behalf before 1975. It was the coming of the Equal Pay Act and the company's unilateral proposals on job evaluation that provided the trigger for the dispute. In one sense, therefore, the dispute centred on the Electrolux women's determination to secure their entitlement to equal pay and equal opportunities under new legislation. The three-week strike was fought over just that issue, but it failed to solve either the immediate problem of equal pay or the more fundamental underlying issue — namely, the company's chronic failure to tackle the root causes of its bad labour relations. The three-week strike, followed within 12 months by the outcome of the Hutchinson tribunal, finally persuaded Electrolux management to give more serious attention to its long-range industrial relations strategy, rather than its short-range production and quality problems. The three-week strike was a turning point in the company's history. It dramatized the women's discontent and led the men to reject the company's equal pay proposals. This, in turn, paved the way for the comprehensive job evaluation programme that finally began the serious voluntary reform of the company's industrial relations.

(2) How important was the context?

1975 had been a bad year for Electrolux, but 1976 was even worse. Quite apart from the Hutchinson appeal and the 700 remaining cases waiting to be heard at Industrial Tribunals, the company's domestic sales were badly hit by sales of imported vacuum cleaners and white goods. The strike may have brought employee discontent to a head, but it severely disrupted the rhythm of production and adversely affected product quality. Management time, which should have gone into resolving these problems, was diverted by the outcome of the two Bedford Tribunal cases.

The Electrolux dispute thus had three contextual dimensions: first, the ten-year saga of management's largely cosmetic attempts to bring some order into its industrial relations; second, the important new statutory requirement that the company confront the equal pay issues; and third, the unprecedented women's strike, which precipitated the company's first major all-out stoppage in 1975. Although the strike was important, it was the aftermath of the strike that provided the crucial context for the dispute and its eventual resolution in the New Wage Structure Agreement of 1978.

(3) Why did workplace relations degenerate at Electrolux?

No single employer can ever typify a whole industry, yet Electrolux was not significantly different from many other middle-size engineering establishments that suffered from a progressive degeneration in its employee relations throughout the 1960s and 1970s. The causes of that degeneration are not difficult to discern. They are to be found in that malign management neglect to which the Donovan Commissioners referred, when they precisely pin-pointed management's prime responsibility for the reform of workplace industrial relations. The crucially important question for management is why it had neglected to discharge that prime responsibility. The answer is almost invariably to be found in two factors:

(i)   the fact that for 25 years in post-war Britain, most engineering (and other manufacturing) companies were operating in a highly profitable seller's market, disposing without difficulty of almost everything they produced and passing on additional costs to their customers. For that reason, employers concentrated on production and selling, seriously neglecting their important responsibilities towards the management of their human resources;

(ii) the fact that the employees in most engineering (and other manufacturing) companies enjoyed a higher living standard than ever before and were relatively content to extract whatever concessions they could from their employers whilst the good times lasted.

Whenever a company, like Electrolux, suffered a sudden rise in the volume of small-scale industrial disruption, management took short-term, palliative steps to reduce the scale of the problem but did nothing to tackle its underlying causes. The Donovan Commissioners sharply reminded management and unions that, whilst they appeared content with their existing institutions and arrangements, they were in effect cutting their own economic throats by failing to deal with their problems. Unfortunately, the Donovan analysis probably came too late and its prescriptions were, in any case, unpalatable to most British managements, for Donovan placed on management the prime responsibility for the reform of workplace relations — of overcoming the barriers of entrenched tradition, an immense task of cultural change for which most British managers were untrained and totally unprepared. Many British managers believed that the prime responsibility for reform lay with the unions or with government. As Sir Terence Beckett, Managing Director of Ford of Britain (later CBI Director General), explained to a House of Commons Committee that was seeking to explain this earlier neglect:

> *Over the years, a whole set of panaceas have been advanced on this, and we joined in the national feeling that such-and-such would solve the problem. But in the end we have come down to the basic situation that we, the unions and our own workforce together have got to sort the thing out. Government will not do it for us and it was probably unreasonable to expect that they ever would. We have really got to sort the thing out for ourselves.* [10]

If Ford, in the top league of manufacturing multinationals, could make that admission, it is hardly surprising that smaller, second-league companies like Electrolux had done even less to put its industrial relations house in order. In practice, Electrolux had made some valiant efforts at superficial reform. As noted in Section 2(1) above, it had called upon a variety of third-party change agents to assist its reforming efforts, but few lasting benefits came of these interventions. Degeneration set in early, was allowed to secure a hold and gradually encroached upon the whole of the company's industrial relations.

(4) Did the strike settle the dispute?

Most industrial disputes *culminate* in a strike, at the end of which the parties succeed in resolving their differences by means of a compromise solution that allows them to resume a new or modified relationship. In this respect, the Electrolux dispute was exceptional. Far from settling the dispute, the strike served first to unite the workforce in its opposition to the company's attempt to impose a unilateral, management-evaluated wage structure on its employees, and second, to raise the political consciousness and self-confidence of women employees to the point where all seven hundred were subsequently willing to file complaints at an Industrial Tribunal, alleging company breach of the Equal Pay and Sex Discrimination Acts.

The Electrolux strike lasted three weeks in May 1975 but it was not until January 1979 that the dispute was finally resolved, with the implementation of a New Wage Structure Agreement. However, it took a further three years for grading appeals to be heard, for mistakes in the wage structure to be corrected and for the new structure to become fully accepted. In short, the return to work marked the end of the strike but the continuation of the dispute by other means.

(5) Who won?

To the extent that both management and unions had suffered the disruptive effects of a degenerate system of industrial relations for many years, the end of the dispute marked achievements for both sides. It is difficult to say which side achieved more in terms of long-lasting, predominant gains. The implementation of the New Wage Structure Agreement, on 1 January 1979, seemed to place management in the ascendancy. It had devoted much time, money and effort to the reconstruction of its payments system and appeared to have emerged with almost all of its objectives achieved. Having been frustrated in so many past initiatives, not least at the time of the Heath Government's incomes policy U-turn in November 1972, the company viewed the signing and implementation of that Agreement as a historic turning point in its history.

From a union standpoint, however, the 1979 Agreement was equally significant, for it not only gave women equal pay and conditions of employment with men but it also secured substantial pay increases for all hourly-paid employees; it provided a new range of fringe benefits, including a greatly enhanced pension plan, as well as the prospect of a reformed incentive payments system, to follow within the year.

But the deepening world recession of the late 1970s had already hit Electrolux. By 1980, the imposition of 15% Value Added Tax by the incoming Thatcher Government severely retarded an anticipated sales recovery. By 1981, the domestic electrical appliance market was severely affected by rising unemployment. By 1982, the Electrolux order book was so depleted that the company was forced to introduce short-time working. By 1985, almost half the workforce had been made redundant.

Despite these catastrophic developments and their effects on management and employee morale, the company was able to survive and compete by virtue of the new, innovatory culture that emerged at Electrolux. Despite the recession, the British company's economic performance was transformed, as measured in terms of higher labour productivity and reduced unit labour costs. This encouraged the parent company to invest in new technology and to launch new products from its British subsidiary. Electrolux profits fell sharply over the decade since 1978, but considerably less than for comparable companies of its size and product range.

(6) Costs and benefits of the dispute

The severe costs of the Electrolux dispute have been emphasized sufficiently. The benefits accruing to management and workers from this programme of voluntary reform are best summarized as follows:

1. Within a 12-month period of January 1978, virtually all of the equal pay problems at Electrolux were resolved:
   (i)   The old discriminatory grade and basic pay structure was abolished and replaced by a new 'unisex' structure under which workers automatically took the grade and pay rate of the job they were doing, without regard to sex.
   (ii)   Women employees, who now enjoyed equal pay for 'the same or broadly similar work' as established by job evaluation, were required to undertake all of the corresponding obligations as men who did that work, including night shifts, overtime, weekend work, etc.
   (iii)   Women employees played a full and equal part alongside men in the reform programme. The team of job analysts always included two women shop stewards; the JEC included the senior woman GMWU representative; the union negotiating team always included one or more women; the Job Evaluation Secretariat also included a woman.
   Conversely, women were given no special consideration in the evaluation of their jobs (i.e. there was no reverse discrimination against men). The opportunities for discrimination were thereby minimized — a view supported by the fact that not a single case of alleged discrimination was reported to the EOC during the entire reform programme.
2. The application of the new wage structure from 1 January 1979 removed most, but by no means all, of the dissatisfaction amongst Electrolux workers over alleged inequitable pay differentials. The salient features of the new wage structure that contributed to this outcome were:
   (i)   the consistent application of the job evaluation rules without concessions to bargaining pressures and without sacrificing the integrity of the evaluated gradings, but with full acceptance of the need for periodic adjustments to correct mistakes made in the early months of the scheme's operation;
   (ii)   the removal of such mistakes during a 'Benchmark Review', carried out after two years' operating experience, and at the same time adjusting job analyses to incorporate significant changes in job content that had occurred through the passage of time;
   (iii)   the maintenance of a highly-trained, well-motivated team of job analysts, plus a high stability factor amongst the

members of the JEC, to provide the essential continuity of policy and procedures required for consistency;

(iv) the establishment and operation of an agreed procedure for investigating all prima facie legitimate grading grievances. During the first two years of the new wages structure, 157 grading appeals were investigated by the JEC. These resulted in 62 (40%) upgradings, 92 (59%) confirmations of existing grades and 3 (2%) downgradings of the job (but with many more individuals affected), without loss to the jobholders;

(v) the incorporation of a final grading arbitration stage, carried out by the consultant who continued to advise management and unions on the scheme's maintenance. Some 28 arbitrations were completed during the wage structure's first year (1979–80), resulting in 20 (71%) upgradings and 8 (29%) confirmations of existing gradings, with no downgradings.

3. The economic gains achieved by women workers at Electrolux as a result of removing the former discriminatory grade and basic pay structure are shown in Table 4.2.

Table 4.2 Distribution of total manual workforce by grade and sex, December 1980

Grade	Total	Percentage	Men	Percentage	Women	Percentage
1	179	8.9	31	2.4	148	20.6
2	709	35.1	343	26.4	366	51.0
3	598	29.6	408	31.4	190	26.5
4	255	12.6	241	18.5	14	1.9
5	67	3.3	67	5.2	Nil	Nil
6	84	4.2	84	6.5	Nil	Nil
7	126	6.2	126	9.7	Nil	Nil
Total	2018	100.0	1300	100.0	718	100.0

Notes:

(a) Although women took their rightful place alongside men in those grades in which they were represented, as determined by job evaluation, there were proportionately far more women than men in the lower grades. This partly reflected *direct discrimination* by management in filling higher-grade vacancies and partly the unwillingness of women to undertake such jobs with the special working conditions that are attached to them.

(b) There were still no women in the top three grades, reflecting the continued failure of women to be selected, trained and appointed to higher-grade jobs by reason of *indirect discrimination*, i.e. the inability of women to secure the same treatment as men by virtue of previous discriminatory practices.

4. An examination of the relative earnings of men and women in the same grade revealed no difference in basic (time) rates and earnings, *except* those that arise from the fact that few women work

night shifts, overtime or weekends; and no significant differences in bonus earnings, except insofar as men have been able to secure a greater share of the higher-paid bonus work.

5. Both men and women appellants were successful in prosecuting grading grievances and thus advancing in the grade structure. The extent to which changes in job content were reflected in subsequent upgradings is shown in Table 4.3.

Table 4.3. Changes in the distribution of total manual workforce by grade and sex — December 1978, 1979, 1980

Total workforce	Distribution by grade								
	1	2	3	4	5	6	7	Balance	Total
Men									
December 1978	9.7	41.6	20.8	9.2	3.7	4.8	6.8	3.5	100.0
December 1979	7.5	35.5	26.0	12.4	4.3	5.5	8.7	–	100.0
December 1980	2.4	26.4	31.4	18.5	5.2	6.5	9.7	–	100.0
Women									
December 1978	31.5	57.7	5.8	1.7	Nil	Nil	Nil	–	100.0
December 1979	28.4	60.5	10.0	1.0	Nil	Nil	Nil	–	100.0
December 1980	20.6	51.0	26.5	1.9	Nil	Nil	Nil	–	100.0

Source: Company documentation, unpublished.

Notes

(1) The proportion of men in the lowest grade dropped more significantly and faster than the proportion of women.

(2) The proportion of men in Grades 4–7, inclusive, almost doubled, whilst the proportion of women in those grades remained almost constant.

(3) The greatest shift amongst men has been out of Grade 1 (down from 9.7 to 2.4%) and Grade 2 (down from 41.6 to 26.4%) and into Grade 3 (up from 20.8 to 31.4%) and Grade 4 (up from 9.2 to 18.5%).

(4) The greatest shift amongst women has been out of Grade 1 (down) from 31.5 to 20.6%) and into Grade 3 (up from 5.8 to 26.5%), with no women into Grades 4–6.

6. From the company's viewpoint, bonus earnings were brought under progressively closer control and the worst anomalies of the incentive earnings scheme had been eliminated. Over the three-year period 1978–80, the company introduced an improved form of work study — Method Time Measurement (MTM) — requiring the complete revision and validation of job timings and piecework prices for some hundreds of separate piecework jobs. This signifi-

cant improvement in control of unit labour costs reduced Electrolux wage drift from the level of 12–15%, cited in the Management Consultants' 1973 Report, to <1.0% in 1980. Incentive earnings were also stable at around 25–30% of total gross pay, compared with an average 75% cited in the CIR's 1971 Report.

7. The virtual elimination of the former endemic disruption helped to stabilize earnings and so contributed significantly to maintaining a more united workforce. This unity is attributable to two separate but linked factors:
   (i) the need to work together to reform the wage structure and bonus system;
   (ii) the need to control costs and remain competitive under the growing threat of redundancy following the onset of the recession of the late 1970s and early 1980s.

8. More indirect benefits flowing from the transformation of industrial relations have been:
   (i) improved and more consistent product quality,
   (ii) reduced scrap levels,
   (iii) the removal of some major production bottlenecks,
   (iv) more flexible working practices amongst both craftsmen and production workers,
   (v) the achievement of more delivery targets,
   (vi) the introduction of new models without major dislocation to existing production,
   (vii) the acceptance and timely completion of completely new layouts,
   (viii) the re-equipment of several major departments as part of the 1979–80 investment programme.

(7) Lessons of the dispute

The most significant lesson of the dispute for Electrolux management was that the company's earlier efforts to reform its degenerate wage structure had failed because that reconstruction could not be separated from the need to reform the company's entire system of industrial relations. In seeking to comply with the Equal Pay Act, and to meet the women employees' legitimate grievances on employment discrimination, the company was compelled to renegotiate its entire collective bargaining agreements and to widen the range of its fringe benefit programmes. That reform of workplace relations could only be carried out with the willing agreement and active cooperation of the entire workforce. The company paid a high price for its earlier failure to effectively manage its human resources and its industrial relations. The costs of the reform programme were not recouped, in fact, until after 1979, when the impact of the recession, coupled with the arrival of the new 'enterprise culture' enabled Electrolux to cut its workforce by half, whilst maintaining full production and reducing manufacturing unit costs.

The Electrolux shopfloor workforce paid most of the cost of that failure. The most important lessons for the unions were largely those identified much earlier by the Commission on Industrial Relations Report — namely, the neglect of inter-union cooperation and the failure of full-time union officers to support and guide the workforce. In a town like Luton, dominated by two of Britain's largest motor corporations (Vauxhall and BL), it was difficult for union officers of the AEU and the GMU to devote sufficiently close attention to Electrolux. By taking strike action in the summer of 1975, the Electrolux women concentrated the attention of both management and unions on the fundamental problems of fragmented bargaining and the long-neglected grievances of women workers, which underlay much of the company's poor industrial relations.

A third lesson for both sides was the somewhat bewildered realization that the law per se can achieve little by way of help in the reform of workplace relations. As management and unions found elsewhere in Britain, the only realistic and assured road to reform is that which the parties build for themselves, within a strong, prosperous economy and a supportive national framework.

There is no fundamental conflict between voluntarism and the use of the law. As demonstrated in this chapter, they are complementary modes of social action. The Electrolux case has taken the Equal Pay Act 1970 as an example of the *catalytic legislation* that appears essential in order to stimulate both management and unions to undertake a fundamental review of long-neglected policies and practices, as the first step towards their effective reform. Other examples might have been chosen from the Health and Safety at Work Act 1974, the Race Relations Act 1976, or the Employment Protection Act 1975, amended 1978. It should be emphasized, however, that all these laws were intended to provide *individual* employment rights. The 1980 and 1982 Employment Acts and the 1984 and 1987 Trade Union Acts, by contrast, were intended to deal with aspects of *collective* labour law — a much more contentious area of legislative reform, which we shall not deal with here.

Whilst catalytic legislation per se cannot produce the desired changes in practice that are required at workplace level, the *declaratory effect* of such legislation is nevertheless significant. It serves as a clarion call on public policy, demanding responsive action by management and unions. Attempts by either side to exploit such new legislation to secure short-term tactical gains over the other are doomed from the outset. For that reason alone, catalytic legislation like the Equal Pay Act 1970 calls for the greatest possible measure of shopfloor participation — and for direct action, where necessary — to ensure that the reforming intention of the legislation is not subverted by collusive action between an evasive management and a cynical union bureaucracy.

After a decade of *legislative* reform, it may be argued that an energetic programme of *voluntary* reform along the lines advocated by the Donovan Report, supplemented by the application of the new 'floor of individual employment rights' legislation, still hold out the best hope for improved industrial relations in Britain. Attempts to transplant concepts, institutions and laws developed in other countries at other times for other industrial societies are unlikely to 'take root' in the special soil of our own industrial relations, or to flourish in our peculiar industrial relations climate. The voluntary tradition is not merely deep-rooted in the institutions of British industrial relations, it is also tenacious in the consciousness and experience of the principal actors who operate the system. The law has, at best, a supplementary role to play in securing the fundamental shift in industrial structure, attitudes and behaviour that a regenerated British economy so urgently needs. Breaking out of the vicious circles of degenerate industrial relations is not simply a matter of managerial determination, as Donovan implied.

Breaking into the first circle of voluntary reform leads almost invariably into other virtuous circles. The gains and losses of such reform may not be equal but they are by no means one-sided either. Indeed, there is substantial evidence from Electrolux, and from experience elsewhere, that the mutual benefits of voluntary reform are long-lasting and irreversible, because they tap human resources and change psychological attitudes in a way that the mere application of the law can never do.

SECTION 4: CONCLUSIONS AND 1987 POSTSCRIPT

This account of successful negotiated reform of industrial relations at Electrolux in the period 1975–78 demonstrates a number of fundamental features of the British system of industrial relations that are not confined to Electrolux or to the British engineering industry. The fact that the company was a wholly-owned subsidiary of an important Swedish multinational firm seems to have had little immediate effect on the conduct of the dispute. But, in retrospect, the outcome of the dispute and its all-important aftermath had a significant effect on the parent company's willingness to continue to invest in its British subsidiary.

Thanks to that continued investment, Electrolux Limited has continued to prosper with the restoration of improved profitability and sustained employment levels throughout the 1980s. Industrial relations have been transformed through a management strategy of negotiated change. This is not to deny that the company was forced to act decisively — some would say ruthlessly — to achieve its objectives. But there is no indication of massive discontent amongst the company's workforce. On the contrary, many would argue — from members of senior management down to men and women on the shopfloor — that the company has never been in better shape to face the future.

CHRONOLOGY OF THE DISPUTE

December 1974	Management make unilateral proposals on equal pay
January 1975	Unions make unilateral counter-proposals on equal pay
May	Management issues Statement on Equal Pay
9 May	Entire hourly-paid female workforce walks out on all-out strike
1 June	Strike ends with resumption of full normal working
31 December	Equal Pay Act 1970 and Sex Discrimination Act 1975 take effect
May 1976	Bedford Industrial Tribunal upholds complaint by Mrs Hutchinson of pay discrimination by company
July	Bedford Tribunal rejects complaint by Mrs Peckett of pay discrimination by company
November	Employment Appeal Tribunal rejects company appeal against Bedford Tribunal findings on Hutchinson complaint
January 1977	Equal Opportunity Commission begins inquiry into discrimination at Electrolux
September	Management and unions agree to work with independent consultant in reforming wage structure
January – December 1978	Joint Evaluation Committee complete evaluation of all hourly-paid jobs
December	Management and unions agree new wage structure and fringe benefits package
1 January 1979	New Wage Structure Agreement takes effect

WHO'S WHO IN THE DISPUTE

Cox, Colin	Union Convener, Electrolux Limited, 1977 to date
Hutchinson, Mrs Ann	AEU Shop Steward, Refrigerator Assembly Department, Electrolux Limited
Martin, H	Union convener, Electrolux Limited, 1965–77
McCarthy, Lord	Special Commissioner, Equal Opportunities Commission
Philips, Mr Justice	President, Employment Appeal Tribunal
Phipps, Ray	Director of Industrial Relations, Electrolux Limited, 1972–85
Sjogren, A	Luton District Officer, AEU

REFERENCES

1   Mr Justice Philips, President, Employment Appeal Tribunal: Report of Findings, Hutchinson Appeal, November 1976.
2   Otto Kahn-Freund: 'Legal Framework', in Allan Flanders and H. A. Clegg: *The System of Industrial Relations in Great Britain*, Blackwell, Oxford, 1967, p. 44.
3   *Report of Royal Commission on Trade Unions and Employers' Associations (The Donovan Report)*, Cmd. 6323, HMSO, London, 1968, Terms of Reference, p. 1.
4   See *The Donovan Report*, Ch. XVI, paras 1018–9.
5   Commission on Industrial Relations: *Report on Electrolux Limited*, HMSO, London, 1971.
6   Electrolux Joint Management–Shop Stewards' Working Group Report, Company documentation, unpublished, 1971.
7   For a concise account of this legislation, see 'The Coming of Equal Pay and Equal Opportunity', in Friedman and Meredeen: *The Dynamics of Industrial Conflict: Lessons from Ford*, Croom Helm, London, 1980, pp. 288–308.
8   Electrolux Limited: Draft Equal Pay Agreement Company documentation, unpublished, 1974.
9   Company Submission to Equal Opportunities Commission, Formal Investigation at Electrolux Limited, January 1977.
10 Terry Beckett, cited by Meredeen in Friedman and Meredeen, *The Dynamics of Industrial Conflict: Lessons from Ford*, Croom Helm, London, p. 236.

STUDY QUESTIONS

1.   Consider Mr Justice Philips remarks on the Hutchinson appeal findings and explain why he considered the law inadequate to deal with the industrial relations problems at Electrolux Limited.
2.   What special problems face (a) management, (b) employees and (c) unions in carrying out the joint reconstruction of a degenerate payment system?
3.   Why was the aftermath of the Electrolux pay dispute more important than the strike itself?
4.   Why should management accept the prime responsibility for the reform of degenerate workplace industrial relations?
5.   What are the arguments for and against the retention of incentive payments as a method of sustaining and increasing worker productivity in manufacturing industry?
6.   To what extent does the dispute at Electrolux illustrate the types of industrial relations problems of the 1960s and 1970s, as portrayed by the analysis and prescription of the 1968 Donovan Commission?

SUGGESTIONS FOR FURTHER READING

Report of Royal Commission on Trade Unions and Employers' Associations (The Donovan Report), HMSO, London, 1968.

Commission on Industrial Relations: *Report on Electrolux Limited,* HMSO, London, 1971.

Equal Opportunities Commission: Report of Formal Investigation into Electrolux Limited, 1981.

CHAPTER 5

■ Work and the new technology —

THE DISPUTE AT TIMES NEWSPAPERS LIMITED, 1978–79

The outcome of the war over new technology will be determined by the battle at The Times — of that I am sure. So there is no going back. There can be no surrender. We fight for our members. We fight for our union. We fight until we have won.

Joe Wade, General Secretary
National Graphical Association

We are not going to surrender to the incoherent immobility of some of the unions . . . To do so would be to accept that we must produce newspapers with gross inefficiency for the indefinite future . . . We are not going to abandon The Times. The Times will not surrender and The Times will not be destroyed.

William Rees-Mogg, Editor, The Times

INTRODUCTION: THE TIMES RUNS OUT OF TIME

On 30 November 1978, after 194 years of continuous publication, *The Times* of London — the world's oldest and most respected newspaper — suspended publication of all its titles. For almost a full year its presses remained silent in one of the most complex and intractable labour disputes in Britain. Like the monarchy or St Paul's Cathedral, *The Times* was a national institution. Civil strife, political and economic upheaval, and two World Wars had failed to silence its authoritative voice. Now, after years of management neglect, mounting disruption and financial loss, Times Newspapers Limited (TNL) decided to take a stand. In April, TNL told the unions representing its 6000 employees that unless they sat down and thrashed out new agreements on a wide-ranging set of proposals designed to achieve higher productivity through the introduction of new equipment, the reduction of manning and the elimination of unnecessary disputes, then 'publication of all our newspapers will be suspended'.

That ultimatum sent a shock wave through Fleet Street. For years *The Times* had castigated other employers for their weak handling of industrial relations. Now it had turned the spotlight on itself and was determined to put its own house in order. The shutdown threat caused intense speculation: Did *The Times* mean what it said? Would its owners — the powerful International Thompson Organization — withdraw its financial support? How would the unions react?

Of the many problems facing *The Times* in 1978, none was more urgent than securing union acceptance of the new electronic printing technology which, almost literally at a stroke, would reduce unit labour costs and remove one of the prime sources of disruption — the compositors' historic monopoly on typesetting. More than a decade earlier, American newspaper proprietors had persuaded their print unions to accept the new computer-linked technology, which greatly increased their productivity. *The Times* now sought to introduce that technology in order to reduce costs and increase profitability. But Times management was also determined to resolve other controversial and long-neglected issues: a revised disputes procedure to eliminate unnecessary work stoppages; a more rational wage structure to reflect changing job content; and an end to the interminable inter-union wrangles, which regularly disrupted the rhythm of high-speed production runs and which now threatened *The Times* itself. But the most difficult and potentially explosive issue was new technology.

SECTION 1: TECHNOLOGY AND WORKPLACE RELATIONS

All human societies are 'technological' in the sense that humans are distinguished by a unique capacity to construct, improve and utilize tools of every description. The sword and the ploughshare are more than biblical symbols of mankind's destructive and constructive urges, they bear witness to man's transformative skill: the capacity to subdue and exploit much of his natural environment, to extract useful materials from the earth's crust and to apply hard-won technical skills to meet the needs and wants of an increasingly scientific and materialistic world.

Advanced industrial societies rely on the application of scientific knowledge for the production and distribution of high-technology goods and services, which they so conspiciously and voraciously consume. It was not until the middle of the nineteenth century, however, that Western man consistently applied his mind to the systematic development of more durable, accurate and productive machine-tools. These rapidly superceded the hand-tools of earlier handicraft production: 'manufacture' began to be displaced by 'machinofacture'. It was these machine-tools — the machines for making machines — that provided the indispensable foundation for advanced technological economies. By releasing the latent energy in coal and harnessing it to the steam engine, the pioneers of the industrial revolution set in motion the machine age — an irreversible historical process of technological innovation, which progressively transformed the agrarian economy of eighteenth century Europe with its small-scale production for local markets into an industrial economy, concentrated into manufacturing units of ever-increasing size and technical complexity. The application of mass-production methods in the late nineteenth and twentieth centuries achieved unprecedented economies of scale, thereby supplying the needs of an expanding world economy.

Technological change has not simply transformed the material basis of our everday lives, it has also had the most profound effect on our economic, social and political systems. The word 'technology' is derived from two innocuous Greek words, corresponding closely with our modern term 'know-how'. But, as Toynbee observed, behind every technology there is an implied ideology.[1] When considering the social implications of technological change, we should not assume that technology is somehow 'neutral' or that technological advance is either inevitable or self-evidently beneficial to human development. Environmental pollution, excessive use of chemical fertilizers and pesticides, occupational health hazards from toxic substances and the prescription of inadequately tested drugs are familiar examples of the risks attendant on technological innovation, to say nothing of the risk of nuclear catastrophe, whether by accident or design.

This is not to deny that technological advances have stimulated economic development, thereby increasing employment and generating improved living standards for most people. If workers have not always welcomed new technology it is because its effects are not always beneficial to their interests. To understand the potential clash between those promoting and those resisting new technology, we need to examine the motives that underlie technological innovation, as well as its consequences.

In a major study of technological innovation, Landes speaks of the two essential elements that characterize any modern industrial system:

> *rationality, which is the spirit of the institution: and change, which is rationality's logical corollary, for the appropriation of means to ends which is the essence of rationality implies a process of continuous adaptation.*[2]

The rationality that has shaped our world is that of capitalist econimics, i.e. the pursuit of efficiency, productivity and private profit in accordance with the principles of *laisser faire* economics. Landes is arguing that the logic of capitalist rationality leads entrepreneurs to promote and invest in new technology when it helps them to become and remain more profitable: conversely, they will stop investing in new technology when it appears less profitable than investing elsewhere.

Just as entrepreneurs exploited the economic opportunities of new technology in order to enrich themselves, so workers reacted by forming trade unions to defend and advance their own interests, as they perceived them. For the most part, workers cooperated willingly in operating the new technology. Machines that threatened established jobs and traditional ways of working were sometimes resisted, but colourful accounts of armies of 'Luddites' engaged in a blind orgy of destructive hatred against the new machines are now thought to have been greatly exaggerated.[3]

The 'new model' unions of the 1850s were never anticapitalist in character but were 'exclusive brotherhoods' of skilled workers, organized into 'trade clubs' to secure higher wages and better working conditions for their members. Naturally enough, they opposed unilateral changes introduced by employers that appeared to threaten their job or income security. Throughout the Victorian era, the engineering unions engaged the employers in a continuous debate over the so-called 'machine question', which included such matters as the manning, speed of work, and the training and use of semi-skilled workers on new machines. But they were not opposed in principle to new technology.[4]

By contrast, the 'new unionism' that developed amongst less-skilled workers after 1880 was more overtly socialist in its ideology. However, since unskilled workers lacked the bargaining power of their more-skilled colleagues, they offered little sustained resistance to new technology. Under the influence of radical, socialist and syndicalist ideas, many union members sought to oppose and overthrow the capitalist economic system and to replace it with some form of socialism. Where capitalist economic rationality argued for the private ownership and control of the means of production, distribution and exchange, socailists argued for public ownership and the popular administration of the economy. Whereas under capitalism, profits would be retained in the business or distributed to shareholders as the reward for the loan of risk capital, under socialism any 'economic surplus' would either be ploughed back into the economy or distributed in accordance with some more egalitarian formulation (e.g. 'from each according to his capacity; to each according to his need or work contribution'[5]).

These competing ideologies and economic rationalities must be borne in mind when considering both the motivation for technological innovation and the reactions to it. During the present century, under the constraints of state intervention and the pressures of organized labour, employers have generally adopted less overtly exploitative policies in the management of their workforces. But trade unions in Britain and elsewhere continue to exhibit acutely ambivalent attitudes towards capitalism: they remain critical of its fundamentally exploitative character but no longer seek its overthrow, *provided* it can be made to yield material gains for their members. Rank-and-file members have sometimes been willing to challenge the unilateral exercise of managerial prerogative, but few contest management's fundamental right to manage the enterprise efficiently. The most significant resistance has been offered by those whose jobs and income security have come under threat from new technology.

Against this background, the managerial motives for technological innovation may be summarized briefly as follows:

(i) *to increase productivity* at a time when existing technology can no longer keep pace with rising demand, despite more intensive machine utilization (e.g. mechanization of cotton spinning in the 1820s followed by the replacement of hand-loom weaving by power-loom weaving between 1830 and 1850);

(ii) *to reduce costs* at a time of increasing competition and the availability of new labour-saving machines. Other things being equal, as the amount of labour needed to produce an article decreases, its cost falls and the demand for that article will increase (e.g. the adoption of the Bessemer converter for steel making in the 1860s);

(iii) *to improve quality* at a time when existing machines cannot sustain a consistently high standard of production or attain higher technical specifications (e.g. the development of improved machine-tools for the mass-production industries of the 1890s);

(iv) *to produce new goods and services* at a time when existing machines cannot be adapted for that purpose (e.g. the rise of the chemical, pharmaceutical and electronics industries after World War II);

(v) *to reduce conflict* in periods when organized workers threaten continuity of production with frequent or protracted work stoppages; managers seek to reduce their dependence on worker cooperation by substituting capital for labour (e.g. contrast the lack of modernization before 1939 with the labour rationalization schemes of the post-war period).

Where a significantly higher rate of profit cannot be achieved despite such innovation, entrepreneurs will switch investment from declining sectors into growth sectors, which further stimulates the pace of technological innovation.

The impact of new technology on workers and their families will vary with the stage of economic development, the state of product and labour markets and the balance of bargaining power between management and workers. This, in turn, reflects the balance of power in the wider society. The three principal economic and social effects of technological innovation may be summarized as:

1. *The productivity effect* — which is usually strongly positive, hence the managerial motivation to invest in new machinery and equipment. At crucial stages in the process of industrialization, the productivity effect of new technology has been spectacularly positive (e.g. the substitution of steam power for human/animal/water/wind power in the late eighteenth century; or the adoption of mechanical typewriters to replace laborious manuscript in the early years of this century).

Other things being equal, an overall increase in productivity will reduce unit costs, thereby increasing the quantity of the product/ service sold. It is important, but by no means easy, to distinguish between the share of increased productivity that is attributable to capital investment in new technology and that due to faster or better working. An employer who invests successfully in new technology may derive a strong initial advantage over his competitors by capturing a dominant share of the market. Whether the employer shares the economic gains of such increased productivity with his workforce depends on their relative bargaining power. Trade unions frequently cite increased productivity and profitability as important indices of an employer's ability to meet the cost of wage claims.

2. *The employment effect* — which may be positive or negative, depending on the relative levels of demand in product and labour markets at the time when the new technology comes 'on stream' (e.g. the power-loom displaced hand-loom weavers from employment when product demand was rising but labour supply outstripped labour demand; conversely, when linotype printing machines were introduced around 1900, the demand for printers increased because the product market for printed matter, especially newspapers, grew faster than labour supply).

3. *The industrial relations effect* — which is less easy to explain but which is associated with a loss of individual identity and personal significance experienced by workers subjected to the continuous pressure and discipline of modern industrial working life. Dissatisfaction at work produces widespread frustration, which, in turn, may lead to absenteeism, lower quality, more accidents and a higher propensity to raise grievances or to resort to strike action. In the words of Marx, 'the worker is not at home in his work' but is 'alienated' or 'distanced' from the primary sources of psychological satisfaction and personal growth. When Marxists refer to 'alienation' they use the word in this technical sense to describe the experience of workers under capitalist modes of production who are alienated:

(i)   from the means of production, which they neither own nor control;

(ii) from the products of their labour, which they neither control nor dispose of according to their own estimate of its market value;

(iii) from their own 'true nature', i.e. their capacity to develop into mature, moral and socially cooperative citizens.

Amongst the prime manifestations of such alienation is the propensity of workers:

(i)   to demand higher money wages to compensate for a lack of intrinsic satisfaction at work;

(ii) to resort to strike action;

(iii) to resist technological change, which is perceived as a threat to traditional ways of working and hard-won living standards.

It is an example of this third manifestation — the propensity of workers to defend themselves against what they perceive as the adverse effects of technological change — that provides the substance of the rest of this chapter.

SECTION 2: THE DISPUTE AT TIMES NEWSPAPERS LIMITED (TNL)

(1) The pre-dispute context

According to Routledge, the TNL dispute 'had its roots in years of unrest and apprehension about manpower economies and the impact of new printing technology'[6], but the more immediate causes of the dispute are to be found in its organizational context. When Roy (later Lord) Thomson, the Canadian entrepreneur, who already owned the *Sunday Times*, bought *The Times* from the Astor family in 1966 for £2 million plus, his motives were complex:

> It would probably not be disputed that ownership of The Times *and* The Sunday Times *was useful for Thomson in getting his oil licences. Thomson, who was always open about his social ambitions, also hoped that ownership of an establishment paper like* The Times *would get him a seat in the Lords.*[7]

That judgement proved correct. Raised to a peerage, Thomson soon secured licences for his independent television company (the notorious 'licence to print money') and a significant stake in North Sea oil. Paradoxically, he did not apply his business acumen to improving the performance of TNL. The inefficiency, poor industrial relations, frequent disruption and mounting losses that characterized Fleet Street continued to be tolerated.

When Thomson added *The Sunday Times* to his list of newspaper holdings, it was already highly profitable thanks to its glossy and much-imitated colour supplement with its associated advertising revenues. Circulation rose from about 900 000 to over 1.5 million copies, with annual profits consistently surpassing £1 million. For this reason, TNL continued to turn a blind eye to gross inefficiencies in labour utilization at the *The Sunday Times*: overmanning; the notorious system of employing casual labour; many ludicrous restrictive practices; and frequent surrender to union pressure for higher wages, without any corresponding increase in effort or productivity. Disputes were quickly settled by the simple expedient of capitulation:

The old proprietors generally paid up. Their motives — a mixture of political power-seeking and rivalry — compelled them to observe one priority above all else: to publish.[8]

Since Caxton set up his first moveable-type press in Westminster in 1476, the printing industry has been characterized by closely-controlled entry into the mysteries of the printers' craft. Print unions have been amongst the best-organized and most powerful in the world, especially in the newspaper industry. Since newspapers operate in a uniquely competitive product market, selling a highly perishable commodity, almost everything is sacrificed to production deadlines. If a labour dispute threatens production, management has traditionally bought itself out of trouble by expensive piecemeal concessions in wages, conditions, manning and working practices. For decades, Fleet Street management had tolerated the traditional 'customs and practices' of the trade rather than accept the certain losses of a head-on confrontation with the print unions. For years, wealthy newspaper proprietors had subsidized their heavy publishing losses. *The Times* was the prestigious flagship heading Lord Thompson's armada of highly profitable commercial and industrial enterprises. By the mid-1970s, however, its crew were under new orders: Halt the chaos and financial losses at *The Times* or its days are numbered.

By 1976, the organization had grown in size and scope to include book and magazine publishing, travel, television and, perhaps most important, oil. Unlike his father, the second Lord Thomson saw TNL as a minor part of the International Thomson Organization (ITO). In 1977, TNL contributed only £1.9 million in profits to ITO, compared with £4 million from travel, £10 million from provincial newspapers and no less than £82 million from oil revenues. But Thomson, based in Toronto, clearly recognized the need for new printing technology at TNL and at his other printing houses in Britain. He therefore brought into the business a team of younger, more professional managers, several of whom were destined to play prominent roles in the TNL dispute.

Two of the most important decisions taken by the new team were to install a new technology section on the third floor of *The Sunday Times* building in the Gray's Inn Road, even though they had no clear plan or timetable for its introduction, and to relocate *The Times* away from its historic home in Old Printing House Square, near St Paul's Cathedral, to a new site adjacent to, and physically linked with, *The Sunday Times* building. In theory, this physical proximity gave TNL management greater control over both publications, but equally it offered the chapels (print union workplace branches) better opportunities to compare wages and working conditions, to devise and implement common strategies or, when it suited them, to take unilateral action against the management of each newspaper in turn. Table 5.1 identifies the six main unions that TNL recognized for collective bargaining purposes in different departments of the newspaper.

Table 5.1 Trade union recognition at Times Newspapers Ltd, 1978

Trade union	Main departments/chapels*
NGA	Typesetting; foundry/hot metal; machine-room print managers
NATSOPA	Machine-room print assistants; packing and despatch
SOGAT	Clerical and ancillary workers
AUEW	Mechanical maintenance workers
EEPTU	Electrical maintenance workers
NUJ	Journalists (including some editorial staff)

* Print union workplace branches.

By 1978, both *The Times* and *The Sunday Times* were losing money: production costs soared, competition was more intense and TNL had failed to tackle its bad labour relations. The ITO took the precaution of separating the financial structure of TNL from other ITO operations in the UK and placed them under the direct control of Gordon Brunton, Chief Executive of the Thomson Organization in Britain. Concerned about growing financial losses at TNL and the rising incidence of unofficial stoppages, Lord Thomson applied pressure on Brunton to put his TNL house in order; Brunton, in turn, warned the TNL board of the likely consequences of their failure to reverse the losses at TNL.

(2) The challenge

On 10 April 1978, Marmaduke ('Duke') Hussey, Managing Director and Chief Executive of TNL, addressed a letter to every employee in the company. He reported that in the first 3 months of 1978, unofficial strikes had cost TNL some £2 million through its failure to publish 7.7 million copies or a staggering 20% of normal output. 'No newspaper' wrote Hussey 'even one as strong as *The Sunday Times* can withstand such losses'. From January to March of 1978, *The Times* had failed to complete its full production run on no less than 21 occasions. It lost four complete issues in February and five in March. *The Sunday Times* had lost one complete issue in March and another in April with nine separate incomplete runs. *The Times'* sister publications *The Times Education, Higher Education* and *Literary Supplement* failed to complete their runs on seven occasions. Such losses were not unfamiliar in Fleet Street, but they were a continuous drain not only on TNL's financial resources but also on management's time, energy and creativity:

> *It is not an exaggeration that almost the total working hours of our board and senior managers are now occupied with*

trying to prevent disputes, solving disputes and repairing the damage they cause. Virtually no effort is going into improving the turnover and profitability of the company.[9]

The TNL board finally decided it could no longer stand aside from the crisis. On 26 April it presented the unions with a clear-cut ultimatum: either they cooperate with TNL to secure agreement to end the disruption, raise efficiency and introduce the new technology or TNL would suspend publication of all its titles. Such an ultimatum had to be taken seriously. At mid-April meetings with union leaders, Hussey spelled out the facts: if the disruption continued and editions were lost, advertisers would shift their spending elsewhere, leaving TNL with a prospective £4 million drop in revenue. To prevent that happening, the company had identified five basic objectives on which it sought the unions' cooperation:

(i)   absolute continuity of production, with the removal of all arbitrary restrictions on output;

(ii)   negotiation of a new fast-acting and effective disputes procedure;

(iii) acceptance of new technology;

(iv) the negotiation of a new wage structure;

(v)   efficient manning in all departments.[10]

Hussey called on union leaders for 'urgent discussions' on these objectives, reaffirming that if negotiations were not successfully concluded by 30 November 1978, the shutdown would be implemented and would continue 'until we are satisfied that publication can be restarted on a basis of reasonable staffing, efficient working and uninterrupted production'. In full-page advertisements in the national press, TNL explained that it had offered the unions fair and wide-ranging proposals:

(i)   a new disputes procedure 'that will be honoured by everyone before, not after, copies are lost or production disrupted';

(ii)   the replacement of old machinery and equipment and the phasing in of new technology that 'many papers elsewhere in the world have been using effectively for the last ten years';

(iii) the reduction of heavy overmanning.

In return, TNL promised to spend two-thirds of projected savings to improve pay, sick pay, pensions and holidays. No compulsory redundancies would result from the adoption of the new technology; those who volunteered to go would receive compensation on a scale described as 'the best offer ever made in British industry'. An optimistic note added:

We are working hard to reach a fair and effective agreement. And when we get it, which we will, all our readers, newsagents, advertisers and (above all) our staff, will have something to celebrate.[11]

Paul Routledge, Labour Editor of *The Times*, later made clear precisely what the company was demanding from each of the principal unions concerned:

> *From the National Graphical Association (NGA):*
>
> *Abandonment of the printers' monopoly of the typesetting keyboard, with shared access for journalists and tele-ad girls to the new computerized photocomposition system through desk-top visual display terminals.*
>
> *From the National Society of Operative Printers and Assistants (NATSOPA):*
>
> *A cut of 40% in* The Sunday Times *machine-room numbers, no work restrictions and the efficient operation of new equipment.*
>
> *From the Society of Graphical and Allied Trades (SOGAT):*
>
> *The operation of new machinery, fewer men at work and abolition of the 'Toby' system which allowed members to supplement their pay packets by supplying additional copies to London newsagents to top up their supplies.*
>
> *From other unions:*
>
> *A contribution towards higher productivity.*[10]

(3) Initial responses

According to Eric Jacobs, Labour Editor of *The Sunday Times*, the union leaders privately agreed with Hussey that the 'Fleet Street anarchy' had to be stopped. They appeared to be strongly in favour of TNL's shutdown strategy, 'even to the point of encouraging the board to set a deadline for November there and then'.[12] Since 'Fleet Street anarchy' was as much a challenge to their authority as it was to the company's they declared themselves ready to enter negotiations, but as months went by and TNL failed to translate its basic objectives into specific plans, their enthusiasm evaporated. Joe Wade, General Secretary, NGA, accused TNL of wanting 'to provoke a major confrontation with the unions by trying to do a deal with the union leaders over the heads of the chapels'. TNL repeatedly denied this, but Hussey allowed five months to elapse before starting the 'urgent discussions' he had asked for in April. During this hiatus, TNL's proposals were closely scrutinized in Fleet Street, not least by NGA printers whose jobs were at greatest risk. According to Wade, the rest of Fleet Street and the provincial press were 'waiting like vultures' for his union to capitulate on new technology at TNL. Wade's response was characteristic of the man and of the NGA:

> *In industrial life, as elsewhere, there are some battles you win and others you lose — and if you lose a battle, it doesn't necessarily mean that you have lost the war. But the outcome*

of the war over new technology will now be determined by the battle at The Times *— of that I am sure. So there is no going back. There can be no surrender. We fight for our members. We fight for our union. We fight until we have won.*[13]

At a meeting with Hussey on 18 September, Wade refused to discuss new technology. He was ready to agree a conventional 'back-end' system (i.e. one in which his members would continue to operate typesetting keyboards) but he refused to consider TNL's 'front-end' system of single keystroking (i.e. one in which members of other unions, including journalists and phone-advertising staff, would share access to the keyboards). His union was 'determined to fight this issue to the bitter end.'[14]

One commentator read Wade's remarks as 'the customary sabre-rattling of trade union leaders at the onset of a dispute'. But Routledge notes:

In the industry, we knew that the NGA was in deadly earnest: a tough, disciplined and comparatively wealthy union, it was well placed to ensure that new technology was installed only on its terms.[15]

In late September, Hussey produced TNL's New Agreement Proposals (NAPs), at the heart of which was a draft disputes procedure intended to stamp out unofficial action. If any chapel took unconstitutional strike action (i.e. stopped work before first exhausting every stage of the disputes procedure) then employees in *all* TNL chapels in that establishment would be taken off pay until normal working was resumed. Such 'penalty clauses', designed to bring maximum union pressure to bear on recalcitrant chapels were not new. They were introduced by Ford of Britain in 1969 [16] but they were ambitious and without precedent in Fleet Street, where they were accurately perceived by the Fathers of the Chapels (FOCs) as a provocative challenge to their traditional power to 'take the lads down the road'. According to Jacobs:

This was, indeed, the underlying theme of The Times *strategy. The company had set out deliberately to reduce the power of the fathers and increase the power of its own managers with, it believed, the support of the staff's own union leaders and that of the whole of the trade union establishment. But the plans represented a challenge to the fathers, and they did not fail to rise to it.*[17]

Much earlier, in May, Reg Brady (FOC, NATSOPA, ST machine room, 540-strong) had written to Hussey, protesting bitterly against the threatened lock-out. In July, eleven NATSOPA Fathers addressed a joint letter to Hussey, rejecting his ultimatum and demanding the right to take part in direct negotiations with their own management —

an attempt to outflank the national union officers. Brady accused the company of being in breach of the Employment Protection Act (1975) by withholding bargaining information on future company plans. Ten days before the November deadline, in a desperate bid to defer the shutdown and secure more negotiating time for their national leaders, Brady's chapel lifted the overtime ban that it had operated all summer, but to no avail. Hussey refused to concede an inch, even in response to direct approaches from the TUC and the Labour Government's Employment Secretary, Albert Booth.

On the eve of the deadline, only four of the 65 TNL chapels had reached agreement with management. Given the deadlock between TNL and the NGA, it was hardly surprising that other chapels dragged their feet. The delay was fatal. *The Times* took some pride in saying what it meant; on this occasion, its ultimatum clearly meant what it said. Up to the last hour, management tried without success to get the NGA to take part in the talks. In the words of Bill Booroff, Secretary of the NGA's London Region:

> *If they shut the paper, we will have to accept it. But we will not negotiate under the threat of close-down, and that's final.*[18]

The Times kept its word. On 30 November 1978, all TNL publications were suspended. The presses stopped turning and an unfamiliar, year-long silence fell upon New Printing House Square.

(4) Consequences

The first results of the shutdown were entirely predictable: as readers and advertisers transferred their custom elsewhere, financial losses at TNL mounted even faster. Its accountants had estimated that every month's closure would cost the Thomson Organization almost £4 million. Having locked out its workforce to secure certain conditions, TNL was unlikely to relent and resume publication until those conditions had been met, whatever the cost. Management nevertheless withheld staff dismissal notices for two weeks to allow talks to continue, but its attempt to buy time came to nothing. When the NGA proposed a round-table conference, chaired by the Employment Secretary, provided that single keystroking was not on the agenda, TNL refused to accept any pre-conditions. Lord Thomson himself had said that for management to concede on keystroking would be to give up a basic objective. So the deadlock continued.

On 14 December, notices were duly issued and in early January 1979 the first dismissals took effect. TNL employees responded by forming an All-Union Liaison Committee (AULC) to represent rank-and-file views and resolved to boycott further discussions with management until all those dismissed had been reinstated. Since there was no prospect of an early settlement, some unions set about finding alternative work for their displaced members. The NGA chapels, totalling some 600 men, decided not to move but stayed on, eventually to picket TNL buildings, living on their savings plus £60 a week strike pay from the NGA and another £40 from a levy on other NGA members. By contrast, SOGAT and NATSOPA members were gradually found work in and around Fleet Street, even though this sometimes meant displacing temporary print workers elsewhere in Fleet Street.

In March, after four months' closure, Employment Secretary Albert Booth succeeded in getting the parties together for the first time. Although the issues were unchanged, the question of new technology was left for later and the FOCs were now also involved in negotiations. The NGA agreed to accept the new technology and to surrender up to 40% of compositors' jobs, *provided* that it retained its exclusive right to typesetting. But it would not agree to go to arbitration on keystroking. In the words of the NGA President, Les Dixon:

> It's a matter of principle and you can't arbitrate on a principle.[19]

Since the TNL shutdown, the NGA had reached agreement with management at *The Glasgow Herald*, *The Observer* and *The Daily Express*. In each case, new technology was accepted but the NGA retained its monopoly of typesetting. It would settle for nothing less. Meanwhile, at *The Times*, the deadlock remained unresolved:

> In April, as in November, the company failed to establish its credibility with the unions, persuading them neither of the benefits of its innovations nor of the penalties for rejecting them. Technology exercised psychological dominion over every other issue: as a result, only a trickle of staff were induced to make settlements.[20]

By Easter it became clear that TNL had devised a new publishing tactic. On 20 April, *The Times*' editor, William Rees-Mogg, disclosed that TNL intended to publish a weekly international edition on secret presses somewhere in Europe. The NGA immediately despatched an official to the International Graphical Federation (IGF) urging it to instruct its affiliates in Germany, Portugal and even as far away as Turkey, not to handle TNL material. In the event, more direct action produced the desired result. When the secret location in Frankfurt was identified, members of the German print and engineering unions physically prevented publication. Rather than risk an embarrasing and violent confrontation, TNL abandoned the venture, but a new bitterness was now injected into the dispute: the NGA stepped up its campaign by mounting a 24-hour picket on all TNL buildings. As a result, the search for a solution became all the more difficult.

By the end of April, the dispute had entered its sixth month. As often happens in protracted disputes, both sides now began to reveal divisions within their own ranks. TNL directors were divided between those who adhered to the shutdown strategy, and who there-fore favoured battling it out to the bitter end, and those who wished to adopt a more conciliatory strategy, viz:

(i)   There should be no more dramatic attempts to break the dead-lock, like the Frankfurt fiasco.
(ii)   If keystroking was the only remaining impediment to resumed publication, it should be set aside for later resolution.
(iii) TNL must start to devise a piecemeal solution with each union, in turn.
(iv)   TNL should no longer rely on national officials but must open discussions with the FOCs, since they alone could deliver the desired agreements and make them stick.

It was this latter view that prevailed at the TNL board meeting in early May. Meanwhile, frustrated journalists began direct talks with the NGA on the crucial issue of keystroking. According to Jacobs, this seemed to be quite distinct from all other issues in dispute:

> It was really an argument between unions about how to handle a new species of print technology, not a parochial squabble within one company. The unions themselves, I thought, should sort out questions of who did what, perhaps through the TUC, one of whose functions was to settle just this kind of argument.[21]

Jacobs wrote privately to Len Murray, General Secretary of the TUC, setting out the journalists' ideas for a compromise solution that involved shared keystroking, but nothing came of this initiative. The AULC then picked up the idea and requested a meeting with Hussey. He declined to meet them but judged the moment right for a move of his own. On 2 May he wrote to the NGA offering an important concession: all original typesetting would be reserved for NGA members, with journalists allowed access for editing purposes only; the whole system to be reviewed after two years with no prior commit-ment other than a TNL guarantee that no NGA jobs would be lost. The NGA rejected the compromise outright.

By June, TNL management were compelled to acknowledge that every approach to the NGA for a compromise on keystroking had failed. They reluctantly concluded that this issue would have to be deferred until after publication had been resumed. The target now was to get the men back to work, and that meant direct talks with the chapels. On 12 June, a top management team met the AULC for the first time since the dispute began. Sir Dennis Hamilton, Chairman of TNL, was brought in as a catalyst to get the talks restarted:

> I don't think we have been seeing enough of each other; many of us, including myself, have got out of touch. We want strong unions with authority. But things have changed over the past few years, FOCs have won more power, but I don't believe

*that the movement has realized its responsibilities. I want our
FOCs to use their power with us constructively.*[22]

By publicly acknowledging this shift of power, Sir Dennis had set the
scene for realistic bargaining. But, according to Routledge, the real
breakthrough did not come until Lord Thomson himself intervened
at the highest level. Addressing the AGM of the Thomson Organization in London on 27 June, he emphasized the great importance that
TNL attached to the new technology:

*Ultimately this new modern equipment should be used to its
full potential.*[23]

Whether deliberately or not, by his use of the word 'ultimately', Lord
Thomson transformed single keystroking from an immediate into
an ultimate objective, thereby offering the basis for a compromise
resolution of the dispute. As Jacobs confirms:

*Evans had been in Bedford talking to Joe Wade and Les Dixon.
Over lunch they had settled on a formula for dealing with the
new technology. Under the formula, keystroking would be 'set
aside', to be settled after the newspapers were restarted.*[24]

With new technology temporarily shelved, a second meeting was
held between directors and FOCs, on 4 July, at which the company
produced a 9-point plan, spelling out its 'minimum practical
conditions' for restarting publication and a return to work. According
to TNL, speedy negotiations were essential if the company's publications were to be saved. In the event, it took four months of tedious
bargaining with the separate chapels and unions before the necessary
agreements were reached. The three main questions to be resolved
were:

(i)   re-instatement terms for those dismissed,
(ii) manning requirements for start-up,
(iii) wage rates for start-up.

Discussion of these vexed questions could not be rushed, particularly
since the national union leaders were not prepared for TNL directors
to negotiate directly with FOCs in their absence. Not surprisingly,
TNL's first proposals on all three outstanding points were rejected by
the chapels and unions, who presented their own counter-demands.
On 20 July, TNL came back with revised proposals, spelling out its
detailed requirements on new machinery and systems. TNL apparently wanted full agreement on the operation of all new equipment —
other than keystroking — *before* publication resumed, whereas the
unions thought that all such questions should be left until *after* publication had resumed.

      At the end of August, the NGA members threatened to with-
draw from the discussions and find work for its TNL members elsewhere in Fleet Street, thereby jeopardizing any chance of any early

start-up. By mid-September, the NGA was back in discussions. So the bargaining dragged on through the summer into autumn.

(5) The climax

According to Jacobs, by October:

> *the conviction was growing that if the newspapers did not return soon, they might never return at all . . . The company now decided to build up pressure in every way it could.*[25]

On 8 October, Dixon flew back from Stockholm to take personal charge of the union side of the negotiations. On 12 October, Brunton issued a statement pointing out that the consequences of failure in the negotiations would be 'the certainty of the loss of thousands of jobs within the company and possibly elsewhere too'. He added the ominous note that TNL had no intention of selling the titles. During the following week, the dispute was built up by both sides to its well-orchestrated climax:

> *Management deliberately stepped up the pressure so as to remove any lingering doubt that this week was positively the last chance to save the newspapers and the jobs they provided.*[26]

On Sunday 14 October, Hussey got the General Secretaries together for resumed talks at New Printing House Square. With the TNL deadline set for midnight on Wednesday 17 October, there followed four days of almost continuous negotiations. On Monday 15 October, TNL warned the Departments of Trade and Employment 'that there might soon be a final closure'. On Tuesday 16 October, Hussey told the General Secretaries that if there was no agreement by Wednesday, the TNL board would meet on Thursday to take its fateful decisions, and these would be conveyed to the unions on Friday.

Wednesday 17 October proved to be the crucial day of the entire dispute. Three TNL external directors were recalled from the United States; Lord Thomson himself flew into London from Toronto. Although some progress had been made, not one of the fourteen deals that the unions had to make was within sight. In Jacob's words:

> *The fate of two great newspapers and thousands of jobs depended on the NGA's ability to make a deal.*[26]

Under the pressure of the deadline, the NGA began to crumble. But by Wednesday evening it was obvious that there would be no agreement that night. In the early hours of Thursday 18 October, Dixon walked out on hearing that TNL had finally offered NATSOPA's *semi-skilled* machine assistants £207 per week (for a 45½-hour week, mainly on nights) compared with only £204 per week for his NGA *skilled* machine managers (albeit for a 34-hour, four day-week, with six weeks paid annual holiday). Bill Keys, Chairman of the TUC

Printing Industry Committee and General Secretary of SOGAT, helped to restore some order on the union side. He also called in other leaders of the print unions to spell out the repercussions of permanent closures at TNL. If *The Sunday Times* closed, Sun Printers of Watford would lose the contract to print the colour supplement. Sun was an important component of the British Printing Corporation. According to Jacobs:

> *The loss of jobs at Gray's Inn Road would be serious; the loss elsewhere would be catastrophic.*[27]

(6) The settlement

On the evening of Thursday 18 October, Keys asked Brunton to meet him with other print union leaders at the TUC in a desperate attempt to retrieve the situation. He appealled for an extension of the deadline. Brunton eventually agreed: Lord Thomson had granted a 3-day stay of execution. If agreement was not complete by 4 p.m. on Sunday 21 October, the great axe would fall.

The final round of talks occupied the whole weekend of 20/21 October. On Friday 19 October, the atmosphere around the negotiating table was described by Jacobs as 'intense, serious, sober'. Even strong drink had been banished from the room![28]

At 9.30 a.m. on Saturday, not one of the fourteen outstanding agreements had been finalized. At 1 a.m. on Sunday, two fundamental problems were still outstanding: there was no agreement on resumption pay and no concessions by the machine minder's chapel on manning:

> *From the start the machine-room chapels had been the toughest nuts of all on one issue: jobs. Every other chapel that had been asked had made some concessions but the [NGA] machine minders had consistently refused. And they still refused.*[29]

At this point, Hussey reshuffled his negotiating team, putting Nisbet-Smith into the top management chair. He, in turn, invited Dixon to help him to coordinate the last stages of negotiation by meeting the FOCs of each department, in turn, to resolve outstanding issues. At 7 a.m. that Sunday morning, this last stumbling block had still not been overcome. Nisbet-Smith and Dixon had been negotiating all that night and most of the previous day. Nisbet-Smith decided to take a gamble and proposed that the one outstanding issue of machine-room manning should be referred to ACAS arbitration. At first Dixon refused; then he had second thoughts and agreed. But by now the TNL directors were divided. Knowing that the noise levels in the machine-room 'verged on the unlawful'[30], some feared that the NGA might persuade ACAS that *more* men were justified on health grounds alone. Rees-Mogg supported Nisbet-Smith but it took some time to persuade other directors that whilst arbitration might not be perfect, it was better than losing the newspapers.

Since single keystroking was still outstanding, the board wanted all other negotiating issues out of the way. At 11 a. m. it decided to give way and accepted the NGA's figures on machine-room manning. With that decision, the last brick was in place. There was agreement at last . . . Champagne corks popped:

The Times and The Sunday Times were saved.[31]

(7) Aftermath

The return to work was orderly and good-humoured. Harsh jokes were a Fleet Street institution and there was bound to be some bitter recrimination, but the FOCs resumed their traditional 'love-hate' relationship and soon closed ranks against their common enemy: the management. In the first weeks following the strike, production runs were tense. When small disputes erupted, they were side-stepped or bought out by shopfloor management. Nobody wanted another all-out stoppage. According to Jacobs, it did not take long for journalists to recognize that the strike had changed nothing.[32] Times Newspapers had paid a very heavy price for a widely-publicized pyrrhic victory. Thomson International was a wealthy corporation, but its directors had no intention of continuing to subsidize the world's most presitigious newspaper. Within months, ITO had sold all its newspaper titles to Rupert Murdoch's News International.

SECTION 3: ANALYSIS OF THE DISPUTE

(1) What was the dispute about?

From the outset, TNL used its unique position to publicize what it saw as the central issues of the dispute. It repeatedly stressed that it was neither anti-union nor seeking a confrontation with its workforce:

> This has not therefore been a struggle by the management of Times Newspapers against the unions; it has been a struggle to reach a more productive relationship with the unions, a relationship more advantageous to both sides. That it involves a major bargain against a fixed deadline is true, but how else could such a change of relationship be achieved? . . . Low productivity is our central economic failure. It can only be overcome by strong managements dealing with strong trade unions [which] should accept the role of management in increasing the efficiency of the business because that is what earns trade unions their pay . . . . A union which adopts a pure adversary position cannot look after its members and all great or even good leaders of trade unions in history have known that.[33]

TNL management sensed that it was embarking on a national crusade; that its own domestic dispute was 'in some ways a symbol of a national crisis and that if it can be resolved successfully it will be national good news'. For TNL, the dispute centred on three familiar themes of British industrial relations:

> *These historic themes — that unofficial strikes are a mortal danger to effective trade unionism; that new technology is the inevitable future of the printing industry and is already the present of the printing industry of the United States; that the battle for higher productivity means concern for higher real pay and not higher paper wages — are what the negotiation in Times Newspapers is concerned with. They are not easy issues, and indeed such major issues never are easy. Yet they must be resolved.*[33]

If the unions at TNL failed to present a coherent collective view of the dispute from their viewpoint it was not because they lacked the flair for publicity or polemics but, like most other British unions, they were divided on both ideological and practical issues. Initially, there was no concerted union counter-strategy against TNL's threat to suspend publication. Indeed, multi-unionism was one of the issues that Rees-Mogg complained about most bitterly in January 1979:

> *Our basic negotiation aims to achieve regular production without unofficial strikes, more efficient manning and the introduction of new technology . . . What we are trying to achieve is better (sic) for all our staff: higher pay, better holidays, safer jobs, bigger pensions. We need higher real earnings to achieve these obviously desirable objectives. Yet the militants say 'No'. This has not surprised me, but what has surprised me is the sheer incapacity of most of the trade unions with which we have to deal to carry out coherent negotiations, let alone negotiations of some complexity.*[34]

Although Rees-Mogg sought to blame the unions for the deadlocked negotiations, Routledge detected from the outset a second powerful motive behind TNL's ultimatum:

> *the privately-held but rarely publicized objective of restoring management's right to manage in an industry that has seen this prerogative increasingly challenged by the trade unions.*[35]

The reassertion of 'management's right to manage' is a recurring rhetorical theme in British industrial relations. (See Chapter 8, Section 2). Fleet Street proprietors frequently lamented their lost right to manage yet they condoned and encouraged 'the Fleet Street disease' of continuous disruption. As Hussey admitted in a television interview shortly before the dispute:

> *We've allowed situations to develop, Fleet Street's allowed situations to develop, which it should never have done, that we're trying to deal with now. . . The right to manage is one of the issues at stake . . . it is a Fleet Street problem.*[39]

More precisely, it was management's failure to exercise 'the duty to manage' that had brought TNL to its knees. The reason for this was chapel power: the ability of the FOCs to extract concessions from management by the threat of a walk-out at strategic points in the daily or weekly production cycle. As Louis Heren, a deputy editor on *The Times*, explained:

> *This industrial warfare, as I tend to think of it in darker moments, is terribly damaging because a newspaper is so vulnerable. Unlike a car plant, which can build up stocks and, if they are exhausted during a strike, can hope to catch up when production is resumed, nothing is more unsaleable than yesterday's newspapers. Perishable products such as milk and bread can be kept for a day or two but not newspapers.*[36]

The fact is that, with few exceptions, Fleet Street proprietors had long neglected the strategic management of their businesses. This was the nature of the crisis that *The Times* finally recognized when its editor wrote:

> *Something had to be done if* The Times *was to survive and prosper.*[33]

The extent of the crisis is revealed by TNL's decision to wage a one-company, unilateral campaign against the unions and to issue an ultimatum to suspend publication if comprehensive agreement was not reached by November. In Routledge's words, it was 'an unprecedented move, as bold as it was fraught with the risk of failure'.[35] As another authority on Fleet Street has noted:

> *The management in Fleet Street have no real sanctions. The ultimate sanction is to close the newspaper but for obvious reasons this is self–defeating.*[37]

(2) How significant was the context?

The historical context of the dispute was important but it was not entirely of TNL's own choosing. Over the previous twenty years, Fleet Street had earned a reputation for appalling industrial relations. Supremely unaware of the inherent irony, its leader writers fulminated regularly against the disastrous strike record and poor labour productivity of other industries. When the management of certain printing houses tried their hand at some half-hearted reforms, they came up against the implacable hostility of the print unions and soon abandoned their labour-saving and cost-cutting plans. During the 1960s and early 1970s, newspaper proprietors around the world had compelled their managers and employees to meet the challenge of automation and advanced printing technology. In the United States and Canada, Germany, Sweden and some other Scandinavian countries, print unions had surrendered jobs in return for very large financial compensation.[38] Elsewhere, as in Italy, France, The Netherlands,

Belgium and Britain, these unions had dug in their heels and refused to surrender their historical monopoly of typesetting, despite the attractive financial inducements on offer.

By the late 1970s, Thomson International was determined to break the stranglehold that British print unions exercised over newspaper printing in Fleet Street and the provincial press. There seemed no better place to launch the assault than at the biggest loss-maker of all — *The Times* itself.

(3) Why did TNL adopt the shutdown strategy?

When the board of TNL met in late March 1978, it had three clear objectives: first, to restore TNL to profitability within the year or risk the sale of the titles; second, to achieve a significant improvement in productivity in all departments of TNL, which required a comprehensive productivity bargain with all the unions; and third, to devise some unmistakably clear signal to let the unions and the world know that it meant business. The shutdown strategy of April 1978 emerged from these considerations.

According to Rees-Mogg, in a phrase destined to achieve much wider currency, TNL chose the shutdown strategy because 'there was no alternative'.[34] Precisely how and when it emerged is impossible to say. Jacobs believed that it had been discussed as far back as 1971, when Hussey joined the company. But two things are clear: first, TNL was determined to install the new technology and so match the best performance of the North American press; second, since single keystroking constituted a direct threat to the printers' monopoly of typesetting, the NGA would inevitably mount a powerful and sustained campaign of resistance to any attempt by British management to break that monopoly as the American, Canadian, German and Scandinavian newspaper proprietors had successfully done in the previous decade.

The shutdown strategy was therefore designed to mobilize the six other unions at TNL against the NGA, since the New Agreement Proposals (NAPs) offered greater benefits to their members in return for the surrender of customary practices than was required from the NGA. TNL made clear that the signatures of *all* the unions with members at TNL were required on the NAPs by 30 November if the shutdown was to be averted. It thereby signalled its intention to apply massive union pressure on the NGA to secure its eventual agreement or acquiescence to single keystroking. Failing that, the NGA would be isolated and exposed as the 'luddite' union, which persistently blocked progress and so denied other union members the improved wages and working conditions that TNL was offering in return for improved efficiency and the acceptance of new technology.

Routledge acknowledges that 'the multiplicity of unions was certainly an exacerbating factor in the delay in reaching a workable peace formula to end the shutdown', and he goes much further in his analysis:

> *No proprietor had hitherto contemplated a limited, one-company lock-out to win back managerial prerogatives long since surrendered to the unions, and while it was rarely stated openly, that was clearly a major company objective.*[35]

But, as Routledge pointed out in 1981, 'the lock-out is enjoying something of a new vogue'. It had certainly been used to great effect by the German newspaper proprietors earlier in the year; it was to be used by the British engineering employers in their 1979 dispute over shorter working time (See Chapter 6, Section 2) and it was threatened by commercial television companies in their autumn dispute of 1979.

In this connection, it is worth noting that, in the early months of 1978, just before the shutdown strategy was adopted, the eyes of newspaper executives and unions around the world were focused on the German press. According to Anthony Smith, after a series of sporadic strikes by the German print unions in opposition to the threatened introduction of new printing technology:

> *The employers replied with a massive lock-out that shut down almost the entire daily newspaper industry, inducing the federal government to step in and mediate. The final agreement permits journalists to use VDTs (i.e. single keystroking) only on their own stories. . . and by editors at the copy desk. The period of transition between old and new contracts of employment is to be eight years (instead of the five hoped for) during which time all layout and makeup work, all photocomposition and correction work is at first to be performed by the traditional workers. At the end of this period (viz. 1986) management may decide which group of workers is to use which machine.*[38]

(4) Did the shutdown strategy fail?

By midsummer 1978, TNL must have felt that its shutdown strategy was fully vindicated. Its first half-year losses had more than swallowed up the entire profits made in 1977, its most successful trading year. With five months to go until the ultimatum expired, it had every reason to believe that the NAPs would be constructively discussed, perhaps amended, but finally agreed and signed by all the unions concerned before the 30 November deadline. In the event, the strategy proved counter-productive and was eventually abandoned. But does that mean it failed?

The first point to be considered in implementing a successful strategy is timing. Even assuming that the shutdown strategy was inherently correct (i.e. a rational choice of the most effective means of achieving its pre-determined policy objectives), why did TNL unilaterally announce the November deadline in April?

Rees-Mogg cited TNL's earlier experience to justify the announcement of 'a firm but realistic deadline':

In at least two parts of this negotiation — the commercial computer and the 80-page Sunday Times *— we have already been in negotiation for so long that the equipment we originally installed is now obsolete. It will go out of the building without ever having been used. Those negotiations have taken 4 years and 12 years respectively, and so far without any success.*[34]

Seen from the TNL boardroom, the November deadline seemed to offer management sufficient time to secure all the necessary agreements. Both Hussey and Rees-Mogg failed to comprehend shop floor anxieties and the time needed to overcome them and to achieve anything approaching a worthwhile productivity agreement:

Six weeks is a long time to negotiate anything, if there is a willingness to negotiate. We are prepared to talk day and night, weekends, anytime.[39]

If TNL management had engaged in the tortuous productivity bargaining in vogue in the mid-1960s and early 1970s, it might have recognized that its timetable was wildly over-ambitious and unrealistic:

Some shop floor leaders complained that they had been given no more than six weeks to study and accept the detailed management proposals.[39]

The Secretary of the NGA's London Region, Bill Booroff, was a professional union negotiator. He did not refuse to negotiate with TNL. He simply refused to negotiate under the duress of an artificial and unilateral ultimatum:

I suppose this deadline is meant to be an exercise in firm management. It is a mistaken exercise and will not work. If they withdraw the deadline we will negotiate immediately. [18]

As the November deadline approached and the deadlock remained unbroken, TNL found itself trapped by its own shutdown strategy. It had set its face against a compromise and feared that any offer to defer the deadline would be interpreted as a sign of weakness. So the shutdown went ahead. Eleven months later, having lost more than £30 million, TNL was forced to acknowledge that the shutdown strategy had failed. It set aside its former insistence on single keystroking and adopted the more realistic strategy of securing whatever productivity improvements it could obtain from the chapels.

In Jacobs' view, the strategy failed because TNL had not made up its mind whether to be tough or tender:

Having chosen a strategy whose essence was persuasion, the company failed to persuade. Neither its promises nor its threats were forceful enough. It declared a crisis in April, but the staff heard little more than rumour until September. Thereafter management's eagerness to appear reasonable gave the impression of weakness. It did not lock out its members (sic) but gave them notice: a quarter of TNL's employees were not in danger of dismissal, and half were paid for more than three months after the newspapers were shut . . . (In short) the company did not live up to the tough image it had cultivated. [40]

(5) Who won?

On the day the dispute was settled, both sides argued that victory was theirs. The agreements signed on 21 October 1979 covered every issue tabled by TNL in the April letter: productivity, manning, pay, working arrangements and the use of new equipment. Since TNL's primary objective was to secure union agreement on all those issues, it could argue, from a management perspective, that it had achieved most, if not all, of its objectives. The only exception was single keystroking, on which there were to be further discussions. But the unions could argue, with equal conviction, that having held out for almost a full year against the threats and blandishments of TNL, their members had gone back to work on their own terms, as in the case of the NGA without having surrendered its monopoly on typesetting.

Paul Routledge, Labour Editor of *The Times*, summarizes his view of the outcome in this way:

If the test of success and failure of the lock-out is judged to be the recovery of managerial hegemony at Gray's Inn Road, then the strategy must be deemed a failure . . . The outcome of the TNL dispute lends credence to the NGA view that the union is 'winning the war of the new technology' . . . The importance of this withdrawal from the 'front end' battle cannot be overemphasized. Where the unions lost in the USA and West Germany, they won in Britain. [15]

Jacobs agrees with Routledge:

The real victor of the shutdown was . . . the fact of chapel power . . . it had not been overridden, either by the company or by the unions; so it had to be propitiated. And when the newspapers were back in print, the chapels continued to bestride the company's operations and to be the arbiters of production . . . Paradoxically, if the Organization had stuck to a balance-sheet view of its problems, it might have achieved more of its abstract aims, particularly the elusive right to manage. As it was, the long dispute confirmed the power of the unions and, in many parts of the business, reduced managerial authority. [41]

(6) Costs and benefits of the dispute

On 13 November 1979, the day of resumed publication, Rees-Mogg gave TNL's definitive assessment of the costs and benefits of the dispute under the dramatic headline *The terrible price we have paid.* By this account, the settlement represented a historic productivity bargain. It was:

> *Obviously of substantial benefit to the commercial future of our newspapers, a benefit which will continue to grow in future years as labour costs continue to rise . . . In the production areas Times Newspapers will have a 20 per cent reduction in manning and a 10 per cent increase in capacity. If 80 per cent of the work force produce 110 per cent of their previous output, the productivity per head rises by 37.5 per cent . . . Obviously these gains depend on the agreements being successfully carried out.* [42]

Rees-Mogg unfortunately omitted to say precisely who was to be responsible for ensuring that the agreements were carried out, and the criteria for measuring their 'success' were left conveniently obscure. In return for these concessions, said Rees-Mogg, 'staff pay had been brought from well below Fleet Street levels to the level of the higher, though not the highest, Fleet Street rates'.

But if the outcome was a mutually beneficial productivity agreement, why had it taken nearly two years to negotiate, including nearly a year of suspended publication? Rees-Mogg dismissed the idea that these benefits could have been achieved without a stoppage: 'There was no evidence to support such a view'. TNL had been trying to negotiate some parts of the new agreements for years, in at least one case since the mid-1960s. 'Such negotiations had been quite fruitless'.

Perhaps the best guide to TNL's thinking was provided by Rees-Mogg in his address to the EEF in January 1979:

> *The productivity deal we are proposing should not be very difficult to negotiate. It is in line with the policy both of the Government and the TUC. Indeed, if I understand the Concordat*, the idea of raising the technological efficiency and the productivity of British industry by negotiation is central to it . . . We are therefore seeking to carry out what is, as I understand it, the official policy of the whole labour movement. We gave seven months notice of our desire to negotiate new contracts and have steadily offered to negotiate them without pre-conditions in the three months that we have been closed. Yet we are still in the situation that two of the major*

---

* Early in 1979, in the last stages of the 'winter of discontent', the Labour Government and the TUC signed a jointly-agreed 'Concordat', intended to provide guidelines for the conduct of industrial disputes.

> *print unions (NGA and NATSOPA) will not even talk to us.*
> *That must be wrong; it must be right to talk . . . Yet we have*
> *to go on and we have to succeed. We are not going to surrender*
> *to the incoherent immobility of some of these trade unions.*
> *To do so would be to accept that we must produce newspapers*
> *with gross inefficiency for the indefinite future. It would also*
> *hand over union power to the militants, because it is the*
> *rational men in The Times unions who have been on our side.*
> *We have no intention of proving the wise men wrong and the*
> *wild men right.* [34]

Rees-Mogg here reveals the extent of TNL's self-deception. How else may one explain the misplaced optimism or hopeless naivety of a management which apparently believed that 'it should not be very difficult to negotiate' a highly complex package of productivity improvements with six different unions in one of Britain's most chaotic and unreformed bargaining structures, within the space of a few months, under the threat of suspension and dismissal notices?

At the end of the dispute, Rees-Mogg declined to attribute TNL's frustration in achieving a settlement to 'the small number of trade union officials involved in the dispute (who) held militant left-wing views, to which they are perfectly entitled'. For one thing, the majority of TNL employees did not share those views. And, in any case, he did not believe that 'the actual conduct of trade union nego-tiators was mainly determined by their political philosophies . . . (It) was primarily determined by a competitive search for benefits for their members'. [42]

In an adjacent column, Barry Fitzpatrick, Chairman of the AULC and Father of the SOGAT clerical chapel at *The Sunday Times*, offered a more concise evaluation. He chose not to dwell on 'the mistakes and attitudes of the past 11 months' but regretted:

> *that the £30m to £40m so far spent by Times Newspapers on*
> *the dispute does not represent a penny invested in either plant*
> *or employees. It has simply been money squandered. A fraction*
> *of it well-spent could have secured the new technology and*
> *many of the benefits and social improvements that we all want*
> *to see.* [43]

According to Jacobs, 'the most authoritative verdict on the material outcome of the dispute' [44] was contained in a memor-andum prepared for the TNL board on 21 November 1979. This put the total cost of the dispute to TNL at some £46 million, made up as follows:

Item	Cost (£ million)
(1) Wages and salaries paid out during suspension	33.4
(2) Settlement terms	3.5

| (3) | Relaunch publicity | 1.0 |
| (4) | Lost advertising revenue | 8.1 |

Total   46.0

To offset these costs, TNL could claim some significant, if not all quantifiable, gains:

(i)   an overall reduction in manning of perhaps 15%
(ii)   virtual elimination of unnecessary overtime working
(iii)   faster press speeds
(iv)   increased publication size of 10%
(v)   introduction of new labour-saving equipment

Unfortunately, it is impossible to strike a neat balance between these costs and benefits — first, because operational changes on resumed publication throw doubt on the quantification; and second, because some of the potential gains were never fully realized. An arithmetical balance did emerge, however, from ITO's consolidated accounts for 1979, which showed a trading loss of £39.3 million at TNL for that financial year. But the ITO Group profits nevertheless rose by over 30% from £146.5 million to £172 million. The Thomson policy of industrial diversification had clearly paid off.

As to the prospective gains, Jacobs notes that TNL's estimated overall productivity improvement factor at the end of the dispute amounted to only 30% compared with its target figure of 40–45%. The balance sheet of gains and losses prepared on 21 October 1979 was therefore:

in a sense an idealized picture . . . a kind of snapshot of things as they looked on the day it was written rather than things as they actually were. [45]

In other words, the losses were known but the gains still had to be realized: manpower reductions; the smooth transition from old to new technology; and the crucial test, as Jacobs says, was 'making the agreements stick'.

Routledge offers his own interim balance sheet, as follows:

The shutdown cost an estimated £30 million, which will take six years to recoup from £5 million a year reductions in wage costs. Top management argues that it will be two years (viz. 1981/82) before it will be clear whether it was all worth it. . . . Whilst it is still too early to draw up a final balance sheet, some gains and losses are already clear:
(1) The NGA has hung on to its monopoly of the typesetting keyboard for a year at least and probably for the foreseeable future.
(2) 'Chapel power' in Fleet Street has been confirmed and consolidated; the final deals were struck with chapel leaders.

(3) *TNL management has accepted that there must be a radical shift in attitudes towards the workforce. Change must be negotiated, not imposed.*

(4) *The unions have accepted some de-manning, though not in all areas (40% fewer men in the new electronic photocomposition room; fewer men in machine room, etc.).*

(5) *A new disputes procedure has been signed; whether it will be honoured remains to be seen.* [46]

Whether 'the game is worth the candle' depends here, as everywhere else, on one's perception of the risks and opportunities involved. Perhaps the best short verdict on the dispute was that offered by Owen O'Brien, General Secretary of NATSOPA, the largest union at TNL:

> *I believe what has happened would have happened without closing.* [47]

(7) Lessons of the dispute

For the lessons of the dispute, we need look no further than the columns of *The Times* itself. On the day of resumed publication, the anonymous leader–writer (probably Rees-Mogg), returned from his 'Year of Agony', to reflect ruefully and at length on the lessons and implications of the dispute:

> *If at the beginning we had foreseen that the stoppage would last fifty weeks . . . it must be doubtful whether we would have gone ahead . . . Yet during our absent year it has not been the productivity of Fleet Street but that of Britain which has become the essential question . . . The Fleet Street disease is only the British disease in a more acute form . . . British output per man is probably no more than a third of the normal international competitive level. Indeed, that seems to be the crisis point . . . In the 1980s this disparity of productivity will probably become much greater . . .*
>
> *Britain is already an industrial country with such low industrial productivity that we are rapidly becoming disindustrialized. Low productivity is actually threatening our existing standard of living, let alone our capacity to increase it. Low productivity is the central issue of our political life, as it underlies the others; it is the issue of our national future.*
>
> *Low productivity is killing Britain . . . It is perhaps easy for a newspaper to write such things, though not all do so; on* The Times *we have at least been willing to live our beliefs, and it is the urgency of the national issue which justifies that experience. But it has been a sad way to spend our one hundred and ninety fifth year.* [48]

Three days later *The Times* published a short reply from Reg Brady (FOC, NATSOPA, *The Sunday Times* machine room):

It seems to me you have not learned a thing in the last 11 months ... You say that you 'believe it (higher productivity) leads to better rather than worse relations with our staff' ... May I give you a thought for today: 'Lord, help my words to be tender and gracious today, for tomorrow I may have to eat them'. [49]

In the next day's issue, a letter from Professor Friedrich von Hayek, Mrs Thatcher's economic guru, congratulated *The Times* on its leading article:

If The Times *has learned all that and will persist in teaching it, its calamities may prove a blessing for Britain.* [50]

In another letter, Lord Young of Dartington wrote that few would disagree with *The Times* that Britain desperately needed raised productivity and that the unions were stopping us getting it:

But you are, just as you accept Mrs Thatcher is, more motivated than motivating in your here-we-die stand. There is no hint of any sympathy for those who support the unions. Why should they accept new technology when it can produce so much unemployment? Employers should follow the Japanese model and wherever it is feasible guarantee employment in return for acceptance of new technology. [51]

But the most telling response probably came from a Miss Margaret Cooke who complained that *The Times'* leader writers had become cold-hearted and abstract in their approach to industrial relations. Miss Cooke went on finally to expose the:

totally illogical assertion that 'increased productivity means more jobs'. Increased productivity may well mean bigger and better profits but that does not ipso facto *mean more jobs. It may lead to more jobs, given good management and a progressive approach to society and the need to create more jobs. Alternatively, it can mean an ... increasing preoccupation by the upper income brackets with bigger and better profits through new technology at the expense of the people, man's essential dignity and the need to work ... The present Conservative Government's blind faith in market forces, free collective bargaining, and increased profitability will perpetuate a class-ridden society where the weakest goes to the wall and people are forgotten in a blind rush for increased 'productivity' and new technology.* [52]

SECTION 4: CONCLUSIONS AND 1987 POSTSCRIPT

This chapter on the dispute at TNL in 1978–79 has focused on the well-intentioned, if belated, efforts by TNL management to set its industrial relations house in order after decades of neglect. More specifically, it has shown the management of Fleet Street's once most distinguished newspaper struggling desperately to secure union acceptance of the new electronic printing technology by negotiation if possible, by coercion if necessary. If desperate measures reveal desperate men, then TNL's strategists were suicidal in their desperation to recapture control of the business from the chapels, to whom they had long since surrendered it.

The TNL dispute was in no sense a typical British dispute of the late 1970s or even a typical printing industry dispute, for Fleet Street is not to be equated with that industry. It does, however, contain some distinctive elements of British conflict management in the late 1970s. It clearly demonstrates what happens when an inherently conservative management attempts to achieve higher productivity, restore control and reassert managerial prerogatives. At the end of the dispute, TNL put a bold face on its year-long crusade, claiming that the outcome fully justified its actions. If the judgements of Jacobs and Routledge are accepted, TNL lost more than it gained. We have independent evidence to corroborate their view. Within four months of its reappearance, TNL was once more embattled against the chapels:

> *Unrest and disruption were loosed again. The appearance of smooth relations had been deceptive. All the old tensions were still there, lurking beneath the surface. If one chapel could threaten production, so could all sixty-five . . . We were back to living dangerously again . . . wildcat disruptions were what had led the company to its shutdown strategy two years before. After all the agony of the time since then, had nothing changed?* [32]

TNL evidently shared that judgement. Within one year of resumed publication, the Thompson Organization sold all its titles to News International, the Murdoch Organization.

To the detached observer, indulging the luxury of hindsight, the TNL dispute seems unproductive of significant and sustained achievement in improving industrial relations. Headlined at the time as 'the battle over new technology', the dispute now emerges as a ritualized confrontation between a multinational employer under new ownership, fighting to re-establish the cherished 'right to manage', and an uncoordinated collection of unions, fighting for the reciprocal right of workers to defend and improve their living standards through job security and regular incomes. It was not so much a dispute over new technology as a struggle between competing ideologies, represented by protagonists who had utterly failed to develop the consensual attitudes and the skills needed to achieve an integrative solution to their mutual problems. New technology offered a unique opportunity for the restructuring of attitudes on both sides and for a major breakthrough in Fleet Street. In a dialogue of the blind and the deaf, that opportunity was lost.

The final word must be about single keystroking. Despite its costly and protracted shutdown in 1978–79, TNL failed to secure union acceptance of direct inputting by employees other than NGA members. By 1986, *The Times* and its sister papers under Rupert Murdoch's more aggressive management had still not brought the new electronic typesetting equipment into full operation. Meanwhile, its Fleet Street rivals have done little better: the Mirror Group did best under the Reed management, securing union acceptance of new technology — but with NGA members controlling all direct inputting into the computer-typesetting equipment. *The Financial Times* gave up the struggle to win union acceptance for its new technology and continues to use NGA members on traditional typesetting.

In 1985, News International sacked all 5000 of its print workers, taking advantage of Mrs Thatcher's new labour laws to transfer production to a new, fully-automated, highly-protected publishing site, 'Fortress Wapping', well away from Fleet Street. The story of the bitter and protracted Wapping dispute cannot be told here. But in many commentators' eyes, it marked the beginning of the end of the print unions' power in Fleet Street: by abandoning Fleet Street in favour of new printing locations, where old traditions could be forgotten and new traditions established alongside profitable new technology.

CHRONOLOGY OF THE DISPUTE

10 April 1978	Hussey letter to all TNL employees
13 April	General Secretaries meet TNL executives
26 April	Hussey letter to General Secretaries
July	Employment Secretary's unsuccessful intervention
August	TNL produce New Agreement Proposals
30 November	Deadline expires; TNL suspends publications
14 December	TNL issues notices to first 3000 staff
January 1979	Rees-Mogg's lunchtime speech to EEF
January	First notices expire; 580 staff dismissed
March	Employment Secretary gets two sides together
9 March	TNL agrees:
	(i) to re-engage dismissed staff
	(ii) to extend notices of remaining staff
	(iii) to leave keystroking for later discussion
	(iv) to bring FOCs into direct negotiations
20 April	TNL reveals plans to publish abroad; NGA mounts 24-hour picket around TNL premises
2 May	NGA rejects TNL's keystroking compromise
12 June	TNL initiates talks with General Secretaries and FOCs; Hamilton and TNL executives meet AULC

27 June	Lord Thomson addresses AGM of ITO
4 July	TNL proposes 9-point compromise plan
17 July	Unions present counter-proposals
20 July	TNL amplifies original start-up proposals; unions reject them outright
August	NGA threatens to withdraw from negotiations
16 September	NGA resumes negotiations
17 October	TNL revised deadline for final agreement
18 October	Lord Thomson extends deadline by three days
21 October	All agreements signed and dispute settled

WHO'S WHO IN THE DISPUTE

Booroff, Bill	Secretary, London Region, NGA
Booth, Albert	Secretary of State for Employment
Brady, Reg	FOC, NATSOPA, ST machine room
Brunton, Gordon	Chief Executive, Thomson Organization (GB)
Dixon, Les	President, NGA
Fitzpatrick, Barry	FOC, SOGAT, ST clerical chapel Chairman, AULC
Hamilton, Denis (Sir)	Chairman and Editor-in-Chief, TNL
Hussey, 'Duke'	Managing Director and Chief Executive, Times Newspapers Limited (now Chairman, BBC Board of Governors)
Keys, Bill	Chairman, TUC Printing Industry Committee
Nisbet-Smith, Dugal	General Manager, Times Newspapers
Rees-Mogg, William	Editor, *The Times*
Thomson, Roy (Lord)	Canadian entrepreneur and newspaper proprietor Bought *The Times* 1966
Thomson, Kenneth (Lord)	Son of Roy Thomson Owner of *The Times* in 1979
Wade, Joe	General Secretary, National Graphical Association

REFERENCES

1 Arnold J. Toynbee: *The World and the West* (BBC Reith Lectures, 1952), Oxford University Press, Oxford, 1953.

2 David Landes: *The Unbound Prometheus: Technological Change and Industrial Development in Western Europe from 1730 to the Present*, Cambridge University Press, Cambridge, 1969.

3 The Earl of Halsbury: 'Integration of Social with Technological Change', Institute of Personnel Management, London, Occasional Papers No. 11, 1957.

4 Eric Wigham: *The Power to Manage: A History of the Engineering Employers' Association*, Macmillan, London, 1973.

5 Karl Marx: *Communist Manifesto, (1848)*, ed. H. Laski, Allen & Unwin, London, 1948.

6 Paul Routledge: 'Months of hope and despair', *The Times*, 13 November 1979, p. 14.

7 Charles Raw: *The Sunday Times Reporter*, Issue No. 3, 1979.

8 Eric Jacobs: *Stop Press: The Inside Story of* The Times *dispute*, Andre Deutsch, London, 1980, p. 36.

9 'Duke' Hussey: Letter to print industry General Secretaries, quoted by Routledge, *The Times*, 13 November 1979, p. 14.

10 Paul Routledge: 'The dispute at Times Newspapers Limited: a view from inside', *Industrial Relations Journal*, Winter 1979, p. 6.

11 *The Times*: 'What forces us to contemplate suspending, etc.', 28 November 1978.

12 Eric Jacobs: *Stop Press: The Inside Story of* The Times *Dispute*, Andre Deutsch, London, 1980, p. 8.

13 Joe Wade: *Print*, November 1978, quoted by Jacobs, *Stop Press: The Inside Story of* The Times *Dispute*, Andre Deutsch, London, 1980, p. 55.

14 Eric Jacobs: *Stop Press: The Inside Story of* The Times *Dispute*, Andre Deutsch, London, 1980, p. 55.

15 Paul Routledge: 'The dispute at Times Newspapers Limited: a view from inside', *Industrial Relations Journal*, Winter 1979, p. 7.

16 See Henry Friedman and Sander Meredeen: *The Dynamics of Industrial Conflict: Lessons from Ford*, Croom Helm, London, 1981, p. 225 et seq.

17 Eric Jacobs: *Stop Press: The Inside Story of* The Times *Dispute*, Andre Deutsch, London, 1980, pp. 59–9.

18 William Booroff, quoted by Christopher Thomas: 'The crucial day when *The Times* could be silenced', *The Times*, 27 November 1978, p. 12.

19 Les Dixon, quoted by Jacobs: *Stop Press: The Inside Story of* The Times *Dispute*, Andre Deutsch, London, 1980.

20 Eric Jacobs: *Stop Press: The Inside Story of* The Times *Dispute*, Andre Deutsch, London, 1980, p. 85.

21 Eric Jacobs: *Stop Press: The Inside Story of* The Times *Dispute*, Andre Deutsch, London, 1980, p. 117.

22 Sir Dennis Hamilton, quoted by Routledge: 'Months of hope and despair' *The Times*, 13 November 1979, p. 14.

23 Lord Thomson, quoted by Routledge: 'Months of hope and despair' *The Times*, 13 November 1979, p. 14.

24 Eric Jacobs: *Stop Press: The Inside Story of* The Times *Dispute*, Andre Deutsch, London, 1980, p. 121.

25 Eric Jacobs: *Stop Press: The Inside Story of* The Times *Dispute*, Andre Deutsch, London, 1980, p. 134.

26 Eric Jacobs: *Stop Press: The Inside Story of* The Times *Dispute*, Andre Deutsch, London, 1980, p. 135.

27 Eric Jacobs: *Stop Press: The Inside Story of* The Times *Dispute*, Andre Deutsch, London, 1980, p. 138.

28 Eric Jacobs: *Stop Press: The Inside Story of* The Times *Dispute*, Andre Deutsch, London, 1980, p. 140.

29 Eric Jacobs: *Stop Press: The Inside Story of* The Times *Dispute*, Andre Deutsch, London, 1980, p. 142.

30 Eric Jacobs: *Stop Press: The Inside Story of* The Times *Dispute*, Andre Deutsch, London, 1980, p. 143.

31 Eric Jacobs: *Stop Press: The Inside Story of* The Times *Dispute*, Andre Deutsch, London, 1980, p. 145.

32 Eric Jacobs: *Stop Press: The Inside Story of* The Times *Dispute*, Andre Deutsch, London, 1980, p. 147.

33 William Rees-Mogg: 'The Issues at *The Times*', *The Times*, 24 November 1978.

34 William Rees-Mogg, Lunchtime speech to EEF Conference, February 1979, unpublished EEF Notes.

35 Paul Routledge, 'The dispute at Times Newspapers Limited; a view from inside', *Industrial Relations Journal*, Winter 1979, p. 5.

36 Louis Heren: 'War and peace and a happy shop', *The Times*, 27 November 1978, p. 12.

37 Keith Sisson: *Industrial Relations in Fleet Street*, Blackwell, Oxford, 1975, p. 138.

38 See Anthony Smith: *Goodbye, Gutenberg: The Newspaper Revolution of the 1980s*, Oxford University Press, Oxford, 1980.

39 'Duke' Hussey, quoted by Christopher Thomas: 'The crucial day when *The Times* could be silenced', *The Times*, 27 November 1978, p. 12.

40 Eric Jacobs: Stop Press: *The Inside Story of* The Times *Dispute*, Andre Deutsch, London, 1980.

41 Eric Jacobs: Stop Press: *The Inside Story of* The Times *Dispute*, Andre Deutsch, London, 1980.

42 William Rees-Mogg: 'The terrible price we have paid', *The Times*, 13 November 1979.

43 Barry Fitzpatrick: 'Why both sides must change their attitudes', *The Times*, 13 November 1979.

44 Donald Cruickshank, quoted by Jacobs: Stop Press: *The Inside Story of* The Times *Dispute*, Andre Deutsch, London, 1980, p. 149.

45 Eric Jacobs: Stop Press: *The Inside Story of* The Times *Dispute*, Andre Deutsch, London, 1980, p. 150.

46 Paul Routledge, 'The dispute at Times Newspapers Limited: a view from inside', *Industrial Relations Journal*, Winter 1979.

47 Owen O'Brien, quoted by Routledge: 'The dispute at Times Newspapers Limited: a view from inside', *Industrial Relations Journal*, Winter 1979, p. 9.

48 William Rees-Mogg, *The Times*, 13 November 1979.

49 Reg Brady, *The Times*, 16 November 1979.

50 Friedrich von Hayek, *The Times*, 17 November 1979.

51 Lord Young, *The Times*, 17 November 1979.

52 Miss Margaret Cooke, *The Times*, 17 November 1979.

STUDY QUESTIONS

1. Examine the range of strategic choices available to the management of Times Newspapers Limited in its attempt to introduce new printing technology. Why did TNL decide on the shutdown strategy?
2. 'The public is being persuaded that new technology can only happen in a narrow technological and business fashion — the human implications are being ignored, international competition is the issue.' Barry Fitzpatrick (Chairman of the All-Union Liaison Committee, *The Times*, 27 November 1978).
   Consider the case for and against this judgement.
3. (a) Why are there so many unions in the British printing industry?
   (b) Does the multiplicity of unions explain why they failed to produce an effective counter-strategy to the TNL shutdown threat?
4. At the end of the dispute, both sides claimed to have won 'the battle over new technology' in Fleet Street. From your knowledge of what has happened subsequently at *The Times* and elsewhere, which side should now be given the credit for having won that battle?
5. Summarize the arguments put forward (a) by William Rees-Mogg and (b) by Miss Cooke in Section 4(7) for and against higher labour productivity as the key to Britain's economic regeneration.
6. 'Technology is one of the key variables — perhaps the critical variable — in determining the character of workplace industrial relations.' Discuss.

SUGGESTIONS FOR FURTHER READING

On new technology in general:

David Landes: *The Unbound Prometheus: Technological Change and Industrial Development in Western Europe from 1730 to the Present*, Cambridge University Press, Cambridge, 1969.
Trades Union Congress: *Technology and Employment*, TUC, London, 1979.

On industrial relations in Fleet Street:

Royal Commission on the Press, 1965.
Keith Sisson: *Industrial Relations in Fleet Street*, Blackwell, Oxford, 1975.

On the impact of new printing technology:

John Gennard and Steve Dunn: 'The Impact of New Technology on the Structure and Organisation of Craft Unions in the Printing

Industry', *British Journal of Industrial Relations*, Vol. XXI, No. 1, 1983.

John Gennard: 'The Implications of the NGA and Messenger Groups of Newspapers Dispute', *Industrial Relations Journal*, Autumn 1984.

John Gennard: 'The Impact of Front-End Systems on the NGA', *Employment, Work and Technology*, July 1987.

Roderick Martin: *New Technology and Industrial Relations in Fleet Street*, Oxford University Press, Oxford, 1985.

Anthony Smith: *Goodbye, Gutenberg: The Newspaper Revolution of the 1980s*, Oxford University Press, Oxford, 1980.

On the Times Newspapers Limited dispute:

Eric Jacobs: *Stop Press: The Inside Story of* The Times *Dispute*, Andre Deutsch, London, 1980.

Paul Routledge: 'The dispute at Times Newspapers Limited: a view from inside', *Industrial Relations Journal*, Winter 1979.

CHAPTER 6

■ Shorter working time in Britain —

THE NATIONAL ENGINEERING DISPUTE, 1979

We need a shorter working week like a hole in the head.
Pat Lowry
Personnel Director, BL

The shorter working week is now on the collective bargaining agenda of the international trade union movement as never before. Time, for the industrial worker, is the most precious currency he can trade in. Extra time off gained by workers cannot be devalued. It is fully inflation-proofed.
Herman Rebhan, General Secretary
International Metalworkers Federation

INTRODUCTION: THE COMING OF THE 39-HOUR WEEK

On the morning of 4 October 1979, union and management representatives emerged bleary-eyed from all-night negotiations at the Gatwick Airport Hotel, Sussex, to announce that the British engineering industry's longest and most costly dispute this century was over. Not since the great engineering lockout of 1897, which lasted over six months, had the unions succeeded in imposing such pressure on the employers to enforce their demands. For more than 15 years the Engineering Employers' Federation (EEF) had resisted claims by the Confederation of Shipbuilding and Engineering Unions (the CSEU or 'Confed') for a shorter working week of less than 40 hours. Now, after 10 weeks of intermittent disruption and increasingly bitter conflict, the EEF had apparently collapsed and conceded a 39-hour week from 1981.

Terry Duffy, President of the largest engineering union, the Amalgamated Union of Engineering Workers (AUEW), hailed the outcome as:

A historic settlement involving a significant breakthrough for the trade union movement . . . a great inspiration for organized workers throughout Britain and Europe. [1]

That judgement was quickly endorsed by Herman Rebhan, General Secretary of the International Metalworkers' Federation, who declared that the outcome was:

> *One of the most important trade union victories since the war for industrial workers throughout the world.* [2]

The employers and their allies did not share those views. The EEF's Director General, Anthony Frodsham, said:

> *All in all, it is a good agreement . . . If we get four years peace from it, it is a good deal.* [3]

The EEF President, Sir Geoffrey Hawkings, was less sanguine:

> *It has been an extremely damaging dispute. There are no winners, only losers.* [4]

The Financial Times, which consistently supported the employers, saw the entire dispute as:

> *a classic case of how not to manage a full-scale confrontation.* [5]

Which of these judgements was more correct? Was the 39-hour week a 'significant breakthrough' as the unions claimed? Would it help to create additional jobs, as the unions hoped? Or was their victory more symbolic than real? In what sense was the settlement 'a good deal' for the employers? And was their President right when he said there were 'no winners, only losers'? How should we evaluate such a dispute and assess its implications? This chapter seeks to answer these questions.

SECTION 1: WORK, LEISURE AND SHORTER WORKING TIME

In the world of work, wages and hours represent two sides of the 'wage–effort bargain'. For the worker, wages are the prime source of satisfaction, the reward for leisure foregone. Hours are the 'currency' in which purchasing power is earned and later consumed in the form of leisure. For the employer, wages (plus social security taxes) represent the cost of labour, normally expressed in 'time rates' per hour/week/month/year. Wages are the price paid for the worker's skill, experience and cooperation at a 'normal' rate of working. He may also be offered some additional incentive (e.g. piecework) payments for above-normal effort or output, or a fixed sum for the job to be completed faster ('job and finish') with the incentive of more paid work or more leisure or both.

This 'trade off' between money wages and hours of work is the central focus of collective bargaining and industrial relations

around the world. For economists, 'economic man' is a rational opti-
mizer: he works to earn money and works harder or longer for more
money up to the point at which marginal increments of money and
leisure are roughly equal. Thereafter, the worker's 'leisure preference'
takes precedence over his 'income preference' — the desire to increase
his money income. Psychologists remind us that workers have always
sought intrinsic as well as extrinsic satisfaction at work. The fewer
the worker's opportunities for intrinsic satisfaction, the more 'instrumental' are his attitudes to work and the stronger his demands for
extrinsic satisfaction in the form of more money and leisure. When
such leisure pursuits make more physical and/or mental demands than
paid employment, they may be described, somewhat paradoxically,
as 'preferred work'. Some sociologists link this higher leisure preference with the alienation of workers under capitalist modes of
production, where production for private profit robs work of its
meaning by denying its essential social purpose.

By contrast, historians are more likely to explain the trend
towards Shorter Working Time (SWT) as a function of rising affluence
and the growth of trade union bargaining power in most advanced
industrial societies. They point out that, in pre-industrial societies,
there is no meaningful distinction between work and leisure: land is
cultivated, woods are husbanded, cattle are reared and flocks tended
to feed, clothe and shelter a stable population. For, despite the rich
diversity of their cultures, peasant societies are essentially static with
short life spans, low material expectations, low productivity and little
technical innovation.

In the painful transition from an agrarian to an industrial
economy ('industrialization'), many peasants maintain some contact
with the land, which supplements subsistence wages and offers some
relief from the new pressures of factory life. As the pace of industrialization quickens, villages are submerged in industrial conurbations and
even these links with the rural past are gradually lost. With full
industrialization, the countryside has been left far behind as workers
are caught up in the urban round of getting and spending. Most,
though perhaps not all, industrial societies seem obsessively preoccupied with innovation and the search for greater abundance: more
production and consumption; more investment; higher productivity;
and bigger profits. Such societies are frequently characterized by their
'conspicuous consumption'. The combination of rampant materi-
alism, private affluence and public squalor may contribute to a widespread feeling of alienation, which leads workers to demand higher
money wages and more leisure in which to enjoy the fruits of their
labour and, potentially at least, to restore some dignity and significance to their otherwise drab and uncreative lives.

The prospect of the 'post-industrial' society based on automation and microtechnology promises unlimited abundance for those
in work, coupled with a permanent decline in employment levels,

bringing with it new social problems of relative deprivation in terms of both work and leisure. Those who cannot find work are deprived of its psychological value in conferring significance on their lives; but they also lack the financial means, above the level of subsistence, to enjoy their enforced leisure. This profound social and economic transformation presents trade unions with severe problems. Yet they have generally been slow to recognize that their best hope of preserving their members' jobs and income security may be to assist employers in promoting greater productivity in return for SWT and in ensuring that government makes adequate provision for those without work. Social justice and productive efficiency are not necessarily antithetical: many would argue that economic realism plus human compassion are the essential hallmarks of a liberal — some would say a truly socialist — society.

The reduction in working time may take many forms. Initially it means cutting the standard working week, with fewer hours worked each day or week. The next logical step is longer annual holidays, with additional public holidays during the year (e.g. New Year's Day or the days between Christmas and the New Year); or the novel concept in industry — more familiar to academics — of an extended period of sabbatical leave for longer-service employees. The final step is to reduce the total working lifetime of all workers, beginning with those engaged in more arduous, dangerous or responsible jobs, like underground miners, continuous assembly-line workers, airline pilots, members of the armed forces and the police. It implies special or voluntary early retirement for all those who want, need and can afford it. 'Sixty and out' was the slogan adopted in the 1960s by American auto workers when pressing their case for early retirement on full pension when their age in years added to their length of service achieved that magic figure.

All these alternative elements, together with additional personal relief time, paid mealbreaks, preparation and washing time, etc., contribute towards the overall objective of SWT, but the most significant element to date remains the Shorter Working Week (SWW).

For those lucky enough to have a job, the days of the working week are too many and too long, with holidays too few and far between. From earliest times, the pattern of rural working life followed the annual cycle of the seasons. Agricultural labour was regulated by the availability of natural daylight: in midwinter, outdoor work was limited, but at lambing and harvest times, work continued from dawn to dusk, with few breaks for refreshment. A 'lucky' harvest moon could mean working in the fields for 15 or more hours a day on the six working days of the week.

But workers took their pleasures equally seriously. Wilensky records that in the thirteenth century skilled artisans rarely worked more than 194 days in a year (53% of available time). Even before 1761 there were 47 recognized holy days (often holidays) in England.

Contemporary historians noted that when trade was brisk, the self-employed nailer or framework-knitter could religiously worship St Monday, St Tuesday and perhaps St Wednesday in the alehouse. [6]

The domestic (or putting-out) system of production in the early textile and clothing industries meant that handicraft workers enjoyed some measure of independence and could regulate their own hours of work. But we should not be misled: the picture of happy handloom weavers, stockingers or tailors, exercising the mysteries of their craft within easy reach of 'home comforts', is a romantic illusion. Domestic labour was always sweated labour — erratic, badly paid, often insanitary, unhealthy and dangerous. Women suffered most: in addition to their traditional unpaid domestic labour — combining household management, child-rearing, cooking and cleaning — women regularly shared men's work in both agricultural and domestic production. The image of the 'contented housewife', spinning her yarn at the cottage door, surrounded by roses in the evening sunlight, is a grossly misleading, if charming, Victorian myth.

The coming of the factory system at the start of the nineteenth century did little to alleviate those conditions and much to exacerbate them. Eighteenth century working customs and practices were often carried over into the new century:

> *Many of the conditions of work common during the first half of the century and more of industrialization were inherited from the pre-industrial context. Child and women's labour are an example of this. The 12-hour shifts common in the textile mills in 1800 existed in the original Lombe silk factory in 1718. Equally, the worst examples of long hours, evil conditions (etc.) in the factories can be matched by those in the industries that remained organized on the putting-out system into the late 19th century.* [7]

In practice, men, women and children often worked 12 or 14 hours a day, six days per week, for subsistence wages or less. As a result, skilled workers organized themselves into 'trade clubs' and used their new-found bargaining strength to secure higher wages and shorter working hours for the same pay. But since most workers were unskilled and lacked both organization and bargaining power, they were usually at the mercy of the employers.

> *For a large part of the nineteenth century, the overwhelming majority of jobs came before the workers on a take-it-or-leave-it basis. Employers regarded the determination of pay and conditions as their own sole prerogative and were guided in these matters by the state of the local labour market, by their own estimate of what they could afford and by prevailing conventional ideas of what was reasonable.* [8]

In textiles, for example, working conditions were so bad that in 1860 Parliament intervened to impose a legal maximum of 60 hours per week, further reduced to 55.5 hours in 1865. But it should not be supposed that workers were always in favour of external intervention to enforce the compulsory reduction in working time:

> *Up to the 1820s, the main pressure for limiting hours of work and imposing a minimum age for work in the mills did not come from the workers themselves but from external sources — humanitarians, doctors, enlightened employers, occasionally Tory radicals ... The 1833 Factory Act limited the hours of work of children between 9 and 13 to 8 hours per day, those between 14 and 18 to 12 hours per day (with no night work) ... Labour reactions were initially to demand either bringing down adult working hours to those of the adolescents, or a 12-hour day for the children. Then the movement swung behind the campaign for the 10-hour day. This was gained in 1847, and the traditional forebodings of employers about the loss of export markets were not realized.* [9]

During the 1860s the International Association of Working Men mounted its first coordinated campaign for a statutory working week of 48 hours: Its demands were explicitly clear:

> *We require 8 hours for work; 8 hours for our own instruction; and 8 hours for repose.* [10]

It is important to recognize that, whilst mechanization relieved many workers of some physically back-breaking tasks, the adoption by employers of faster machinery greatly increased the pace and the intensity of labour. To counteract this added fatigue, workers developed strategies of self-protection. As Stearns points out:

> *Many workers kept alive a rhythm of work that could be punctuated by a variety of interruptions ... Absenteeism was common in a variety of settings. British metallurgical workers, on the piece rate, earned enough not to work a full week; here is one explanation for the widespread endurance of twelve-hour shifts amid the intense heat ... Frequent change of jobs constituted another widely-used weapon ... [But] the most obvious means of limiting work was to reduce its hours, and this was one of the leading developments of the decades before World War I.* [11]

Unions in the engineering industry led the drive for the 8-hour day. In 1866, one of their leaders, Tom Mann, published his famous pamphlet *What a compulsory 8-hour day means to the workers* [12] to mobilize support for a general statutory limitation of working hours. From its first meeting in 1868, the TUC passed resolutions, year after year, in support of that objective. The Eight Hours League, ensured that the question of working hours remained a lively and contentious issue for the rest of the century.

In the booming Victorian engineering industry, the employer's traditional claim to fix wages and hours by exercising the prerogative rights of ownership or management were seriously challenged for the first time by well-organized and strongly-led craft unions like the Amalgamated Society of Engineers (ASE), forerunner of today's Amalgamated Engineering Union (AEU). The employers responded by setting up local defensive organizations, which came together in 1894 to form the Engineering Employers' Federation (EEF), with the express purpose of enabling member firms to manage their own establishments without union interference. [13]

Hours of work in the engineering industry varied considerably with the state of trade and the region concerned. In 1866, for example, in the flourishing Clydeside shipbuilding industry, workers demanded a reduction from 60 to 55 hours per week, as against the normal 57 hours worked elsewhere in Scotland. The employers conceded a 57-hour week but with reduced pay, a pattern generally established throughout British manufacturing industry during the 1870s and 1880s.

Workers might seek reduced hours to curtail the intensity of work but they almost always failed. Employers compensated by raising the pace during the hours that remained; their ability to do so was one reason why they granted reductions as readily as they did. And workers, often somewhat divided on the importance of limiting hours further in the first place, had an obvious need to respond: they must keep up their earnings. [14]

In May 1897, the ASE joined with other skilled engineering trades to present their demand for a reduction in the working week from 57 to 48 hours on behalf of some 20 000 members in the London area. The timing seemed right: unemployment was falling, overtime rising and the battle for the 8-hour day already half-won in London, having been conceded gradually by 'progressive' employers throughout the 1890s. When the EEF's London Association rejected their demand outright, the skilled trades pleaded for a reduction to at least 51 hours. The Association again refused any concession, instructing its federated members to stand firm. By early July 1897, the skilled trades were ready for strike action. The EEF responded by threatening to sack 25% of union men in every federated plant if there was strike action against any one of its members. By mid-July the first stoppage took place. The employers duly posted notices of dismissal and all union members promptly stopped work. The great engineering lock-out had begun. It lasted almost seven months, from July 1897 to February 1898, ending in humiliating defeat for the unions whose members went back to work on terms dictated by the EEF. [13]

Uncrushed by this defeat, the unions were nevertheless divided between those that favoured a general and uniform reduction in working hours from 57 to 53 or 54 hours by means of a statutory 8-hour day and those that favoured a breakthrough wherever possible. But workers everywhere resented the employers' insistence on cutting pay or introducing compulsory overtime in return for any reduction in working hours. The unions therefore recommended that the 'customary limit' on overtime working should be reduced from 40 to 32 hours per month, producing a new maximum of one hour's overtime per day to be paid at enhanced premium rates. When trade was brisk, this meant, in effect, a maximum of 60 hours *worked* per week (i.e. 54 hours of normal time + 6 hours of overtime) but 66 hours *paid* (i.e. 54 hours at plain time + 8 hours at the premium rate of, say, time and a half).

But, as Stearns points out:

> It must not be assumed that workers had found a reduction in working time inevitably desirable. It went against their own interests to control their own efforts on a more regular basis, according to individual need. [15]

At the turn of the century, the normal 10-hour day in engineering was generally from 6 a.m. to 6 p.m. with an early breakfast break and a midday meal break, each of one hour, both unpaid. Since productivity was low on the pre-breakfast shift, employers began to adopt the 'single-break' system, which effectively reduced the working week to below 50 hours. In 1907, the EEF finally approved this system, but only where firms maintained a 51-hour week.

In 1913, the engineering unions resurrected their claim for a 48-hour week, now outstanding for more than 50 years. In 1914, when the EEF seemed on the point of concession, war was declared and the whole question deferred for the duration of hostilities. In the first post-war agreement of 1918, union leaders held out for a 47-hour week, pointing to the risk of unconstitutional action by leaders of the militant rank-and-file movement, which had sprung up at wartime engineering centres like London and Clydeside.

Describing the battle for the 47-hour week in Glasgow in 1919, Harry McShane told how:

> The ASE were negotiating with the employers for the 47-hour week at the time. The hours of labour before the war had been 54, starting at six o'clock in the morning and finishing at 5.30 p.m. and working until 12 a.m. on Saturdays. This was known as the nine-hour day: 6 a.m. to 5.30 p.m. [less 1¾ hours] Monday – Friday = 48¾ hours; 6 a.m. to 12 a.m. [less ¾ hour] Saturday = 5¼ hours. [16]

To help union executives to defeat this threat to their constitutional authority, the EEF conceded an official 47-hour week — a historic agreement that was to remain in force for no less than 28 years, as shown in Table 6.1.

Table 6.1. Reduction in the normal working week in engineering

Year	Normal hours/week	Reduction in hours	No of years since last reduction
1900	55 plus	–	–
1907	51 *	4	4
1918	47	4	9
1946	44	3	28
1959	42	2	13
1964	41	1	5
1965	40	1	1
1981	39	1	16

* 54 hours in shipbuilding.

Within one year of signing the 47-hour week agreement of 1918 — with the ink barely dry on the paper, as the EEF bitterly complained — the ASE attempted to exploit the post-war boom by pressing ahead with their next demand for a 44-hour week. The EEF deflected the claim by persuading the unions to take part in a joint examination of the economic relationship between working hours, methods of work and efficiency in British engineering and shipbuilding, compared with its foreign competitors.

In 1925, the EEF launched a counter-offensive, offering to increase wages if the unions would agree to revert to a 50-hour week. The unions refused to consider the suggestion and instead lobbied Parliament to press for Britain's ratification of the 48 Hours Convention, adopted by the International Labour Organization in 1921, as an essential first step towards their 44-hour claim. In this, they were to be disappointed. After the defeat of the 1926 General Strike and the fall in union membership during the depression of the 1920s and 1930s, those fortunate enough to be in work at the outbreak of war in 1939 were still employed on a 47-hour week.

It took the Second World War and the lapse of 28 years to achieve the next significant breakthrough. In the first post-war negotiations on wages and hours in 1946, the EEF conceded a 44-hour week to be worked over 5 or 5½ days, thereby ending the long-standing argument over an old EEF rule that the working week must be spread over 5½ days. But the last had not been heard of that problem.

Between 1956 and 1964, the EEF continued to resist the 40-hour claim by offering higher wage settlements instead. In March 1959, it was finally prevailed upon to concede a working week of 42 hours, still to be worked over 5 days. Night-shift workers in the motor industry now began to campaign for four nights of 10½ hours (42 hours) rather than five nights of 9 hours (45 hours). At the Ford Halewood plant on Merseyside, union activists adopted the famous shampoo advertising slogan of the day — *Friday night's Amami night* — to rally support behind the claim aimed at a four-day weekend break from 6 a.m. Friday until 10 p.m. the following

Monday. Unions and employers both strongly opposed the demand, the unions because it would undermine their case for any further reduction in hours, and the employers because the four-night week was seen as a stepping-stone to the four-day week.

By 1963, the Confed was determined to reject any further wage offer unless it was accompanied by a 40-hour week, but once again the EEF bought off the claim with a higher monetary settlement. Meantime the shipbuilding employers, who were in a much tighter economic situation but faced with a similar claim for more money and shorter hours, settled independently by offering a smaller wage increase and a 40-hour week by stages. Having split the employers, the Confed came back to the EEF with an irresistible claim for 40 hours, based on direct comparability with shipbuilding. In reply, the EEF offered a 3-year package deal covering wages and hours, in which the working week would be reduced to 41 hours by December 1964 and to 40 hours by July 1965. This new standard week of 40 hours, pioneered by the engineering unions, became the norm in British manufacturing industry during the 1960s and remained the norm throughout the 1970s.

It is important to distinguish the normal (or standard) working week of 40 hours from the number of actual hours worked, which often vary from week to week with the state of trade in particular industries, companies and establishments. The 'normal working week' defines the standard number of hours worked and paid at 'plain time' or 'straight time' rates of pay. Hours worked in excess of that standard are technically 'overtime hours', which attract 'overtime premia' (i.e. they are paid at enhanced or 'overtime rates' negotiated by the unions in different industries periodically). 'Time and a half' for all overtime hours worked between 6 a.m. Monday and 10 p.m. Saturday evening and 'double time' for hours worked between 10 p.m. Saturday and 6 a.m. Monday is now the generally accepted norm. Despite the gradual reduction in the normal working week in the post-war period, actual hours worked in Britain remained unusually high when compared with the rest of Europe, due to the persistence of high levels of overtime working, as shown in Fig. 6.1.

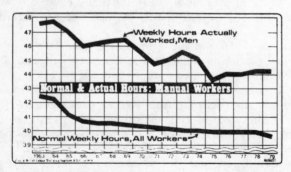

Fig. 6.1. Actual versus normal working hours.

As Sam Brittan noted in 1979:

When the last major reduction from 42 to 40 hours was made for most manual workers in 1964–66, over 40% of the effect was offset by more overtime, even though it occurred during the downswing of the business cycle. [17]

In other words, employers adopted an explicit policy of habitual overtime working, partly to boost the earnings and so retain the services of skilled workers, and partly to utilize existing workers more extensively instead of hiring additional labour. Mortimer notes the debilitating effects of habitual overtime working on productivity in British shipbuilding and engineering, most of which he attributes to managerial incompetence:

It is one thing to complain of this phenomenon [habitual overtime] in Britain since the Second World War; it is another to understand how it arose and how the opportunity in earlier years to develop a tradition of joint overtime control was thrown away. For this responsibility rests principally with the employers. They refused in engineering and shipbuilding to join with the unions in establishing effective joint machinery for the control of overtime. Instead they demonstrated an ideological commitment to what they believed was a right of management. In many cases it proved to be no more than a facade behind which there was managerial inefficiency. [18]

Since the shorter working week increased neither leisure nor employment, employers argued that it was an inflationary device used by trade unions to increase the earnings of existing workers. But it did nothing for the growing number of unemployed workers in the mid-1970s. It was the problem of unemployment that increasingly preoccuped the unions and the TUC, and led them to press for a shorter working week as one means of containing the rise in unemployment in the early 1980s. This was the situation that prevailed when, early in 1979, the Confed presented its claim for a 35-hour week on behalf of its two and a half million members.

SECTION 2: THE NATIONAL ENGINEERING DISPUTE, 1979

(1) The pre-strike context

The Confed's wages and conditions claim — the immediate cause of the dispute — was probably the most complex and ambitious ever presented to the EEF. To appreciate its impact on the employers, it must be seen in its economic and social context.

Following the collapse of Stage 3 of the Social Contract in 1979, workers whose living standards had been hardest hit by successive incomes policies, notably those in the public sector, attempted to restore the purchasing power of their pay packets by presenting claims for large increases in money wages. Within a few weeks, lorry and tanker drivers, local authority manual workers, hospital workers and even motor industry workers (hardly low-paid) were all out on strike, inaugurating the 'winter of discontent' and precipitating the fall of the Labour Government.

In February 1979 the Callaghan Labour Government and the TUC initialled a *Concordat* whose rules were designed to allay public concern about the conduct of industrial disputes, especially those liable to cause major disruption in public services: electricity, gas, food and water supplies, hospitals, schools and so on. But the Concordat came too late. The Conservative Opposition, the Confederation of British Industry (CBI) and the Press mounted an effective campaign to persuade the electorate that Britain's immediate crisis and general economic decline was due to the abuse of trade union power, which must be curtailed by every possible means, including legislation. The CBI urged employers to resist inflationary pay claims and to act with greater solidarity in the face of strike threats. [19] In March 1979 the EEF published a set of *Guidelines*, with one paramount intention:

> to help employers achieve a greater measure of confidence and coherence in the practice of collective bargaining and in responding to the threat or fact of industrial action. [20]

The EEF also arranged a series of conferences for its members, urging them to stand closer together against the 'mindless militancy (of) blind union power'. In a democracy, workers had the right to strike, but that right was qualified by an obligation on the strikers to ensure that no irreperable harm was done to the fabric of society and that the weak and defenceless should not suffer. Strikes should be used as a weapon of last, not first, resort.

That view appeared to be shared by Terry Duffy who said, on his election as AUEW President in 1978:

> The strike is a very delicate weapon. Sometimes a short sharp strike is a good safety valve. But long strikes are of no use to union or nation. I will strive to reduce them. [21]

If Duffy's moderate words lulled engineering employers into a false sense of security, they were shortly due for a rude awakening, for the AUEW decided to launch an all-out assault on the psychological barrier of the 40-hour week. It was 16 years since the industry last reduced working hours, from 41 to 40 hours in 1965. In Ford and some other parts of the motor industry there had been a 40-hour week since 1928. Total working hours in the British engineering industry were generally less than those in other sectors of British manufacturing but they lagged behind many countries in the rest of Europe, where the length of the working week had been reduced generally to around 40 hours but the concession of additional paid holidays had significantly reduced the total number of working hours per year.

But it was the steady growth in unemployment amongst British engineering workers that compelled the Executive Committee of the AUEW to give the highest priority to a shorter working week, in 1981, as one means of generating additional jobs for their members already on the dole or on short-time working.

(2) The challenge

The claim presented by the Confed on 12 February 1979 is best summarized under four headings:

(i) *Pay:* an increase of 33% in national minimum time rates (NMRs) from £60 to £80 per week for skilled workers, with pro rata increases for semi-skilled and unskilled workers and apprentices.

(ii) *Common implementation date:* all new pay and conditions agreements to take effect simultaneously on a common anniversary date.

(iii) *Hours and holidays:* a planned reduction in the working week from 40 to 39 hours in 1979–80 and to 35 hours in 1982-83; an additional 5 days of paid holiday in 1979, bringing the annual total to 25 days (exclusive of six statutory Bank Holidays: New Year's Day, Easter Bank Holiday, Spring Bank Holiday, Late Summer Bank Holiday, Christmas Day and Boxing Day).

(iv) *Other demands:* increased overtime and holiday working premia; a guaranteed week agreement; a maternity leave agreement; adult rates of pay for production workers at age 18; and abolition of qualifying days for holidays.

It soon emerged that the 'Other demands' summarized above were less important than the claim on wages, hours and holidays. For reasons of space alone, they will not be dealt with in this chapter.

(3) Initial responses

When accepting the claim for consideration, the EEF at once made it clear that the industry could not afford the substantial additional costs of a SWW at a time when its manufacturing costs were rising faster than those of its foreign competitors. In June the EEF gave its carefully considered reply. It offered to increase the skilled NMR from £60 to £68 per week and proposed that a Joint Working Party should be set up to examine the implications of the SWW claim and the relationship between staff and hourly conditions of employment in the industry. When negotiations resumed in July, the Confed said that it was willing to settle the skilled wage rate for £70 and was ready to discard some other points of its claim, but it rejected the idea of a working party because:

the problem of the SWW has now reached such magnitude, particularly because of the new techniques following the introduction of micro-electronics, which are beginning to bite, that we feel we must renew our claim for a SWW in 1979. [21]

When negotiations broke down on 10 July, the Confed ordered an immediate national overtime ban and a series of three separate one-day token strikes per month, commencing in August. The EEF was determined to stand firm.

(4) Consequences

The first day's stoppage on 6 August was only a qualified success, since half of the industry's workers were still on annual holidays. When the Confed announced that its claim had been met in full by more than one hundred firms, of whom a dozen were federated, the EEF denied the allegation, saying that only five federated firms had exceeded the national offer and that these were all expected to withdraw their offers or resign from the Federation.

At its AGM in August, the Confed decided to step up its industrial action with a series of weekly two-day stoppages, commencing in September. There was massive support for the first two-day strike on 3 and 4 September, when an estimated 2 million out of a potential total of 2.5 million engineering workers came out on strike. Several leading companies spoke out against any further stoppages. British Leyland (BL) was reported to be running out of money, production had been less than half the norm and lay-offs were inevitable. Rolls Royce urged its employees to put the 'greatest possible pressure' on the unions to settle the dispute, in order to prevent the 'stagnation and decline of the company and its workforce'. Later that week, when lobbied by angry members of his union, demanding an all-out strike, Duffy told them that the two-day strikes would continue every Monday and Tuesday until the employers had met the claim in full.

Before the second two-day stoppage on 10 and 11 September, the EEF advised its members to keep their factories open in the hope that some workers might still report for work. But many employers doubted whether it was worth opening at all that week. The unions' response was that if workers were laid off for the rest of that week, they would be regarded as having been locked out.

On 14 September *The Financial Times* presented a detailed explanation of *Why the dispute must end*. It had become:

an out-and-out trial of strength between two powerful organizations whose credibility and self respect were at stake . . . another example of the British tendency to inflict unnecessary damage on themselves. [22]

According to *The Financial Times*, the central issue was no longer wages but the SWW, although the FT doubted the rank-and-file commitment to that objective. The unions hoped that the SWW would oblige firms to hire more workers, and were anxious to harmonize conditions between manual workers and salaried staff. But the SWW, it conceded, would have one of two effects: either the same hours would be worked but overtime increased; or the industry's assets would be under-utilized through less time worked each week, thus adding to costs by reducing productivity. *The Financial Times* considered that the proposed change would impose a cost penalty that the industry could not afford. It made no sense when all Britain's industrial competitors (e.g. West Germany) had strenuously resisted it. Nevertheless:

> *there has to be a negotiated end to the dispute if the damage to the industry is not to reach disastrous proportions.* [22]

On 17 September, ACAS brought both sides together but could find no basis for resuming negotiations. The Confed made its position clear:

> *We have not indicated in any way to ACAS that our resolve had weakened. We are as strong as ever.* [23]

The EEF forecast that up to half a million engineering workers would defy the call to join the third two-day strike. The employers intended to 'stand absolutely firm'. Many were 'almost suicidal' in their determination to resist the unions' demands. The third two-day stoppage went ahead as planned on 17 and 18 September.

On 17 September, *The Guardian* offered its first comments on the failure of collective bargaining to resolve the issue:

> *The main impression is of bewildered men, each side hoping the other's nerve will crack first ... National wage bargains are not best for either side ... In the end ... the terms and conditions of almost 20% of all private sector workers affiliated to the TUC will thus be decided as a result of one gigantic centralized deal. It might be, in a formal sense, 'free collective bargaining' with no government norm; no government pressure; and no government interference. But this battle of the dinosaurs bears precious little relevance to the free play of genuinely competitive labour markets.* [24]

According to *The Guardian*, the over-centralized struggle that was being fought out at growing cost to the nation was:

> *a damaging mix of the worst of free collective bargaining and the worst of centralized negotiations.* [24]

On 20 September the EEF announced that its earlier estimate of the cost of conceding the whole claim had been too low: it would add not 35% but 50% to direct labour costs (viz. £2300 million per annum for federated firms and £3800 million per annum for the industry as a whole). According to the EEF there was no way that companies could remotely afford to meet the claim:

> *It is in the vital economic interests of employers to stand firm against the claim and they have to stand together to resist it, or next year there will be another enormous claim, and another the year after that.* [25]

Increasing the skilled NMR from £60 to £80 per week would add 33.3% to basic rates, with local incentive and other plus payments on top; granting a SWW would bring that total up to 50%. The offer of £70 for skilled men and a Joint Working Party to consider improvements in hours and conditions might add between 15% and 16% to labour costs in 1979. The EEF estimated that the dispute had already cost the industry over £2 million and predicted that lay-offs might soon affect 100 000 workers. Only 15 federated firms had met the claim in full and all had been expelled or asked to resign. [25]

(5) The climax

After the fourth two-day strike on 24 and 25 September, the dispute took on an increasingly bitter tone, with divisions on both sides helping to build the climax of the dispute. On 26 September, two engineering companies announced their resignation from the EEF: Metro-Cammell in Manchester conceded the 39–hour week at an estimated additional cost of only 2.5% on its wages bill. D. J. Brown Engineering decided that the SWW was not an issue on which the employers should stake so much:

> *We are only debating when it should come in, and not if.* [26]

Both firms decided to resign from the EEF with dignity rather than await expulsion.

By 28 September, leading employers were deeply divided on the EEF's handling of the dispute. Sir Arnold (now Lord) Weinstock, Managing Director of GEC, Britain's largest engineering company, let it be known that his company was considering leaving the EEF because national negotiations were no longer the appropriate means in the long term for settling basic rates and conditions of employment. But GEC continued to support the EEF:

> *in its refusal to submit to the irrational demands of the Confed, based on the escalating application of force, irrespective of the short- and long-term consequences to the industry and to its employees . . . The rigid and totally unconstructive approach of the CSEU must call into question the Confed's quality as a negotiating partner.* [27]

The AUEW's General Secretary was stung to reply: his union's members were suffering 'a most vicious attack' on their freedom to strike. The EEF had displayed 'venom and hatred' towards the unions. It aimed to:

> *impoverish the workers into submission and bleed the unions to death.* [28]

On 1 and 2 October, the fifth and final two-day strike took place amid mounting confusion and disillusion amongst both workers and management. Was it possible that the dispute had got completely out of control? In its leading article of 3 October, *The Financial Times* wrote:

> *On the basis of past experience, it seems unlikely that the dispute will end in total victory for one side or the other. There are certainly some situations in which a confrontation between employers and employees is unavoidable; the chronic tendency of employers to make threats which they do not carry out — and to give in to threats from the other side — has made a major contribution to this country's poor labour relations and low productivity. But the ground for confrontation has to be chosen rather carefully. Above all, it is essential that the issues involved in the dispute are crystal clear to all. These conditions do not apply to the engineering dispute . . . (The EEF was) extremely unlikely to concede the unions' demand for a move to 39 hours. The practical question was not how many hours a week will eventually be worked but how much more employers will have to pay for roughly the same number of hours worked. (The SWW) to all intents and purposes is a disguised wage claim.* [29]

Whether firms could afford to pay depended on their own particular productivity and profitability:

> *The diversity of conditions cannot possibly be catered for by national negotiations. That is why local bargaining has always been regarded as more important; indeed it is hard to think of any industry less suited to industry-wide wage bargaining than engineering.* [29]

That hard-hitting article, read by engineering directors throughout the country, may well have marked the turning point in the dispute. It drove home the futility of the conflict, asking why the SWW had become the battlefield on which the future of the British engineering industry was to be decided. Although negotiations had been broken off and the two sides were out of touch, the EEF had already hinted that it was ready to improve its offer on wages and holidays and was now reported to be seriously considering how best to phase in the SWW over a longer time period. The divisions within both camps were now plainly visible to all: employers in the London Association sent a compromise peace formula to the EEF urging an immediate resumption of negotiations to settle the dispute; the Electricians' Union (EEPTU) was considering a ballot of its members, asking whether they were in favour of accepting the latest offer and a return to work.

On the morning of 4 October, the press detected the first real signs of a breakthrough. Both sides were to resume talks at a Gatwick Airport hotel. *The Guardian* commented tartly:

> *Whatever the outcome of today's talks, the fact is that both the employers' federation and the union confederation will be weaker in future — thank goodness. Free collective bargaining ought to mean local negotiations related to basic local issues like productivity, profits, labour supply and so on. It should not mean a battle to the death between dinosaurs.* [30]

On the same day, *The Financial Times* was even less flattering: it was the end of a 'a battle of coelacanths, between species soon to be extinct'. [31]

(6) The settlement

Next morning, the Gatwick Airport Agreement stole the national headlines: *Engineering workers win shorter week and historic break-through on hours.* Table 6.2 compares the terms of the original claim with successive offers and the final settlement.

(7) Aftermath

The end of the dispute left a bitter taste in many mouths on both sides. Amongst the unions of the Confed there were many examples of harsh recrimination between those unions whose members had conscientiously and enthusiastically supported the selective strike action and those whose members had given only token support. There were calls for tighter discipline and control by union leaders over their more independent and wayward members.

But the employers' side was no less divided between those companies whose directors recognized the inevitability of the shorter working week and who wished to 'get the agony over quickly' by negotiating modest concessions in return for more flexible working practices, and those companies for whom any significant increase in labour costs might prove economically disastrous and whose directors therefore urged the strongest possible resistance to the Confed's claim, at almost any cost. It was precisely the directors of those marginally efficient firms who howled the loudest when the selective strike action hit their production schedules and profits. Hence the bitterness generated by the final settlement and the accusations of a 'sell-out' by the employers. This led Anthony Fordsham, the EEF's Director-General, to take the unprecedented step of publishing a letter in *The Financial Times*, defending the EEF's concessions:

> *The CSEU wanted to buy something — a shorter working week — for which it was prepared to pay very dearly. Everything has its price and the price paid by the CSEU was considerable . . . On balance, the terms of the agreement are a considerable achievement for employers, justifying their deter-*

Table 6.2. 1979 engineering claim, offers and settlement terms

1979	Wages (NMRs)	Wage increase	Hours per week	Paid holidays
Pre-claim	Skilled £60 Unskilled £40		40 (from 1965)	20 plus statutory Bank Holidays
Feb. claim *	Skilled £80 Unskilled £60	33%	39 in 1979–80 35 in 1982–83	5 extra days holiday
June offer **	Skilled £68 Unskilled £49	13%	Joint working party to consider implications	
July offer	Skilled £70 Unskilled £50	17%	Joint working party to consider implications	5 extra days holiday
Oct. offer	Skilled £72 Unskilled £51.5	20%	39 in 1982–83	1 extra in 1979 1 extra in 1980 1 extra in 1981 1 extra in 1982 (Total 24)
Final offer and settlement	Skilled £73 Unskilled £52.	21.7% 16.7%	39 in 1981–82 No further reduction before 1985	2 extra in 1979 (Total 22) 1 extra in 1980 1 extra in 1981 1 extra in 1982 (Total 25)

* Common implementation date.
** Staggered implementation date.

mined stand through a long and damaging series of strikes. [32]

SECTION 3: ANALYSIS OF THE DISPUTE

(1) What was the dispute about?

The engineering unions had pioneered the shorter working week (SWW) in Britain for more than a century, but a further reduction in hours had not been one of the Confed's priority bargaining objectives in the early 1970s. Salaried engineering staff (as distinct from manual workers) had enjoyed a normal working week of less than 40 hours for more than ten years. Amongst manual workers in Britain, underground miners, telephone engineers, firemen, nurses and midwives had already won a 37.5 hour week by 1979, but these were all exceptional groups in special circumstances. In the manufacturing industry, the unions at Ford had presented management with a closely-reasoned case for the 35-hour week in 1977 and 1978. On both occasions, the claims were rejected outright on grounds of cost. [33]

In formulating its 1979 claim, the Confed came under considerable pressure from its affiliated unions to secure a 35-hour week for engineering manual workers. There were two objectives:

(i)   to breach the '40 hour barrier', which had withstood union assault for more than 15 years;
(ii) to help engineering and other unions to combat unemployment and to resist further job losses by a policy of 'job creation' through the shorter working week and less overtime working.

In 1965, when the 40-hour week had been conceded, unemployment in the British manufacturing industry had stood at around 3%. By the end of the 1970s, it had climbed to almost 10%. In engineering, the recession had cut deep: hundreds of firms had already gone out of business; thousands of engineering workers had been forced to accept short-time working or redundancy. The Confed argued that since many thousands of its skilled members were unemployed in 1979, the shorter working week would help their re-employment.

The cause of the dispute was therefore unequivocally clear: the unions' claim for a shorter working week in 1979 was based on a genuine desire to reduce working hours. The employers' reaction was based on an equally genuine desire to control costs and remain competitive. Whilst other elements in the 1979 claim might be negotiable, the Confed was determined to overcome the '40-hour barrier'. The EEF felt obliged to defend this barrier because the claim for a 35-hour week represented an exceptionally costly claim at a time when international competition and a deepening recession were threatening future prospects in the industry. In short, the employers were in the worst possible economic situation in which to respond positively to the claim.

(2) How significant was the context?

The context of the dispute was as important as its content. The Labour Party and the TUC had used the four years of the Heath Conservative Government (1970–74) to learn some of the painful economic and political lessons of Labour's six years in office (1964–70). The results of this self-criticism emerged when Labour was returned to power in February 1974. In addition to abolishing the Conservative Government's 1971 Industrial Relations Act, Labour introduced the Social Contract, a complex, controversial and informal economic and social package deal between the Labour Party and the TUC, intended to help to regenerate the lagging British economy, to reduce inflation and to heal the wounds inflicted on both wings of the labour movement by the previous Labour Government's attempt to introduce industrial relations legislation in 1969. The first three phases of this 'Social Contract', which included a voluntary incomes policy designed to control the rate of domestically-induced inflation, had enjoyed a fair measure of success, but by the autumn of 1978 the Callaghan Government had not only missed the window of opportunity of securing the re-election of a Labour Government, it had also lost the support of the majority of ordinary trade union members, which was essential to the success of its incomes policy. Phase 4 of the Social Contract proved a disastrous failure.

In the so-called 'winter of discontent' that ensued — so eagerly reported by the media — successive groups of workers in strategic parts of the economy abandoned any pretence at supporting the Government's 7% voluntary limit on pay increases and took industrial action in support of their claims. Faced with an increasingly chaotic economic situation and widespread strikes, which crippled many parts of the economy, the Confederation of British Industry (CBI) and the Engineering Employers Federation (EEF) mounted a major joint initiative to bolster employers' morale, urging them to stiffen their resolve to 'stand up to trade union power'. This was the turbulent context in which the constituent unions of the Confed got down to prioritizing their annual pay claim for 1979. Terry Duffy, newly-elected President of the AUEW, leading his first major negotiations with the EEF, was determined to demonstrate to his members and employers alike that he was no moderate 'push-over'. When the Confed formally presented its claim in February 1979, both sides were distracted by the winter of discontent, which left the trade unions at their lowest ebb. The EEF delayed making its reply to the claim during the spring of 1979, which marked the run-up to the General Election. In May, the Conservatives swept back to power with a landslide majority, leaving the labour movement bitterly divided as it prepared to face the radical right-wing policies of the Thatcher Government. But the election of a friendly government, half-way through the dispute, gave an immense psychological boost to the employers' morale. All these contextual factors influenced the conduct of the dispute and helped to shape its outcome. One year earlier — or later – and the result might have been quite different; we shall never know.*

Although the engineering industry was known to have suffered worst from the onset of the world recesssion in the late 1970s, Duffy argued that the Confed needed a SWW if only to ensure that the employers took on additional labour and so contributed to a reduction in unemployment and short-time working amongst their members. The strongest case for a reduced working week came from an international comparison of the total working hours in metalworking industries around the world. According to the TUC, the evidence showed that, whilst most of the advanced industrial countries of Europe had harmonized their working week around 40 hours, the concession of more paid holidays and more public holidays had significantly reduced the total working hours per annum in other countries below the total in Britain.

(3) Why did the Confed choose the 'intermittent' strike strategy?

The Confed presented what it considered to be an irrefutable case for the shorter working week (SWW) in 1979 and was determined to achieve a breakthrough in that year. As Terry Duffy told his union's conference the previous autumn:

> *Somebody somewhere has got to take on the employing class on the shorter working week.* [34]

Having made the SWW a key bargaining objective for 1979 and having raised their members' expectations by setting the ambitious target of a 35-hour week by 1982, unions in the Confed could not easily abandon that element in their claim without risking a mass revolt amongst their rank-and-file memberships. Conversely, the EEF had come under equally strong pressure from the CBI to resist the claim on their own behalf and on behalf of employers in general. Thus, both sides invested the dispute with a symbolic significance quite disproportionate to the objective value or intrinsic cost of the claim.

A 39-hour week or 12 minutes off the normal working day of 480 minutes — a reduction of 2.5% — could hardly justify ten weeks of bitter disruptive conflict, the loss of important orders or customers, the loss of members' earnings, and the risk to jobs and to firms that a protracted dispute inevitably entailed. The Confed knew the employers were too weak to withstand an all-out strike and so adopted the less dramatic but no less effective strategy of a complete ban on overtime working, coupled with intermittent stoppages designed to impose the maximum disruptive pressure and the heaviest

---

* For a discussion of the timing of industrial disputes, see Part I, Chapter 2, pp. 12–19.

cost penalties on the employers, at least cost to their own members and to individual unions' strike funds. Unless the employers acted with unusual solidarity and imposed a collective lock-out, which the EEF's rhetoric urged them to do, the Confed had adopted a winning strategy.

(4) Did the EEF capitulate?

The EEF initially resisted the Confed claim, believing that it could count on its members' new-found solidarity, but this soon melted away. The Confed calculated that in any long drawn-out struggle the employers' nerve would crack first — a calculation which proved to be correct. By October, after 10 weeks of costly disruptive action, with no end to the dispute in sight and no apparent weakening of support for the two-day stoppage on 1 and 2 October, the Federation's strategists got together to find a compromise peace formula. The question that now preoccupied them was how much of the original claim could be conceded without too much loss of face? A report to the EEF's Management Board by its Negotiating Committee provides a unique insight into the employers' thinking during the final stages of the Gatwick negotiations:

(i)   Despite the slow return to work, some 0.75 million workers were still on strike out of a total of 2.5 million; so there was no prospect of an imminent collapse of the strike.

(ii)   Even if a Joint Working Party had been set up, the employers would have come under heavy pressure to bring manual workers' hours (40) into line with staff hours (39) but at a faster rate than could have been negotiated at Gatwick. Such a concession would then have led staff unions to press for the restoration of the hour's differential, at considerable cost.

(iii)   Although the Confed had been determined that new pay rates should take effect simultaneously, as in the past, from a common implementation date (viz. the settlement date, if possible), they were forced to abandon that point and to accept the EEF's counter-demand that the new rates should be implemented on a staggered basis of 'domestic anniversary dates' (i.e. to coincide with each firm's annual domestic bargaining settlement). So the immediate impact of the settlement cost was deferred for many employers.

(iv)   By reason of this 'substantial achievement', the Committee felt able to increase NMRs by 21.7% for skilled workers, by 16.7% for unskilled and by 17.5% for semi-skilled workers, thereby widening wage differentials in the face of substantial union opposition.

(v)   Despite its initial reluctance to enter into any agreement exceeding 3 years, the Confed was persuaded to sign a 4-year agreement which:

    (a) deferred the 'inevitable introduction of a 39-hour week' for two years to 1981;

    (b) held it there for another four years to 1985, thereby ensuring a long period of stability for the industry.

(vi) The Four-Year Agreement was therefore a good agreement for the employers, as favourable as any that might have emerged from a Joint Working Party. Annual hours of work under the new timetable would still be more favourable than those in West Germany, at every stage of the Agreement. [35]

Thus, far from being an abject capitulation to Confed pressure, the EEF could argue that the settlement terms represented a catalogue of deliberate concessions, carefully calculated to minimize the costs of a more protracted dispute, with guaranteed freedom from further economic demands on the employers for four more years.

(5) Who won?

Whenever a major dispute ends, each side draws up a balance sheet of strike gains and losses, taking care to present the outcomes in the most favourable light to itself. There is evidently a strong psychological need to demonstrate that the gains achieved fully justify the sacrifices made. Thus, the EEF argued that the unprecedented solidarity shown by the employers had enabled it to drive away 'the most damaging elements' of a 'colossal claim'; the 4-year deal would 'ensure harmony through the difficult period ahead of us'; it gave the industry time in which to find ways of offsetting, by increased productivity, the cost of the eventual one-hour reduction in the working week.

    When challenged to explain its fierce initial resistance and eventual retreat, the EEF began by denying that the unions had won a major victory:

> *Acceptance of the 39-hour week by the end of 1981 has been emotively hailed as a victory by one side and seen dejectedly by some as a surrender to union forces. In reality it is neither ... Clause by clause, the agreement is a good one for our members. But one salutary question remains — could an equally favourable agreement have been reached earlier if we had offered to reduce the working week over a four-year period? The answer is categorically no.* [36]

Defending the EEF's position in *The Financial Times*, the EEF's Director-General wrote:

> *We have not and do not seek to claim a victory — how could anyone sensibly do so after a dispute in which individual union members have lost up to £350 each in wages; employers have lost or delayed sales worth over £2bn; and our industry has lost reputation and competitiveness in world markets? But*

there is no justification for dismissing the settlement as a defeat for employers. [32]

The *Financial Times* rejected the EEF's reasoning as implausible:

In terms of the politics of wage bargaining . . . the settlement is heavily damaging. Bluntly the employers misjudged the mood of the shopfloor and the solidarity of their own members . . . Because it was a symbolic dispute, the symbolic victory is all-important. The 40-hour barrier has been breached in a huge industry by unions whose actions have repercussions in many other industries. [37]

Most commentators expected that the first effect of the engineering settlement would be to convert demands for a SWW in other industries from a theoretical into a practical and attainable objective. Herman Rebhan of the IMF was in no doubt about that:

The SWW is now on the collective bargaining agenda of the international trade union movement as never before. Time, for the industrial worker, is the most precious currency he can trade in. Extra time off gained by workers cannot be devalued. It is fully inflation-proofed. [38]

In practice, comparatively few other groups of workers were successful in citing the engineering settlement of 1979 as a precedent for obtaining a SWW for themselves. The two-year delay in implementing the reduction from 40 to 39 hours in engineering detracted from the Confed's achievement in breaching the '40-hour barrier'. During this period, British manufacturing industry experienced increasingly severe competition as the world recession bit deeper. Employers in other industries were able to point to the growing list of bankruptcies and rising levels of unemployment in engineering as reasons for rejecting claims for a SWW. The CBI mounted a renewed campaign to close the gap in the dyke created by the EEF concession. Comparisons with SWT in other European manufacturing countries were rejected by the CBI as unfounded and irrelevant — until the German unions won their long and bitter dispute in the German metal-working industry for a shorter working week of 38.5 hours in 1982.

By any strict reckoning, the EEF failed to sustain its resistance to the Confed's assault on the '40-hour barrier', but equally, the Confed failed to achieve its initial, ambitious claim for a 39-hour week in 1979 and a 35-hour week by 1982–83. It took two more years to breach the '40-hour barrier' in 1981–82 and no further progress was achieved towards SWW before 1987 (see Conclusions and Postscript in Section 4). If neither side was entitled to claim outright victory, each side could console itself by estimating its prospective gains, compared with the potential losses of an increasingly bitter dispute.

(6) Costs and benefits of the dispute

According to the EEF, the strike cost engineering workers up to £350 each in lost wages and employers more than £2000 million in lost orders. [32] But these were only the immediate and measurable costs; the longer-term costs of industrial disputes are less tangible. After some disputes, strike losses are soon recovered by both sides: employers catch up on late deliveries by heavy overtime working, which also helps workers to restore depleted savings, especially at new rates of pay. In other disputes, a valuable customer or an entire market may be lost to domestic or foreign competition. Some firms may be forced out of business, with heavy job losses. In assessing the final cost of the engineering dispute, the psychological damage sustained by the engineering industry's long-established collective bargaining machinery must be added to the cost of the economic concessions (viz. the SWW, longer holidays, higher wages, etc.) For, as in all important disputes, in addition to the well-publicized differences between the unions and the employers, there were substantial disagreements amongst the parties themselves on the handling of the dispute and its settlement terms. Leading employers resigned (or threatened to resign) from the EEF both during and after the dispute. Many workers felt themselves betrayed by their leaders' failure to secure the 35-hour week promised for 1979.

As noted elsewhere*, the true costs of a major dispute are notoriously difficult to assess, partly because of potential offsetting gains, partly because they are not all quantifiable, and partly because of disinformation (i.e. deliberate misinformation) presented by both sides as part of their psychological warfare. For a more impartial assessment of the cost of this particular dispute, we turn to leading commentators in the media. *The Financial Times* noted that the final pay settlement was 'not too far above the first offer made'; that the SWW had been delayed for 2 years and was then to be made in smaller stages than had been demanded; and that the 4-year agreement promised some stability to the industry. *The Guardian* found the EEF deal most complicated to cost. According to the EEF, the pay increases of 21.7%, 17.5% and 16.7% to skilled, semi-skilled and unskilled workers, came down to 14%, 12% and 11%, respectively, on an annual basis. But, as *The Guardian* perceptively observed:

> Only about 5% of EEF employees earn the minimum. The other 95% are covered by additional bonuses negotiated at plant level. Matchstick mathematics aside, one point is clear: the EEF, bargaining on behalf of 6500 very different concerns, has reached a pace-setting settlement without any productivity concessions whatsoever. [39]

* See Part I, Chapter 2, p. 22, on problems of estimating the true costs and benefits of industrial disputes.

The Observer contented itself with noting that:

> the most inefficient, unproductive and unprofitable engineering
> industry in western Europe is pioneering a reduction in
> working time. [40]

The unions did not conceal their evident satisfaction at the
outcome of the dispute. Writing in the December issue of the *AUEW
Journal*, Sir John Boyd ridiculed what the unions saw as the patent
dishonesty of the EEF. During August and September it had conducted
a publicity campaign in the media 'telling the country our claim would
increase their direct labour costs by 50%'. These allegations had been
proved mischieviously erroneous — by the EEF itself, which had
belatedly published the truth in *EEF News*:

> Increased overtime and shift payments are unlikely to add more
> than 1% to direct labour costs ... The percentage increase in
> the rates are clearly not inflationary ... The extra holidays
> and 1-hour reduction in the working week would add 8% to
> direct labour costs by November 1983 ... And as the union
> members intend to cooperate in raising productivity the actual
> effects will be negligible for companies which make full use of
> this commitment ...
> ... Well! Well! Well! Would you believe it? Every federated
> employer must become more involved with the affairs of the
> EEF and never again allow their leadership to drag the industry
> into such damaging confrontation. [28]

Perhaps the EEF's estimates and Sir John Boyd's comments
were both misleading. On 15 October, the Government published
figures that gave the first official estimate of the cost of the dispute.
Manufacturing output in August had dropped by 6% to over 2.5%
below the level recorded in 1974, after the miners' strike of that year
had put the whole country on a 3-day week. During 1979–80, many
manufacturing companies closed or reported heavy trading losses,
which they attributed in large measure to rising raw material and
labour costs and the impact of the engineering dispute.

(7) Lessons of the dispute

Both during and after the dispute, the engineering industry's collective
bargaining machinery came in for severe criticism, with greatly
reduced confidence amongst those who count most, namely, the directors of engineering firms — from the high-technology, high-
productivity industrial giants to the labour-intensive backstreet
jobbing firms — and the 2.5 million rank-and-file engineering workers
whom they employed. Since the 1920s, when the industry's first
national negotiations took place, a two-tier system of bargaining had
been developed, which had once served the industry well. At that
time, NMRs accounted for over 90% of weekly take-home pay. With

the post-war shift to plant bargaining — associated with the spread of incentive payments, productivity bargaining and supplementary payments of all kinds, including larger elements of overtime and shift premia payments — NMRs had become little more than a bargaining floor — a theoretical starting point for plant bargaining about actual rates, far above the NMRs.

Not surprisingly, the EEF clings tenaciously to national bargaining over major terms and conditions of employment — such as normal working hours, overtime and shift premia and the number of paid annual holidays — because they wish to avoid the embarrassment of leap-frogging concessions by their affiliated member firms. The unions naturally wish to preserve two-tier bargaining because it allows their members to strike local plant or company bargains over and above already-agreed national minima, thereby providing the basis for future national claims. There was therefore considerable justification for the lack of public confidence in the industry's bargaining system. In the considered view of *The Financial Times*:

> *The apparent lesson is that determined industrial action can still break the most determined employer. [The unions had] at last demonstrated that they were able to mount large-scale coordinated industrial action in the highly diverse industry . . . Whatever role the EEF retains after the dispute is over, a good many companies will prefer to fight their own battles without being entangled in national arguments over which they have little control or influence. Their main aim must be to achieve higher productivity and that, too, can only be done through local negotiations.*

Immediately following the dispute, there was much talk of changing the industry's national bargaining structure, the only realistic alternative being that different sectors of engineering (e.g. heavy, light, electical, domestic appliance, motors, etc.) should each conduct their own bargaining within some overall national framework, to be followed later by detailed plant bargaining on domestic issues. However, at the time of writing (1987), no substantive changes have yet taken place in the bargaining structure of the engineering industry.

SECTION 4: CONCLUSIONS AND 1987 POSTSCRIPT

The national engineering dispute of 1979 focused the public mind on shorter working time in the 1980s as no other dispute before or since. The urgency of the whole issue was strongly reinforced by the spate of closures, redundancies and short-time working in engineering during 1980 and 1981. In April 1979, the TUC launched its campaign to fight against unemployment by backing the demand for the 35-hour week:

> *The TUC, as well as joining with other union organizations within the European Trades Union Congress (ETUC) in pursuing an internationally coordinated reduction of working time, has the clear objective of achieving a 35-hour normal working week throughout the UK economy, and it is anticipated that this issue will become increasingly prominent on the bargaining agenda.* [41]

In January 1980, the CBI put forward for joint discussion with the TUC its proposals for creating 2.5 million new jobs over the next decade. One of its ideas was that working hours might be calculated on an 'annual time budget' instead of on a weekly basis because:

> *in certain cases, increased holiday entitlement or an extra shift can be more easily absorbed in cost and production terms than a reduction in the length of the shift or working day.*

A joint CBI–TUC approach was necessary to the whole problem, since otherwise:

> *bargaining pressures will force through reductions in hours — perhaps after damaging disputes — which will make British industry less competitive.* [42]

Although the Gatwick Agreement promised that increased productivity would be forthcoming at plant level to help offset the cost of the concessions made, the fact is that poor productivity in British engineering has been the principal cause of its deteriorating performance over many years. The industry's share of home and export markets fell throughout the 1970s, for which the lower output per worker in the British industry as against its overseas competitors — not all of which was necessarily attributable to the workers themselves — bears much of the responsibility. An independent report published in 1980 estimated that output per man fell by 7% in engineering in the five years ending in 1979; it was sceptical about the productivity promised in return for the SWW. [43]

Any genuine improvement in labour productivity achieved at plant level following the Gatwick Agreement was probably wiped out by the dramatic fall in the utilization of installed capacity in engineering firms due to the recession. It is ironic to record that when the 39-hour week was due for implementation in November 1981, tens of thousands of jobs had already disappeared from the industry whilst those workers who remained were already working less than 32 hours per week, due to short-time working. [44]

In July 1986, in a renewed attempt to further reduce the working week towards 35 hours, Bill Jordan, the newly-elected General Secretary of the AUEW, tabled on behalf of the Confed a revolutionary package of proposals. *The Financial Times* noted that the negotiations were:

> *within sight of one of the most dramatic industrial relations deals of the decade; the engineering unions, in a bid to win shorter hours, have told employers that they would concede complete flexibility, the employers' right to organize working time, and an end to demarcation.*

The Financial Times went on to explain that the Confed was:

> *seeking to persuade the employers to agree to a cut in the working week when they are in no position to force an hours cut through industrial action.* [45]

Despite the attractions of the deal for the employers, the EEF was reported as being unwilling to cut hours unless the unions also agreed a comprehensive revision of the industry's collective bargaining arrangements, which would dramatically reduce the number of bargaining units and so pave the way towards single-unionism in the industry.

In November 1986, the unions rejected an employers' offer to increase minimum rates by 3.7% to bring the basic pay for an unskilled worker to £75.80 for a 37.5 hour week. According to Dr James Macfarlane, Director of the EEF, the offer was well above inflation. It reflected low profitability in the manufacturing industry where the rate of return was only 7.2% on total capital employed, well below both the level of the 1960s and the 12% risk-free return available in a building society. He nevertheless accepted that manufacturing profitability had risen by 180% since 1981 and that, over broadly the same period, productivity had risen by 25%. But that still left UK productivity between 50% and 100% below US and Japanese levels. The EEF's offer to reduce the basic working week by 1.5 hours in phases from 39 hours to 37.5 hours was made despite the fact that the total number of hours worked by British engineering workers (1778 for manual workers and 1710 for non-manual workers) was less than the total worked by their opposite numbers in many other countries, as shown in Table 6.3.

In June 1987, Gavin Laird, AEU President and incoming President of the Confed, told a national press conference that agreement had been all but reached in principle between the Confed and the EEF, but that the EEF must agree to implement the phased reduction in the working week from 39 to 37.5 hours in two unified stages (viz. November 1988 and November 1989) and not over three years, as proposed by the EEF, with each of the 5000 federated companies making its own reduction to coincide with its annual pay rounds. [46] When the agreement was finally signed on that basis, the Confed was still far from securing the 35-hour week that had led to its national strike in 1979.

Table 6.3. International comparison of basic and total hours of full-time manual workers in engineering

Country	Normal hours per week (basic)	Holiday entitlement (basic)	Public holidays	Total holidays	Net annual working hours*
Australia	38	20	11	31	1748
Austria	38.5	25	11	36	1789
Belgium	37	20	10	30	1709
Denmark	39	25	10.5	35.5	1799
France	38.5	25	9	34	1748
Germany	38.5	30	11.7	41.7	1689
Italy	40	25	8	33	1784
Japan	40	20	10	30	1848
Netherlands	40	22	7	29	1752
Spain	40	26	14	40	1820
Sweden	40	25	12	37	1792
Switzerland	41	20	9	29	1902
UK	39	25	8	33	1778**
USA	40	10***	11	21	1920

Source: Engineering Employers' Federation, October 1986.

*Net annual working hours	=	365 days
minus Saturdays and Sundays		104
	=	261
minus total holidays		33
	=	228 days
divided by 5 working days/week	=	45.6 weeks
multiplied by 39 hours/week	=	1778.4

** Non-manual = 1710 hours.

*** General basic entitlement. Some company agreements provide for additional holidays related to service, etc.

CHRONOLOGY OF THE DISPUTE

12 February 1979	Confed presents claim
June	EEF first offer rejects SWW claim
July	Confed reaffirms demand for SWW in 1979
10 July	Negotiations break down; Confed imposes national overtime ban and decides on series of intermittent one-day stoppages
6 August	First one-day stoppage
August	Confed AGM decides on two-day stoppages
3/4 September	First two-day stoppage
10/11 September	Second two-day stoppage
17 September	ACAS brings both sides together
17/18 September	Third two-day stoppage

24/25 September	Fourth two-day stoppage
1/2 October	Final two-day stoppage
5 October	Gatwick Agreement settles dispute

WHO'S WHO IN THE DISPUTE

Boyd, John (Sir)	General Secretary, AUEW
Duffy, Terry	President, AUEW
Frodsham, Anthony	Director General, EEF
Rebhan, Herman	General Secretary, International Metalworkers' Federation
Hawkings, Geoffrey (Sir)	President, EEF

REFERENCES

1 Terry Duffy, quoted in *The Guardian*, 5 October 1979.

2 Herman Rebhan, quoted in *The Financial Times*, 6 October 1979.

3 Anthony Frodsham, quoted in *The Financial Times*, 8 October 1979.

4 Sir Geoffrey Hawkings, quoted in *The Financial Times*, 5 October 1979.

5 *The Financial Times*, 5 October 1979.

6 Wilensky, quoted by William Ashworth: *An Economic History of England, 1870–1939*, Methuen, London, 1960, p. 204.

7 Peter Matthias: *The First Industrial Nation*, Methuen, London, 1969, p. 201.

8 William Ashworth: *An Economic History of England, 1870–1939*, Methuen, London, 1960, p. 204.

9 Peter Matthias: *The First Industrial Nation*, Methuen, London, p. 253.

10 See B. C. Roberts: *Centenary History of the TUC*, TUC, London, 1968.

11 Peter N. Stearns: *Lives of Labour: Work in a Maturing Industrial Society*, Croom Helm, London, 1975, p. 241 et seq.

12 Tom Mann's pamphlet had a much more significant influence than its circulation might suggest. See B. C. Roberts: *Centenary History of the TUC*, TUC, London, 1968.

13 See Eric Wigham: *The Power to Manage: A History of the Engineering Employers' Association*, Macmillan, London, 1973.

14 Peter N. Stearns: *Lives of Labour: Work in a Maturing Industrial Society*, Croom Helm, London, 1975, p. 253.

15 Peter N. Stearns: *Lives of Labour: Work in a Maturing Industrial Society*, Croom Helm, London, 1975, p. 249.

16 Harry McShane: 'Introduction to Glasgow, 1919', quoted by R. A. Leeson: *Strike: A Live History, 1887–1971*, 1973.

17 Sam Brittan: 'The bogus hours battle of the coelacanths', *The Financial Times*, 4 October 1979.

18 James E. Mortimer: *A History of the Boilermakers Society*, Allen & Unwin, London, 1982, Vol. 2, p. 260.

19 Confederation of British Industry: unpublished report, February 1979.

20   Engineering Employers' Federation: *Guidelines on Collective Bargaining and Response to Industrial Action*, March 1979.

21   Terry Duffy, quoted in the *The Financial Times*, 17 September 1979.

22   *The Financial Times*, 14 September 1979.

23   The Confed, quoted in *The Financial Times*, 17 September 1979.

24   *The Guardian*, 17 September 1979.

25   Engineering Employers' Federation, quoted in *The Financial Times*, 20 September 1979.

26   David Brown: Managing Director of D. J. Brown Engineering, quoted in *The Financial Times*, 28 September 1979.

27   Sir Arnold Weinstock, quoted in *The Financial Times*, 28 September 1979.

28   Sir John Boyd: *AUEW Journal*, December 1979.

29   *The Financial Times*, 3 October 1979.

30   *The Guardian*, 4 October 1979.

31   *The Financial Times*, 4 October 1979.

32   Anthony Frodsham, letter in *The Financial Times*, 15 November 1979.

33   See Ford National Joint Negotiating Committee (Trade Union Side) Claims to Ford Motor Company Limited for Shorter Working Week, 1977 and 1978.

34   Terry Duffy in April 1979, quoted by Rosemary Collins: 'Trouble — by two votes', *The Guardian*, 17 September 1979.

35   Engineering Employers' Federation: Circular Letter No. 387, 12 October 1979.

36   Engineering Employers' Federation: 'Whose victory?', *EEF News*, October 1979.

37   *The Financial Times*, 6 October 1979.

38   Herman Rebhan, quoted in *The Financial Times*, 6 October 1979.

39   *The Guardian*, 6 October 1979.

40   *The Observer*, 7 October 1979.

41   Trades Union Congress: *Employment and Technology*, Report by the TUC General Council to the 1979 Congress, TUC Publication, September 1979.

42   Confederation of British Industry: *Jobs — Facing the Future*, January 1980.

43   Report on Engineering Productivity, quoted in *The Times*, 21 May 1980.

44   The engineering and shipbuilding industries were amongst the worst hit by the recession of the later 1970s and early 1980s. For full statistics, see *Annual Survey of Employment and Unemployment*, in Department of Employment Gazette, 1979–80;

45   *The Financial Times*, 28 July 1986.

46   *The Financial Times*, 23 June 1987.

STUDY QUESTIONS

1.   Summarize the arguments for and against shorter working time as a method of creating jobs and reducing unemployment.

2.   What are the costs and benefits of overtime working to the parties involved?

3.   'A short sharp strike is a good safety valve. But long strikes are of no use to union or nation.' (Terry Duffy) Discuss.

4.   To what extent has the decline in the British engineering industry been brought about by poor industrial relations?

5. Make a critical review of the strategic and tactical choices available to both sides during the national engineering industry dispute, 1979.
6. Summarize the case to be made by (a) the unions in the Confed and (b) the employers in the EEF when negotiating further reductions in the length of the working week.

SUGGESTIONS FOR FURTHER READING

John Atkinson: *Work Organization and Working Time*, Institute of Manpower Studies, London, 1985.

Eugene Consijn: 'European patterns in working time', *Personnel Management*, Vol. 7, No. 7, September 1985.

Trades Union Congress: *Employment and Technology*, Report by TUC General Council, 1979.

Trades Union Congress: *Campaign for Reduced Working Time: Objectives and Guidelines for Trade Union Negotiations, 1984–85 Pay Round*, TUC, London, October 1984.

John Hughes: 'Shiftwork and the shorter working week: two ways to make jobs', *Personnel Management*, Vol. 9, No. 5, May 1977.

Eric Wigham: *The Power to Manage: A History of the Engineering Employers' Association*, Macmillan, London, 1973.

CHAPTER 7

■ Crisis in product and labour markets —

THE NATIONAL STEEL STRIKE, 1980

> *Sir Keith (Joseph) told an industrial correspondents' lunch that the unions were the main threat to employment if they do not heed the danger of pricing themselves and their mates out of jobs. That is what is going to happen.*
>
> The Times
> December 1979

> *We have never failed to recognize and face up to the realities of new technology, declining markets, booms and slumps; and we have never reneged on an agreement to which we are party and which was tailored to overcome the industry's problems.*
>
> Steelworkers' Banner No. 5
> Iron and Steel Trades Confederation

INTRODUCTION: THE END OF AN ERA IN BRITISH STEEL

On 7 December 1979, the Executive Committee of the Iron and Steel Trades Confederation (ISTC), the biggest union in the British steel industry, issued an all-out strike call to its 80 000 members, employed by the British Steel Corporation (BSC) in over one hundred publicly-owned iron and steel plants across the country. By calling the first national steel strike for more than 70 years, the union not only shattered the industry's proud record of 'good industrial relations': it triggered a 13-week strike which was to transform the industry and its industrial relations. British steel had come to the end of an era.

Over the years, there had been many small local strikes in the industry, but there had not been a national industry-wide stoppage of work since the General Strike of 1926, and that had lasted only a few days. What, then, was the nature of the crisis that provoked the leadership of this traditionally moderate union to call an all-out strike in an industry where both management and unions took special pride in their harmonious working relationships?

Three months earlier, in September 1979, the steel unions had presented their annual wage claim in the usual manner. In December, the BSC rejected the wage claim outright and launched a major proposal to change the industry's long-established system of collective bargaining. Before the unions had time to recover, the BSC delivered a second, more devastating, blow by announcing plans to close all its inefficient and unprofitable plants in 1980, with the loss of some 50 000 jobs.

Britain's steel workers were never industrial firebrands. Their leaders were not militants but gritty pragmatists and responsible bargainers. They were certainly not spoiling for a confrontation with the BSC or the government. With the industry in sharp recession, they had probably not expected their 1979 wage claim to be met in full without some tough negotiations, but they were determined to do their best for their members and felt entitled to expect some flexibility in the BSC's bargaining position. The zero wage offer was therefore seen as both derisory and inflammatory, but it was the BSC's announcement on plant closures and job losses that led the ISTC Executive to take its fateful strike decision. Nothing in British steel would ever be quite the same again.

SECTION 1: THE DECLINE IN BRITAIN'S INDUSTRIAL COMPETITIVENESS

The success of Britain's first industrial revolution — the model for the industrializing world of the second half of the nineteenth century — was largely due to the pioneering achievements of its self-educated technical innovators in the iron and steel industry. In earlier times, the demand for iron and steel was limited by production being geared mainly towards local markets. By the third quarter of the eighteenth century, when Abraham Darby successfully replaced charcoal with coking coal for iron-smelting in Coalbrookdale, Shropshire, the iron and steel industry began its first great period of expansion.

By the early nineteenth century, British engineers had harnessed new sources of power to produce new materials for a new age — the age of coal, iron and steel. In their search for cheaper, stronger, more durable construction materials, they perfected the mining, smelting, refining and shaping of metals of every kind, but especially iron and steel, bronze and brass. At the turn of the century, important engineering or shipbuilding centres had been established on new coalfield sites in the Midlands, in Scotland and South Wales, in Sheffield and on the North-East coast. During the Napoleonic Wars (1800–1815), engineering came of age. The lessons of wartime production — the design, testing and mass production of standardized components for reliable guns — were applied to the booming post-war economy of Europe. From Britain's improved and enlarged foundries, forges and rolling mills, streamed an endless flow of metal goods that were to make Britain 'the workshop of the world'.

By mid-century, Britain was the world's leading manufacturing and exporting nation. The Great Exhibition of 1851 served as a brilliant showcase for an unprecedented range of well-designed, high quality and, above all, low-cost engineering products. Britain's reputation as the source of value-for-money metal manufactures laid the foundation for almost a century of national prosperity, which lasted until the First World War.

In 1900, Britain still dominated international markets with over 30% of all trade in manufactured goods. France, Germany and the United States had made substantial strides towards industrialization, but largely for home consumption. After 1900, and despite the ravages of two World Wars, Germany held its export share over the next 80 years, whilst Britain's share dropped to 15% by 1960 and to only 8% by 1982. Conversely, the volume of goods imported into Britain gradually rose after the Second World War and has more than trebled in the last 20 years. With the accelerated decline of its manufacturing industry since 1980, Britain now imports as many manufactured goods as she exports.

> *British industry produced 60% more in 1939 than in 1914, 100% more by 1950, 250% more by 1970. These increases brought a better standard of living and higher real earnings, more government services and improved working conditions. But when set against the progress of other countries, the record has not been impressive. In the 1920s Britain failed to match growth in Europe and North America. In the 1930s she performed better, with the help of [trade] tariffs. During the 1950s and 1960s the gap widened. Britain's economy was growing at 2% a year, that of West Germany at 6%, France at 5%, Japan at 7%. Productivity was certainly rising, but far more slowly than in other countries. As a result, many British goods became less competitive, and there was less to spend on re-equipment, which in turn left [Britain's] productivity further behind.* [1]

How is this decline in Britain's industrial competitiveness to be explained? One school of thought stresses the class divisions in British society, which continue to produce social attitudes that breed poor industrial relations, inefficiency and resistance to change. Another school points to an elitist education system, which fails to produce sufficient scientists, engineers and professionally-trained managers; yet another school concentrates on the failure of public policy to tackle the structure of British industry and the lack of consistent investment in new high technology.

Whichever explanations we favour, there appears to be nothing novel in Britain's continuing economic decline. Dahrendorf dates it from as far back as the end of the last century, certainly from the end of the First World War. [2] The iron and steel industry provides an excellent illustration of the nature and extent of this national decline.

Before 1900, Britain was the world's leading producer of iron and steel and its leading creditor nation. Britain remained a world creditor until 1939. After 1945, with the loss of empire, she became a net debtor, overtaken by the United States and later by the reconstructed and revitalized German and Japanese economies. Steel production was an index of domestic prosperity, economic self-confidence and international prestige. After 1900, Britain's steel industry was overtaken, first by that of the United States and then by that of Germany, due to a combination of lower production costs and the economic protection of trade tariffs.

The economic health of newly-industrialized nations of the twentieth century has often been judged by their consumption of steel: 'As steel goes, so goes the nation' — for steel is the key to the vital construction industry and source of the most important raw material for producer goods (e.g. machine-tools and other engineering equipment) and domestic consumer goods (e.g. motor cars, refrigerators, dishwashers and washing machines). Significant investment in steel may produce a major 'multiplier effect', creating jobs and generating incomes throughout the national economy. Conversely, any downturn in business confidence is likely to make itself felt first in the steel industry.

The very fact that Britain pioneered the first industrial revolution of the eighteenth century meant that the growth of its iron and steel industry was completely unplanned, with widely-scattered, small, uneconomic units, based on local iron-ore and coal deposits. The need for a more rational industrial structure was widely recognized:

> At the war's end [1918], a government inquiry recommended a 'radical reconstruction' of the old iron and steel industry. What was needed, as a matter of great national importance, were 'large and well-designed new units for cheap production upon modern lines', and they had to be on new sites and close to raw materials and transport, with space to develop. It was only the first of many such calls to rebuild the industry, for an end to hallowed traditions and old-fashioned methods, and it provided the central theme in the story of steel. [3]

Throughout the interwar period, competition between steelmakers was intense but, despite some mergers in the 1920s, most production was from small units, which lacked the economic advantages of integration. British steelmakers recognized the need for investment and modernization but complained that they lacked the necessary capital to carry it out without government financial support. As a result, British steelworks were smaller in scale and less efficient than those of the United States or of the reconstructed Germany industry. In an industry characterized by heat, noise, dirt and heavy physical work, conditions were made even worse by the retention of outdated plant and equipment. British steelmakers spent much less on research and development than their foreign competitors but they displayed particular pride in the close, cooperative working relationships between steelmasters and men:

> *Traditionally, labour relations in the steel industry had been good and wages high. There was a well-established conciliation procedure. Pay was linked to the price of steel on a sliding scale. In the 1920s a blast furnaceman could be on £3 a week, three times what a farm labourer would get. Strikes were almost unknown, and even the General Strike in 1926 met with a mixed reception in the steelworks. Managers complained, in a rather general fashion, about restriction of output, and about the number of trade unions who represented the various crafts. But they accepted the rigid divisions and hierarchies, and many of the steel bosses were liked and respected.* [4]

During the economic recession of the late 1920s, steel output was severely reduced, with unemployment running at 25%. By 1931, with steel output halved, some 90 000 steelworkers were on the dole. In South Wales only one blast furnace out of 22 was still working and in Scotland only one out of 89. When the older, least profitable works closed down, unemployment in parts of South Wales reached 73%. By 1932, almost half of the workers in heavy iron and steel were without work. In response to foreign competition, British steelmakers pleaded with government to reintroduce the tariff protection of the 1920s. Despite some forced amalgamations, twenty separate major steel companies survived into the late 1930s. In an attempt to raise efficiency, the government commissioned American consultants who recommended a regrouping and concentration of the industry into five or six key plants. In return for the industry's pledge to reorganize and modernize itself under the self-regulation of a newly-formed Iron and Steel Federation, the government imposed a 33% tariff on imported iron and steel products. But although efficiency increased, employment in the industry remained severely depressed until it began to rise in the late 1930s with the call for rearmament:

> *Although many steelworks were modernized, and working conditions improved as a result, the most radical solutions were put aside again. Most development was 'patched in', to extend the life of existing plants, wherever they might be. 'Relocation' for the sake of the future, on entirely new sites, usually threatened the interests of existing steel companies who felt there was too much capacity anyway.* [5]

Throughout this period the steel unions came out strongly for the nationalization of the industry, arguing that centralized planning and the major investment that the industry required to raise its overall efficiency could only be achieved by public ownership, to replace the greed, inefficiency and neglect of the private owners.

During the Second World War, the industry's obsolete plant and equipment was driven to breaking point. In the post-war decade, the unprecedented demand for steel of every kind clearly pointed to the need for modernization and rationalization. The industry was quickly identified as being amongst the 'commanding heights of the economy', which the incoming Attlee Government was committed to take into public ownership, but iron and steel took second place to the coal-mines, railways, gas, water and electricity. Yet, in the words of the Cabinet Minister responsible for steel nationalization in 1948:

> *The steel industry was in a bad way. It was disorganized. It consisted of a large number of independent and warring units, no coordination, no effort to ensure that the work was done in the most efficient plant. Something more drastic we felt had to be done to make this industry really efficient and to meet the national needs.* [6]

Labour's plans for steel nationalization provoked the most bitter political controversy of the Attlee administration. The steel masters organized a fierce campaign of resistance, which precipitated a constitutional battle to curtail the delaying power of the House of Lords. Speaking against the nationalization Bill in the House of Commons, Winston Churchill cited the industry's good record on industrial relations as a further reason for leaving it in private hands:

> *There has been no serious dispute or stoppage between the employers and the employed during this tumultuous century. It has been one of the islands of peace and progress in the wrack and ruin of our time. Yet this same steel industry is the one which the Socialist government has selected for the utmost exercise of its malice.* [7]

Within fifteen months of the industry's nationalization in 1951, the first post-war Conservative Government was in power, pledged to the industry's denationalization. The Labour Government's Iron and Steel Corporation was replaced in 1953 by an Iron and Steel Board to supervise the industry. Capacity expanded rapidly from 11 million tons at the end of the war to 27 million tons by the early 1960s:

> *Many of the targets had been met — greater fuel economy, larger blast furnaces and mills. But, as in the 1930s there were limits to what the steel industry would do of its own accord. Nothing like the relocation and expansion, that had been advocated before the war, was achieved. Instead, there was more grafting of the new onto the old.* [8]

The most spectacular of these post-war developments was the Abbey Works in Port Talbot, South Wales. To meet the increased demand for flat-rolled steel sheet for consumer durables, a new fast rolling mill was commissioned in 1951 by squeezing the new development onto an existing overcrowded site. As a result, many of the traditional labour practices and manning levels were transferred from the old works to the new. In the words of one senior manager:

> It was a very good time for the steel industry. They had no problems selling their steel. Growth was high. So the great thing to do was to make a profit. As the labour cost per ton was comparatively small, somewhere in the region of 17 to 20 per cent, I think the very top management felt it was not worth closing the plant to make your point, or to hold out against a strike, because this would destroy far more profits than they could see it fulfilling. [9]

This failure by top management to tackle the underlying industrial relations issues of the industry led to gross overmanning, the toleration of traditional restrictive labour practices and wage levels that reflected the overall inefficiency and self-indulgence of the post-war industry. In 1950, British iron and steel plants employed some 300 000 workers. By 1960, that number had risen by 30 000, despite new investment and the introduction of new, supposedly labour-saving equipment. Steel output continued to increase but steel costs rose because productivity failed to keep pace with rising labour costs.

In 1957, a genuine opportunity presented itself for a complete break with the past. The continued demand for sheet steel led to plans for the construction of a new, fully-integrated, high-technology steelworks on a greenfield site, close to deep-water docking facilities for imported iron-ore, with the full economies of large-scale, high-speed production. There was only one site that met all these criteria — Llanwern, near Newport, in South Wales — but the Macmillan Government fudged the issue by splitting the new investment between Llanwern and Ravenscraig in Scotland, simply to placate local interests.

The return of a Labour Government in 1964, pledged to re-nationalize the industry, produced further frustrating delays in modernization and rationalization. The British Steel Corportion (BSC), set up in 1967 with the responsibility for managing the re-nationalized industry, began well by restructuring the industry into new product divisions under strong local management. But it still faced one traditional British problem: How to raise the overall productivity of a poorly-located, under-invested, under-equipped industry, steeped in traditional labour practices, saddled with an outdated, historical structure — all in the teeth of intense foreign competition? In Japan, for example, where steel output had increased tenfold since 1945, output per man employed was roughly three times that in Britain, thanks to large, modern, integrated steelworks, each with an annual capacity of more than 6 million tons, compared with only one works in Britain — Llanwern — with an annual capacity of 3 million tons.

If there was to be any future for British steel, the BSC clearly had a battle with the unions on its hands over rationalization, productivity and demanning — a battle likely to be more complex and more fiercely fought because the BSC faced a deeply-divided workforce, represented by some twenty different unions, the most important of which are shown in Table 7.1.

Table 7.1. Major unions in the British iron and steel industry, 1979–80

1. Iron and Steel Trades Confederation (ISTC)
2. National Union of Blastfurnacemen (NUB)
3. Transport and General Workers Union (TGWU)
4. General and Municipal Workers Union
   (GMWU — now GMBATU)
5. Union of Construction Allied Trades and Technicians (UCATT)
6. National Craftsmen's Coordinating Committee representing craft maintenance unions including:
   (a) Amalgamated Union of Engineering Workers — Engineering Section (AUEW)
   (b) Electrical, Electronic, Plumbing and Telecommunications Union (EEPTU)
   (c) Amalgamated Society of Boilermakers, Shipwrights, Blacksmiths and Structural Workers (ASBSBSW)
   (d) National Union of Sheet Metal Workers, Coppersmiths, Heating and Domestic Engineers (NUSMWCHDE)

By the early 1970s, the BSC had devised a strategy for tackling its long-neglected and intertwined problems of underinvestment, low productivity, concealed overmanning and poor utilization of labour. That strategy derived from the BSC's analysis of the state of industrial relations in the industry, based on five major factors:

(i)   overfragmented representation of manual and staff employees amongst too many unions;
(ii) a long-established system of joint consultation, rounded off in the 1970s with an experimental Worker–Director scheme of industrial democracy, which had not been a conspicuous success;
(iii) an excessively complex, multi-tiered hourly-paid wage structure requiring complete overhaul and modernization;
(iv) historically-based but currently indefensible differentials in the terms and conditions of employment as between staff and hourly-paid employees;
(v)   a catalogue of poor industrial relations including: much higher manning levels than comparable foreign plants; unsystematic

work organization; frequent labour disputes; high absenteeism; low outputs.

The BSC's two-pronged strategy for overcoming these multiple handicaps to efficient operations was deceptively simple:

(i)   the devolution of pay bargaining from the traditional pattern of national industry-wide negotiations to local plant bargaining, with greater scope for local union involvement and local management initiative;

(ii) the phased implementation of productivity improvement policies designed to achieve a significant increase in plant performance, with increased employee participation in plant-level decision-making and some kind of performance or demanning bonus where proven labour productivity improvements were obtained.

With these clear objectives, the BSC strategists set in train a series of consultative discussions in 1977, aimed at securing agreement in principle with the steel unions on what needed to be done to change the traditional machinery of collective bargaining and an outmoded wage structure. Whether this proposed restructuring would have produced the desired reforms remains an open question. For, like many other well-intentioned initiatives taken by British management, the plan came too late, was overtaken by events and was therefore never implemented.

This persistent failure of top management in British iron and steel to overcome its historical legacy by taking a firm grip on the industry and forcing it 'through the iron gates of life' into the twenty-first century was symptomatic of much that was wrong with the British economy. Iron and steel symbolized and exemplified the decline in Britain's industrial competitiveness in the second half of the twentieth century. It therefore raises general issues of most profound importance for economic development, which can only be touched on briefly here:

(i)   What special combination of economic, social, political and psychological factors ensure the continuing economic growth, social development and political stability of a nation? What impedes an economy's capacity to respond effectively to economic and political changes in the wider world? The Netherlands, Spain and Portugal were once amongst the world's leading trading nations. Is Britain destined for a similar fate?

(ii) What should government do to secure an appropriate cultural environment, supportive of innovation, high investment, high productivity and sustained economic growth, to facilitate continuing economic success? Throughout the post-war period, both Labour and Conservative Governments had paid lip service to securing such an environment. Yet the British economy has continued to decline. By 1987, Italy had overtaken Britain in the international league table of national income.

(iii)   What responsibility rests on management and unions for tackling the fundamental labour and productivity problems underlying the performance of their own industries? Why has Britain not succeeded in generating and sustaining that essential minimum framework of cooperation required to weather the storms of technological advance and economic restructuring? Steel was no doubt a special case, but it was certainly not unique or untypical of Britain's failure to manage its industrial economy through a period of rapid change.

SECTION 2: THE NATIONAL STEEL STRIKE, 1980

(1) The pre-dispute context

By the mid-1970s, the BSC's top management faced a major crisis in the industry's product and labour markets, derived from a combination of five underlying problems:

(i) **Surplus production capacity.**   Following thirty years of post-war prosperity, the western world's steel producers were struck a double blow in the mid-1970s:

(a)   a grossly excessive world iron and steelworking capacity, attributable to high and sustained capital investment by the advanced steel-producing economies, with the exception of Britain;
(b)   an overproduction crisis, brought about by a collapse in world demand for steel in the construction, shipbuilding and engineering industries following the most severe international economic recession to hit the capitalist world since the Wall Street collapse of 1929.

(ii) **Lack of sustained investment.**   The renationalized British Steel Corporation (BSC) was not a market-oriented corporation but a politically-inspired social institution required to operate in the harshly competitive economic climate of the 1970s. Throughout its post-war history, British Steel lacked the political backing required to undertake a radical and effective modernization and rationalization programme. Improved efficiency was long overdue but rationalization was postponed by successive governments because it was electorally unpopular and so bound to cause severe political embarrassment to the government of the day. British Steel suffered more than any other publicly-owned corporation from the worst type of political interference in its long-term development planning. Throughout the 1960s and early 1970s, the BSC failed to convince both Labour and Conservative governments to implement the massive modernization and re-investment programme, essential to enable it to compete successfully against the world's intensely competitive steel producers.

(iii) **Technological backwardness.**   The rate of technical change in ferrous metallurgy had left Britain's post-war steel industry far behind those of its foreign competitors and acutely vulnerable in terms of high production costs. In a limited number of areas (e.g. sintering; high top-pressure working of blast furnaces; top-blown LD oxygen steel-making; continuous casting; and high-speed rolling) the BSC had begun to invest in the latest technology in the 1960s, but it was too little and it came too late — a perennial feature of Britain's investment record in the previous one hundred years.

(iv) **Uneconomic dispersion of production.** By 1978, Britain's steelmaking capacity remained fragmented and scattered amongst 105 UK sites, with the heaviest concentrations in Scotland, the North-East, North and South Wales and a number of small but important sites in the Midlands. In the mid-1970s, the BSC had forecast that by 1980 it would need only eight of the twenty-two blast furnaces operating in five or six of its one hundred sites. The social consequences for workers in the doomed plants were likely to be devastating amongst steel communities that had suffered the worst effects of the inter-war depression only thirty years earlier.

(v) **Poor labour productivity.** The Benson Report of 1966, commissioned by the independent steel companies on the eve of rena-tionalization [10], forecast that the industry's labour force could fall by one-third during the proposed rationalization of 1965–75. Four years later, the BSC presented the incoming Heath Conservative Government with its first Business Proposal. This envisaged a 10-year phased reduction of the BSC's total workforce from 259 000 in 1970 to 167 000 by 1980 — a reduction of some 92 000 jobs or 40% of the workforce.

In February 1973, the BSC announced a revised Ten-Year Development Strategy [11] with three principal objectives:

(i)   concentration of steel production within five or six of the BSC's high-productivity plants;
(ii) a reduction in steelmaking capacity from 50/55 to 36/38 million metric tonnes by 1983;
(iii) closure of all old, obsolescent or loss-making plants by 1980.

The unions' immediate response to the Ten-Year Strategy was hardly enthusiastic but it was certainly not obstructive. The steel unions cooperated with the TUC in setting up the TUC Iron and Steel Industry Committee (TUCISC) in 1967, to monitor the rationalization plan and to assist the unions in coping with the worst effects of its implementation. The TUCISC was given the power to consult and negotiate with the BSC on behalf of these unions on all matters affecting working conditions in the industry (e.g. manning levels, hours, holidays, sick pay and pensions) *other than pay*, which was left for autonomous negotiation by the individual unions and the BSC. In the early 1970s, when a fully-extended economy offered reasonable prospects of alternative jobs for displaced steelworkers, the unions and the TUC had been willing to cooperate in the BSC's plan for a phased reduction of its workforce. Even as late as 1973, alternative job prospects still seemed reasonable.

In 1974, the incoming Wilson Government asked Lord Beswick, a former Labour Cabinet Minister, to review the BSC's proposed closure programme. This Steel Closure Review, whose Interim Report was published in 1975 [12], recommended the deferment of many closures and called for more generous redundancy compensation when the plants were eventually forced to close. But by 1975, the international steel market had begun to collapse, shortly followed by much of Britain's manufacturing industry. The ensuing economic crisis compelled the Callaghan Labour Government to seek financial aid from the International Monetary Fund, whose help was forthcoming only on condition that the government stopped further subsidization of loss-making public enterprises. What began as a trickle of job losses in the steel industry of the mid-1970s soon turned into the haemorrhage of the late 1970s, as shown in Table 7.2.

Table 7.2. Plant closures under the BSC's 10-Year Strategy, 1970–80

Plant	Date of closure
1. Clyde Ironworks	Late 1977
2. Hartlepool Steelworks	End 1977
3. East Moors (Cardiff)	March/April 1978
4. Ebbw Vale Iron and Steelworks	March/April 1978
5. Glengarnock Iron Works	1978
6. Shelton Iron Works	June 1978
7. Bilston Ironworks	1979
8. Consett Iron and Steelworks	1979
9. Corby Iron and Steel Works	1979
10. Shotton Iron and Steel Works	1979
11. Cleveland Ironworks	1979

Source: Martin Upham: 'The British Steel Corporation: retrospect and prospect', *Industrial Relations Journal*, Vol. 11, No. 3, 1980.

In 1970, the BSC employed a total of 259 450, of whom roughly 75% were engaged in manual iron- and steelmaking and related operations, the remaining 25% in white-collar jobs throughout the industry. By 1979, the total number of employees had been reduced by some 75 000 — mostly manual workers — leaving the proportion of staff at around 30%, as shown in Table 7.3.

It was in this context and against this background of savage cut-backs and the consequent death of entire steel communities like Corby, Shotton, Ebbw Vale and Consett that the ensuing national steel dispute must be seen.

Table 7.3. BSC employment in iron and steel activities, 1970–79

Year	Total BSC employees (thousands)	White-collar staff (% of total employees)
1970	259	26
1971	240	27
1972	229	27
1973	226	27
1974	222	28
1975	220	30
1976	210	29
1977	206	29
1978	190	30
1979	184	30

Source: Bamber: *Employee Relations*, Vol. 6, No. 1, 1984.

(2) The challenge

On 25 September 1979, the steel unions' Joint Central Negotiating Committee (JCNC), representing some 100 000 production workers, presented the BSC with a pay claim that was ambitious but not wildly extravagant. It called for a 20% increase in basic rates at a time when inflation was running at more than 17% p.a. and when steelworkers' take-home pay had been held back by successive phases of government incomes policy. Morale amongst the unions' membership was low due to a new sense of insecurity, engendered by the BSC's long-term plans to close inefficient steelworks with consequential heavy job losses.

The leading production workers' union, the ISTC, argued that, between 1975 and 1979, its members' basic pay had fallen seriously behind that of their traditional comparators — miners, dockers, newspaper printers and other high-paid manual workers. The annual percentage increase in steelworkers' pay had fluctuated since 1975 from 15% under Phase I of the Social Contract (1976) to 5% under Phase II (1977) and to 10% under Phase III (1978). The ISTC therefore set what it saw as a 'realistic negotiating target' of a 20% increase on basic rates in 1979 to restore its members' earnings to the 1975 level.

On 3 December, the BSC gave its considered reply to the claim. Dr David Grieves, Managing Director of Personnel and Social Policy, made clear that the Conservative Government's policy of cash limits on nationalized industries meant that, in future, the only allowable pay increases would be those that were self-financing, i.e. fully justified by a corresponding increase in productivity. Furthermore, the BSC had decided that any such increase would have to be negotiated separately at each of the BSC plants around the country and not, as hitherto, collectively around the steel industry's national bargaining table:

> *The main plank of our offer is that we should depart from the traditional approach of a national pay award and reach an enabling agreement to allow works or a division to earn local increases of up to a further 10% where these could be justified by improved financial performance.* [13]

Dr Grieves made it clear that, although the BSC had no new money to put on the table, it would honour an earlier undertaking to consolidate into basic pay rates an existing 5% pay supplement, agreed under previous incomes policy. Apart from that consolidation, worth roughly 2% p.a., the reply to the general pay claim was 'Nil'. In the words of Dr Grieves: 'The cupboard is bare'. [14]

The BSC's rejection of the claim was perceived by the unions at both national and local level as brutally and uncharacteristically harsh. According to Bill Sirs, General Secretary of the ISTC and chief union side negotiator: 'The claim was rejected outright by BSC with no offer forthcoming'. [15] Since the BSC's response was so out of keeping with its normal bargaining style, the iron hand of government was detected behind the BSC's normally velvet glove.

Dr Grieves' stark revelation that the BSC was virtually bankrupt may well have shaken union leaders, but within three days came a second devastating bombshell. On 6 December 1979, the BSC announced plans to halt the industry's mounting financial losses and to break even in 1980. To meet growing international competition and the slump in world steel demand, the BSC intended to mount a three-pronged attack on inefficiency and overmanning:

(i) a reduction in steel output of 25% from 20 million to 15 million tons in 1980;
(ii) the closure of all inefficient and loss-making plants as soon as possible;
(iii) a reduction in manpower of some 30% from 150 000 to 100 000 in 1980.

To save the industry from total destruction, the BSC invited the steel unions to cooperate in securing these objectives of concentrating production on the five high-technology plants where productivity compared favourably with that of foreign competitors.

(3) Initial responses

The ISTC Executive met on the following day, 7 December, to take its fateful strike decision — an unambiguous response to the double humiliation of its rejected pay claim and the massive threat to jobs. Sirs felt personally humiliated by the ferocity of the BSC's counter-offensive:

They are trying to make us look small and we have no intention of accepting it . . . It is important for us to cripple the industry as quickly as we can and get it over as quickly as we can. [16]

The ISTC called on its members in all the BSC plants to stop work on 2 January, thereby honouring to the letter its obligations under the industry's long-standing disputes procedure. In effect, the union was giving the BSC three weeks' strike notice in which to withdraw its zero wage offer and to begin negotiating before the die was cast. There was still time to avert disaster.

When Bill Sirs and Len Murray, TUC General Secretary, met the Industry Secretary, Sir Keith Joseph, on 16 December 1979 to put the unions' case, Sir Keith simply repeated the Thatcher Cabinet's policy: no further government financial aid would be forthcoming for the steel industry. But when steel union leaders and Murray met the BSC on 21 December, the Corporation shifted away from its initial bargaining position by making a second offer, worth a further 3% increase in basic rates, on top of the existing 2% offer, *provided* that the unions were willing:

(i)   to scrap the industry's long-standing Guaranteed Week Agreement (GWA), which provided that steelworkers would not be laid off without pay without prior notice;

(ii)   to accept the BSC's right to bring in non-unionized contract labour at the same time as it reduced the size of its permanent unionized workforce.

The production unions rejected the offer outright and the National Union of Blastfurnacemen (NUB) decided to throw in its lot with the ISTC, giving the BSC formal notice of all-out strike action from 2 January.

On 28 December, the BSC came forward with a third, so-called 'final' offer of 6% on basic rates plus a plant productivity bonus, together with an unexpected offer to reduce the length of the working week by one hour. Sirs described this improved offer to his members as follows:

2% consolidation, plus 4% with strings (surrender of the Guaranteed Week Agreement, plus unlimited bonus from local demanning deals, plus talks on a 39-hour week). This definitely was to be their final offer. ISTC negotiators rejected it. [17]

The timing of the BSC's third and 'final' offer on 28 December could hardly have been worse. On the same day, the National Coal Board offered the miners — with whom the steel unions regularly compared data on performance and pay — a straight 20% increase on basic rates, without productivity strings of any kind. When the miners voted to accept this offer, despite the NUM Executive's advice to their members to reject it, and when the government greeted their decision as evidence of success in its campaign to bring home to workers 'the realities of economic life', the steel unions took off their gloves and began to fight in earnest.

(4) Consequences

For many observers, Bill Sirs personified 'the acceptable face' of British trade unionism. He was frequently in the limelight on public policy issues and well known for his down-to-earth, no-nonsense approach to economic problems, his devotion to his union and its members, his early-morning jogging and his successful campaign to ban smoking at meetings of the General Council of the TUC. Sirs epitomized the quietly-spoken, pragmatic, centre-of-the-road trade unionist who had risen from the shopfloor to the top of his union, with a seat on the General Council of the TUC. He was by no means the darling of his union's left-wing, but when he called on his members for whole-hearted support for the strike, he certainly got it. On 2 January 1980, the strike was 100% effective. Virtually the whole of the publicly-owned British steel industry was forced to halt production. Unlike the proverbial phoenix, worldwide symbol of resurgence, the BSC would never again rise in splendour from the ashes of this dispute.

   Having never before led an all-out national strike and needing all the support he could muster, Sirs forged an immediate alliance with Hector Smith, General Secretary of the National Union of Blastfurnacemen, thereby uniting the two principal production unions. He then launched an effective publicity campaign to challenge the BSC's case. He appeared frequently on TV and radio, gave regular press interviews and took every opportunity to put across the union side's case. A popular union broadsheet *Steelworkers' Banner* was launched, which summarized the ISTC case under the heading *What We Want*:

(i)   *a settlement with the BSC on behalf of all our members which at least keeps us up with the cost of living (now rising at more than 17 per cent);*

(ii) *an enquiry into the blundering corporation management which has lost £1.4 billion in four years, tossed away more than 15 per cent of the home market for steel and now proposes to withdraw from export markets;*

(iii) *an end to the destruction of the industry by closures and redundancies which have claimed 26 000 jobs in two years and threaten 53 000 more;*

(iv) *the building of a viable integrated BSC not held to insane financial targets, not under pressure to hive off its more profitable parts, but which is capable of meeting the needs of British industry.* [18]

When the BSC attempted to defend and justify its closure policy, Sirs challenged the BSC's facts as well as their theories:

Some [of the plants closed in the past five years] were older, like the Open Hearth plants. Some were newer, like Corby which made steel by the B.O.S. (basic oxygen) route. BSC wants to close Consett which also has a B.O.S. plant. Twelve significant steel-making sites have now been shut. In the period March 1975 to November 1979 (less than five years) BSC shed about 30 000 jobs (not 22 000). 13 000 more are marked down at Corby, Shotton and Cleveland. [18]

When the strike was seen to be 100% effective on 2 January, the TUCISC resumed its pre-Christmas pressure on the BSC and the government to secure a negotiated solution to the dispute. On 4 January, the TUCISC made its first counter-proposal, calling on the BSC to increase its offer of 2% by a further 6%, to give steelworkers a total increase of 8% in basic rates, plus a further 3% guaranteed bonus from local demanning agreements, plus a further 1% lump sum bonus as a lead-in payment or 'pump-priming operation'. The Corporation rejected this counter-proposal outright.

On 7 January, undeterred by the BSC's rebuff, the TUCISC was back with a second counter-proposal, which called for a general increase of 8% on basic rates, plus a further 5% 'lead-in payment' towards local productivity agreements, totalling 13%, plus talks on a shorter working week with effect from 1 January 1981.

Once again the BSC rejected the TUCISC's peace formula but this time came back with a fourth offer worth 12% – namely, an 8% increase in basic rates without any productivity conditions attached, plus a 4% bonus from local demanning agreements. This was later increased to 13% (viz. 9% plus 4%) without commitment to a shorter working week or a 5% guaranteed lead-in payment as sought by the TUCISC.

On 8 January, this final offer by the BSC was rejected by the unions and negotiations were broken off. But the production unions were far from disheartened for the TGWU and the GMWU, with substantial but minority membership in the industry — together with the National Craftsmen's Coordinating Committee (NCCC), repre-senting several thousand maintenance and ancillary workers — threw their support behind the strike. The stoppage was now 100% solid, with every single one of the Corporation's 100 plants at a standstill and no union labour at work except for skeleton safety crews.

On 16 January, in the third week of the strike, the ISTC Executive Council decided to extend the strike from public sector BSC plants to its 1000 members in the private sector (i.e. non-nation-alized) steel plants with effect from 27 January.

On 25 January, having taking legal advice, the 16 private steel companies, all members of the British Iron and Steel Producers'

Association (BISPA), sought an injunction in the High Court to restrain the ISTC from involving its members in the strike action on the grounds that since there was no trade dispute between the Association and its employees, 'secondary action' (i.e. industrial action taken in support of a strike in another establishment) at BISPA plants was unlawful under the Employment Act 1980. The High Court ruled that the ISTC had acted legally throughout the dispute and refused to grant an injunction.

Next day, 26 January, the Master of the Rolls, Lord Denning, sitting as President of the Court of Appeal, reversed the High Court ruling by granting BISPA their injunction and refusing the ISTC leave to appeal to the House of Lords. Denning's judgement faced the ISTC's Executive Council with the most difficult decision of the entire dispute: whether to obey the law and withdraw its strike orders to members in the private steel plants; or to defy the injunction, thereby placing themselves in contempt of the High Court, with the risk of imprisonment for the union's principal officers and/or fines on the union until they had 'purged' their contempt.

On 29 January, the Executive Council chose discretion by deciding to obey the law as defined by Lord Denning. Next day, the relevant instructions were despatched to the branches by the union's Head Office in Gray's Inn Road, London, to give effect to the Denning Judgement.

Three days later, on 1 February, the ISTC scored a notable legal victory. By appealing directly to the House of Lords, over the head of Lord Denning, it secured a reversal of the Denning Judgement. [20] This enabled it once again to issue lawful instructions to its private sector members to withdraw their labour from 3 February. The overturning of Lord Denning's Judgement put fresh heart into the striking steelworkers but it also led Conservative MPs to put pressure on the Thatcher Government to tighten the law on secondary industrial action. On 8 February, having disposed of the legal issues, Bill Sirs and Hector Smith were invited to Bob Scholey, BSC's Chief Executive, to meet him privately to discuss a further improved pay offer. The union leaders were given to understand that the BSC proposed a new package deal worth 13% on current earnings, payable from the first day of resumed working, and comprising three elements:

(i)   a 7% increase in basic rates;
(ii)   a further 4% guaranteed 'lead-in' payment for local productivity agreements;
(iii) the 2% consolidation of the 5% Phase II supplement.

On 8 February, the two sides met to allow the Corporation to spell out the terms of this new offer. The BSC's new Chairman, Sir Charles Villiers, a merchant banker brought into the industry for his financial expertise, described the new offer as 'a many splendoured thing' — shortly rechristened by the unions 'a many splendoured sting'. The splendours soon faded when union leaders were told that the 4% guaranteed bonus would not be incorporated into basic rates but paid as a quarterly lump sum payment, on condition that local productivity targets had been achieved to the full satisfaction of BSC management.

The meeting ended before noon. According to Sirs, the Corporation had no intention of moving towards a settlement that day and the ISTC deplored such tactics:

> *The Corporation deliberately misled the unions into resuming negotiations in the hope that after six weeks on strike we would be prepared to settle for anything, or that someone would step in at the 11th hour to prevent a settlement . . . The gulf between us is now wider than ever. Only a substantial offer, without strings, and written down in unambiguous terms will get us to the negotiating table again.* [21]

On 10 February, in the ninth week of the strike, the NCCC informed the BSC that its members were ready to settle their own pay dispute for a 10% increase in basic rates, plus a further 4% from local productivity bargaining. The BSC immediately recognized the opportunity to split the strikers and quickly decided to settle with the craftsmen on those terms. The unions' solidaristic strike front had begun to crumble.

On 22 February, in the tenth week of the strike, the unions produced fresh evidence from the Government's New Earnings Survey to show that manufacturing earnings had increased on average by 15% – 16% since the last survey. The unions informed the BSC that they were now ready to settle the dispute for an increase in basic rates of 15%, plus a 5% guaranteed lead-in payment for prospective local productivity gains. But the BSC refused to entertain such a claim.

The unions suffered a further set-back when their members gave up the strike in the private sector plants. Seizing the initiative, the BSC came forward on 3 March with the novel suggestion that there should be a ballot of striking steelworkers to discover the strength of feeling in favour of an early settlement. Full-page advertisements appeared in the national press, under banner headlines, urging the strikers to press for a ballot:

STEELMEN: BRITISH STEEL
OFFER YOU A DEMOCRATIC WAY
TO END THE STRIKE.
DO YOU WANT TO VOTE?

When the ballot initiative failed, both sides recognized that the dispute was again deadlocked, with no prospect of a peace initiative in sight. Behind the scenes, however, the unions kept up their pressure on the government to intervene and save the industry from self-destruction.

(5) The climax

It took three further weeks of strike action to persuade the Government to act. On 24 March, the Employment Secretary, Mr James Prior, announced that he had asked Lord Lever, a former Labour Treasury Secretary, to chair an Independent Committee of Inquiry, under the Industrial Courts Act 1919, to look only into the pay aspects of the dispute and to report. Within five days, the Inquiry began its work. Within three more days it issued its Report. The Lever Committee recommended that a further 1% should be added to the BSC's final 10% offer on basic rates, bringing the increase up to 11%, plus a further 4.5% increase with productivity strings attached, producing an overall increase of 15.5%. [22]

(6) The settlement

On Tuesday 1 April — April Fool's Day, which many strikers found ironically appropriate — the lay members of the unions' negotiating team decided by 41 votes to 27 to accept the findings of the Lever Committee. This vote, unanimously endorsed by a joint meeting of the Executive Councils of the ISTC and NUB, officially brought the strike to an end. Later that night, outside the ISTC's Head Office in Gray's Inn Road, London, there were turbulent scenes in the pouring rain as militant pickets, bitterly opposed to the Lever settlement — which they saw as a 'sell-out' of the unions' 20% claim — jostled Executive Council members on their way home. But the strike was over.

(7) Aftermath

Many steelworkers returned to their jobs with a sense of betrayal and despair. They had taken their first national stand on a matter of principle and fought the combined strength of the BSC and the Thatcher Government for 13 weeks. They had seen themselves as defending their jobs and their industry against the recklessness and inefficiency of the BSC's top management. Over the years they had persuaded themselves that they were amongst 'the best steelmakers in Europe', if not the world. Now they had not merely lost their battle to maintain their living standards but thousands were faced with the bleak prospect of redundancy.

Throughout the strike, members of management, non-manual unions and some staff sections of the manual workers' unions had stayed at work, despite initial mass picketing. Following the return to work, there were inevitable recriminations and accusations of 'blacklegging', with the usual reported incidents of refusal to work with 'scabs'. According to Bamber, members of the Steel Industry Managers' Association (SIMA) were represented by militant strikers as:

a scapegoat to blame for the length of the strike, and a symbolic focus for enmity, which helped the activist strike leaders to maintain a high degree of group cohesion. [23]

But there were others who came in for blame, notably the ISTC national leadership, BSC top management, and ISTC members in the private sector, as well as members of unions outside the industry who had been conspicuously unsupportive during the strike. But these understandable emotions were soon overtaken by even greater anxieties about personal redundancy and the industry's survival.

SECTION 3: ANALYSIS OF THE DISPUTE

(1) What was the dispute about?

When the ISTC called its all-out strike on 2 January 1980, Bill Sirs evidently believed that there would be a brief if bitter battle with the BSC, followed by a quick union victory:

> *It is important for us to cripple the industry as quickly as we can and get it over as quickly as possible.* [16]

As late as March 1980, ISTC's Research Officer, Martin Upham, still refused to accept that his union was engaged in an all-out struggle for survival with the BSC:

> *The ISTC is engaged in a protracted pay dispute. It is not involved in a 'run-down strike' of the kind which we had expected to fight at the end of 1979.* [24]

It would be simplistic, however, to characterize the national steel strike as either a 'pay dispute' or a 'run-down strike'. What began as a dispute over pay soon became a life-and-death struggle for the future of Britain's steel industry. The election of the first Thatcher Government in June 1979, and the appointment of Sir Keith Joseph as Industry Secretary, put pressure on the BSC to implement its rationalization plans for the industry at a much faster rate than had been intended. The BSC's 'Business Plan' and its ideas for a new 'Steel Contract' with the unions failed to satisfy Mrs Thatcher's ideas for cutting back the public sector. Her Government wanted the industry returned to profitability as soon as possible, by whatever draconian means were deemed necessary, as the first step towards its return to private ownership.

The BSC was instructed to act accordingly. Its challenge to the unions on pay and jobs was part of a deliberate radical strategy to secure an efficient and competitive British steel industry by tackling the long-neglected, complex, interrelated issues of poor plant productivity, low investment, overmanning, and an out-of-date bargaining structure. The BSC therefore was not content with rejecting the unions' wage claim but went on to propose a significant, unilateral and long-overdue change in the industry's traditional national bargaining system, imposing that change under the duress of imminent plant closures and job losses.

In a letter to *The Times*, in December 1979, Dr Grieves explained the reasoning behind the BSC's strategy for rationalizing the industry's pay and productivity problems:

> *The Corporation's management and trade unions have, during the past two years, agreed to the closure of a number of works and negotiated agreements covering the commissioning of major new items of plant, e.g. the Redcar blast-furnace. But overall, we have failed to make any significant progress in streamlining manning and working arrangements at our existing works ... We feel that works' costs must become more competitive and that it is only at works level that the improvements can take place and where the broad interests of the Corporation and its employees can be seen as identical.* [13]

In the words of *The Financial Times*' Labour Editor:

> *British Steel had concluded that this year's earnings increase had to be paid for out of negotiated job losses and more efficient working down in the plants.* [25]

(2) How important was the context?

An understanding of the context provides the key to understanding the national steel strike. At the time of renationalization in 1967, the industry comprised 13 separate steel companies, remnants of a much larger and more fragmented industrial structure that had survived nationalization and denationalization in the two previous decades. From 1967, the BSC had aimed to close the productivity gap between the most efficient and least efficient of these inherited plants. Until 1973, its commercial policy had been one of expansion, with a size-able investment programme intended to assist the industry to achieve an annual export target of around 35 million metric tonnes by 1980. Then came the oil crisis of late 1973, leading to a rapid increase in the industry's manufacturing costs, combined with the collapse of the home market for steel and the devastating recession in Britain's manufacturing industry.

Given the sharp intensification of international competition in steel prices and a rapidly contracting market, the steel industries in countries like Japan, Korea and Brazil, with their more modern, advanced and well-tested technology, were far better placed to ride out the economic storm than the BSC.

Whether the BSC's top management were adequately briefed by their economists is unclear. Union General Secretaries and Execu-tive Councilmen may have understood the changed realities of inter-national steel markets in the late 1970s, but the Corporation manifestly failed to get across its message of an impending crisis to the majority of its shopfloor workers, many of whom were still operating capital equipment that was inefficient, run-down, and technically obsolete. At the top of the productivity range, new plant and equipment was slowly coming on stream (e.g. the new steelmaking complex at Redcar on Tyneside) as the result of an investment programme of £2.7 billion in the five years 1973–78. At the other end of the range, there had been some large-scale redundancies in the same period amongst workers in the oldest and least efficient plants (e.g. Clyde, Shelton and East Moors Cardiff Works), with the loss of some 26 000 jobs through voluntary redundancies in the 2½ years up to 1979. Such closures attracted little publicity because the unions accepted their inevitability and offered only token resistance to BSC plans. In effect, the steel unions had 'colluded' or 'cooperated' with management by encouraging steelworkers to accept voluntary redundancy, with lump sum payments of up to £20 000 (in the best cases), and to seek alternative employment, which was still generally available in the early 1970s.

The BSC failed, however, to get to grips with the middle-range plants, whose productivity remained depressingly low due to the luxuriant overmanning of the 1960s. In the BSC's Scunthorpe plants, for example, Dr Grieves estimated that overmanning was around 60% higher than acceptable for the given level of technology. These remaining low-productivity plants drove up the average cost per ton of the BSC's finished steel, draining the profitability of the BSC's high-productivity plants at Llanwern, Scunthorpe and Ravenscraig.

One of the BSC's most urgent tasks was to tackle the grievous problem of multi-unionism, but the BSC signally failed in its efforts to encourage, persuade or cajole the industry's two dozen separate unions to sit down together and discuss, let alone resolve, the key problems associated with low productivity and overmanning in the industry.

By 1979, three factors came together to accelerate the pace of change:

(i)　the election in June 1979 of a Conservative Government, which issued a directive to the BSC requiring it to restore the industry to profitability within one year (viz. by March 1980), after which date severe cash limits on expenditure would be applied;

(ii)　the catastrophic world recession in the late 1970s, which forced the BSC to drastically reduce its estimates of steel demand both at home and abroad. Against this background, even the most optimistic union leaders found it difficult to sustain the campaign to save inefficient plants with the argument that they might be needed to cope with any sudden revival in world steel demand;

(iii)　the replacement of BSC's Chairman, Sir Monty Finneston — a metallurgist who had spent his working life in the industry — by Sir Charles Villiers, a merchant banker, who insisted on making early and draconian cut-backs against the opposition of nearly all other Board members, who were determined to show that they could manage the business more vigorously and so resist the proposed cuts.

The severity of the cuts called for by Villiers was largely the result of BSC's failure to rationalize the industry in the 1960s and early 1970s, when a more favourable economic climate and full employment would have allowed the workforce to be streamlined without the need for compulsory redundancies. As always, the case for rationalization turned on the political sensitivity of plant closures and job losses in steel communities that had borne more than their fair share of the misery of unemployment in the 1930s. Steel towns like Ebbw Vale, Consett and Hartlepool enjoyed something of a protected status during the post-war decades. Such considerations had led the Beswick Committee to recommend a temporary reprieve for most of these plants in 1975. Their economic life was thus artificially and expensively prolonged. By 1979, the prevarication was no longer tolerable.

(3) Why did the unions call an all-out strike?

Given the depressed economic condition of the industry and the lack of militancy amongst steelworkers in general, the question arises: Why did the steel unions decide on an all-out strike when negotiations on their wage claim had hardly begun, when there still seemed scope for manoeuvre and when steel supplies far exceeded demand?

The first explanation is to be found in the so-called 'Ridley Report', prepared by the Conservative Opposition's policy group on nationalized industries and leaked by *The Economist* in May 1978. The report included some inspired guesswork on those industries in which a future Conservative Government might pick a showdown battle with the unions, on a ground of its own choosing. Since steel headed that list, it was hardly surprising that Bill Sirs should respond to the report in his union journal:

> I realize that for certain Tory MPs union-bashing, like a hairy chest, demonstrates virility. But their memories are short: they ought to recall that even Mr Heath in 1970 declared himself to be ready to face a general strike if the unions resisted him. Yet when he did try to take on the trade union movement he was rebuffed time and time again ... The Trade Union movement has no wish to fight a pitched battle with any government, but it would be a fatal error for the Tories to talk themselves into over-confidence. We in this union will stand by what has been achieved, much of it by patient negotiation ... But if there should be a Tory Government after the next election I can only issue its likely members with a solemn warning not to delude themselves that steelworkers would be a soft touch. [26]

At the beginning of the strike, Sirs' comments were reprinted in the January/February 1980 issue of the union's journal, together with some additional editorial remarks:

> *At the time, Bill Sirs warned the Tories not to get carried away. Some of their MPs easily drift into an ideal dream world where no trade unions hinder their stampede for profits. But with steelmaking at a standstill, and industry rapidly running out of supplies, they may have a rude awakening ... Britain is about to pay a very heavy price for the education of this Tory government.* [27]

The steel unions inevitably, and correctly, interpreted the BSC's counter-offensive on pay and productivity as the opening round of that predicted battle between the newly-elected Thatcher Government and the trade union movement. Despite their members' record of non-militancy, the steel unions concluded that they had no option but to wage total industrial war against the BSC.

A second explanation for the all-out strike decision is to be found in the BSC's deliberate and personal humiliation of Sirs and Smith, the General Secretaries of the two most powerful unions in the industry, who had cooperated, battled and compromised with management over the years and who were deeply wounded by the BSC's insulting initial offer and subsequent refusal to negotiate:

> *British Steel made the error of demanding too much too quickly. Its offer of 2% at national level and up to 10% in local bargaining was a slap in the face of the trade union ... It underestimated the character of Mr Bill Sirs ... and the militancy of the men who stood behind him. Disillusioned, demoralized, and fearful for their jobs, they blamed management incompetence for British Steel's financial difficulties and were determined not to pay for the mistakes.* [25]

The unions took the deliberate risk of calling their first all-out strike for reasons both of expediency and rationality. They selected this tactic because they accurately calculated that only a total stoppage and no lesser economic sanction would bring home their determination to fight plant closures and job losses. But they miscalculated the likely response of both the Government and the BSC to the disruptive, short sharp strike that they had planned. Instead of achieving an early government intervention of the kind so familiar during the Labour Governments of 1964–70 and 1974–79, they found themselves the first to face the Thatcher Government's tough monetarist policy, including drastic cuts in the Public Sector Borrowing Requirement to be achieved by ending subsidies to corporations in the loss-making public sector.

Committed to an all-out strike against the combined forces of the Government and the BSC, and despite the clear warnings of the

'Ridley Report', the steel unions waged their campaign with less than the wholehearted determination required to win:

(i) they failed to involve the craft and general unions, representing steel maintenance workers, until the third week of the strike. The strike thus was never fully supported by all the industry's own workers, and it was the craft unions who undermined the strike's solidarity by making the first negotiated settlement;

(ii) by giving three weeks' notice of the strike, they allowed steel stockholders sufficient time to stockpile normal supplies for a six-week strike and reduced supplies for up to 18 weeks. The intended disruption of the economy simply did not occur;

(iii) they did not aim to prevent private steel being made but simply picketed the private plants to prevent deliveries to customers. When that tactic failed, they called out their members in the private sector, only to be confronted with the threat of contempt for defiance of the law. Had the appeal to the Lords been unsuccessful, there is little doubt that the private sector would not have become involved and the strike might have crumbled sooner than it did.

On the first point above, what of the role played by the other unions directly involved in the dispute? In the words of one commentator:

> Almost from the start, Mr Sirs and Mr Smith were harried by leaders of some of the smaller British Steel unions' officials for whom steel is only one part of life and who resent Mr Sirs' imperious style of leadership. Powerless to affect the result, yet appalled at the way things were going, they justified their breaking of the ranks as necessary to 'save Bill (Sirs) from himself'. [25]

The craft unions' approach to the BSC in February for a separate negotiated deal evidently presented the BSC with an acute dilemma: whether to make such an independent agreement with the NCCC, thereby effectively undermining the strike and hastening its end by splitting the union side and isolating the production unions; or whether to insist on a simultaneous package settlement with all the unions in the industry and, by maintaining the union side's solidarity, help to end the traditional sectionalism that bedevilled the industry. By means of the NCCC settlement, the BSC succeeded in blunting the edge of the strikers' resistance for the first time, and so the strike was initially undermined.

On point (ii) above, since they still hoped for a quick constitutional settlement of the dispute without the need for an all-out strike, for which they realized their members were ill-prepared, the unions felt obliged to give three weeks' strike notice. Once steel stocks had been built up in that period, nobody outside the industry and few inside could accurately predict how long those stocks might last.

In practice, given the low level of steel demand at the time, the stocks virtually outlasted the strikers.

On point (iii) above, the ideological divisions between members of the steel unions working in the private and publicly-owned sectors of the industry were clearly brought out during the dispute. At the outset, the steel unions appeared not to take seriously the private sector loophole in steel supplies. They then found themselves involved in an expensive and unnecessary legal battle, which drained their energies and distracted their attention from the main issue.

(4) A 'failure of communications'?

To what extent was the steel strike a 'failure of communications', as claimed by some commentators? The first point to be noted is that, having decided on its closure strategy, the BSC may well have failed, in some formal or technical sense, to meet its statutory obligation to consult with the trade unions. Under paragraph 5, subsection (2) of the Iron and Steel Act 1975, the BSC had the duty 'before reaching conclusions' on such major policy decisions to 'seek consultations with organizations appearing to them to represent substantial proportions of the persons employed by the Corporation'. The question was raised by Sirs during the dispute, but was never tested in the Courts [19].

The second point is that both sides deployed half-truths in their attempt to win the propaganda battle of words. In his pamphlet *Sense or Non-Sense*, published in February 1980, Bill Sirs attacked Dr Grieves' *Management Newsletter* of 17 January 1980 for its lack of truthfulness:

> It is essential that any discussions that take place ... should at least be based upon truth. [28]

The BSC, for its part, sought to persuade the unions and the public that the unions were the prime obstacle to improved efficiency because they refused to sit down together with the Corporation to negotiate a more rational and coordinated pay and productivity agreement. The unions, in reply, accused the BSC of deliberately manipulating the strike for its own ends:

> BSC's financial crisis is self-inflicted. It was caused by the ineptitude of higher management ... What BSC plans to do is to underpay the steelworkers, sack one-third of them, cook its books by reconstructing its capital, thus appearing to make a profit, and then claim that the sackings and low pay offer make profit possible ... The major issue in the present steel strike is an attempt by BSC management to introduce a complete change into the process of collective bargaining that has become established over many years. This change is a refusal to accept that any increase in wages can be paid unless it is funded by so-called 'productivity agreements'. These

'productivity agreements' are in effect no more than crude demanning exercises. [19]

This mutual misunderstanding might be construed as a 'failure of communication' in the sense that neither party was willing to accept the basic premises from which the other was arguing its case. In practice, both sides operated on the assumption that the other side had made up its mind and was unwilling to listen to alternative arguments that might lead it to change its views.

(5) Who won?

The steel strike was the first serious challenge to face the Thatcher Government following its election in June 1979. It was widely seen, therefore, as a crucial test of the Government's policy towards strikes in nationalized industries. In the words of one commentator:

> *It became imperative for the Tories, facing the first industrial upheaval of their administration, to preserve ideological purity by refusing to intervene and to demonstrate to employers and unions everywhere that the Government's financial constraints could not be broken, however painful the consequences for bank balances, jobs and workers' living standards.* [25]

The Times took a very different view:

> *It was obvious from the first that the strike would be a difficult one to win: the uncompetitive position of the industry was too glaring, its monopoly status too diluted, and its products, unlike water or electricity, would not instantly be missed by the public. Others may be in a stronger position. But they will not, as they might have done before, expect to win almost as a matter of course ... (The outcome is) the most significant success that the Government has had in the domestic field since it took office. It is a success achieved by a resolute refusal to act. Much of its significance lies in that very act.* [29]

That judgement was tempered by *The Financial Times*:

> *The Government, which is the one party to the dispute that could conceivably claim the outcome of the strike as a victory for its policies, can scarcely be satisfied with the length of time it has taken for its message to get across to the strikers. If the unions could not celebrate the end of the strike as a triumphant victory, they were not yet ready to acknowledge it as a defeat. For the ISTC, the outcome of the long and bitter dispute was 'an honourable draw rather than a defeat'.* [30]

As Sirs told the final press conference of the dispute:

> *I am tremendously proud of the qualities that have emerged among iron and steelworkers ... I have been very proud to*

*lead them in this struggle, in which we have achieved tremen-
dous progress . . . Some people will be disgruntled. They have
been on picket lines in foul weather looking for a victory of
20% without strings, but they should not be disheartened . . .
If we accept to go back to work, it is only to gird our loins
so that the next struggle we will be fighting comes over jobs,
which is more important. I only hope that the whole of the
trade union movement will be prepared to stand and fight as
we have been.* [31]

That 'next struggle' never materialized. By 1982, the steel
workforce had been reduced to 92 000 employees — just half its
1979 level — with Ebbw Vale, Shotton and Consett added to the list
of steel ghost towns. By 1984, British iron and steel production was
concentrated in five remaining sites: Llanwern, Ravenscraig, Scunthorpe, Port Talbot and Redcar. 'Thatcherism' plus the BSC strategy
had triumphed. The British steel industry would never be the same
again.

(6) Costs and benefits of the dispute

Addressing a press conference at the end of the 13-week dispute, Sirs
said that he calculated the value of the settlement at 11% across the
board, plus 4.95% on productivity bonus, plus a further 1% on
pensions and holidays, plus a £50 lump sum to strikers on their return
to work as an advance payment for prospective productivity increases.
[31]

In simple economic terms, *The Times* calculated that:

*Each striker, on average, has sacrificed some £700 in wages
to secure a pay increase of about £150. The gains made since
the early days of the strike have scarcely offset the price
inflation day by day over the same period. Even if they had
won the 20% they sought, they would still have been badly
out of pocket. Every worker contemplating strike action should
make calculations such as these and draw the conclusions, and
make sure that his leaders do so on his behalf.* [29]

The *Financial Times* did its own arithmetic:

*The ISTC and NUB have emerged from the longest strike for
decades with a face-saving, third-party settlement — neither a
victory, nor a defeat. Their members have lost £1300 in wages
on average which it will take years to recover, yet scarcely a
voice was raised against the action. The Government and
British Steel must now ponder whether the strike was the last
throw of a demoralized workforce, or a dress rehearsal for
next time.* [30]

In wider social and economic terms, some 90 000 steelworkers
lost their jobs and their incomes. Since the majority were over 50

years of age, it is unlikely that they would ever find regular work again. For example, at the Shotton Steelworks in North Wales — *'the biggest ever BSC redundancy and possibly the largest of its kind on any one site anywhere in the UK'* — the average age of the 6200 men made redundant was 46, half of these aged 48 or over with an average length of service of 18 years in steel. Research shows that amongst the youngest age-group, aged 18 – 20, some 70% remained unemployed after six months, but amongst those aged 54 or over, the figure was as high as 90%. [32]

In devising its closure strategy and calculating the financial cost of its redundancy offers, the BSC was aware that whereas only 8% of EEC steelworkers were aged 55+, some 20% of BSC's total workforce were over 55, due to the promotion-by-seniority rule traditionally operated in British steelworks. The BSC could argue that it had paid out some £250 million in compensation and redundancy payments to reduce its workforce by one-third in three years.

Reflecting on the costs of the dispute, *The Financial Times* asked:

> What has British Steel won? It has preserved the principle that the whole pay rise must be earned through higher productivity [and] emerged with an arbitrated settlement only 1½ per cent more than its own final offer ... The ISTC and NUB have emerged from the longest strike for decades with a face-saving third-party settlement — neither a victory, nor a defeat ... [But] they have fulfilled the predictions of [the Ridley Report which] ranked steelworkers as among those public sector employees least able to win a confrontation with the Government. [30]

(7) Lessons of the dispute

The Times was quick to point at the first major lesson of the steel dispute:

> The tragedy of the steel strike is that it could so easily have been avoided by a little more imagination on both sides.... Both unions and management were fatally confused in their objectives and out of their depth; in the industry itself, the history of the dispute gives no grounds for jubilation to either side. [29]

With the benefit of hindsight, that judgement still seems correct. On the management side, Dr Grieves fiercely defended the BSC's strategy throughout the strike. Once it was over, however, he freely admitted its tactical errors [33], listing some of the lessons of the dispute for the BSC:

(i)   The BSC failed to make the union side negotiators 'totally aware' of the national and international economic scene for steel.

(ii)　The BSC failed to make its story stick with the media, who conveyed a false impression of the seriousness of the crisis in steel. It had also perpetuated a set of 'half-truths' about average earnings in the industry.

(iii)　The unions had chosen the 'short sharp strike' strategy but, having failed to secure an early government intervention, they then had no alternative strategy to fall back on. In particular, they failed to realize that the British economy could survive for 13 weeks without steel supplies and without suffering great economic hardship.

(iv)　Once the strike had begun, the industry's traditionally moderate union officials lost control of the dispute, which was virtually taken over by militant rank-and-file leaders who refused to settle for anything less than the original claim of a 20% increase in basic rates.

(v)　The TUC had made some well-meaning interventions but contributed nothing to the resolution of the dispute.

(vi)　ACAS had been equally powerless and unhelpful.

(vii)　Throughout the dispute, management had been forced by time-pressures to take decisions — for better or for worse — that required more time for mature judgement to be exercised.

(viii)　The legal action by BISPA had achieved nothing but distracted the parties from the major issues of the dispute.

(ix)　The Lever Inquiry had provided a final settlement but the BSC (and presumably the unions) had been given only three days in which to prepare its complicated case.

(x)　Wage settlements by other organizations (e.g. the engineering industry's 1979 settlement of 22% or the coal-mining industry settlement of 20% in December 1979) adversely affected the BSC's bargaining position.

(xi)　Since arbitration had been available from the outset of the dispute — and was finally used to resolve it — some means must be found of building arbitration into the conflict resolution processes used in the industry.

On the union side, Upham was prepared to make what he described as 'the damaging admission' that the strike had proved 'an expensive learning process' for the unions, largely brought about by their inexperience of running a successful national strike and, in particular, by their failure to develop an alternative strategy to combat management's attack on pay and productivity levels. [24]

The Times insisted that:

It is important to be clear just what general lessons can be drawn from this and what cannot. Since 1974 there has been a danger that a convention would establish itself in British political life that a Government could not survive an all-out challenge by a major union. The steel strike has gone some way towards redressing the balance. But the result should not be interpreted on either side as a crude victory for industrial machismo. [29]

For *The Financial Times*:

Management and unions have emerged with little credit from this strike and both must share the blame for the damage which their industry has sustained — estimated by BSC as a 10 to 12 per cent loss of market share, half of which will probably not be recovered . . . (Nevertheless) some important principles have been established. A nationalized industry has been forced to bargain over wages on the same basis as private employers: a pay settlement must ultimately be determined by an industry's ability to earn the money it requires in the market.

For employers, there are some lessons to be drawn even from the BSC's generally unimpressive bargaining performance. The opening offer, which appeared to be 2%, was both unrealistic and ineptly presented. To have given the impression that all the industry's mistakes would have to be visited on the workforce within the course of a single year, with massive redundancies and large cuts in real wages was little short of provocative . . .

But the most important lesson of the strike is addressed to the unions. In the present atmosphere of industrial crisis in Britain many workers will find that productivity improvements provide the only hope for increasing or even maintaining their living standards. It was argument about the productivity conditions, as much as about the size of the total offer, which kept the steelworkers out of work for three months. Their attempts to win an offer with 'no strings' was doomed to failure. [30]

SECTION 4: CONCLUSIONS AND 1987 POSTSCRIPT

The national steel strike was as conclusive as it was unexpected. In an industry notorious for its traditional ways of 'managing around' its problems — all too frequently by sweeping them under the carpet or by the resort to short-sighted expedients — the BSC's ferocious assault on its long-neglected problems of loss-making production, overmanning and poor productivity took union leaders, rank-and-file steelworkers and most commentators by surprise. Within a couple of years of the end of the dispute, with the industry's workforce virtually halved, it became clear just how high a price rank-and-file steel-workers had paid for the failure of union leaders and corporate managers to cooperate in achieving a modern, efficient and profitable industry.

Every industry has its traditional 'customs and practices' — the long-established, familiar folkways of working life, which endow each industry with its unique and cherished character. Iron and steel, one of Britain's oldest and most conservative industries, was burdened by more than its fair share of customary duties. Even the boldest and most courageous of the industry's younger managers seemed to hit a wall of complacency when they tried to bring about the significant 'change of practice' that the industry so obviously required. By the time the economic recession finally struck, the industry's managers and union leaders seemed incapable of generating last-minute solutions. Once the dispute had begun, it moved ineluctably, like a classic Greek tragedy, to its cathartic conclusion.

CHRONOLOGY OF THE DISPUTE

25 September 1979	Steel unions present annual wage claim – amount unspecified
3 December	The BSC rejects wage claim but offers 2% for consolidation of 5% supplement into basic rates; unions reject first offer
6 December	The BSC announces unilateral plans to cut: (a) steel output by 20% (from 20 million to 15 million tons in 1980) (b) employment by 30% (from 150 000 to 100 000 in 1980)
7 December	The ISTC gives three-weeks' notice of all-out strike action from 2 January 1980
17 December	Steel unions and the TUC General Secretary meet Industry Secretary, Sir Keith Joseph
21 December	Steel unions and the TUC General Secretary meet the BSC senior management; BSC makes second offer: 3% on basic rates plus up to 10% plant productivity bonus for demanning (= 13% but 10% not guaranteed); unions reject second offer; the NUB gives notice of strike action from 2 January 1980
28 December	The BSC makes 'third and final offer': 2% on basic rates, plus plant productivity bonus, plus talks on a 39-hour week; unions reject third offer
2 January 1980	Strike takes effect in all of the BSC plants in the UK
4 January	TUCISC makes first counter-proposal: 8% on basic rates, plus 3% guaranteed productivity bonus, plus 1% lead-in payment (= 12% total); the BSC rejects first counter-proposal
7 January	TUCISC makes second counter-proposal: 8% on basic rates, plus 5% lead-in payment (=13% total), plus talks on 39-hour week from January 1981; the BSC rejects second counter-proposal

7 January	The BSC makes fourth offer: 8% on basic rates, plus 4% guaranteed productivity bonus (= 12% total without commitment on 39-hour week)
8 January	Unions reject fourth offer; negotiations break down; the TGWU, GMWU and NCCC join official strike; strike now 100% effective in public sector
16 January	The ISTC instructs its members in 16 BISPA companies to join the strike from 27 January
19 January	Industry Secretary meets union leaders but refuses additional cash for pay settlement
21 January	Prime Minister Thatcher meets separately with both sides
25 January	BISPA seeks High Court injunction against ISTC; High Court refuses BISPA injunction against ISTC
26 January	Court of Appeal reverses High Court decision and grants injunction to BISPA
29 January	The ISTC obeys injunction, withdraws strike notice to BISPA but appeals to House of Lords
1 February	House of Lords reverses Appeal Court decision; the ISTC reinstates strike notice
8 February	The BSC calls in senior union leaders, the BSC makes fifth offer: 7% on basic rates, plus 4% guaranteed productivity bonus, plus 2% consolidated supplement into basic rates [= 13% total without commitment on 39-hour week)
10 February	The BSC makes sixth and final offer: 10% on basic rates, plus 4% productivity bonus (= 14% total); the NCCC and TGWU accept sixth offer
22 February	TUCISC makes third counter-proposal: 15% on basic rates, plus 5% productivity bonus (= 20% total); the BSC rejects third counter-proposal
3 March	The BSC calls for a 'ballot about a ballot'
24 March	Employment Secretary, James Prior, appoints Lord Lever to chair Committee of Inquiry into pay dispute
29 March	Lever Committee begins work on Inquiry
1 April	Lever Committee recommends settlement: 11.0% on basic rates, plus 4.5% productivity bonus (= 15.5% total); TUCISC recommends steel unions to accept Lever proposals; steel unions recommend members to accept Lever proposals
3 April	Strike ends when steelworkers return to work

WHO'S WHO IN THE DISPUTE

Denning, Lord Master of the Rolls
       President, Court of Appeal
Finneston, Monty Chairman, BSC (1974–79)
 (Sir)
Grieves, David   Managing Director,
       Personnel and Social Policy, BSC
Joseph, Keith (Sir) Secretary of State for Industry
Lever, Lord   Former Labour Cabinet Minister
       Chairman, Lever Court of Inquiry
Sirs, Bill   General Secretary, ISTC
Smith, Horace   General Secretary, NUB
Villiers, Charles (Sir) Chairman, BSC (1979–80)

REFERENCES

1 Peter Pagnamenta and Richard Overy: *All Our Working Lives*, BBC, London, 1983, p. 267.
2 See Ralf Dahrendorf: 'On Britain', television series, January 1983; also see 'Why Britain failed', unpublished public lecture, London School of Economics and Political Science, November 1982.
3 Peter Pagnamenta and Richard Overy: *All Our Working Lives*, BBC, London, 1983, p. 78.
4 Peter Pagnamenta and Richard Overy: *All Our Working Lives*, BBC, London, 1983, p. 82.
5 Peter Pagnamenta and Richard Overy: *All Our Working Lives*, BBC, London, 1983, p. 84.
6 Lord Strauss, cited by Pagnamenta and Overy: *All Our Working Lives*, BBC, London, 1983, p. 87.
7 Winston Churchill, cited by Pagnamenta and Overy: *All Our Working Lives*, BBC, London, 1983, p. 88.
8 Peter Pagnamenta and Richard Overy: *All Our Working Lives*, BBC, London, 1983, p. 88.
9 Sir Campbell Adamson, cited by Pagnamenta and Overy: *All Our Working Lives*, BBC, London, 1983, p. 92.
10 Sir Henry Benson: *The Steel Industry: The Stage 1 Report of the Development and Co-ordinating Committee*, British Iron and Steel Federation, 1966.
11 *British Steel Corporation: Ten Year Development Strategy*, Department of Trade and Industry, Cmnd. 5226, February 1973.
12 Lord Beswick: *Steel Closure Review: Interim Report*, HMSO, 1975.
13 David Grieves: Letter to *The Times*, 12 December 1979.
14 David Grieves, quoted in *The Times*, 4 December 1979.
15 Bill Sirs: *Sense or Non-sense?*, ISTC, London, February 1980.
16 Bill Sirs, quoted in *The Times*, 8 December 1979.
17 Bill Sirs: 'Notes and Comments', *Man and Metal*, Vol. 57, No. 1, 1980, p. 1.
18 Bill Sirs: 'What We Want', *Man and Metal*, Vol. 57, No. 1, 1980, p. 13.
19 Bill Sirs: *Sense or Non-sense?*, ISTC, London, February 1980, p. 6.

20 On the Denning Judgement, see Duport Steels v. Sirs, I.C.R. 161, 1980, p. 193.

21 ISTC: 'A Many Splendoured Sting', *Steelworkers Banner*, No. 7, 1980.

22 Report of a Committee of Inquiry into Iron and Steel Industry Dispute (The Lever Committee Report), HMSO, London, April 1980.

23 Greg Bamber: 'Relations between British Steel and its Employees, especially Managerial Employees', *Employee Relations*, Vol. 6, No. 1, 1984.

24 Martin Upham, at an academic seminar in London, 3 March 1980.

25 Christian Tyler: *The Financial Times*, 2 April 1980.

26 Bill Sirs: *Man and Metal*, June 1978.

27 Editorial, *Man and Metal*, January/February 1980.

28 David Grieves: *Management Newsletter*, BSC, 17 January 1980.

29 *The Times*, 2 April 1980.

30 *The Financial Times*, 2 April 1980.

31 Bill Sirs, quoted in *The Times*, 2 April 1980.

32 See S. P. Chakravatry, D. R. Jones and R. R. Mackay: *Redundancy at Shotton – The Place of Steel*, Institute of Economic Research, Clwyd County Council, cited in Department of Employment Gazette, December 1981.

33 David Grieves, at an academic seminar in London, 11 May 1980.

STUDY QUESTIONS

1. Comment on the steel unions' choice of strategy in their dispute with BSC management in the 1980 national steel strike.
2. Examine the relative responsibilities of (a) the management and (b) the unions and workers for the decline of the British steel industry since the Second World War.
3. Were the steel unions wise to advise their members to cooperate with management by accepting redundancy payments as part of the cut-back in the British steel industry in the early 1980s?
4. Identify and comment on the principal problems facing the management of the British Steel Corporation in the mid-1970s.
5. How far does the personality of top managers or union officials matter to the conduct and outcomes of a major industrial dispute? Examine the role of Mr Bill Sirs, General Secretary of the ISTC, in the 1980 national steel dispute.
6. What are the arguments for and against the use of plant productivity bonus payments (as against national pay increases), which were at the heart of the 1980 national pay dispute?

SUGGESTIONS FOR FURTHER READING

Greg Bamber: 'Relations between British Steel and its Employees, especially Managerial Employees', *Employee Relations*, Vol. 6, No. 1, 1984.

Jean Hartley, John Kelly and Nigel Nicholson: *Steel Strike: A Case Study in Industrial Relations*, Batsford, London, 1983.

Ken Jones: *The Human Face of Change: Social Responsibility and*

Rationalization at British Steel, Institute of Personnel Management, 1974.

Keith Ovenden: *The Politics of Steel*, Macmillan, London, 1978.

Martin Upham: 'The British Steel Corporation: retrospect and prospect', *Industrial Relations Journal*, Vol. 11, No. 3, 1980.

John Vaizey: *The History of British Steel*, Weidenfeld and Nicholson, London, 1974.

CHAPTER 8

■ Trade unions and the right to manage —

THE MINERS' STRIKE, 1984–85

The issue, whichever way it was dressed up in words, was the right to manage the industry. When it came down to it — whatever other items there were in the solution to the dispute — it had to contain an element that recognized the NCB's authority and indeed responsibility for making the final decision about which pits we closed, why and when.

Ian MacGregor
The Enemies Within

All collieries must eventually die, but the decision to end the life of one of them prematurely must not be taken without regard to the effect on the community and the social assets dependent on or associated with it.

National Coal Board
Revised Plan for Coal (1959)

INTRODUCTION: 'THE STRIKE IS OVER BUT THE STRUGGLE GOES ON'

At dawn on Monday 5 March 1985, at the end of a year-long dispute, over 100 000 coal-miners assembled behind their lodge banners and colliery bands in dozens of pit villages throughout the length and breadth of Britain's coalfields and set off to march back to their pits with heads held high and spirits undefeated.

After a national overtime ban lasting 16 months and an all-out 12-month strike that was never 100% effective, and after endless abortive negotiations between the parties and repeated interventions by ACAS, the TUC and the Labour Opposition, the miners had failed to win their case. But they went back to work undefeated. The irresistible union force – the National Union of Mineworkers (NUM) — had come up against two unmoveable obstacles: the National Coal Board (NCB) and the Thatcher Government. The 180 000 members of the NUM — the most solidaristic union in Britain and political scourge of successive governments — had allowed themselves to become divided to the point at which almost half of their number had remained at work or returned to work in defiance of the strike leadership. Others had initiated action in the High Court against their own union leaders or even threatened to form their own breakaway union.

On the morning of the return to work, Arthur Scargill, President of the NUM, told eager journalists:

> *The strike is over; but the struggle goes on until we have won the battle for pits, for jobs and for our communities.* [1]

The message was clear for all to hear: after their two historic and successful national wage strikes of 1972 and 1974, the miners had this time failed to achieve their two principal objectives: first, to get the NCB to abandon its plan to close twenty so-called 'uneconomic' pits; and second, to preserve the national *Plan for Coal*.

But if the NUM had failed, the NCB had been equally unsuccessful in getting the miners to accept its unilateral right to manage the industry and to close pits without prior consultation. The strike had ground itself to a year-long stalemate.

How had the NUM sustained a national 12-month strike on the divisive issue of pit closures? How had the NCB kept the industry going throughout those 12 months with a majority of miners out on strike? How had the Government managed to stand aside, allowing the dispute to run for over a year without directly intervening or finding some other means to end one of the most bitter and violent industrial conflicts in British history? This chapter seeks to answer these questions by concentrating on selected issues in the year-long dispute.

SECTION 1: IDEOLOGICAL CONFLICT OVER THE RIGHT TO MANAGE

In liberal democratic theory, 'rights' are an assertion or statement of fundamental claims on society, by individuals and groups, to the enjoyment of certain *positive* freedoms or liberties to act in particular ways without external interference*. [2] Such rights are of two basic kinds:

(i) moral rights, i.e. general claims of the widest applicability, founded upon some metaphysical or ideological notion, such as 'the right to life, liberty and the pursuit of happiness', enshrined in the American Declaration of Independence of 1766; or of 'the

---

* For examples of managerial claims to exercise 'the right to manage' in industrial disputes, see Part II, Chapter 1, on the Ford Motor Company's claim to the prerogative right to manage its establishments without union interference; Chapter 5 on the newspaper publishers' claim to the prerogative right to introduce new printing technology in Fleet Street; Chapter 6 on the engineering industry employers' claim to the prerogative right to determine hours of work in that industry.

rights of the citizen' enshrined in the French Declaration of the Rights of Man of 1792; or of the so-called 'Beveridge principles' of 1944, including the five *negative* rights to freedom *from* poverty, disease, ignorance, squalor and fear, as well as the *positive* rights to freedom *for* work, travel, free expression, etc.

When religious-minded people speak of 'moral rights' or of 'natural justice', they are asserting that such rights derive from a so-called 'moral law', which they regard as divinely inspired. Non-believers will sometimes refer to 'the law of nature' or 'the law of right reason'.

(ii) legal rights, i.e. claims to the enjoyment of specific liberties, which may have their origins in moral rights, but which now carry the added endorsement and protection of the law of the land, e.g. the right to own private property and to dispose of it as one wishes without interference by others, except under the law. Thus, most citizens have the legal right to enjoy the fruits of their labour (i.e. to spend their own earnings as they choose) provided that they have met their legal duties (i.e. declaring those earnings and paying appropriate income taxes).

Rights and duties, both moral and legal, are collateral and inseparable. Thus, my right to own property (e.g. a factory) carries with it a corresponding set of duties (including the common law duty of care towards my employees and visitors to the factory, supplemented by statutory duties imposed by the Health and Safety at Work Act 1974 or similar legislation affecting employment conditions).

The 'right to manage' begins as a moral right — a claim derived from the ownership or control of property in the means of production, taken in its widest sense. It is a right, buttressed by tradition as well as by the law, to exercise day-to-day and final control over an enterprise (e.g. a business, a hospital, a university, etc.), carrying with it the corresponding duty to manage that enterprise in the interests of those to whom the business belongs or on whose behalf the enterprise exists. Business enterprises are managed in ways that suit the owners of the business or their representatives and are of principal economic benefit to the owners and their representatives.

By this argument, the ownership of an enterprise is said to confer on its owners and managers a wide-ranging set of 'managerial prerogatives', i.e. a set of inalienable rights to exercise an unquestionable decision-making power in the enterprise, including the prior right to decide each and every important issue that may affect the efficient and profitable running of that business in the interest of the individual owner (in the case of a private company), or of the shareholders (in the case of a public company).

Before nationalization, Britain's private mine-owners undoubtedly exercised such prerogative rights to manage their collieries in their own richly beneficial interest. Following nationalization in 1947, the National Coal Board (NCB) was vested with the rights and duties of managing Britain's mines on behalf of the State, i.e. on behalf of the people of Britain. Board Members were given the legal right to take day-to-day decisions and to run the industry as they saw fit, subject to the will of Parliament, which laid down guiding principles for the management of the industry in the Coal Industry Act 1946, as modified from time to time by subsequent legislative guidelines, most recently by the Coal Industry Act 1984.

During the first forty years of public ownership, the NCB published a series of reports, setting out its broad intentions for the future running of the coal industry. These reports — such as *Plan for Coal (1950)*, *The Fleck Report (1955)*, *Investing in Coal (1956)*, *The First Ten Years (1957)*, *Revised Plan for Coal (1959)*, *Plan for Coal (1974)* — are of crucial importance to Parliament, to the coal-consuming, tax-paying community and, above all, to those who work and who give their lives — sometimes literally — to the coal industry. Quite apart from its legal duty to negotiate pay and conditions of employment with representatives of the miners' own choosing, the NCB has recognized certain trade unions (viz: the NUM, NACODS, COSA) for the purpose of allowing consultation to take place on vital issues affecting job and income security, such as investment, development and closure plans.

In effect, these recognition and procedure agreements amount to the acceptance by management of a restraining or delaying power upon their unilateral right to manage. They embody concessions by management, which confer on trade unions:

(i)   the right to challenge management if it should seek to decide issues unilaterally which are the proper subject of consultation and negotiation

(ii)   the right to oppose management's decisions where they perceive that such decisions conflict with their members' own interests.

Collective agreements are (normally) the product of bilateral (sometimes multilateral) negotiation. They confer on the parties rights and duties that cannot simply be overlooked or broken without the risk of corresponding penalties. Such agreements are not normally enforceable under current British law but they carry with them a morally binding obligation. Failure to observe the detailed terms of such agreements brings the risk of economic sanctions, which may be applied by either party in the ultimate form of a collective withdrawal of labour by workers or the enforcement of a collective lock-out by management.

By recognizing trade unions and negotiating collective agreements with them, the NCB has given up what would otherwise have remained the unilateral right to manage the industry without challenge from its employees. Having signed such collective agreements, the NCB has accepted the right of the unions to challenge, to contest and ultimately to frustrate management's decisions by withdrawing the labour of its members in opposition to any managerial decisions that union members feel are inimical to their immediate or longer-term interests.

As with other employers in both the private and public sectors, however, the NCB reserves what it would regard as the exclusive and unilateral right to take managerial decisions in a specified area of managerial competence or technical expertise, e.g. decisions on product pricing, marketing, or investment in new mining equipment. But on matters that directly or indirectly affect the welfare of its employees, the NCB, like most other employers, recognizes the right of the union to be consulted before such decisions are taken or implemented. Whilst these consultative rights are analytically distinct from negotiating rights, in practice they merge into a more general right to negotiate and to reach agreement on certain key decisions, notably those affecting working arrangements, job and income security and, above all, pit openings, pit developments and pit closures. The NCB's 'right to manage' the industry includes the right to plan pit closures. It is not, however, an absolute right but one that is qualified by the duty to consult employee representatives, and implies an equal and opposite right of the NUM and other unions to oppose such closure plans.

In the light of their experience of NCB policy on pit closures during thirty post-war years, the unions finally succeeded in negotiating a new agreement with the NCB and the Labour Government in 1974, specifically dealing with the rights and duties of management and unions on the subject of pit closures. This agreement, known as the Colliery Review Procedure (CRP), is an elaborate set of formal steps that must be followed by the NCB *before* it proceeds to close any pit. It therefore allows the unions to put forward their own representations and objections to each proposed closure, should they so wish. The CRP was thus at the centre of 'the right to manage' in the British coal-mining industry after 1974. In the words of R. L. Turner, the CRP was intended to be:

> *the agency through which such closures could be processed . . . Through it, the NUM could object to proposals covering particular pits. On occasions, however, such objections merely resulted in the delay of closure.* [3]

The appointment of Ian McGregor as NCB Chairman in 1983 appeared to change all that. The NCB's pit closure plan, announced on 1 March 1984, was an attempt to reassert the NCB's unilateral right to decide which pits to close and when, thereby seeking to ignore or to circumvent the CRP. Whether the NCB intended to dispense with the CRP altogether is unclear, but it invoked the state of the industry's finances and the Government's insistence that the Board must break even financially before the year-end, in support of its decision to close up to 20 pits with the loss of some 20 000 jobs within a few months. It was this fundamental clash of ideological values — this conflict of industrial rights and duties — that gave rise to the miners' strike of 1984–85.

When is an economic pit no longer 'economic'? Whereas manufacturing industry normally conserves and increases its capital stock through investment, extractive industries like coal-mining are in a continuous state of flux, as mines are first sunk, then exploited, then exhausted and finally abandoned as their natural reserves run out. At this point, they are normally regarded as 'uneconomic' unless, as in wartime, the cost of getting coal is less important than its availability, in which case the expenditure of additional funds on, say, improved ventilation or drainage, may restore the economic viability of an otherwise exhausted and 'uneconomic' pit.

Throughout forty years of public ownership, both sides of the coal-mining industry adopted a realistic and mostly cooperative approach to the closure of 'uneconomic' pits. From the late 1950s to the late 1960s, as the demand for coal fell and pits were progressively closed due to their exhaustion, some 200 000 miners left the industry. This contraction of manpower in Britain's major basic industry was carried out without a single major strike on the issue of closures. By the late 1960s, however, with major economic and social changes in the wider society, attitudes towards pit closures and voluntary redundancies began to change:

> *Throughout the 1950s, the 1960s and most of the 1970s, the position adopted by the NUM towards pit closures was one of compliance and cooperation with the NCB and the government of the day. It was only in the 1980s that this position was superseded by one of resistance.* [3]

In a detailed analysis of post-war pit closures, R. L. Turner distinguishes five distinct phases in the post-war history of British pit closures, as shown in Table 8.1.

According to Turner, the NUM leadership of the late 1950s and the 1960s accepted much of the logic of the case for de-industrialization. Sidney Ford, NUM President, told his members:

> *If we are to obtain the reforms and improvements to which we believe our members are entitled, the industry will have to sell its products, and this will have to be done in the face of keen competition, especially from oil.* [4]

In short, the NUM Executive went along with the NCB's policy of producing cheaper coal by achieving a smaller, more competitive and compact industry. As early as 1947, the NUM President, Will Lawther, had told the miners' annual conference that nationalization meant that 'There are now no opposing sides of the industry.' That policy remained virtually unchallenged until the mid-1960s when a militant minority began to make its voice heard, challenging the union's policy of full cooperation with the management of the nationalized industry. By 1964, the Derbyshire area of the NUM set out the

Table 8.1. Post-war pit closures in Britain's coal-mining industry

Phase	Year	No. pits working	No. miners working	Coal extracted (million tonnes)	Inland coal consumption (million tonnes)
1	1947	980 (a)	(31 078) (b)	197 (c)	
	1956				218.4 (d)
2	1957	822	704 000	207	213.2
	1959		(97 924) (e)		
	1963				
3	1965		571 000		
	1968		(44 160) (e)		
	1969				
4	1970			133	
	1974		(30 300) (b)		
	1975	241	245 000	114.7	
	1978				
5	1979				
	1984	174	189 000 (f)	110 (h)	
	(Nov.)		178 000 (g)		
	1985			135–150 (i)	100

Notes: (a) inherited by NCB at nationalization; (b) Nottinghamshire area only, (c) Tony Hall: King Coal, 1981, p. 28; (d) Post-war peak; (e) Durham area only; (f) total manual workers; (g) total working in pits; (h) 1980–84 average; (i) NCB projection.

case for resisting pit closures in a pamphlet *A Plan for the Miners*. Three years later, an unknown rank-and-file delegate from Yorkshire, Arthur Scargill, responded to a speech by Richard Marsh, Labour's Minister of Power, at the NUM's 1967 Annual Conference, as follows:

> *I can honestly say that I never heard flannel like we got from the Minister ... he said we have got nuclear power stations with us, whether we like it or not. I suggest to this Conference that we have got coal-mines with us ... but they did something about this problem: they closed them down. This was a complete reversal of the policy ... that was promised by the Labour Government before it was put into office ... this represents a betrayal of the mining industry.* [5]

It was from such obscure and unpromising origins that the militant minority in the NUM set out to break the ideological bond between those who advocated adherence to capitalist logic — successive governments, union leaders such as Will Lawther and Sidney Ford, and the NCB — and the NUM itself.

During the third phase of the 1970s, pits continued to be closed despite the post-1973 oil shocks and the NCB's 1974 *Plan for Coal* — enthusiastically endorsed by the NUM and the incoming second Wilson Labour Government — for expanding the coal industry throughout the 1970s and into the 1980s. Thus, in the last five years of the 1970s, the NUM accepted the closure of 27 collieries, involving the loss of 14 000 jobs.

Between 1957 and 1975, the number of working collieries fell from 822 to 241 and the number of working miners from 704 000 to 245 000 — a reduction no less than 65% over 18 years. The worst phase was between 1965 and 1969 when 200 collieries were closed at an average rate of one per week for over four years. The Wilberforce Inquiry, set up by the Heath Government to examine the miners' 1972 pay claim, commented on the severity of the contraction and on the NUM's exemplary compliance in this achievement:

> *The rundown, which was brought about with the cooperation of the miners and the union, is without parallel in British industry in terms of the social and economic costs it has inevitably entailed for the mining community as a whole.* [6]

Turner regards the events of 1957, the year following the Suez Canal Crisis, as 'the beginning of the turning point in the history of the British coal industry'. In 1956, inland coal consumption in Britain reached its post-war annual peak of 218 million tonnes. By the following year (1957), it had fallen by 5 million tonnes to 213.2 million tonnes and was to fall by a further 35 million tonnes in each of the three successive years, to reach an all-time low of 109 million tonnes at the end of 1959:

> *The real villain of this piece was the emergence of cheap oil. As the price of oil fell relative to coal, coal was allowed to be squeezed out of the market for electricity production.* [3]

And as the demand for coal fell, the NCB closed collieries and reduced manpower under both Conservative (1951–64 and 1970–74) and Labour Governments (1964–70 and 1974–79). The NUM said that it opposed this catastrophic rundown. Why, then, did it actively cooperate, or at least acquiesce, in the policy of contraction rather than mounting an effective campaign of resistance to the cuts? Turner offers a convincing explanation:

> *In an era of full employment, displaced miners could still find jobs elsewhere. Many were pleased to have the opportunity of getting out of the pits and into more salubrious sectors. Furthermore, as different regions were affected to different extents by the closures, there was little chance at this time that any unity of action could have been forged on the issue, even*

had elements of the rank-and-file membership and the leadership wished it to be so. But the third aspect which should be recognized was that the leaders of the NUM themselves did not believe in assertive trade unionism; at least not for the purpose of maintaining the size of their industry. The reduction of the size and capacity of the industry was considered to be outside the ambit of trade unionism. [3]

With the fall of the Wilson Labour Government in 1970, the Conservatives were returned to power under the leadership of Edward Heath. His single term of office was abruptly ended in February 1974 when, following the second miners' pay strike in two years, he appealed to the electorate by calling a 'snap' General Election on the key issue of 'Who governs Britain?', and lost. The miners' pay strikes of 1972 and 1974 traumatized the Conservative Party and its future leader, Margaret Thatcher.

The massive programme of pit closures and progressively declining real wages had left the miners demoralized and bitter. But, according to Turner:

Although the 1974 strike had the more spectacular political results, it was actually the 1972 strike which had the most profound effects on relations between government and the miners ... First, the self-confidence of the miners and their Union, following years of passivity, was restored ... Secondly, as protagonist in the organization and mobilization of 'flying pickets', the 1972 strike was to give Arthur Scargill, who still did not hold an official position in the Union, his first public platform. The building of the 'counter-hegemony' developed in earnest after the miners' victory of 1972. From that moment on, the left, with its espousal of trade union assertiveness and industrial action, was in the ascendancy. [3]

The building of a 'counter-hegemony' against the dominant managerial ideology of the NCB illustrates in dramatic fashion the ideological conflict over the right to manage in British industry. Coal-mining is, of course, a unique industry and there are few other industries that demonstrate so clearly the deep, traditional hostility between employers and employees, managers and unions, as British coal-mining. It is against this historical background that the miners' strike must be seen.

SECTION 2: THE MINERS' STRIKE, 1984–85

(1) The pre-dispute context

The 1978–79 'winter of discontent' was followed by the election of the Thatcher Government in June 1979, committed to reducing the power of organized labour by the imposition of stark monetarist economic policies: the substitution of free market forces for a planned economy; restoration of profitability to the public sector industries in order to cut back the Public Sector Borrowing Requirement, thereby reducing inflation; and the reduction in total government spending by savage cuts in the public sector, including rate-capping of local authority spending.

1980 had been a good year for the NCB: deep-mined coal output rose by over 4.5 million tonnes; employment and absenteeism were down; therefore labour productivity was rising. Two factors, however, militated against the NCB's success: first, the recession was biting deep into coal demand, which fell by over 20% amongst domestic consumers and by over 15% amongst industrial customers; and second, the truncated steel industry, the Board's second largest customer after the electricity generating industry, had reduced its requirement for coking coal by almost 25%.

The NCB responded by appealing to the Government for the type of help envisaged by *Plan for Coal*, but the Thatcher Government refused financial help and insisted that the coal industry must break even financially by 1984. The NCB therefore postponed further expansion schemes and looked around for ways to cut costs.

In the autumn of 1980, the NCB told the NUM that 'un-economic' pits must close, that jobs would be lost and that the wage deal for 1981 could not exceed 13%. In February, NCB Chairman, Derek Ezra, told NUM President, Joe Gormley, that between 20 and 30 pits would have to close on grounds of exhaustion, bad geology or other adverse working conditions that reduced productivity and profitability. Over a longer period, the total could reach 50 pits.

Within one week, some 23 pit closures had been announced by the separate Area Boards. If piecemeal disclosure was intended to soften the blow, it had just the opposite effect: unofficial strikes began in South Wales, the most threatened area. Other areas quickly followed. By the end of that same week, the miners of Kent, Durham and Scotland had stopped work and those in Yorkshire were due to follow. A third head-on confrontration between the Government and the miners now seemed unavoidable.

But, on 18 February, against all her previous policy pronounce-ments, Mrs Thatcher executed her first significant U-turn since assuming office in 1979. The Government capitulated to the miners' strike threat: the NCB withdrew its closure plan after being granted an extension of its cash limit from £834 million in 1980–81 to £882 million in 1981–82. According, to Gormley, the miners had achieved a 'victory without tears'.

With the advantage of hindsight, the miners' strike of 1984–85 may be seen clearly as having been triggered by the NCB in the aftermath of that humiliating defeat for the Thatcher government in 1981.

(2) The challenge

On 1 September 1983, fresh from his 'triumphs' at the British Steel Corporation (BSC), Ian MacGregor assumed office as NCB Chairman, having been selected by Mrs Thatcher to take charge of both of these tough assignments at a compensatory management fee to his banking employers, Lazard Freres, of some £2 million. On his arrival at the NCB, he quickly imposed his will on the organization, replacing 'unsuitable' Board members and setting up the Office of the Chief Executive, which he shared with a fellow-Scot, James Cowan, the NCB's Deputy Chairman.

In 1981, the NCB had produced a Development Plan showing 25 million tonnes of new capacity, including the prestigious new Selby (Yorkshire) pit, coming on stream between 1984 and 1990 against the projected demand for some 100 million tonnes per annum of sales throughout that period. With an existing capacity of about 110 million tonnes p.a. in 1984, the Plan aimed to reduce higher cost capacity by about 26 million tonnes over seven years or 4 million tonnes p.a. to accommodate the new capacity. The level of pit closures achieved in 1983–84 and planned for 1984–85 would have to continue into 1990 and beyond.

During 1983–84, the NCB pressed ahead with the closure of 15 pits. Of the 1800 miners made redundant in that year, fewer than 300 were under 55 years of age and all of them left on voluntary redundancy terms. The NUM Executive failed to bring all its members out on strike in opposition to such closures at Kinneal (Scotland), Snowdown (Kent) and Tymawr-Lewis Merthyr (South Wales). When this last pit was threatened with closure in March 1983, the miners voted at a pithead ballot by 61% to 39% *against* a national strike. For the Thatcher Government, this outcome demonstrated that the miners had recognized 'the realities of economic life' by rejecting their leaders' strike call for the second time in six months.

On 31 October 1983, the NUM ordered a national overtime ban in protest against the NCB's offer to increase wages by 5.5% in 1984. At first, the NCB appeared willing to ride out a possible 'winter of discontent', but on 23 January 1984, some 19 000 miners were sent home by management for persisting in their refusal to work 'reasonable overtime', triggering a rash of strikes throughout the British coalfield, called spontaneously at local pithead ballots. Finally, on 20 February, the national scene was prepared when the traditionally militant Scottish miners called an all-out strike, north of the border.

On 1 March 1984, the NCB announced its plan to close Cortonwood Colliery (Yorkshire) on economic grounds. The 55 000 Yorkshire miners responded enthusiastically to an Area strike call in defence of the local mining community at Cortonwood, whose members had received recent assurances of its long-term future. That intended closure provided the NUM nationally with the first hard evidence of an 'NCB hit-list' of some 20 pits destined for closure, with the loss of some 20 000 jobs. Within five days, on 6 March, the NCB confirmed that it also intended to reduce national coal capacity by 4 million tonnes in 1985. These two announcements, taken together, gave the NUM Executive its cue for action. The strike had begun.

(3) Initial responses

On 8 March, the NUM Executive gave its official backing to the Yorkshire and Scottish strikes. By 12 March, the strike was effective in both coalfields. Next day, the NCB reported that some 100 000 miners out of a total of 183 000 were on strike in more than 90 of its 174 pits. In other words, almost two-thirds of Britain's miners were on strike, principally in Scotland, Wales, Kent and Yorkshire, whilst one-third remained at work, principally in the Derbyshire and Nottingham coalfields. Miners in the latter fields argued that they had stayed at work awaiting the outcome of a national pithead ballot and they reacted fiercely against the arrival of mass 'flying pickets' from Yorkshire — Arthur Scargill's so-called 'Red Guards' — determined to prevent them from getting to work. Within 48 hours, the battle-lines had been drawn and the pattern of the strike settled for the duration of the dispute.

(4) Consequences

On 14 March, the NCB obtained an injunction in the High Court under the Employment Act 1980, requiring the NUM to call off its 'flying pickets' because they were interfering with the right of other miners to go to work and were picketing other than at their 'own place of work'. But the NUM ignored this injunction. Throughout the remainder of March, the media reported violent incidents at working pits as unprecedented numbers of police, estimated in hundreds, were bussed and flown at dawn into the Nottingham and Derbyshire coalfields. These movements were directed by the police from a new National Reporting Centre in Whitehall, set up by the Home Secretary as part of a carefully-constructed and nationally-coordinated contingency plan to meet any repetition of the violent events surrounding the 1972 and 1974 miners' strikes. The tactics and conduct of these 'flying policemen' led to allegations in Parliament by Labour MPs that they amounted to nothing less than violent attacks on striking miners and their supporters. The allegations were initially discounted, but when clear evidence appeared on television screens, night after night, it soon became a matter of national concern. Police were obviously being deployed in very large numbers, using force and with unprecedented powers to frustrate the attempt by both peaceful and some violent pickets to demonstrate at working pits in the Midlands coalfield. In particular, questions were asked in Parliament about the legality of police action in stopping and turning back private cars said to contain would-be peaceful pickets in order, as they said, 'to prevent any anticipated breach of the peace'.

Since the NUM had secured what amounted to a national stoppage without recourse to a national ballot, the NCB and the Government denounced the strike as unconstitutional as well as unlawful and urged both the strikers and the working miners to press for a national ballot, on the grounds that it would either legitimate the NUM Executive's position or fail to produce a clear majority of 55% in favour of the strike. In practice, the greater the clamour for a ballot, the greater the determination of the NUM to resist one.

Early in April 1984, the moderates on the NUM Executive were claiming a 14–10 majority in favour of calling a ballot, but at a crucial meeting of the Executive on 12 April, Scargill skilfully avoided the ballot call and the Executive voted instead for a special National Delegate Conference on 19 April, which predictably voted against a ballot.

Recognizing that his members were fatally divided, the NUM President turned elsewhere for union allies who might help him win the strike. There were three key groups whose support was vital to success: the power station and steel workers, who are the NCB's two major industrial customers; the railwaymen, who transported the bulk of coal supplies to both steelworks and power stations: and the dockers, who handled supplies of imported coal at various ports around the country.

Scargill argued that, since the miners had offered assistance to the steelworkers in their 1980 strike by blacking supplies of coal to the stricken steelworks, steelworkers should now refuse to handle NCB coal or foreign ore supplies, despite any threat to the steelworks so affected. At the Llanwern Steelworks in Monmouthshire, the South Wales NUM reached agreement with the steel unions on guaranteed coke supplies to maintain some 4000 steelworkers' jobs. At Immingham in North Lincolnshire, dockers were asked to 'black (i.e. to boycott and refuse to handle) imported iron-ore supplies, thereby crippling the Scunthorpe steelworks. At Ravenscraig, the only remaining Scottish steelworks — already under threat of closure — the National Union of Railwaymen (NUR) began blacking supplies of coal to the plant on 3 April. When the NCB arranged to meet its commercial contract to supply coal to the BSC by road deliveries, the NUM relented and allowed a resumption of minimum coal supplies by rail. This agreement later broke down when Scottish train drivers refused to deliver imported iron-ore to Ravenscraig from the BSC's Hunterston Depot unless the steel unions agreed to reduce coal consumption. Later, in June, when the Iron and Steel Trades Confederation (ISTC), which was determined to preserve the Ravenscraig Works, refused further cutbacks in steel production, the NUM attempted to mount a total road and rail blockade on supplies into and out of the plant. Ugly scenes were recorded both in Scotland and South Wales as serried ranks of miners and their supporters bombarded road convoys with missiles of every kind in an attempt to prevent supplies from reaching the steelworks.

On 9 July, a national dock strike was called by the Transport and General Workers Union (TGWU) in protest against the BSC's alleged use of non-union labour to unload iron-ore at Immingham Docks. Despite media allegations that the union had deliberately instigated the strike to help the miners topple the Government, the TGWU denied the charge and the strike was soon settled with the withdrawal of non-union dock labour. A second dock strike began on 21 July, again in protest against the use of non-union labour, but this took rather longer to settle.

On 29 May, scenes of unprecedented violence took place at the Orgreave (Yorkshire) coke depot when several hundred pickets clashed with mounted riot police. Witnessed by millions of television viewers, the clash showed heavy casualties on both sides and hundreds of pickets and demonstrators were arrested for obstructing the police or for causing a breach of the peace. Mounted police were seen in military-style attacks, swinging truncheons onto the heads of unarmed and peaceful pickets; police wearing full riot gear, drummed on their riots shields as they advanced menacingly on unprotected miners.

Whilst the NUM Area Councils continued their action to involve other groups of workers in support of the strike, the NUM Executive prepared for its first round of negotiations with the NCB. Meanwhile, the Executive's refusal to hold a national ballot continued to dominate the dispute. In the words of one commentator:

> the absence of the ballot — the centre piece of the NUM constitution — was poisoning the dispute. The moral legitimacy of the strike and therefore its potentially explosive political power was crippled. [1]

Throughout the early summer, various peace initiatives were launched to resolve the dispute by peaceful negotiation. A first round of direct talks between the NUM and the NCB in May quickly collapsed without any significant progress. A second round of talks at Rotherham in mid-June similarly failed, mainly because of deadlock over the use of the word 'uneconomic' to describe 'high-cost' pits that the NCB wished to close and the NUM's refusal to acknowledge the validity of the very concept of an 'uneconomic' pit.

In July, a third round of talks began in London, but these were as sterile as the earlier rounds. After a seven-week negotiating deadlock, an attempt by Fleet Street publisher, Robert Maxwell, to bring the parties together failed before it even got started. Direct talks between the NUM and the NCB had been arranged for 6 September when the NCB made clear that it was unwilling to re-open negotiations unless the NUM accepted that closure of 'uneconomic' pits was on the agenda. When told that Scargill had accused the Board of scuppering the talks, MacGregor replied: 'That would be normal for Mr Scargill. He lies through his teeth.' When MacGregor proclaimed that he was 'ready at any time to meet people, to discuss constructive views to settle the dispute,' Scargill retorted: 'I think Mr MacGregor needs a long rest.' In this atmosphere of personal recrimination, it proved impossible to secure a resumption of direct talks between the two sides.

Throughout these early abortive meetings, the two sides maintained their initial bargaining positions. The NUM demanded:

(i)   that the NCB should withdraw the 6 March plan to cut 4 million tonnes p.a. of production and to close 20 pits;

(ii)   that it should guarantee the survival of the five named collieries (viz. Snowdon, Polmaise, Herrington, Cortonwood and Bulcliffe Wood);

(iii)   that it should abandon the accounting notion of what constituted an 'uneconomic' pit.

The NCB had been adamant that loss-making pits must close when their 'beneficial' reserves were exhausted. But by July it had indicated what it was ready to concede:

(i)   it agreed to review the 6 March plan, though without giving any prior assurances;

(ii)   it agreed to maintain production at the five named pits;

(iii)   it would not shift its position on 'uneconomic' pits because it regarded that as the essence of its re-established 'right to manage' the industry according to strict economic criteria.

Between 9 – 14 September, the NCB and NUM held a series of meetings to thrash out a revised Colliery Review Procedure (CRP), specifying the procedure to be followed in the case of pit closures. It was agreed, within the provisions of the *Plan for Coal*, that:

(i)   collieries that were deemed exhausted should be closed by joint agreement;

(ii)   collieries facing severe geological difficulties (e.g. on safety grounds) should also be closed by joint agreement.

The main point of contention was the NCB proposal that 'exhausted' pits should include those containing no further minable reserves that could be 'beneficially developed'. The NCB's proposed formulation read:

> *It is agreed that since the advent of* Plan for Coal *there have been colliery closures which do not fall within the definition of exhaustion or safety, and in accordance with the principles of the plan, it is acknowledged that this procedure will continue to apply ... In the case of a colliery where a report of an examination by the respective NCB and NUM qualified mining engineers establishes there are no further reserves which can be developed to provide the Board, in line with their responsibilities, with a basis for continuing operations, there will be*

agreement between the board and the unions that such a colliery will be deemed exhausted. [7]

The NUM proposed, in place of the last lines of the above, the wording:

. . . enabling the board in line with Plan for Coal to continue operations . . .

Further talks were held under the auspices of ACAS from 11 to 13 October, but broke down on 15 October. The NCB favoured wording which stated that discussion of a possible pit closure under the modified CRP should take place 'in line with the principles of the *Plan for Coal*' rather than the NUM wording 'in line with *Plan for Coal*'. The NUM also opposed restricting the scope of a proposed independent review body to the consideration of references from either side only on matters relating to pit closures.

The next crisis points in the dispute came in September, with the Brighton TUC and the Labour Party Conference at Blackpool. At the TUC, Scargill was persuaded by his Vice-President, Mick McGahey, that the NUM was in danger of losing even left-wing support at Congress by his refusal to allow the TUC's senior statesmen on the General Council to provide some positive assistance to help the miners to secure a negotiated solution. Scargill had worked untiringly for an industrial solution to the dispute and had asked the TUC not to intervene. He was now prevailed upon to acknowledge that, since all attempts to open up a 'second front' with the steelworkers had failed, the NUM was in dire need of official TUC help to bring the dispute to a climax.

In one of his last official engagements before his early retirement on health grounds, Len Murray, TUC General Secretary, provided a formula whereby, in return for TUC help, Scargill was allowed to appeal to all union members to refuse to cross picket lines and to discuss other ways, including industrial action, to bring the dispute to a head. Scargill scored an undisputed personal triumph at Congress but when the official TUC message eventually went forth, calling on all union members to back the miners, the support was seen to be little more than a paper promise.

At the Labour Party Conference, Scargill again won a diplomatic victory by upstaging party leaders, thereby ensuring that the miners' strike crowded out other matters of perhaps even greater political importance. The Labour leader, Neil Kinnock, son of a Welsh miner and representing a former mining constituency, found himself in an exquisite dilemma. He had quickly condemned the violence of the dispute, from whatever quarter it came, but for electoral considerations he had declined to appear on NUM platforms, giving active support to the strike — partly because he felt it essential to distance himself from Scargill's brand of extra-parliamentary politics and partly because he needed an early peaceful resolution to the dispute that had seriously undermined Labour's showing in the polls. At the start of the dispute, the new Labour leader had taken his party ahead of Mrs Thatcher. By the time it ended, she was once more well in the lead.

(5) The climax

At the end of December, the Secretary of State for Energy, Peter Walker, confidently announced that there would be no power cuts in 1985 — a judgement based on the comparatively mild winter and the relatively high level of coal stocks at power stations. Peter Heathfield, General Secretary of the NUM, agreed with that judgement, saying that he had never expected the NUM to win the dispute by imposing power cuts but by bringing home to the Government the high cost of the strike. In the event, it was the Government's continued willingness to meet that cost, combined with the Electricity Board's ability to maintain supplies, which finally defeated the NUM.

On 7 January 1985, the first working day following the Christmas and New Year holiday, some 1200 more miners were reported by the NCB as having returned to work. These so-called 'new faces' brought home to the miners' leadership the crisis they now faced. Following a promising preliminary meeting between Peter Heathfield (NUM General Secretary) and Ned Smith (the NCB's Director of Industrial Relations), the Board issued a statement to the effect that:

> The (peace) proposals must establish that the NUM recognize that management must deal with the problem of uneconomic capacity, and that the NUM will cooperate in this essential task. [7]

Not surprisingly, the peace talks were quickly broken off. Late in January, in the closing weeks of the dispute, came another unexpected twist in the tangled skein of events. With the NCB insisting that the NUM must accept the closure of uneconomic pits as a prior condition for final peace talks, the National Association of Colliery Overmen, Deputies and Shotfirers (NACODS), the pit 'deputies' or supervisors' union, suddenly announced on 25 January that it was not prepared to see that prior condition imposed on the NUM. NACODS argued that it had already reached agreement with the Board that a revised Colliery Review Procedure (CPR) would shortly be introduced whereby independent arbitrators would examine and report on each individual case for pit closure before any unilateral closure by the Board. If the NCB insisted on its prior condition to the NUM, what was the value of the NACODS deal? The Prime Minister was unrepentant. In the course of a television interview on 21 January she had said:

> There are an awful lot of uneconomic pits and you don't need to argue about the definition. They are heavily loss-making

pits, the worst 12% cost £275 million a year. You don't need to argue about them . . . You have to go through a procedure with the NUM and they have to be shut down. [8]

Events came to a head on 18 February when the Prime Minister finally agreed to meet members of the TUC Liaison Group, headed by TUC General Secretary, Norman Willis. He sought to persuade her that there might still be some alternative to total, unconditional surrender, with its prospects of enduring bitterness. Mrs Thatcher was unmoved: Any agreement must be 'absolutely clear and unequivocal' if it were to avoid sowing the seeds of future disputes. The wording of the final settlement must include reference to the working of the revised CRP, and this must be made transparently clear to the miners and the public. The NCB must retain the right to manage the industry.

(6) The settlement

At the end of February, in the absence of a negotiated solution to the dispute — and with an accelerating return to work by miners in most of Britain's coalfields — Emlyn Williams, South Wales President of the NUM, proposed a face-saving formula to the Executive. Rather than see the ignominious collapse of the strike, the miners should vote for a dignified return to work *without* signing any peace settlement and *without* agreeing any of the terms required by the NCB. This proposal recommended itself to the vast majority of striking miners as the only acceptable way of bringing the year-long strike to an honourable end without admission of defeat by either side.

(7) Aftermath

In the days immediately following the return to work, there were genuine fears at the NCB that the bitterness of the 12-month dispute would spill over into the workplace, with non-cooperation and vindictiveness between working and non-working miners. Though some incidents were reported, the vast majority of striking miners resumed their work in a dignified and subdued fashion. Since the strike had exhausted their savings, most miners seemed glad to be back at work and happy to have a job to go back to.

But the NCB refused to allow miners to resume work if they were deemed to have been involved in any form of violent incidents, as reported by local NCB management. This resulted in several hundred trade union activists — including some of the most prominent local strike leaders — losing their jobs for no other reason, as they saw it, than their active participation in the dispute. This was to become the most bitter legacy of the whole dispute. The NUM protested against the NCB's deliberate policy of petty discrimination against some of its most loyal members, who remained unemployed on the suspect evidence of NCB staff who had themselves been highly active partisans throughout the dispute. The NCB replied that, whilst it was willing to reconsider every appeal from excluded miners on its merits, it was not willing to offer a blanket amnesty to those miners whom it judged unfit for further employment following their reported activities during the strike. If miners were not satisfied with the outcome of these appeals, it was open to them to bring complaints of unfair dismissal to an Industrial Tribunal. Of the hundreds of such complaints eventually heard, the vast majority were upheld by the Tribunals. But this still did not always persuade the NCB to reinstate all successful complainants. In Britain, employers may still lawfully discriminate between those returning strikers whom they will, or will not, continue to employ. Tribunals have no powers to require employers to reinstate employees, but may award compensation against employers who refuse to do so.

Meanwhile, the NUM began to make overtures to the Union of Democratic Mineworkers (UDM) on how to bring the breakaway union's members back into the fold. The atmosphere immediately following the strike was anything but fraternal and no accommodation was possible between the two sides, either then or since.

SECTION 2: ANALYSIS OF THE DISPUTE

(1) What was the dispute about?

In Mrs Thatchers's Britain of 1984–85, there were few people without strong views on the miners' strike. According to your judgement and ideological standpoint, the strike was:

(i)   *the most prolonged, bitter and courageous mass industrial struggle Britain has witnessed this century*; [9]
(ii) *the country's most wasteful and unnecessary strike of all time*; [10]
(iii) *the longest, bloodiest and costliest dispute in the nation's history.* [11]

Despite their very different assessment, all three commentators would no doubt have agreed that:

> *Although ostensibly about no more than the further slimming down of an industry which had already been in decline for over three decades, it was, in fact, about much, much more.* [12]

It could be argued that the dispute was about *industrial* power and the conflict of industrial rights: the right of the NCB to exercise its traditional managerial prerogative in deciding which pits to close and when, *versus* the right of the NUM to mobilize its members by every means at its disposal, to oppose pit closures, job losses and the collapse of mining communities.

Ian MacGregor had been clear from the outset what the dispute was about:

The issue, whichever way it was dressed up in words, was the right to manage the industry. When it came down to it — whatever other items there were in the solution to the dispute — it had to contain an element that recognized the NCB's authority and indeed responsibility for making the final decision about which pits we closed, why and when. [13]

If this first view is correct, the dispute centred on two competing rationalities: the economic rationality of efficiency, cost reduction and the restoration of profitability to coal-mining *versus* the humanistic rationality of workers' jobs, the lives of miners and their families and of the communities in which they spend their lives — in short, the rationality of defending, in John Lloyd's words, 'a culture besieged'. [14]

Community isolation, fraternal solidarity and the distinctive culture of pit villages are recurring themes amongst academic analysts of the inter-industry propensity to strike. Kerr and Siegel concluded from their study of the subject that:

the miners [and the longshoremen] form isolated masses, almost a 'race apart'. They live on their own in separate communities. [15]

British historians have traced the roots of 'the miners' intense solidarity and loyalty to their unions' to 'their physical and social isolation'. [16] One has identified its origins in 'the emergence of the feeling of community out of a common experience of hardship'. [17] Another has pointed to the inherently romantic and conservative tradition within the miners' union:

The NUM is, like its predecessor the Mineworkers Federation of Great Britain, concerned with the preservation of the individuality of pit villages. [18]

A second interpretation might be that the dispute was about *political* power and the conflict of social objectives in the wider society: the central policy objective of the radical right Conservative Government of Margaret Thatcher being to shift the balance of power in the wider society in favour of the employers' interest, more especially the interest of private sector employers, and against the interest of organized labour in the trade unions. Amongst trade unions, no target was more symbolically important than the NUM, traditionally Britain's most solidaristic industrial union. Since the power of the unions was seen by the Thatcher Government as the biggest single obstacle to economic reform and regeneration, a successful confrontation with the miners would advance the cause of Conservatism in two ways:

(i)   By getting rid of 'uneconomic' pits and the crippling subsidy to the NCB, it would secure a significant reduction in the Public Sector Borrowing Requirement and thereby reduce energy costs.

(ii)   By defeating the NUM, it would purge the humiliating traumas of 1972 and 1974 when the NUM had taken on the government and the country, and won.

For Prime Minister Margaret Thatcher, the NUM (or its leading activists) was identified as 'the enemy within' whose power to subvert the economy must be ruthlessly destroyed, just as the 'enemy without' (the Argentinians in the 1982 Falklands War) had been destroyed, regardless of the casualties suffered on both sides.

Many political commentators subscribed to this second interpretation. According to Peter Riddell, Political Editor of *The Financial Times*:

> *After the downfall of the Heath administration, a miners' strike was regarded as the major industrial challenge for the Thatcher Government.* [19]

Having backed down over pit closures in the face of a threatened strike in 1981, the Government was certainly ready in 1984 to support the NCB in a direct confrontation with the NUM by its announced intention to cut capacity and to close 'uneconomic' pits. In the eyes of a majority of NUM members, that was what the dispute was about. In the words of Dr Kim Howells, Research Officer for South Wales NUM:

> *This strike hasn't been about pit closures. This strike has been about taking on the organized British labour movement — and smashing it.* [20]

One academic commentator made the same point even more explicitly:

> *The dispute in the coal industry is not about 'uneconomic pits'. It is demonstrably about this government's determination to gain total control over the industry in order to force down real wages and to 'reorganize' it, a euphemism that almost certainly implies privatization. But it is something more . . . breaking the miners has become more than a key issue. It has become an obsession.* [21]

A third interpretation might be that whilst the dispute raised a number of important social issues, like violence and democracy, the future of trade unionism, and management's right and duty to manage, the fundamental underlying issue was the price of coal. For, as indicated in *The Financial Times*:

> *This was always supposed to be a dispute about the future of Britain's main source of energy.* [22]

According to this interpretation, the future for British coal would, in practice, be determined in part by its price and in part by the investment decisions of the Coal Board's biggest customer — the Central

Electricity Generating Board (CEGB). By 1984, some 80% of the CEGB's power was generated by coal, but falling oil prices and the availability of cheap and safe nuclear power (before Chernobyl) were seen by the CEGB as likely future sources of its power needs:

> *With world coal in chronic oversupply and extractable cheaply in huge open pit operations, dollar prices of coal, like dollar prices of oil, are unlikely to rise in the next few years. So, if the Coal Board is to improve its finances it can only do so by continuing heavy investment (£750 million a year) and cutting costs, which is where Mr McGregor comes in. The ex-chairman of Amax, the US mining company, has grown up in a nomadic industry where you dig the cheapest coal first and close pits at the drop of a hat if the terms of trade move against you. It could not be further removed from the ethos of the UK coal-mining industry.* [22]

A fourth interpretation might be that the dispute was about trade union democracy and the doubtful legitimacy of a strike that failed to provide NUM members with the opportunity to vote during the year-long dispute. *The Times* saw it in precisely these terms:

> *At its heart, this strike is about a divided union and the struggle by working miners to rescue their union from the Communists and ultra-leftists who have hijacked its leadership.* [10]

(2) How important was the context?

For those employed in the industry, the historical context of the miners' dispute provided an essential clue to the impending confrontation. The long history of pit closures was always closely related to 'the politics of de-industrialization'. By 1979, Britain had a Conservative government whose policy explicitly aimed at ending the post-war economic consensus of Keynesian economic management. Instead, it espoused the radical right policies of economic monetarism and deliberately set out policies for reversing the nation's economic decline by driving back the frontiers of the Welfare State, cutting public services, restoring the free play of market forces and ending subsidies to loss-making nationalized industries.

Having successfully employed Ian MacGregor to cut back the British steel industry to a size commensurate with greatly-reduced world markets, Mrs Thatcher invited MacGregor to turn his attention to the British coal-mining industry with the same broad objectives — namely, to restore the competitiveness of British coal by closing uneconomic pits, reducing labour costs and getting rid of public subsidies. The historical context and the political environment were both ideal for the exercise of his managerial talents. MacGregor relished the task.

(3) Why did the NUM mount a national strike without a ballot?

When the NUM came into existence in 1945, the traditional rivalries and conflicting interests of Britain's miners were theoretically subordinated to the greater good and unity of all the miners nationally. In practice, however, schismatic tendencies inevitably persisted. What unified the miners was a set of common problems and aspirations: a national living wage; reduced working hours; improved working conditions, including better health and safety provisions; and a decent miners' pension. Where common issues were at stake, miners adopted a national stance and accepted restrictions on their freedom of action to strengthen the hand of their National Executive Committee (NEC). But miners remained divided on very real differences in working conditions and pay in different areas, and even between pits within a single area. Geological conditions, the age of the pit, the depth of working, manning levels, heat, dust, noise, and water levels — all these factors affected the mind and temper of the miners in different parts of the country.

Under its new constitution, the NUM Rulebook preserved the right of the area to debate and decide issues of particular local concern. But on national issues, such as wage claims, it also provided for a strong NEC with the right to recommend national strike action, followed by a national pithead ballot requiring a two-thirds majority of those voting before the NEC could call an official strike, at a moment of its own choosing.

In October 1970, the NUM engaged the Electoral Reform Society to supervise the union's first independent national ballot. The result showed only 55.5% of miners in favour of strike action on their annual wage claim, despite the fact that more than two-thirds had voted earlier in favour of strike action in Scotland, Wales, Cumberland and Kent — with Yorkshire just short of the two-thirds majority required. The union was genuinely split on the issue and the strike was narrowly averted. Mick McGahey, communist leader of the militant Scottish miners, urged his members to respect the democratic outcome of the ballot, to remain at work but to campaign inside the union to get the two-thirds rule changed in favour of a simple majority vote. McGahey's movement was finally successful: in 1984, the NUM changed its Rulebook to require a majority of 55% instead of the former two-thirds majority.

In the two successful miners' pay strikes of 1972 and 1974, the pithead ballot produced substantial majorities in favour of strike action. In 1981, unofficial strikes in many areas were backed by a resolution of the NEC recommending a ballot on strike action. The Government capitulated in the face of this threat without the need for a national ballot to be held, but during 1983–84, the NEC's recommendations for national strike action in opposition to the proposed closure of Kinneal colliery in Scotland, Snowdown in Kent and Tymawr-Lewis Merthyr in South Wales were all rejected. In the case of Tymawr-Lewis Merthyr, the result of a national pithead ballot produced a majority of 61% *against* a national strike.

In their analysis of the dispute, *The Guardian* Labour Staff threw new light on the thinking at NUM Headquarters on the use of the 'area strike strategy':

> There is more than anecdotal evidence that Scargill had long intended to ignore the union's constitution and the need for a 55% majority in a national strike ballot. Part of the leadership argued that it could legitimately avoid being 'constitutionalized out of action' by calling each area out on strike, thereby creating a de facto national strike and a de jure series of area strikes. NUM Executive Minutes, leaked in the summer of 1984 but dating back to March 1983, showed that Scargill advocated such an area strike strategy in spring 1983 over the closure of Tymawr-Lewis Merthyr, near Pontypridd, in South Wales. The National Executive rejected his advice, called a national ballot and lost . . . [23]

It thus became clear that the NEC could not rely on an automatic majority in favour of national strike action on pit closures because pit closures, unlike a national pay claim, is an inherently divisive issue. Not all miners, or all coalfields, are affected to the same extent. Which closure should the NUM fight? A national overtime ban, called in defence of Langwith colliery in Derbyshire, failed in 1976, as did similar attempts with Teversal in Nottinghamshire and Tymawr-Lewis Merthyr in 1983. Hence, the relentless pressure on the miners for a national ballot.

The crucial lessons that Scargill learned in his first years as President were applied in the 1984–85 dispute. When the proposed closure of Cortonwood colliery was announced, the NEC avoided the risk of a further rebuff by not recommending a pithead ballot in favour of a national strike. Instead, it decided to await the outcome of unofficial action in the Yorkshire area, which it could then endorse in the hope that other areas would follow suit, thereby producing what amounted in practice to a national strike but without the risk of defeat in a national ballot.

By this means, Scargill and the NUM Executive outwitted Mrs Thatcher's strategists, who assumed that the miners would reject for a third time their Executive's call for a national strike. By refusing to hold a ballot, the NUM Executive outmanoeuvred the opponents of strike action within the NUM and the Government. Conversely, by avoiding the ballot, Scargill opened fatal divisions within his own union, antagonized the general public, deprived the NUM of the financial and moral support of many trade unionists and alienated most members of the General Council of the TUC. What began as a tactical triumph for Scargill brought eventual disaster and defeat for the NUM.

In a round-table discussion in *Marxism Today*, George Bolton,

Vice-President of the Scottish Area NUM, gave his view on what the result of a ballot might have been:

> If the mass picketing in Nottinghamshire ... hadn't taken place, if you'd had a series of mass rallies in Nottingham, together with the special conference and the change of the ballot percentage rule, then in my view we could have won a national ballot and, against that different background, Notts would have come out. [24]

Ken Capstick, an NUM Yorkshire Branch Delegate, agreed:

> We could have won a national ballot hands down. And we probably missed a chance. But the trouble was that the national ballot had been made into an issue in itself. It was like giving in ... Quite honestly, you mentioned the ballot at your peril in miners' clubs and so on ... They looked at it that Margaret Thatcher wanted a ballot, MacGregor wanted a ballot, the media wanted a ballot, and they weren't going to have one. [25]

Alan Baker, Lodge Secretary of South Wales NUM, explained his doubts:

> If we'd had a ballot from cold, nationally, before the strike started, I think it would have gone against us ... But if we'd had one later on, around April–May, I'm positive we could have won with a fairly substantial majority. [26]

Dave Priscott, a member of the Communist Party Executive Committee, summed up the discussion in this way:

> The ballot raised two opposing principles. It was as much a matter of principle to some miners, that they must have a ballot before they struck, as it was a matter of principle to others not to have a ballot. And in the battle of principle around the ballot, the real principle, how to win, got a little bit lost ... [27]

The Guardian's Labour Editor gave his own, rather different, view of the ballot issue:

> The refusal to hold a ballot ran against the populist mood the Government had created amongst union members. It allowed a third of the union's own members to remain at work and, above all, it was probably a self-inflicted wound. A ballot could well have been won in April. [28]

But are ballots the only or, indeed, the best way to establish the popular will of workers in an industrial dispute? However desirable in terms of individual liberty and political theory, ballots may be self-defeating. An American academic has offered an alternative view of strike ballots:

The ballot, as a means to show support for a strike, is a less than perfect device. Many American unions do not conduct strike ballots (nor does the American law require them — one of the few areas in which American law is less restrictive than the UK) and British unions still do not require it. Workers have other ways to demonstrate a willingness to strike other than using a ballot. Every working day workers can 'vote' with their feet; they walk the picket line or punch the clock. Strike ballots in the US are often devices used to instill solidarity, to move people from ambivalence to commitment, and to embolden those who want to go out and shame those who don't. But the new British labour law made the NUM officials criminals: their 'illegal' actions weakened the NUM claims of legitimacy in the eyes of the public. [29]

It was doubts over these 'claims of legitimacy' that became the fatal flaw in the NUM's otherwise winning strategy.

(4) Did the NCB succeed in reasserting the 'right to manage'?

During the course of the dispute, the NCB significantly modified its principal position on pit closures. From the outset, MacGregor was clear that the dispute was about his right to run the coal industry as a business. But the Board was saddled with the Colliery Review Procedure (CRP), a long-standing and well-tested jointly-agreed procedure for deciding the future of pits that the Board felt should be closed. Introduced in the 1960s at a time of substantial pit closures, it enabled the unions to challenge the Board's proposal to close a particular pit where it could show good cause. The procedure comprised an elaborate four-stage review:

(i)   A local colliery review of the pit's economic performance with suggestions from both sides on how performance might be improved to justify keeping the pit open.

(ii) Where such suggestions failed to improve performance, a recommendation by the colliery manager that the pit be closed on economic grounds.

(iii) Where no agreement was reached at Stage (ii), a recommendation for closure by the Area Director to NCB top management, to be followed by a full review at which both unions and area management presented their case.

(iv) A final review by the full Board and a decision whether to endorse or reject the proposed closure.

Over twenty years, this form of CRP had become 'established custom and practice' in the industry. Its skilful use by previous Chairmen had helped the NCB to close hundreds of pits and allowed some 200 000 miners to leave the industry without major conflict over pit closures. Having spent some years in the American coal-mining industry, MacGregor recognized the value attached to the

CRP by both sides of the British mining industry, but his autocratic style had no room for such procedures:

> *Over the years the consultative machinery [on pit closures] at Hobart House [NCB Headquarters] had been distorted and diluted to the point where it was no longer a question of management outlining and consulting on the best way of carrying out its policies . . . [but of] finding some way to get the union to permit the management to take any action at all . . . From the mid-1970s the NUM's interpretation of the consultation process was translated into the idea that nothing could be done without their prior agreement and approval . . There was such a phobia within Hobart House about the power of the NUM that the NCB had to go to absurd lengths to disguise even its gentlest of intentions . . . I thought it was time to put a stop to all this nonsense and to reassert the NCB responsibility to manage the enterprise effectively.* [30]

As a result of NUM opposition and the threat of NACODS joining the strike, the NCB eventually agreed to retain the CRP in modified form, provided that it included provision for the closure of pits on grounds other than exhaustion or safety. On 18 July 1984, the NCB offered to keep open the five pits at the centre of the dispute and produced a revised version of the CRP, which contained just three clauses on future pit closures:

> *In order to establish more clearly the parameters in respect of exhaustion of reserves, in line with the principles of The Plan for Coal, the following categories and procedures will apply:*
> (i)   *Collieries which are exhausted in line with the principles of The Plan for Coal will be closed by joint agreement*
> (ii) *Collieries facing severe geological difficulties, again in line with the principles of The Plan for Coal, will be closed by joint agreement*
> (iii) *The NCB and NUM agree that where a comprehensive and in-depth investigation by their respective mining engineers shows that a colliery has no further minable reserves that are workable and which can be beneficially developed, such a colliery shall be deemed exhausted.* [31]

Negotiations broke down when the NUM refused to accept this third clause in the NCB's revised CRP. On 19 September 1984, MacGregor presented a three-point 'total package deal' to the NUM:

(i)   a stay of execution of the five pits under closure threat;
(ii) the phasing of the proposed cut of 4 million tonnes of capacity over a longer time period;
(iii) some form of words that established the third category of closure on grounds other than exhaustion or safety.

MacGregor presented the proposed deal in these persuasive terms:

> *Gentlemen, it comes as a total package. You don't get the first two things unless we get the third. If we can agree it — then I will give you some things you can use to go off and claim a great victory, provided we can still genuinely say that we have retained, at the end of the day, the right to manage the business.* [32]

Once again the NUM refused to compromise on the issue. It was not until 13 February 1985 that the wording was agreed on a document, drafted by the TUC, which provided for a modified CRP that would include the setting up of a panel of independent qualified arbitrators who would hear the evidence of both sides and adjudicate on the merits of any proposed pit closures.

Despite this vital concession, the NCB insisted at the end of the dispute that its position had been vindicated and that it had maintained its original stance on the right to close 'uneconomic' pits. It conceded that it had modified its original 1 March 1984 closure plan but insisted that it had not surrendered its fundamental 'right to manage'. Indeed, the Board pointed to the collapse of the strike on 2 March 1985 as evidence of its success in having reasserted that right. In the aftermath of the dispute, that judgement seemed premature. Whether it will be confirmed in practice over the next few years remains to be seen.

On the morning of the return to work, *The Financial Times* summed up a widely-held view on the NCB's right to manage the industry:

> *It is important that pit managers should regain the right to manage, but it has to be management by consent. As in other industries faced with structural upheaval, the management has to convince employees that modernization is in their interests, to find imaginative ways of easing the impact of change and to bring new sources of employment to mining communities.* [33]

(5) Who won?

Given the duration of the dispute, the concluding stalemate, and the return to work without an agreement on pit closures, all sides were reluctant to claim an outright victory. On 3 March 1985, the NUM President, whilst refusing to concede defeat, virtually admitted failure when he insisted that, although the strike was over:

> *The dispute goes on. We will continue to fight against pit closures or job losses, make no mistake. Don't underestimate this union's ability to oppose.* [34]

For the NUM leadership, the year-long battle may have been lost, but not the war. Scargill's important distinction between the outcome of the strike and the outcome of the dispute on pit closures was taken up by *The Times* in its own judgement on the outcome:

> *For all the public denials of crowing or gloating, Mrs Thatcher and her colleagues will regard the outcome as a major victory . . . The strike has been defeated. The attempt by Mr Scargill to use industrial muscle to challenge the parliamentary system, the policies of a freely-elected government and the rule of law have been defeated . . . The challenge and menace of Scargillism has been crushed. We have seen the face of defeat. We await the responsibility of victory.* [35]

The Times identified three main reasons for the miners' defeat:

> *First, the uninterrupted production of coal from Nottingham has reduced the cost of oil substitutes.*
>
> *Second, the fact that never fewer than 40 000 miners continued working, which reminded the whole world that the union was divided because its leadership ignored the rules.*
>
> *Third, the fact that the working miners, armed with legal rights, were able to move against Mr Scargill's control of union funds.* [10]

The Financial Times entered a more cautious judgement:

> *Government ministers and the Board alike are not happy that the strike has ended without an agreement on the issue of uneconomic pit closures.*

It noted that there was certain to be fresh pressure on the NUM to accept the principle contained in the TUC document, subsequently thrown out by the NUM Executive, to the effect that:

> *. . . where there are no further reserves which can be developed to provide the Board, in line with their responsibilities, with a satisfactory basis for continuing operation, collieries will be referred to a new review procedure.* [19]

Providing his own explanation for the outcome of the dispute, *The Financial Times* leader–writer concluded:

> *Far from Government seeking a confrontation with the miners, it has won largely because of Mr Scargill's intransigeance . . (He) had confidently predicted victory almost to the last. The Government and the NCB were prepared to make compromises. Indeed there were several times when Mr Scargill could have accepted very attractive terms for his members but turned them down.* [33]

On another page, *The Financial Times*' Industrial Editor, John Lloyd, subjected 'Scargill's intransigeance' to sustained analysis:

> *The mineworkers' president is of a stamp which negates all*

argument — including his own — that personalities do not matter, policies and events do. It is a matter of real doubt if this strike would have been possible, at this breadth and depth, without him ... (For Scargill) no consideration is higher than the pursuit of principle, even the continued existence of a union and supporters who could defend it. [14]

Those who consistently supported the miners' strike offered a very different view of its outcome. In *Marxism Today*, Hywel Francis identified some 'obvious and legitimate reasons why there is a belief circulating that the strike was a "victory" ':

1. The incredible organization and courage that sustained almost half a million miners (including their families) in mining areas for nearly a year.
2. The fact that the Government, with the backing of virtually every arm of the state, failed to compel the NUM to sign the terms that the NCB wished to dictate to the miners.
3. The fact that the NCB had been unable to close the 20 pits and axe the 20 000 jobs, which was its intention in March 1984.
4. The fact that the NCB had been unable to close the five threatened pits, which also sparked off the dispute.
5. The fact that the NCB had been forced to accept an independent appeal body within the Colliery Review Procedure.
6. The fact that the NCB had failed in its attempt to break the NUM and its members' morale.

Having noted those reasons, Francis went on to present a painfully honest analysis of the dispute:

To talk in terms of 'victory' or 'defeat' would be simplistic. There is no doubt however that the miners and the labour movement have suffered a significant setback ... It would be a most appalling exercise in self-delusion to claim that the NUM had achieved its objectives:
1. *The closure programme had not been withdrawn by the NCB.*
2. *The unity of the union had been broken in the course of the struggle.*
3. *Hundreds of union members had been sacked.*
4. *No general amnesty had been won for sacked miners.*
5. *In some coalfields, long-established procedures had not been adhered to and managerial policy had become more aggressive, notably in Scotland.* [9]

Such diverse judgements tempt one to ask whether this particular dispute was capable of being won by either side. Perhaps the miners' strike epitomizes the futility of full-scale industrial warfare, just as the possession of massive nuclear arsenals by the world's superpowers brings home the futility of nuclear warfare in which neither side can possibly 'win'.

Given the uncompromising stance taken by both sides from the outset; given the strategic plans that each side put into effect; given the massive intervention of the state to uphold what Ministers called 'law and order'; given the NUM's refusal to call a national ballot or to put their case into the hands of the TUC; given the NCB's refusal to abandon its closure plans; given the Government's determination to see the NUM defeated — given all these considerations, one is forced to conclude that whilst the NUM did not lose, neither did the NCB win. In different ways, and for quite different reasons, each side acknowledged its own limited defeat. On balance, the NUM lost more than the NCB.

(6) Costs and benefits of the dispute

Replying to a House of Commons question, early in the dispute, Chancellor Nigel Lawson asserted that winning the strike could be worth every penny that it cost the Government and the nation. Yet the final cost of the dispute, estimated by Gavyn Davies, chief economist with stockbrokers Simon & Coates, must have shocked even the Chancellor:

Item	£ billion
1. Substitution of oil for coal by the CEGB	1.200
2. NCB losses in revenue	1.100
3. Income tax lost on miners' earnings	0.300
4. Policing the strike	0.200
5. Additional losses at the NCB	0.200
6. Additional social security payments	0.050
Total	3.050

In national accounting terms, the dispute was officially estimated by the Treasury to have reduced the Gross Domestic Product by between 1% and 1.25% in 1984 alone. But, as *The Financial Times*, amongst others, pointed out:

> *This is mainly confined to miners and their communities, representing the loss of coal production and the reduction in miners' spending power.* [33]

Although such production losses might be made up by the end of 1985, *The Financial Times* saw little point in denying that Britain's national income would be permanently lower than it would have been without the strike.

Against this independent estimate of £3 billion losses, the Government's political arithmetic looked quite different since it showed the likely cost of *not* having fought the NUM on the issue of closures — namely, the perpetuation and further rise in the NCB's annual operating losses, allegedly running at some £350 million in 1983–84, arising mostly from the high cost of producing coal from so-called 'uneconomic' pits.

The NCB's accountants arrived at their own estimate of the costs and benefits of the strike along the following lines:

(i)   loss of coal output (64.5 million tonnes against a planned reduction of 4 million tonnes);
(ii) loss of more than 60 coal faces (equivalent of about 20 pits);
(iii) loss of some £100 million of coal-mining equipment;
(iv) reduction in the workforce of about 10 000 (5% of the total) due to:

(a)	voluntary redundancies	5750
(b)	retirement due to ill-health or death	850
(c)	normal retirements	430
(d)	other reasons, including dismissals	2360

Although Scargill himself put the total cost of the strike to the Government as 'approaching £7 billion', the NUM was less forthcoming on the cost of the strike to its own members through lost earnings, or the drain on NUM funds by way of fines, legal costs, etc., as well as the loss of union dues from reduced NUM membership as a result of pit closures and the formation of the breakaway UDM.

But the true costs of an unprecedentedly long and bitter conflict cannot be measured simply in cold economic terms. A social cost-benefit analysis would have to take account of less tangible, but no less important, costs, which may defy quantification but which are nonetheless real — such as the divisions within the NUM between striking and working miners; the subsequent breakaway of the Nottinghamshire miners; the human suffering in mining communities, including some heart-rending divisions amongst previously united families; the division of the country between those who supported the miners in their stand against the NCB's authoritarian style of imposed change and those who supported the NCB and its desire to quicken the pace of change in Britain.

(7) Lessons of the dispute

The exceptional duration and character of the miners' dispute led many commentators to reflect on its lessons. Given the historic divisions amongst Britain's miners, R. L. Turner was impressed by the very possibility of a national strike on such an issue:

> *The most significant factor of the 1984–85 miners' strike against pit closures was not the substantial minority of workers who continued to work throughout the dispute, nor the number of men who 'drifted back to work', but the fact that a strike over pit closures could have been pursued on a national basis at all.* [3]

For *The Financial Times* there were three important lessons:

(i)   The Government and the country could have stood up to a major strike accompanied by violence and intimidation on a large scale, without caving in and without serious dislocation.

(ii) The power of the big unions had been at least temporarily reduced, which was one of the Government's original aims.

(iii) The balance of forces was tipped in the Government's favour because:
   (a) coal stocks were high;
   (b) the miners were not united;
   (c) there was no energy crisis;
   (d) other unions declined to back the NUM on any significant scale;
   (e) violence on the picket lines never quite led to a complete breakdown in the normal rule of law;
   (f) NACODS did not join the strike, as once seemed possible.
   [33]

From a very different perspective, Hywel Francis in *Marxism Today* carefully weighed the lessons of the miners' achievements against their mistakes:

> *The most important achievement of the year-long strike was the collective national leadership given by Scargill, Heathfield and McGahey to defend jobs, communities and the nationalized coal industry itself . . . [This] evoked a most loyal and courageous response from striking miners, women supporters, their immediate and extended families, mining communities, a support network at home and abroad the like of which Britain has never witnessed. The lessons for other industrial workers are all there to be learned . . .*
>
> *The bitter lesson of the miners' strike is that no section of the trade union movement can mount a successful struggle of its own; that simply going to the TUC and Labour Party Conferences in the traditional way and getting fine-sounding solidarity resolutions is not enough . . . [What we need is] a strategy whereby the NUM is not confronting but cooperating with workers, whether they be in the first instance NACODS or eventually also with power and transport workers as part of a broad energy workers' alliance.*

Francis sharply contrasted the intelligence network of the NCB and the Government, 'based on a serious and scientific assessment of the views of the miners, and other industrial workers and the public at large', with that of the NUM and other unions which:

> *often based their plans on nothing more than hearsay and wishful thinking . . . If the price for 'victory' and 'unity' will be acceptance of the ballot and the abandoning of mass-picketing, then so be it. [9]*

This view clearly reflected much post-strike agonizing on the part of the NUM and its supporters on the value of mass picketing. At the start of the strike, many miners appeared to believe that Nottinghamshire would never be balloted out, but only picketed out. By the end of the strike, Scargill continued to express his faith in the efficacy of flying pickets. But how many miners still shared Scargill's view? In an interview in January 1985, Scargill admitted that, after a while, he had not expected Nottinghamshire miners to join the strike:

> *I knew after two weeks of the dispute that Nottingham would not join us. All my experience is that if workers do not back a strike after a fortnight, they will never be brought out.* [36]

At the end of the strike, Dr Kim Howells, Research Officer for the South Wales miners, articulated some of the lessons that he felt had to be learned from the dispute:

> *The present dispute has taught us that it's not like 1972 and 1974. We're living in a very different age now. We have a much larger police force. The great image of the Saltley Gates situation, where large numbers of miners actually succeeded in turning a Government around, doesn't seem possible now. This Government is very different from that which operated under Edward Heath. The police force is infinitely larger. Miners picketing alone can't actually win. We need the TUC to act, we need the Labour Party to mobilize effectively behind us if we are to win next time.* [37]

Howells concluded that it was no longer possible for the miners to deliver a 'knock-out blow' to the government as they had done in the pay disputes of 1972 and 1974. In future, the miners would need the solidaristic support of the entire labour and trade union movement.

The Industrial Editor of *The Financial Times*, John Lloyd, struck a similar note in his own conclusions on the strike:

> *Very few people indeed now believe in the miners' case without major reservations — believing in the miners' cause may be something different. It is not that the Government has retained the support of the people; it is that the miners have not won it.* [14]

In the view of *The Guardian*, the NUM had made three fateful errors in its handling of the dispute:

(i) the fact that the NUM Executive had refused to hold a ballot, which could have been won in April;

(ii) the fact that Scargill himself refused to condemn outright all forms of violence;

(iii) the fact that the NUM allowed itself to be boxed into a negotiating position where it was seen to be defending 'uneconomic' pits. [1]

Finally, *The Guardian*'s leader–writer spelled out some of the deeper and more wider-ranging political lessons of the dispute:

> *The defeat of the miners will be seen as a landmark in the decline of the industrial working class and the advocates of political strike action. It is unlikely that the unions will again mount such a general and uncoordinated challenge to the authority of the state. The power of the unions to bring down governments appears to have been a phenomenon of the seventies, and is unlikely to re-emerge as long as the labour market remains in its present depressed state . . . After the year of the miners' strike, union leaders will think hard before calling out their members for a strike against industrial policy.* [1]

SECTION 4: CONCLUSIONS AND POSTSCRIPT 1987

The effects of the miners' strike continued to reverberate throughout Britain in the year after the end of the strike. Journalists and academic commentators continued to offer their reflections on the conduct and outcomes of the dispute in a stream of publications (see Suggestions for further reading at the end of this chapter). Ian MacGregor published his own detailed account of the dispute, ominously entitled *The Enemies Within*. [13] Arthur Scargill initially observed a more discreet silence.

The TUC, meeting in Blackpool on 3 September 1985, approved by 4 649 000 votes to 4 585 000 (a majority of only 64 000) a resolution moved by Arthur Scargill calling for a future Labour government to introduce legislation:

(i)   to review the cases of all miners imprisoned as a result of the dispute;
(ii)   to reinstate all miners dismissed by the NCB for activities arising out of the dispute;
(iii) to reimburse the NUM and other unions involved of all monies 'confiscated' as a result of fines, sequestration and receivership;
(iv)   to end all pit closures other than for reasons of exhaustion.

On the previous day, the General Council of the TUC had decided by 25 votes to 16 not to support the NUM resolution on the grounds that 'we cannot and must not put miners in a special situation and claim a special deal from a Labour government in the future'.

The Annual Conference of the Labour Party, meeting in Bournemouth on 2 October 1985, voted by 3 542 000 votes to 2 912 000 in favour of a similar resolution but the majority of 630 000 was less than the two-thirds necessary for its inclusion in the party's next general election manifesto.

At the end of October 1985, agreement was reached between

the NCB, NUM, NACODS, and BACM on a revised Colliery Review Procedure that provided for the appointment of six senior independent arbitrators, of whom three would be nominated by the NCB and three by the unions.

During 1985, industrial tribunals upheld the claims of unfair dismissal brought by large numbers of miners whom the NCB refused to re-employ after the dispute. Notwithstanding these tribunal decisions, the NCB reserved the right not to take back into employment miners whose conduct it deemed to be inconsistent with continued employment. Many of these miners have still not been re-employed by the Board.

By December 1985, the Union of Democratic Mineworkers (UDM) had been formed with a membership made up principally of dissident members of the NUM, concentrated in the Derbyshire and Nottinghamshire coalfields. This breakaway from the NUM was initially encouraged and sponsored by Ian MacGregor, who offered higher wages to members of the UDM who had remained at work during the dispute. Sir Robert Haslam, who replaced Ian MacGregor as Chairman of the renamed *British Coal* in September 1986, took a rather different view, discouraged the breakaway union and worked for reconciliation of the dissidents within the NUM.

In September 1986, the NCB made a unilateral wage award (backdated to November 1985 for those miners who had worked through the dispute) to members of the NUM, even though no agreement had been reached with their union because of a further dispute over the pension rights of miners who had engaged in the earlier major dispute.

In March 1987, the miners of South Wales voted for six-day working at the new coking pit at Margam, despite the bitter opposition of the NUM Executive. By May 1987, thirty months after the end of the strike, the miners were still refusing to negotiate pay and conditions with British Coal. In desperation, British Coal made yet another unilateral wage award.

In the June 1987 general election, the UDM and NUM both worked for the defeat of Mrs Thatcher and the Conservative Government, but the divisions of the 1984–85 miners' strike were still not yet healed. In a series of pre-retirement interviews, Mick McGahey offered his considered reflections on the dispute, together with some advice to his 'young comrade', Arthur Scargill:

> *I have to say to him that anger is not enough. If anger was sufficient, our forefathers would have won the battle long ago ... so we need more than anger. We need tactics and policies that win people: win people to come over to us ...*
>
> *To say that you can go through a year's strike with all the traumatic events we went through from March 1984 to March 1985 and say we'd do all the same things again — No ...*
>
> *The miners never demanded a ballot vote, and the consti-*

tutional process allowed the miners to have a ballot vote had they demanded it . . . I'm not sure that the ballot vote question did not penetrate into people's minds because of the traditional democracy of the British people. They asked — why not a ballot vote? And did that not isolate us? . . .

I do believe that a more critical — and shall I suggest, a more self-critical — approach to the miners' strike, in analysing the lessons for the future, might have been beneficial for young trade unionists . . . If there were mistakes — lessons to be learned — then we're all involved. [38]

In November 1987, Scargill resigned as life President of the NUM and immediately offered himself for re-election — an astute move and a defiant gesture against the Thatcher Government's new trade union laws, which require all major union office-holders to offer themselves for election before assuming office. The miners' dispute of 1984–85 is now long over, but its political and industrial repercussions will continue to be felt in the 1990s.

CHRONOLOGY OF THE DISPUTE

1 September 1983	MacGregor takes over as NCB Chairman
31 October	National overtime ban begins
23 January 1984	Sporadic strikes throughout Scottish coalfields in support of 20 000 miners sent home due to overtime ban
20 February	Scottish pit strike
1 March	NCB announces closure of Cortonwood pit; Yorkshire miners called out on strike
6 March	NCB announces 4 million ton cut-back in output
8 March	Yorkshire and Scottish strikes given official support by NUM Executive
12 March	Official strike begins
14 March	NCB granted High Court injunction against NUM
16 March	Nottingham miners vote against strike
26 March	NACODS accepts 5.2% pay offer
3 April	NUR begin blacking coal supplies
19 April	Special delegate conference votes against ballot
23 May	Talks between NUM and NCB collapse
29 May	Violence at Orgreave coke depot
13 June	Rotherham peace talks break down
18 June	Further violence at Orgreave
20 June	Pickets blockade steelworks; railwaymen halt coal supplies to Llanwern and Ravenscraig
21 June	MacGregor letter to miners
5 July	Peace talks at Rubens Hotel, London
9 July	Docks' protest strike against BSC

11 July	Delegate conference decides to discipline working miners
18 July	Rubens Hotel peace talks collapse
21 July	Docks' protest strike ends
31 July	South Wales Area NUM fined £50 000 for contempt, and assets seized
11 August	NUM Special Conference calls for TUC support
21 August	TUC General Council discusses miners strike
23 August	Second dock strike over unloading of coal
3 September	TUC Congress backs support for miners
9 September	Fresh peace talks
12 September	NACODS decides to ballot members on strike action
14 September	NCB — NUM talks break down in stalemate
15 September	TUC directly involved in peace talks
20 September	Derbyshire miners win injunction against NUM
24 September	Scottish Court declares strike official and lawful
28 September	NACODS votes 82.5% for strike; Yorkshire and Derbyshire strikes ruled unlawful
1 October	Scargill gets strong personal support at Labour Party Conference; Kinnock condemns all violence
3 October	NACODS and NCB go to ACAS
9 October	Conservative Conference supports fight to the finish against miners
10 October	NUM fined £200 000
11 October	NUM and NCB go to ACAS
15 October	ACAS talks break down over revised CRP
16 October	NACODS Executive calls strike for 25 October
21 October	Michael Eaton appointed NCB spokesman
24 October	NACODS calls off proposed strike
25 October	NUM's assets seized after NUM refuses to pay contempt fine
31 October	Second round of ACAS peace talks break down
9 November	Violence at Cortonwood
12 November	NCB claims 1900 more miners back at work
21 November	Government reduces benefits to strikers' families
23 November	NCB offers bounty to returning strikers
7 December	TUC decides against illegal action in support of miners; NCB's Industrial Relations Director to retire early
24 January 1985	Preliminary talks between NUM and NCB
25 January	NACODS backs NUM in refusing NCB precondition to talks
29 January	Preliminary talks break down
19 February	Prime Minister meets TUC Liaison Group
20 February	NUM Executive rejects TUC revised formula to end strike

21 February	NUM Special Delegate Conference rejects but NACODS accepts the TUC formula to end strike
25 February	South Wales strike begins to crumble
1 March	NUM Area Conferences call for return to work without an agreement
2 March	Yorkshire Area NUM votes to continue strike
3 March	Special Delegate Conference votes for return to work; strike ends but 'the struggle goes on'

WHO'S WHO IN THE DISPUTE

Heathfield, Peter	General Secretary, National Union of Mineworkers
MacGregor, Ian	Chairman, National Coal Board
McGahey, Mick	Vice President, National Union of Mineworkers
Murray, Len	General Secretary, TUC
Scargill, Arthur	President, National Union of Mineworkers
Smith, Ned	Director of Industrial Relations, National Coal Board

REFERENCES

1 *The Guardian*, 4 March 1985.
2 For a lucid exposition of the meaning and evolution of the concept of rights, see Alexandre Berenstein: 'The development and scope of economic and social rights', *Labour and Society*, International Labour Organization (International Institute for Labour Studies), Geneva, Vol 7, No. 3, July–September 1982.
3 Royce Logan Turner: 'Post-war pit closures: the politics of de-industrialisation', *Political Quarterly*, Spring 1985.
4 Sidney Ford, quoted by Turner: 'Post-war pit closures: the politics of de-industrialisation', *Political Quarterly*, Spring 1985.
5 Arthur Scargill, quoted by Turner: 'Post-war pit closures: the politics of de-industrialisation', *Political Quarterly*, Spring 1985.
6 Wilberforce Inquiry Report, cited by Turner: 'Post-war pit closures: the politics of de-industrialisation', *Political Quarterly*, Spring 1985.
7 John Lloyd: 'Who said what to whom, when and why', *The Financial Times*, 15 October 1984.
8 Mrs Margaret Thatcher, TV interview, 21 January 1985.
9 Hywel Francis: 'NUM United: A Team in Disarray', *Marxism Today*, April 1985
10 *The Times*, 4 March 1985.
11 Peter Wilsher, Duncan Macintyre and Michael Jones: *Strike: Thatcher, Scargill and The Miners*, Andre Deutsch, London, 1985.
12 Andrew Neil, Editor of *The Sunday Times*, Introduction to Wilsher, Macintyre and Jones: *Strike: Thatcher, Scargill and The Miners*, Andre Deutsch, London, 1985.
13 Ian MacGregor: *The Enemies Within*, Collins, London, pp. 236–7,

14   John Lloyd: *The Financial Times*, 4 March 1985.
15   Kerr and Siegel *The Inter-industry Propensity to Strike*, in Kornhauser, Dubin and Ross: *Industrial Conflict*, McGraw-Hill, New York, 1954, pp. 186–212.
16   V. L. Allen: *The Militancy of British Miners*, The Moor Press, Sheffield, 1981.
17   E. P. Thompson: *Writing by Candlelight*, Merlin, Coventry, 1971.
18   Brian McCormick: *Industrial Relations in the Coal Industry*, Macmillan, London, 1976.
19   Peter Riddell: *The Financial Times*, 4 March 1985.
20   Dr Kim Howells, quoted in *The Financial Times*, 4 March 1985.
21   Colin Sweet, in Huw Beynon (ed.): *Digging Deeper: Issues in the Miners' Strike*, Pluto Press, London, 1985.
22   Ian Hargreaves: *The Financial Times*, 4 March 1985.
23   Keith Harper and Patrick Wintour: *The Guardian*, 4 March 1985.
24   George Bolton: *Marxism Today*, April 1985, pp. 21–4.
25   Ken Capstick: *Marxism Today*, April 1985, pp. 21–4.
26   Alan Baker: *Marxism Today*, April 1985, pp. 21–4.
27   Dave Priscott: *Marxism Today*, April 1985, pp. 21–4.
28   Keith Harper: *The Guardian*, 4 March 1985.
29   Teresa Ghilarducci: 'When management strikes: PATCO and the British miners', *Industrial Relations Journal*, Vol. 17, No. 2, Summer 1986.
30   Ian MacGregor: *The Enemies Within*, Collins, London, p. 237.
31   Ian MacGregor: *The Enemies Within*, Collins, London, p. 250.
32   Ian MacGregor: *The Enemies Within*, Collins, London, p. 288.
33   *The Financial Times*, 4 March 1985.
34   Arthur Scargill, quoted in *The Times*, 3 March 1985.
35   *The Times*, 3 March 1985.
36   Arthur Scargill, quoted by Harper and Wintour: *The Guardian*, 4 March 1985.
37   Kim Howells, BBC Radio 4 interview, March 1985.
38   Mick McGahey, interviewed by Trevor Philips for *This Week*, and reported by John Lloyd and John Sweeney in 'Anger is not enough', *New Statesman*, 3 April 1987, pp. 18–19.

STUDY QUESTIONS

1.   What do you understand by the term 'management prerogatives'?
2.   Are secret postal ballots before strike action the only — or the best — way of ensuring democratic decisions in industrial disputes?
3.   Is it possible to reconcile 'the right to manage' with 'management by consent'?
4.   Examine the arguments for and against the NCB's (British Coal's) refusal to reinstate all miners sacked during the dispute.
5.   Consider what more could (or should) have been done by one or other of the following bodies to help to resolve the miners' strike, 1984–85:

    (a)   the Government,
    (b)   the Labour Party,
    (c)   the TUC,
    (d)   ACAS.

6.   Make an evaluation of the respective strategies and tactics of the NCB and the NUM in their handling of the miners' strike.

SUGGESTIONS FOR FURTHER READING

Martin Adeney and John Lloyd; *The Miners' Strike*, Routledge, London, 1986.

V. L. Allen: *The Militancy of British Miners*, The Moor Press, Sheffield, 1981.

Huw Beynon (ed.): *Digging Deeper: Issues in the Miners' Strike*, Pluto Press, London, 1985.

Alex Callinicos and Mike Simons: *The Great Strike: The Miners' Strike of 1984/5 And Its Lessons*, Socialist Worker Publication, London, 1985.

Jim Coulter: *A State of Siege: Politics and Policy of the Coalfield: Miners' Strike, 1984*, Canary Press, London, 1984.

Jill Dennis: The Miners' Strike 1984–5: a Select Bibliography, London University, 1985.

Bob Fine and Robert Miller: *Policing the Miners' Strike*, Lawrence and Wishart, London, 1985.

Teresa Ghilarducci: 'When management strikes: PATCO and the British miners', *Industrial Relations Journal*, Vol. 17, No. 2, Summer 1986.

Geoffrey Goodman: *The Miners' Strike*, London: Pluto Press, London, 1985.

Tony Hall: *King Coal*, Penguin, Harmondsworth, 1981.

Peter Hain: *Political Strikes*, Viking, London, 1986.

Nicholas Jones: *Strikes and the Media*, Blackwell, Oxford, 1986.

Brian McCormick: *Industrial Relations in the Coal Industry*, Macmillan, London, 1976.

Ian MacGregor: *The Enemies Within*, Collins, London, 1986.

Brian Towers: 'Posing larger questions: the British miners' strike of 1984–85', *Industrial Relations Journal*, Vol 14, No.2, Summer 1985.

Royce Logan Turner: 'Post-war pit closures: the politics of de-industrialisation', *Political Quarterly*, Spring 1985.

Peter Wilsher, Donald Macintyre and Michael Jones: *Strike: Thatcher, Scargill and The Miners*, Andre Deutsch, London, 1985.

CHAPTER 9

■ White-collar militants —

THE TEACHERS' PAY DISPUTE, 1985–87

> *Schoolteachers, especially those in grammar and high schools,*
> *are the economic proletarians of the professions.*
> C Wright Mills
> *White Collar*

INTRODUCTION: COMPROMISE OR CHAOS?

On the afternoon of 11 December 1986, the Secretary of State for
Education and Science, Kenneth Baker, rose in the House of
Commons to open the Third Reading of the Teachers' Pay and
Conditions Bill. This would end the existing arrangements for nego-
tiating teachers' pay and conditions in England and Wales and substi-
tute an Interim Advisory Committee, whose recommendations the
Education Secretary could accept or ignore by imposing pay levels
that the Government thought appropriate.

According to Mr Baker, the Bill marked the end of the
discredited Burnham pay negotiating machinery and the beginning of
the period when teachers' pay and conditions would be negotiated
together. It would help to re-establish the proper role of the Secretary
of State in determining pay:

> *The Bill will bring to an end the negotiating brawl that has*
> *disfigured the education system for the last two years, of which*
> *the children have been the victims.* [1]

Despite nearly 24 hours of continuous debate on 251 amendments
tabled by Opposition parties, the Government refused to offer any
concessions. Giles Radice, the Shadow Education Secretary, described
the Bill as dangerously authoritarian. It removed bargaining rights
and substituted a system of ministerial diktat. The Liberal education
spokesman, Clement Freud, said that 400 000 teachers would lose
the rights they had had in law since 1919:

> *What other section of workers is similarly disadvantaged when*
> *it comes to pay negotiations? We need a new initiative to solve*
> *this dispute and not the strong-arm tactics we have seen.* [2]

Having completed its first Commons stages without changes,
the Bill was given a Third Reading and sent to the House of Lords.
Next day, John Pearman, leader of the local authority employers, told
the Education Secretary that there would be no compromise with the

Government on teachers' pay unless it withdrew or fundamentally altered the Bill. Meanwhile, the TUC had requested a meeting with the Prime Minister to protest against the Bill, which was seen not only as the death knell to collective bargaining between teachers and their employers but as a potentially wider threat to all public sector workers.

Once more, the lives of hundreds of thousands of shoolchildren were about to be disrupted. The question that parents throughout the country asked themselves was whether chaos in the schools was inevitable again or whether some compromise settlement might not be found. How was it possible that an industrial dispute over teachers' pay had been allowed to drag on for over two years? Why had the members of the teaching profession resorted to militant industrial action in support of their pay claim? Why did the Government find it necessary to legislate an end to the dispute? The rest of this chapter seeks to answer these questions.

SECTION 1: PROFESSIONALISM AND MILITANCY

The professions occupy an obscure yet significant place in the occupation structure of advanced industrial societies because the boundaries that surround them are perennially fluid and indistinct. Professionals are neither capitalists nor workers, neither bureaucrats nor administrators. Yet they undoubtedly play an increasingly important strategic role in the development of advanced societies. Talcott Parsons suggests that their emergence:

> *probably constitutes the most important change that has occurred in the occupational structure of modern societies.* [3]

To appreciate the distinctive character of the professions, we must first briefly trace their origins and development. Pre-industrial societies are characterized by a relatively simple occupational and class structure. From the high Middle Ages of the twelfth century to the flowering of the European Renaissance in the sixteenth century, the occupational system of Europe could be contained comfortably within three broad occupational groupings:

(i)   agricultural labourers (i.e. serfs, villeins and peasants who tilled the soil, kept herds, reared cattle for their feudal masters);
(ii)   professional soldiers (i.e. those who fought in the king's army and navy);
(iii)   clergy (i.e. those who prayed for the physical well-being and spiritual salvation of the king and his court).

Within this simple occupational classification, the clergy preserved a well-guarded monopoly of literacy:

> *Back in the Middle Ages, all 'learned men' were in some sense religious specialists . . . In the Judeo-Christian world, the clergy is clearly the primary historical matrix from which the modern professions have differentiated.* [3]

From this handful of 'clerics' or literate scribes, who kept society's books and records, there gradually evolved an occupational elite whose members alone 'professed' the requisite literacy, numeracy, knowledge and skills to minister to society's most pressing needs: spiritual healing (the clergy), physical healing (medicine) and legal remedies (the law).

By the eighteenth century the so-called 'liberal professions' — the church, medicine and the law — emerged as the nucleus around which the professional middle classes of the nineteenth century State were to organize themselves as bastions of the established order:

> *Linked by the bond of classical education, their broad and ill-defined functions covered much that later would crystallize out into new, specialized occupations: that each ultimately derived much of its standing from its connection with the established order in the State, and that for this reason the parsons and the lawyers had a much more certain claim to social recognition than the doctors.* [4]

Social recognition went hand-in-hand with material rewards. But, as W. J. Reader notes, whilst members of the clergy might endure genteel poverty in return for social status, lawyers and doctors preserved their economic advantage at the top of the Victorian occupational hierarchy by establishing professional associations which enforced rigorous control over entry into their professions. Teachers, by contrast, were poorly-paid and poorly-organized. Their numbers grew very much faster, as shown in Table 9.1.

Table 9.1 Growth of certain professional occupations, 1841–1911

	1841	1881	1911
Clergy	14 500	21 600	25 000
Physicians and surgeons	17 500	15 000	23 000
Barristers	2000	4000	4000
Solicitors	12 000	13 000	17 000
Teachers	52 000	169 000	252 000

Source: See ref. 4.

The American sociologist, C. Wright Mills, defines occupations as 'specific functions within a social division of labour, as well as skills sold for income on a labor market'. He notes the dramatic twentieth century shift from an economy dominated by employment in the primary and secondary sectors towards one dominated by the tertiary sector (i.e. the service economy). Wright Mills sees this shift as a 'white-collar revolution', marked by the emergence of a class of workers who are:

> *masters of the commercial, professional and technical relation-ship. The one thing they do not do is live by making things; rather, they live off the social machineries that organize and*

coordinate people who do make things. White-collar people help turn what someone else has made into profit . . . supervising the work of actual manufacture and recording what is done. They are the people who keep track; they man the paper routines involved in distributing what is produced. They provide technical and personal services, and they teach others the skills which they themselves practice, as well as all other skills transmitted by teaching. [5]

According to Wright Mills:

Schoolteachers, especially those in grammar and high schools, are the economic proletarians of the professions. These outlying servants of learning form the largest occupational group of the professional pyramid. [5]

Blanche Greer, another American writer, enters a provocative reservation:

Teachers are not professions in the usual sense. They do not have clients who choose them, terminate the relationship or bring to it the immediate need of help that tempers the client's subordination to the physician or lawyer. In a broader sense they are professions with society for client. We cannot do without the transmissions, however imperfect, of its heritage. It is even probable that society would be quite different had children no opportunity to engage in conflict with their superior, the teacher, and have no opportunity to learn early something of the strengths that collective action brings to subordinates. [6]

So what do we mean today by the term 'professional'? What are the objectives and methods of a professional association? And do all such associations serve the same purpose?

Many definitions and classifications of the professions have been advanced over the years, but six essential features of the professions are noteworthy:

(i) A profession is based upon the existence, preservation and transmission of some body of esoteric theoretical knowledge.

(ii) Entry to a profession requires a protracted period of intellectual and vocational (i.e. technical) training.

(iii) Entry to a profession requires some institutionalized mode of validating both intellectual and practical standards of attainment.

(iv) There must exist some institutional means of ensuring that such professional competence is put to socially responsible use.

(v) Integrity is maintained by adherence to a code of professional conduct.

(vi) The profession must be organized.

One hundred years ago, only doctors, lawyers and members of the clergy satisfied those exacting criteria. By the mid-twentieth century, their professional exclusivity had been reduced by a host of new occupations whose members aspired to comparable professional status:

> *Most of the old professionals have long been free practitioners;*
> *most of the new ones have from their beginnings been salaried*
> *employees. But the old professions, such as medicine and law,*
> *have also been invaded by the managerial demiurge and*
> *surrounded by semi-professionals and assistants. The old prac-*
> *titioner's office is thus supplanted by the medical clinic and*
> *the law factory, while newer professions and skills, such as*
> *engineering and advertising, are directly involved in the new*
> *social organizations of salaried brain power.* [6]

As early as 1915, Beatrice Webb concluded that the National Union of Teachers (NUT) — directly descended from The National Union of Elementary Teachers, formed after the 1870 Education Act — must be classified as a trade union because, like manual worker unions, it used 'mutual insurance and collective bargaining, with the ever-present alternative of the strike' as the means of attaining its objectives. Mrs Webb clearly saw the NUT as something of a 'new model' of future union behaviour:

> *The trade unions of the workers will more and more assume*
> *the character of professional associations . . . each trade union*
> *will find itself, like the NUT, more and more concerned with*
> *raising the standard of competency of its occupation,*
> *improving the professional equipment of its members,*
> *'educating their masters' as to the best way of carrying on the*
> *craft, and endeavouring by every means to increase its status*
> *in public estimation.* [7]

Writing fifty years later, Millerson noted in 1964 that professional associations had concentrated their efforts on elevating their members' status and wondered how professional bodies, like those of the teachers, which were so reluctant to take strike action, could really be considered as trade unions:

> *Professions have always regarded trade unions as dangerous*
> *and unnecessary. The professional does not bargain or discuss*
> *fees. To descend to the market place might disturb the deli-*
> *cately balanced superiority of his position. To quarrel over*
> *payment may destroy the ideal of public service. Bureaucratiz-*
> *ation and mass employment have removed many qualms; in*
> *medicine and teaching, 'union' consciousness grows . . . How*
> *far will professions go before they adopt true trade union*
> *tactics? Strikes, working to rule, compulsory membership,*
> *demarcation disputes — all have been used or threatened, but*

> *such actions can harm the reputation of any professional*
> *group.* [8]

The fact that these observations were made only twenty-five years ago illustrates the rapid development of trade union consciousness amongst many professional workers.

Sociologists of the professions approach their definition of a 'professional' from two different angles:

(i) The *trait approach* to professionalism seeks to isolate a set of distinguishing characteristics for a profession, on the assumption that it comprises 'a relatively homogeneous group whose members share identity, values, definitions of role and interest and who were governed by norms and codes of behaviour'. [9] Flexner, a pioneering exponent of the 'trait approach', isolated six criteria for distinguishing professions from other occupations. According to Flexner, professional activity is:

(a) primarily intellectual and involving great personal responsibility;
(b) essentially learned and not based on routine;
(c) essentially practical rather than purely theoretical or academic;
(d) based upon the mastery of techniques acquired through education;
(e) dependent upon a strong internally-controlled organization;
(f) dependent upon the altruistic motives of its members for the promotion of the general good. [9]

(ii) The *process approach* to professionalism seeks to identify the 'natural history' of an occupation on the assumption that this represents the process of maturity of those occupations that aspire to professional status. A 1972 study by Terry Johnson criticizes exponents of the 'trait approach' for their neglect of the power dimension, i.e. they fail to provide 'any means of analysing real variations in the organization of occupations in culturally and historically distinct societies'.

Johnson seeks to identify and account for those institutionalized forms of control that he sees as the hallmark of professionalism:

> *Professionalism, then, becomes redefined as a peculiar type of*
> *occupational control rather than an expression of the inherent*
> *nature of particular occupations. A profession, then, is not an*
> *occupation, but a means of controlling an occupation. Like-*
> *wise, professionalism is a historically specific process which*
> *some occupations have undergone at a particular time, rather*
> *than a process which certain occupations may always be*
> *expected to undergo because of their 'essential' qualities.* [10]

Other writers classify occupations into 'professional' and 'non-professional' according to the dominant behaviour of their members. According to this school, 'professional' behaviour is predominantly responsible and consultative whereas 'non-professional' behaviour is essentially sectional, self-interested activity. In his 1975 study of educational policy-making, Professor (now Lord) Kogan distinguishes between 'sectional' organizations, which aim to protect and advance the collective interests of their members (i.e. trade unions), and 'promotional' organizations, which advocate some more altruistic cause (i.e. professions). According to Kogan, most of the teacher unions, and more especially the biggest, the NUT, display a duality of aims:

> *First, plainly, they have a clear trade union role, advancing and negotiating salaries and conditions of work for their members. Secondly, the associations are a strong force in creating opinion about the style, organization and content of education . . . the NUT inevitably faces ambiguity between its professional and trade union objectives.* [11]

In its evidence to the House of Commons Expenditure Committee, the NUT saw no ambiguity or contradiction between its various aims:

> *The Union combines the activities and services of a professional organization and a trade union. It has always considered it essential not only to protect and advance the interests of its members in respect of their salaries and conditions of service . . . but also to secure the improvement of educational provision and the reform and development of the education system.* [12]

Why, then, have members of the so-called 'teaching profession' become more militant in recent years, resorting to strike action in pursuit of their perceived legitimate objectives, despite their apparent adherence to a code of professional conduct? According to Coates [13], teacher unions have traditionally adopted professional strategies in pursuit of their educational aims, but changing economic circumstances have forced them to change their strategies in order to accommodate changes in the way government itself operated in the 1960s and early 1970s. The teachers' strike of 1969 demonstrated that the NUT was every bit as much a trade union as it was a professional association. This was confirmed when the NUT followed the lead of the NAS by voting for affiliation to the TUC. In short, Coates argues that teachers have adapted their behaviour to fit changed circumstances, over which they exercised little, if any, control:

Finally Harold Silver has pointed to the diminution in the professional self-esteem of teachers in recent years:

> *For most of their modern history, teachers have combined being relatively underpaid with being relatively secure. The security was for much of this century the justification for the pay. Their security has been an important element in some*

> *public suspicion of the teacher. On the other hand, the teachers' lack of power over their own training and registration has diminished them in the league of professionals.*

Silver goes on to pose a key question:

> *If being a professional involves a state of mind, the acceptance of certain kinds of responsibility, the question has to be asked: Who defines the responsibility? The teachers' accountability structure has come to include not only their own immediate peers and superiors, but networks of inspectors and select committees and government departments and ministers and their frequent public utterances and repercussions. Against such a background it is not surprising that the definition of their 'professional responsibilities' and their relationships with the state, the labour movement, other professions and the public at large, have been the subject of confusion and dispute.*

Silver concludes by noting the two threads of collective action and militancy that make the teachers' brand of professionalism distinctive:

> *As a mass profession, teachers have less uniformity of view than others, and there is a long and interesting story of the changing pattern of teachers' politics. Teachers have been pulled toward and away from the labour movement and joint action with other trade unions . . . 'professional behaviour' has always had to be reconciled with the need for collective action, and in fact to contain it as part of the definition.* [14]

It is against this increasingly stressful background of 'dual consciousness' — of aspiring middle-class professionalism in conflict with traditional proletarian unionism — that the teachers' pay dispute must be viewed.

SECTION 2: THE TEACHERS' PAY DISPUTE, 1985–7

(1) The pre-dispute context

Although the teachers' pay dispute covered the whole of the UK, it would be misleading to describe it as a single homogeneous dispute. To help to place the dispute in context, it is first necessary to identify some important differences between education north and south of the English/Scottish border.

Since the end of the Second World War, the pay of primary and secondary schoolteachers in the UK has been negotiated by two separate committees: (i) the Burnham Committee for England and Wales and (ii) the Scottish Teachers' Salaries Committee. Teachers are represented in these negotiating committees by a variety of different organizations, shown in descending order of membership in Table 9.2.

Table 9.2. Membership of teacher unions, 1987

Trade Union (Abbreviation) [General Secretary]	Approx membership (nearest 1000)	No. of seats on negotiating bodies
England and Wales		
National Union of Teachers (NUT) [Fred Jarvis]	200 000	13
National Association of Schoolmasters and Union of Women Teachers (NAS/UWT) [Fred Smithies]	100 000	7
Assistant Masters and Mistresses Association (AMMA) [Nigel de Gruchy]	100 000	4
Professional Association of Teachers (PAT) [Peter Dawson]	41 000	1
National Association of Head Teachers (NAHT) [David Hart]	27 000	2
Secondary Heads Association (SHA) [Peter Snape]	5000	1
Scotland		
Education Institute of Scotland (EIS) [John Pollock]	43 000	13
Scottish Secondary Teachers Association (SSTA) [Alex Stanley]	7000	3
Professional Association of Teachers (PAT) [John Bell)	5000	1
National Association of Schoolteachers/Union of Women Teachers (NAS/UWT) [Jim O'Neill]	3000	1

Note: Figures should be taken as indicative rather than definitive. A mixture of sources have been used. There is fierce controversy amongst teacher unions on membership.

The annual settlement date for both committees is 1 April, which means that separate claims are usually submitted in the summer of the previous year, for discussion in committee during the autumn, in the hope of achieving a settlement to take effect the following spring. But whereas in Scotland, since 1976, pay and conditions of service have been negotiated together, by the same committee, the Burnham Committee was empowered to deal only with pay, conditions of service being determined elsewhere.

Schoolteaching throughout the UK is in the process of becoming an all-graduate profession. Most, but not all, teachers in England and Wales are professionally qualified, i.e. they have undertaken a course in teacher training, as well as having the required academic qualifications. In Scotland, there is a professional training requirement but not all entrants to the profession are graduates.

In 1974, the Houghton Inquiry reported on teachers' pay in the whole of the UK. The Houghton Report (Houghton) recommended salary increases for teachers that brought them roughly into line with what the Committee felt was their proper place in the hierarchy of professional earnings. The Labour Government accepted and implemented the Houghton recommendations, including an undertaking to keep teachers' pay relativities under periodic review.

In March 1979, the Callaghan Labour Government set up the Clegg Standing Commission on Pay Comparability (Clegg), to examine terms and conditions of employment of particular groups of workers referred to it by the Government, in agreement with the employers and unions concerned. Clegg was required to report, in each case, on the possibility of establishing acceptable bases of comparison with the terms and conditions of employment for other comparable workers and of maintaining appropriate internal relativities.

In July 1979, Clegg was asked to undertake such a comparability study on teachers' pay and not, as with most of its other references, on pay and conditions. However, the Commission felt that this restriction made little difference since the study was to be undertaken:

(i)   'in the light of' the terms and conditions of employment of teachers;
(ii) having regard 'to all relevant principles and considerations relating to the assessment of the value and role of the teaching profession in society'. [15]

Giving evidence to Clegg, English and Welsh employers stressed that teachers should receive a professional salary in return for a professional commitment to their work. They said that it had long been accepted that the professional teacher's duties were not limited to the timetabled day and year. However, whilst most teachers continued to adopt a professional attitude to their work, there was a growing tendency for 'a narrower view' of the job to be adopted. Areas of difficulty included responsibility for:

(i)   care and discipline of pupils before and after the school day;
(ii)   lunchtime supervision;
(iii) involvement in pupils' extracurricular activities;
(iv)   parents' consultation evenings;
(v)   staff meetings and in-service training outside the timetabled day;
(vi)   taking classes for absent colleagues. [15]

The English and Welsh employers therefore asked Clegg to make clear what assumptions it had made about the professional obligation of teachers when considering their pay. By contrast, the Scottish employers emphasized the gradual introduction of written formal conditions of service for Scottish teachers, including stipulated hours of work and the amount of time spent in direct class contact, and were therefore less concerned with the need to specify the expectation of the teachers' professional commitment.

In reply, the teacher unions conceded that certain restricted actions had been taken in the context of industrial disputes, but they strongly contested the employers' assertion that teachers in general were tending to take 'a narrower view' of their job. Furthermore, they protested that the employers were acting improperly in asking Clegg to include any statement on teachers' conditions of service in its report — a view with which the Clegg Commissioners agreed in their report of July 1979, which recommended pay increases to teachers of between 17% and 25%.

Although the incoming Thatcher Government had already committed itself to honouring the Clegg award, it lost no time in dismantling the Standing Commission:

> *It became accepted wisdom within the government machine that the Clegg award fuelled the early inflation which caused the government considerable political embarrassment in its first year or so in office. Independent pay reviews became anathema in government thinking — particularly for teachers because of their numbers. Pay reviews were going to have to be fought for in the future.* [16]

After 1979, the annual pay claims presented by the teaching unions were settled by arbitration at levels below both the current rate of inflation and the rate of settlement for other non-manual workers. By 1984, therefore, teachers' pay was once more significantly out of line with that of comparable professional groups.

(2) The challenge

Early in 1984, the NUT put forward its 1985–86 claim for a minimum increase of £1200 p.a. in the pay of all teachers in England and Wales. The Government had already ruled out unilateral reference to arbitration but, when deadlock was reached in the Burnham Committee, following rejection of the employers offer of 4.6%, both sides agreed to remit the matter to an arbitration panel, chaired by Professor Eric Armstrong (Professor of Industrial Relations, Manchester Business School). The Armstrong Award, published in September 1984, recommended an average increase of 5.1%, but the award was signed by only two members of the arbitration panel. Professor Armstrong made clear that, in his view, arbitration was not the answer to establishing teachers' pay relativities:

> *It is just possible that expectations may have formed that this arbitral body has somehow 'put everything right' in regard to the many issues on which the parties differ. Clearly this cannot be the case given the terms of reference and the important differences that exist between the processes of arbitration and review work ... It is my view that those [earlier] inquiries [Houghton and Clegg] and their results plainly mark off teachers' pay negotiations and settlements from other groups who have not been subjected to the same close, independent and evaluative scrutiny. In short, looked at in that way, teachers form a distinct group.* [17]

Professor John Hughes, Principal of Ruskin College, Oxford, the third member of the panel, representing the teaching unions, explained why he had refused to sign the report, thereby causing a split in the arbitration panel for the first time in its history:

> *The government is insisting that it can apply lower standards for teachers' pay than for that of other professions. I had hoped that an independent arbitration team could have stood out against such double standards. It seemed to me that any recommendation which accepts those double standards could not be a proper deliberation of the merits of the case. In those circumstances, I felt that signing the recommendation would be to the impoverishment of teachers.* [18]

The government immediately accepted the arbitration award of 5.1% but the teachers' unions lost no time in rejecting it and began to develop plans for industrial action to enforce its earlier claim. Meanwhile, in the Burnham Committee, talks on the reform of teachers' pay structure, linked to a new contract of service that had been adjourned during the arbitration, reached deadlock. On 1 November, Sir Keith Joseph, Secretary of State for Education, announced that, if agreement was not forthcoming on the pay and conditions package, the Government would introduce legislation to allow Local Education Authorities to dismiss teachers whose work performance was considered unsatisfactory. On 29 November, the NUT decided that there was an unbridgeable gap between the two sides and used its majority on the union joint panel of the Burnham Committee to force a 16–15 vote in favour of the unions withdrawing from the talks.

Meanwhile, north of the border, the EIS, the biggest teaching union in Scotland, was planning industrial action in support of its own separate but parallel campaign for an independent inquiry into the pay of Scottish teachers. On 5 December, the EIS launched its campaign by organizing the first-ever national one-day strike amongst its members throughout Scotland. This was followed by a series of rolling strikes on 11–13 December and a ballot of all EIS members, seeking support for further industrial action in the new year.

On 11 December, George Younger, Secretary of State for Scotland, rejected the teacher unions' call for an independent inquiry into Scottish teachers' pay:

> *It appears to me that the case being advanced by the Teachers' side depends essentially upon the claims (i) that the salaries of teachers have been eroded in recent years and (ii) that teachers have over the same period experienced considerable increases in workload . . . In the circumstances, I am not persuaded that I should be justified in establishing an independent review of the sort requested.* [19]

On 20 December, the tenth anniversary of the 1974 Houghton Report, the EIS announced that its latest ballot had resulted in an 85% return and an overall 75% majority in favour of escalating industrial action. The EIS leadership were particularly heartened by the support received from the traditionally more moderate primary teachers (64% compared with 86% from secondary teachers) and from the traditionally more moderate rural areas of Scotland.

Towards the end of January 1985, Scottish teachers' leaders met the Scottish Secretary, in a further unsuccessful attempt to persuade him that an independent pay review was the only realistic method of preventing a potentially disruptive dispute throughout the Scottish school system.

On 6 February, members of the EIS began industrial action by boycotting all preparatory work for the Scottish Examination Board and by withdrawing from curriculum development and administrative work connected with the new 16–18 examinations in Scotland (the Munn and Dunning Reports).

On 6 February, south of the border, members of the NUT began to apply sanctions against their employers by refusing to carry out six duties that they regarded as non-contractual:

(i)   to cover for absent colleagues;
(ii)   to supervise pupils at lunchtime;
(iii)   to take part in lunchtime activities,
(iv)   to do any work connected with school meals,
(v)   to attend parents' meetings after school,
(vi)   to attend staff meetings after school.

After a long period of skirmishing, the NUT and the EIS met early in 1985 to coordinate strategy in their respective pay campaigns.

Battle-lines were drawn, resources marshalled and forces brought into play. The 'phoney war' was over; the long war of attrition had begun.

(3) Initial responses

The idea of a teachers' strike had been on the cards for years. Its arrival was greeted with a mixture of disbelief and stoicism. Many, if not most, parents sympathized with the teachers' long-standing and unresolved pay grievance, though few felt it necessary for teachers to disrupt school classes with selective strike action. But their sympathies were initially engaged on the side of the teachers.

The employers — the local education authorities — deplored the teacher unions' decision to impose industrial sanctions. Labour-controlled authorities blamed the Government for its obstinate refusal to fund a reasonable settlement. Conservative-controlled authorities weighed in behind the Government, accusing teacher unions of betraying their professional duty to their pupils.

(4) Consequences

In response to the teachers' application of sanctions, more than 30 employers in England and Wales, controlled by Conservative-dominated councils, announced that they intended to dock the pay of teachers who refused to carry out the six duties listed above. This was to give rise to several court actions, which both complicated and politicized the dispute.

On 18 February, the Solihull (Birmingham) Borough Council — one of strongest Conservative councils in Britain — brought an action in the High Court against the NUT, arguing that the six duties no longer being undertaken by NUT members formed part of the teachers' contracts of employment and that the application of such sanctions was therefore unlawful industrial action under the Trade Union Act 1984 because there had been no pre-strike ballot. On 23 February, the High Court issued an injunction against the NUT, ordering it to call off its industrial action. Two days later, the NUT held a ballot.

On 4 March, Solihull announced that, in addition to stopping the pay of teachers on strike, it intended to deduct a sum of £2 for each separate refusal to carry out duties. The NUT responded by promising to make good the teachers' loss of earnings and began a counter-action against employers who threatened to withhold teachers' pay.

On 11 February, back on the negotiating front, the employers came forward at the Burnham Committee with a renewed pay offer of *either* 4.6% *or* 4% plus arbitration. The unions responded favourably to the proposed new package deal, so long as it excluded teacher assessment. Sir Keith Joseph had let it be known, however, that whilst the Government might be willing to fund the new package deal, this was conditional upon the unions accepting teacher assessment. Once again, the talks were in stalemate.

On 19 February, the NUT announced that over 80% of its members had voted for strike action and that 3-day stoppages would shortly commence in 26 separate Local Authority areas. The employers once again alleged that the strike was unlawful because the ballot had failed to mention that such action would be in breach of the teachers' contracts of employment. The NUT promptly arranged to re-run the ballot on 25 February.

On 26 February, the Prime Minister told Parliament that the Government had ruled out an independent inquiry into the dispute. But next day, the unions responded favourably to the employers' proposal that ACAS should be invited to attempt to conciliate in the dispute. Shortly after, the Education Secretary met local authority leaders who urged him to reform the 'inflexible' Burnham machinery which they held was partly responsible for the bargaining stalemate.

Progress towards a negotiated settlement was now hamstrung by the Education Secretary's warning on 17 March that acceptance of ACAS intervention would not lead to any additional money being made available by the Government to cover any increased cost of a settlement. Nevertheless, talks began at ACAS on 19 March.

Three days later, on 22 March, the NUT announced that its 25 February ballot had produced a majority of 78% in favour of further escalation of the dispute. On the same day, the EIS confirmed its own plans for further disruption of Scottish schools and warned of future coordinated industrial action by teachers throughout the UK. Next day, AMMA, the third largest teachers' union south of the border, announced that its members had balloted in favour of further sanctions in the summer school term. The NAS/UWT, the second biggest union, had already announced on 14 February that its members would apply indefinite selective action, so the campaign south of the border was now almost fully concerted. The one union to remain completely outside the dispute on both sides of the border was PAT.*

During April, when the teaching unions restated their original aim of achieving a substantial pay increase to restore their earnings levels, the Education Secretary repeated that no extra money would be made available unless there was a new contract, including teacher assessment.

On 15 May, Burnham Committee negotiations resumed after an interval of three months, with an improved offer by the employers of 5% plus arbitration — but this offer was again rejected. Following county council elections on 2 May, changes were made to employers'

---

* The Professional Association of Teachers (PAT) was formed in 1970, as a reaction against the attempts by the NUT, the largest teacher Union, to affiliate to the TUC. The constitution of PAT forbids members to take industrial action of any kind that might harm children's educational interests.

representation on the Association of County Councils which, in turn, gave Labour a majority amongst employers on the Burnham Committee. When the Labour majority proposed a resolution on 3 July in support of the teachers' pay claim, the Government used its power of veto to block any pay offer made by the Committee and talks were once more indefinitely adjourned. This led the Education Secretary to announce on 4 July that the Government would now seek to establish new negotiating machinery, covering both pay and conditions, to replace the Burnham Committee, which was restricted to considering pay only.

The Government then announced its intention to alter the balance of representation on the Burnham Committee by reducing the NUT from 16 to 13 seats. This resulted in the NUT temporarily losing its leadership of the union side in the protracted negotiations south of the border.

North of the border, on 29 July, the EIS announced plans to step up industrial action in the next school year. Its members would in future:

(i)   work only to the strict terms of their contract,
(ii)   boycott all school examinations,
(iii) apply a ban on any curriculum development,
(iv)   increase strike action over a wider area.

On 13 September, the EIS produced a ballot result that showed 69% of its members in favour of rejecting a management offer to increase Scottish teachers' pay by an average of 18% over three years. Encouraged by this support, the EIS renewed its campaign to achieve an independent inquiry into Scottish teachers' pay, but this was again refused.

In January 1986, George Younger became Defence Secretary and was replaced as Secretary of State for Scotland by Malcolm Rifkind, whose appointment stimulated renewed lobbying by the Scottish teaching unions for an independent pay review. Within two months they had succeeded. On 6 March, Rifkind appointed an independent Committee of Inquiry (under the chairmanship of Sir Peter Main) into Scottish teachers' pay and conditions of service, in return for the restoration of normal working in all Scottish schools. Peace immediately returned to the schools as union and management sides got down to the preparation of evidence and the Committee began to hear their submissions.

On 9 May, under the resumed leadership of the NUT, a partial breakthrough was achieved at the Burnham Committee when the English and Welsh employers offered an interim pay rise of 5.7% in return for union acceptance of three conditions:

(i)   that there should be an immediate return to 'peace and calm' in the schools;

(ii)   that the NUT should cooperate in achieving a negotiated settlement;

(iii) that the interim payment should be without prejudice to negotiations on a longer-term reform of teachers' pay and contract of service.

The NUT gave the necessary pledges but made clear that whilst the union accepted the requirement that so-called 'voluntary' duties should be resumed during the next phase of talks, there was no guarantee that individual teachers would be prepared to cover for absent colleagues any longer.

On 21 May, Mrs Thatcher reshuffled her Cabinet, appointing Kenneth Baker as Education Secretary in place of Sir Keith Joseph, who had previously announced that he would not be standing for re-election at the next General Election.

On 23 May, the High Court ruled that teachers' obligation to provide cover for absent colleagues formed part of their contracts of employment. Local Education Authorities had therefore acted lawfully in making deductions from the salaries of teachers who had applied such sanctions as part of their pay campaign.

During July, further attempts were made by both sides to move the dispute towards a resolution but the Government made it repeatedly clear that it would offer no further concessions towards funding a more generous pay settlement. On 18 July, the new Education Secretary, Kenneth Baker, let it be known that he, too, favoured the early replacement of the Burnham machinery.

(5) The climax

Throughout the first half of 1986, ACAS had sustained its efforts to obtain a negotiated settlement of the dispute, south of the border, by appointing Sir John Wood to head its panel of conciliators. On 29 July came the long-awaited breakthrough. After several weeks of delicate conciliation by ACAS, the two sides had thrashed out the skeleton of a new salary structure, combined with a new contract of service for all teachers throughout England and Wales. Of the six unions involved, only the NAS/UWT initially refused to sign the new deal but other unions had second thoughts before the year was over.

North of the border, the Main Committee's Report and recommendations on Scottish teachers' pay and conditions was published in October. The Main Report proposed an average 16.4% increase in teachers' salaries, to be implemented in stages over two years, in return for some significant changes in Scottish teachers' conditions of service.

On 23 October, at a historic Special General Meeting, one thousand EIS members voted by 7:1 against acceptance of The Main Report's proposals. Campaigning strongly for a rejection, EIS leaders called for an immediate one-day strike, an intensification of disruptive action and a new campaign linked to demands for tripartite talks between the EIS, the Local Authorities and the Government. Whilst teachers' unions in England and Wales had reluctantly accepted the Government's insistence that any increase in teachers' pay must be linked to a new contract of service, their counterpart unions in Scotland campaigned for outright rejection of any settlement that attempted to link salary increases to what they saw as a worsening of conditions, the unequal distribution of pay rewards, the loss of trade union rights and the educational philosophy behind The Main Report's recommendations.

(6) The settlement

On Monday 17 November 1986, following days of acutely difficult negotiations, details emerged of the draft agreement signed over the previous weekend by four of the six teaching unions in England and Wales (NUT, AMMA, PAT and SHA but not the NAS/UWT or the NAHT). The main features of the deal were as follows:

(i)   within the ceiling prescribed by the Education Secretary, an average increase of 16.4% in teachers' pay over the stipulated two-year period;

(ii)   biggest pay increases to teachers at the bottom of the existing pay scales, with the opportunity for promotion on the two Principal Teacher grades further up the scale;

(iii)   an increase to at least 9.25% of classroom teachers of £779 p.a. for extra responsibilities from October 1987;

(iv)   a graded promotion structure in contrast to the distribution of money proposed in the Baker package, which favoured fewer, but higher, rises;

(v)   new conditions of service attaching to the draft agreement:

(a)   maximum class sizes of 33, subject to availability of teachers, with provision for further reviews;

(b)   guaranteed time away from classroom;

(c)   limit to obligation to cover for absent colleagues;

(d)   appraisal of teacher performance;

(e)   obligation to attend staff meetings, parent meetings, and in-service training for up to four hours per week;

(f)   commitment to out-of-school activities, including preparation and marking;

(g)   a new National Joint Council to determine teachers' pay and conditions of work, to replace the Burnham Committee.

This package deal then became the subject of protracted negotiations before it was finally accepted by all parties early in 1987.

In Scotland, the settlement was equally hard-fought, with last-minute attempts to re-jig the total amount on offer or even to abandon the whole deal. Eventually, in the last days before Christmas 1986, the EIS leaders voted by 21–6 to recommend acceptance of a package that gave Scottish teachers:

(i)   a working year of 190 days, which brought Scottish teachers into line with England and Wales
(ii)   seven days additional holiday
(iii)   16.4% phased increase in salaries
(iv)   80 hours p.a. of 'programmed activities'
(v)   five days p.a. of in-service training
(vi)   an immediate staffing review
(vii)   commitment to better absence cover
(viii) composite classes of no more than 25 pupils when practicable
(ix)   a system of new promoted posts for class teachers.

When this package was put to Scottish teachers early in 1987, it produced a decisive majority in favour of acceptance. Though the details remained to be worked out in protracted discussions, the dispute north of the border was now over.

(7) Aftermath

South of the border, the dispute rumbled on for several months after the settlement was formally agreed. Teachers continued sporadic protest action, with some militant factions accusing their leadership of having sold out under pressure. The bitter aftermath of the dispute served to further alienate many disgruntled parents. The atmosphere of post-dispute recrimination and continued divisions amongst teacher unions enabled the Secretary of State to pose as the man of destiny, determined to prevent any recurrence. The dispute, he claimed, had demonstrated the clear need for a shift in public policy. Legislation would be introduced to curb teachers' bargaining power in England and Wales and to begin the much more radical programme of educational reform to which the Thatcher Government had been long committed. The dispute was over, but the aftermath had only just begun.

SECTION 3: ANALYSIS OF THE DISPUTE

(1) What was the dispute about?

The origins of the teachers' pay dispute throughout Britain lay in the teachers' perception that their pay had fallen significantly behind that of other groups of professional workers. As an EIS car sticker ironically proclaimed:

> *Overtake this teacher. Everybody else has.*

But British teachers had never been politically militant. There was no tradition of sustained industrial campaigning for teacher unions to draw upon in urging their members to take action in defence of their profession. Teachers were certainly aware of the decline in their real living standards. Equally worrying for most teachers, perhaps, was the physical and financial rundown of the entire education system:

> *This dispute has never been exclusively about money. Rather it has been about a collective self-respect which the profession believes it has lost somewhere down the road. Self-respect does not come down to the odd per cent . . . [20]*

The Government's view of what the dispute was about became crystal clear from its evidence to the Main Committee of Inquiry into the Pay and Conditions of Service of School Teachers in Scotland. The Government specifically asked Main to define:

> *which aspects of a teacher's time and duties should be subject to the management of the employers, exercised through the headteacher, and which should be left to the teacher's discretion. [21]*

The Government clearly saw the dispute as not simply being about pay relativities but also about the control and management of the entire school education system. In particular, the Government was determined to replace the Burnham Committee in England and Wales, which it saw as a continuing threat to peace in the schools because its terms of reference precluded it from prescribing the linkage between effort and rewards, pay and conditions of service. But there were other reasons, as René Saran explained:

> *When the education system was reshaped after the Second World War, Burnham salary negotiations were already an established feature of employer–union bargaining relations. The Burnham Committee, established in 1919, was reconstituted in 1945, when certain important changes were made. It became a statutory committee, with the Minister [of Education] determining the number of seats which each of the employer and teacher organizations was given . . .*
>
> *While it is impossible to quantify in any precise way the power of either employers or unions, it is possible to deduce shifts in the balance of power from changes in negotiating machinery. What stands out both in [the enactment of the Remuneration of Teachers Act 1965] and [its demise during the 1986–7 Parliamentary session] is the ultimate power of the Secretary of State, provided support from Cabinet and Parliament is assured. The way the Secretary of State decides to exercise that power affects in turn the power of employers and unions . . .*
>
> *Under the new [1965] legal framework the Secretary of State gave up the power to reject a Burnham settlement, in its place taking up membership of the employers' side of the negotiating committee. Admittedly the two DES representatives were*

greatly outnumbered by those from the local education associ-
ations, but at least central government now had a direct voice
and participated in the important 'withdrawal' meetings of the
Management Panel where the hard decisions are made during
negotiations. Ministerial power was further enhanced by a
'concordat' . . . under [which] it was agreed that the two panel
members from the DES held a veto over global sums that
might be offered to teachers during negotiations and could
exercise a weighted vote of 15 [out of a total of 27] on issues
such as distribution of increases across the salary structure . . .

Teacher union rivalry, and increased use of disruptive sanc-
tions, are among the reasons why the Burnham machinery has
come into disrepute. Another has been the veto of the Secretary
of State, operated under the concordat described above. For
20 years its use was a major cause of very protracted nego-
tiations, often with counter-productive results. Securing
Cabinet approval for an increased employer offer delayed
negotiations by a minimum of three weeks, by which time
union psychology made the revised offer unacceptable. The
power of veto created a ratchet effect because the inability
of employers to settle quickly produced a higher-priced final
settlement.

In order to understand the factors leading up to the
1986 ministerial intervention in Burnham affairs, it is essential
to bear in mind that, in the eyes of the local authority
employers and of the government, the Burnham machinery
had not 'delivered the goods' for some five years. Given the
level of parental (electoral) concern about the disruption of
schools during the 1984 and 1985 salary disputes, and the
high position of education on the political agenda, the scene
was set for a grand ministerial act. Baker had secured extra
money from the Cabinet, but it was to be used on his own
terms . . . [22]

The Secretary of State had evidently persuaded the Cabinet that it
was worth paying a high price to achieve some breakthrough in the
entire education system by ending the Burnham Committee system.
The Government was clearly determined not to fund any pay settlement without such a breakthrough.

Despite the lack of any official report on the dispute in England
and Wales, the Scottish Main Committee's Report brought out very
clearly the issues at the heart of the dispute on both sides of the
border so far as teachers themselves were concerned:

We do not believe that the present difficulties can be attributed
to dissatisfaction about pay levels alone. Behind that dissatis-
faction lies a deeper concern within the profession about their
relative status in society. The teachers' representatives tended
to measure the status of their profession by reference to pay

levels and to the evidence of public support as judged by public expenditure priorities. There can be no doubt that these two factors are valid indicators but arguably they are the symptoms not the causes of that decline in public esteem. Nor have teachers been alone in this respect. We are now a less deferential society, and all professional groups have experienced a decline in public respect. If it is true that teachers have suffered a relatively greater decline than other groups, then we must consider how best to raise public esteem for the profession and the teachers' own morale. [23]

(2) How important was the context?

The teachers' pay campaign was launched in the autumn of 1984 when the eyes of the Government and the general public were still fixed on the unresolved miners' dispute (see Chapter 8). The Government was therefore determined to adhere to its economic strategy of holding down inflation, reducing the public sector borrowing requirement and regenerating the economy by promoting the wealth-creating private sector as against the wealth-consuming public sector. In this context, the teachers' unions were at a double disadvantage: first, the inherent justice of the teachers' case for improved pay, in what the public generally regarded as a secure profession, compared unfavourably with that of the miners, whose claim that they were fighting to defend jobs, pits and mining communities provoked wide public sympathy; second, the disruptive actions taken by teachers, in withdrawing from what they considered to be non-contractual duties, angered parents and alienated the general public. This enabled the Government to condemn industrial disruption of every kind, regardless of its cause.

In this context — without the miners' long history of industrial struggle or of spontaneous public support to sustain them, and in the face of determined government resistance — the teaching unions did well to establish early in their campaign that their members were committed professionals who had sustained a serious deterioration in their living standards and employment conditions and whose patience was rapidly running out.

(3) Why did the unions take selective strike action?

Towards the end of the dispute, a question frequently posed was: Why had the teachers dragged out their industrial action over more than two years, alienating public sympathy for their case, when an all-out strike might have brought the dispute to a head much sooner, without damaging children's education? To answer that question, it is important to note the long-standing debate amongst teachers on whether industrial action could *ever* be justified amongst the members of a profession whose first commitment was to the education and the welfare of their pupils. The persistent failure of successive governments to address teachers' genuine grievances on pay and conditions had led many dedicated teachers to revise their views on the subject over the previous decade and produced sporadic threats or incidents of school disruption. It is highly questionable, however, whether a majority of teachers could have been found anywhere in the UK before 1984 to support industrial action in the schools.

By 1984, union leaders recognized a clear change of mood amongst a majority of their members, the lowest-paid classroom teachers. This enabled them to call upon teachers to apply tough sanctions — directly against their employers but indirectly against the Government — by withdrawing from such traditional duties as lunchtime supervision or after-hours activities.

Commenting on this changed mood, Kathy Finn, the EIS President, described the differences between the current campaign and those preceding the Houghton and Clegg awards:

> *The bulk of action in the past was unofficial. Teachers formed action groups and organized strikes, unpaid of course. This time, action had been organized by the EIS leadership. I do not see this as a sign that teachers are less militant than before; rather that the EIS is much more militant.*
>
> *The changes since I joined the EIS in 1964 have been fairly dramatic. The move from being a 'professional association' to being a trade union has taken place reasonably smoothly. Its passage has been helped by the contempt with which successive Governments have treated teachers.* [24]

Teacher unions in England and Wales had been equally reluctant to adopt a militant strategy before 1984 for the most compelling of reasons — namely, the lack of rank-and-file militancy and therefore very doubtful commitment to what would inevitably be a protracted industrial struggle.

The strategy adopted by the unions on both sides of the border was essentially pragmatic: to persuade a clear majority of members to recognize that the future of education, and therefore their own future, lay in their own hands. In the words of John Pollock, General Secretary of the EIS:

> *This campaign could well be a long one. You have two options. Either you go down on your knees alongside your colleagues in the Professional Association of Teachers (PAT) or you stand up and fight for the profession. If we don't stand up and fight, history will come to condemn Scottish teachers for having sold out Scottish education and Scottish children.* [25]

Having persuaded their members to 'stand up and fight' for their cause, the unions had to devise a strategy that would bring maximum pressure to bear on the Government — the Local Education Authorities' paymaster — to force a major concession on the pay issue. Whilst the strategy and tactics adopted were similar on both sides of the border, the objectives were slightly different. In Scotland, where teachers salaries were already linked to a detailed contract of employment, the tactics were to apply increasingly disruptive sanctions in selected schools in support of an independent inquiry into teachers' pay. In England and Wales, the tactics were similar but the aim was not to secure an independent inquiry but a substantial pay increase achieved through the Burnham machinery without any worsening of teachers' conditions of employment.

The result was a very complex, long, drawn-out campaign of slowly mounting pressure on the Government through the children, the Head Teachers, the parents and Parent Associations, school governors, Local Education Authorities, political pressure groups and directly on Government Ministers in their own constituencies. By organizing selective industrial action over wide areas of the UK, the unions sustained the momentum of the campaign, through rolling strikes, the withholding of cooperation, working to contract and boycotting of new work, all of which increased the pressure on Government though it failed to bring about an early change of heart.

Eventually, in all three countries of the UK, the selective strike strategy paid off. Both north and south of the border, the appointment of a new Minister helped the breakthrough. In Scotland, the new Secretary of State, Malcolm Rifkind, reversed the policy of his predecessor, George Younger, and ordered an independent inquiry within one month of assuming office. In England and Wales, the new Education Secretary, Kenneth Baker, adhered closely to the policies adopted by Keith Joseph, but won Cabinet support for additional money for teachers' pay in return for the promise of a new teachers' contract, including teacher assessment, and the replacement of the Burnham Committee. But all this took time, causing inevitable damage to children's education. With hindsight, it seems most unlikely that the teacher unions would adopt the slow-acting, selective strike strategy in any future confrontation with the Government.

(4) Why did the Government not end the dispute earlier?

Although schoolteachers throughout the UK are employed and paid by Local Education Authorities, their effective paymaster is the Government, which funds roughly half of the cost of national expenditure on education. More specifically, the Education Secretary has the power of veto over any pay settlement reached in the Burnham Committee, just as the Scottish Secretary has over Scottish teachers' pay settlements. The crucial decisions on the employers' side throughout the dispute were therefore not made by the employers' side of the Burnham Committee, nor the Council of Local Education Authorities, nor the employing authorities, but by the Government. Its decision on when to intervene to end the dispute, by making sufficient funds available to enable a compromise settlement to be reached, was entirely a political one.

As in the earlier steel dispute (see Chapter 7) and the concurrent miners' dispute (see Chapter 8), Mrs Thatcher's Cabinet continuously monitored the teachers' dispute, reviewing policy in the light of advice offered by the Education Secretary and his civil servants. That advice seems to have been consistent throughout the dispute: although the teachers saw themselves as a special case, the cost of the settlement would have a severely adverse effect on the public sector pay settlements. Any concession should therefore be kept to the minimum and should only be made in return for the guarantee of a new teachers' contract, to include teacher assessment and clearly-specified contractual obligations.

Whilst the teachers' leaders took every opportunity to castigate the Government for its neglect of the nation's educational priorities, their greatest efforts went into educating the public at large on the financial plight of their members and the justice of their case for a substantial improvement in their pay. The Government was not entirely unsympathetic about teachers' pay but was determined not to make any significant pay concessions without corresponding changes in teachers' contracts of service.

Writing in *The Guardian* on 26 November 1985, John Fairhall noted that, although it had made piecemeal concessions, the Government had stuck to its guns on two points: to get a pay rise teachers must (a) sign a contract and (b) accept pay and conditions of service being negotiated together. There was nevertheless a substantial flaw in the Government's argument:

> But the Scottish teachers have a contract. They have a negotiating body which deals not just with pay but also with conditions of service. The two procedures which Sir Keith (Joseph) suggests could solve the problem in England and Wales have done nothing to soften the anger or the action of teachers in Scotland ... What a by now desperate Sir Keith still will not accept is that the root of the teachers' dispute is just that the ordinary teacher is not paid enough. It is useless for him to appeal to the teachers' professionalism. He has done far more to destroy that than the teacher union leaders. Professionalism comes into play only above a basic salary level. Below that level and you're into survival and the Family Income Supplement and the other welfare benefits for the poor for which some teachers are now eligible. [26]

The Government's policy probably emerged most clearly in Scotland. Towards the end of 1985, after a full year of the dispute, representation of the two main religious bodies in Scotland — the Church of Scotland and the Roman Catholic Church — sent a delegation to the Secretary of State with a letter, setting out their views on ways of ending the disruption and of bringing the dispute to a peaceful end. In his reply to the church leaders' letter, the Scottish Secretary, George Younger, reiterated the Government's position:

> *I have to say that the present conditions of service and con-*
> *tractual arrangements are plainly not working: they satisfy*
> *neither the teachers, nor the employers, nor the public at*
> *large.* [19]

The church leaders then issued a joint statement, saying quite bluntly that, in their view, the Secretary of State:

> *could not consider making a case for extra money for teachers*
> *unless the teachers could give a firm commitment to the*
> *working out of a specification of the teacher's job including*
> *responsibility for examinations, curriculum development and*
> *similar matters. The churches have therefore asked the unions*
> *to enter into discussions on the matter of job specification and*
> *clarification. They wish to make it clear that this is quite*
> *different from renegotiating the teachers' contract and that it*
> *should not entail, certainly at this stage, any discussion issues*
> *such as hours of work and class contact.* [27]

But the only solution acceptable to the Government was one that included a new contract of employment for teachers, linking pay and conditions.

(5) Who won?

If teachers in England and Wales thought that they could secure a worthwhile pay settlement without having to accept a new contract of service — or, if teachers in Scotland thought that they could secure such a settlement without some worsening in the terms of their existing contract — then, in those terms, all UK teachers failed to win the disputes. In the words of John Pollock, General Secretary of the EIS:

> *No-one pretends we've won all we hoped to achieve. But there*
> *is now no question of the loss of negotiating rights for teachers,*
> *no question of draconian powers for head teachers, no mention*
> *of removing teachers' unique protection against dismissal; and*
> *the original, paternalistic senior teacher post has been replaced*
> *by proper promoted posts.* [28]

The proposals recommended for acceptance in Scotland gave teachers a 16.4% increase in salaries from October 1987, with interim payments of half of this amount from 1 January 1987. Individual teachers were guaranteed an increase of not less than 5% on their end-of-1986 salaries and at least 10% from October 1987. Although the Scottish Secretary argued that the amount conceded in the final package had not increased, the distribution of the total amount had been rearranged. Conversely, the teachers had also made some important concessions, linking pay and conditions. As the *Times Education Supplement (Scotland)* had commented earlier:

That is what the unions refuse, above all, to accept. They have said — and they say it more loudly and clearly — that they are ready to talk about conditions of work but only after a pay settlement is made. Pay agreements, as they well know, are quickly eroded. Changes in conditions are permanent. [29]

But teachers are not stupid. From the outset of the dispute in England and Wales, as well as Scotland, they were fully aware of government economic policy in general and of its financial policy towards the public sector in particular. They must also have recognized that some form of compromise settlement was the only reality for both sides. The question is therefore which side gained more on balance from the final compromise settlements?

When the Secretary of State for Scotland reaffirmed that the Government would only fund a settlement based on the re-codification of the teachers' contract, the *Times Education Supplement (Scotland)* commented:

Teachers will be wary of trading conditions for pay . . . They are afraid of being lured into permanent loss of professional freedom in exchange for a pay rise immediately subject to the ravages of inflation. [30]

But what 'conditions' did Scottish teachers have to trade? What 'professional freedom' had teachers retained to defend against 'permanent loss'? If 'professional freedom' was the sticking point, why had Scottish teaching unions campaigned so hard for the contract back in 1976? Part of the answer may be found in the EIS Evidence to the Main Inquiry. Here, it was explained that:

When the EIS conducted a 3-year campaign which led to the teachers' 'contract' of 1976, it did so with a view to establishing a safety net of individual conditions which any teacher could fall back on. There was no intention of restricting the professionalism of teachers and the 'contract' deliberately avoided prescribing, other than in general terms, the activities which should be encompassed within the contractual working hours . . .

Prescription or definitive contracts are unnecessary and would be counter-productive — and invite teachers to work to the letter of such prescription . . .

Teachers would be opposed to giving the [Education] Directorate additional power in the form of a more detailed 'codification' of the teachers' contract. Such powers would be likely to be used to diminish still further the professionalism of teachers and to prescribe their activities beyond the point which would be justified in relation to the teachers' professional role . .

We invite the Committee of Inquiry to reject 'codification' as being inimical to the development of a full professional education service and counter-productive in relations to getting the best out of the teaching force. [31]

Having heard the evidence both for and against 'codification', the Main Committee had no doubts as to why it was now necessary:

> *In their evidence to us, none of the teachers' associations saw any real need to clarify the teacher's job. It was suggested to us that teachers well understood, from their professional training, what would be expected of them and that parents were well aware of the main features of the teacher's work . . .*
>
> *We were also presented, on the other hand, with evidence asserting that a clarification of the teachers' responsibilities was now necessary, though almost all of this was principally concerned with clarifying the teachers' contractual duties . . .*
>
> *We have no doubt that many parents have little understanding of the extensive responsibilities expected of teachers and of the highly professional input now required for teaching. We concluded that the time has now come for a full description of the teachers' professional role, which we hope will help to dispel some of that misunderstanding, and serve as a useful contribution to the continuing public debate on education.* [32]

To the extent that Scottish teachers were reluctantly compelled to concede a much more detailed 'clarification' of their classroom and extracurricular duties, teacher unions north of the border paid a heavy price for their 16% pay increase. But teachers south of the border paid a much heavier price. Not only were they compelled to accept a detailed specification of duties in their contracts of employment, but they were also deprived of collective bargaining rights and representation through unions of their choice as a result of the Teachers' Pay and Conditions Act 1987, which Mr Baker rushed through Parliament immediately after the voluntary settlement was reached in December between the teacher unions and Labour-dominated Local Authorities.

Had the teacher unions failed to select an effective and realistic strategy for achieving their long-held objectives? As early as May 1986, John Wright, in the *New Statesman*, contrasted the conduct of the teachers' dispute with that of the miners:

> *At the start of the teachers' dispute someone high up . . . mooted that a government which had just seen off Scargill and the miners would be able to gobble up the teachers' unions 'before breakfast'. It is now clear that this was a bad misreading, not of the balance of forces as such, but of the nature of the war to be fought . . .*
>
> *Despite the merit of the teachers' case, no one really expected the government to respond. Six intransigent years of cuts in public expenditure and refusing to deal with the unions had made it clear that talk was pointless. The legacy of the miners'*

dispute was not, then, that industrial action would inevitably fail against a Thatcher government, but that nothing else was really worth trying. And by its own policies and behaviour the government had persuaded a large proportion of teachers to this view. If we are counting, this was the first defeat for the government in its psychological war with the teachers. And it was self-inflicted.

The government's second defeat . . . came about as the direct result of Sir Keith Joseph's obsession with tinkering with the state education system . . . Instead of simply saying No and returning to his tinkering . . . he pulls out plans for modifying the conditions of service, altering the salary structure and appraising teachers' work.

As a negotiating ploy, this was dumb. It infuriated and further united teachers and inevitably prolonged the dispute by making the nature of the agreement to be reached between government and unions infinitely more complex than a wages settlement, with its relatively straightforward haggle over percentages and back-dated periods. [33]

(6) Costs and benefits of the dispute

During the course of the dispute, teachers lost pay, schools were disrupted and children's education undoubtedly suffered. The question is: How much had education suffered? And were the gains achieved on both sides of the compromise settlement sufficient to justify the price paid by teachers, by employers and, most important of all, by individual children whose educational losses could perhaps never be made up?

On the adverse effects on children's education, it is worth noting that the Scottish Education Council reported no significant overall deterioration of performance standards amongst candidates for the O grades or Higher School Certificate level examinations in Scotland. This might imply that the disruption in schools had been exaggerated, that Head Teachers found ways of concentrating educational time and effort where it most mattered during the dispute, or that classroom teachers themselves found ways of ensuring that children in general did not suffer the full effects of their 'work to contract' policy.

Teachers both north and south of the border undoubtedly achieved a much better pay settlement than most informed commentators were willing to predict at the beginning of the dispute, but the price paid was considerable. North of the border, the teachers' contract was spelled out in even greater detail and was almost universally perceived to be a more restrictive document than before the Main Committee reported. South of the border, teachers' contracts were spelled out in written detail for the first time. The Secretary of State made use of his existing powers to emasculate teacher unions by virtually removing their future pay bargaining powers. Furthermore he declared war on the unions by taking new measures on the Teachers' Pay and Conditions Act 1987 to begin the total overhaul of the teaching profession within the national school system.

It is clearly too soon to judge the outcome. Partisans on both sides have seen the teachers' strike as a great divide, the last bastion in the crumbling edifice of the old unreformed education system. Nothing can or will ever be the same again in British education.

(7) Lessons of the dispute

John Wright pointed to one of the more practical lessons of the dispute, not only for teachers, perhaps, but for all who engage in industrial action:

> *Perhaps a little market research by the NUT would reveal that good clean simple strike action would be better understood and supported by parents than months on end of withdrawal of 'voluntary' this and that and the other, including so-called 'good-will'.*

Noting that the NUT deployed a campaign fund of half a million pounds, Wright wondered whether the union might not have considered some part of that amount in caring for children affected, citing the lessons to be learned from examining teachers' strikes elsewhere:

> *When the teachers took industrial action in France they made it much easier for us (i.e. the parents) to support them. They said that they would come and look after our children but they wouldn't teach them. In return, we, as parents, agreed to put all kinds of pressure on the education authority to come to a settlement and carry out their legal obligations to educate. The education authorities were very upset at the thought of all those teachers taking the kids on outings and talking to them about the need for industrial action!* [34]

This raises in acute form the familiar question of whether — and, if so, to what extent — teachers, nurses, doctors, police, firemen and others in the public service can or should be free to take industrial action in support of their legitimate employment grievances. The deepening crisis over low pay amongst nurses and ancillary workers in the National Health Service over recent years is a case in point. These workers, unlike most others, find themselves in a most invidious position. They have immense industrial power, which they dare not use. Like teachers, they have chosen or been forced to enter a field of employment where their prime responsibility is to those whom they serve. If they take action in support of their genuine grievances, they are rebuked and scorned for behaving irresponsibly and accused of reneging on their professional trust. If they take no action, their terms and conditions of employment continue to deteriorate by comparison with those of other workers with whom they choose to measure their comparative worth or contribution to society and economy.

Amongst the major lessons of the teachers dispute must be that teachers (nurses and others) are not workers just like any others; that they do fulfil an unusual and demanding role on behalf of the community; that they must not be forced to engage in disruptive industrial action in order to maintain decent living standards; and that the community must somehow find ways in which to ensure that their exceptional social contribution is recognized, continuously monitored and generously rewarded. Public policy requires those basic lessons to be learned.

SECTION 4: CONCLUSIONS AND 1987 POSTSCRIPT

The teachers' pay dispute provides an elementary textbook lesson in how not to manage industrial conflict. The teacher unions were often deeply divided on ideological grounds as well as on the strategies and tactics required to win their dispute; the employers were themselves divided between a majority of Labour-controlled Local Authorities and a vociferous minority of Conservative and Alliance-controlled Authorities; and the Thatcher Cabinet was itself far from united on how best to meet the teachers' irresistible demands for the redress of their long-standing pay demand.

For more than a decade, schoolteachers had agonized, as members of a 'caring profession', over the moral dilemma of taking sustained — as opposed to token — industrial action in pursuit of their legitimate claims for better pay and wider social recognition within a better-funded state school system. Such a moral dilemma should not be belittled or underestimated: the vast majority of schoolteachers enter the profession — knowing its acutely ambivalent position within the British occupational hierarchy — because they are committed to educational objectives. Unlike many other 'professionals', schoolteachers frequently live amongst the members of the communities they serve and are still regarded with respect by most parents and pupils in towns and villages throughout Britain. Though strongly reluctant to take industrial action, many felt morally compelled to follow their union leaders' advice, not simply to protect their own professional interests but also to defend the state school system whose marked deterioration they themselves were best placed to observe.

In a recent paper, Baldry and Lockyer have sought to identify the primary motives underlying the Government's conduct of the dispute. In particular, they highlight some significant consequences, which they see as flowing from the compromise resolution of the dispute:

> *Government and employers are increasingly attempting to apply rigid industrial cost-accounting criteria to a profession whose members have traditionally tended to relate to their work in almost a 'pre-industrial' fashion . . .*
>
> (1) *Work tasks are permeated by a sense of personal obligation and commitment, in addition to any monetary reward.*
> (2) *Tasks are defined by a perception of a generally agreed set of needs that children have rather than by a rigidly defined contract or job description.*
> (3) *There is no clear distinction between work (or sold) time and home (or 'free') time . . .*
>
> *We have called this process the 'industrialization of education' because it seems to consist of two interrelated processes. First, the intensification of the use of contractual time in . . . ways . . . requiring greater 'managerial' control over teachers' labour process via specifically contracted duties and continuous assessment of teachers' performance. Secondly, the introduction of market forces into education wherever possible . . . [35]*

Whether or not one accepts this broad characterization, it captures the spirit of conscientious objection voiced by those teachers who opposed the compromise settlement to the dispute. In Scotland, the settlement proved broadly acceptable to the vast majority of teachers and peace returned to Scottish schools. In England and Wales, where intra-union bargaining compounded the difficulties of securing a compromise settlement, all six teacher unions expressed their outrage at the Secretary of State's announced intention to dispossess teachers of their traditional negotiating rights by legislative enactment. Mr Baker may have succumbed to the combined effect of pressure by the teacher unions and public opinion by finally endorsing the compromise pay and conditions settlement, but he opened up an even more bitter battle over teachers' negotiating rights and the future of the state school system — including the introduction of a national curriculum and the opportunity for schools to opt out of the State system altogether — a battle that continues to rage.

Sporadic protest action followed throughout the early months of 1987 in England and Wales (but not in Scotland, which was not immediately affected by the new legislation on teachers' negotiating rights). Once again, there were marked differences between the unions south of the border on the best tactics to pursue in opposing the Baker Bill. The NUT again took the lead in calling for days of action and withdrawal of cooperation by teachers. Other unions again appeared less enthusiastic in their support, arguing that there was little heart amongst their members for continuing industrial action.

In April 1987, full-page advertisements appeared in the national press, setting out AMMA's decision *not* to resume industrial action, and appealing to the public to stand by the unions in their fight against the Government's action in depriving teachers of their negotiating rights:

A HISTORY LESSON
March 1834
The Tolpuddle Martyrs

Six farm labourers were transported to Australia.
Their crime?
Forming a friendly society to try to improve
their pay and conditions.
Only after widespread protest were they released.

January 1987
Education Secretary Kenneth Baker on
the Value of History Teaching

'Pupils cannot play their full part in operating
the institutions of our society
unless they have a well-developed sense of our national past.
They need to have some feeling for how our present
political attitudes have their roots in
the English Reformation, the Reform Bills,
the Tolpuddle Martyrs . . .'

March 1987
The Government Removed Teachers'
Negotiating Rights With Their Employers

This advertisement has been placed by the 123 000 strong
Assistant Masters and Mistresses Association as an alternative
to strike action.
By rejecting industrial action AMMA members are standing by
the country's children. Please stand by us in our campaign for
the right to negotiate.

English and Welsh teachers continued the fight for the restoration of their negotiating rights by planned days of industrial action right up to and including the week of the General Election on 11 June 1987. However, once it became clear that the Conservative Government had been re-elected for a further five years the NUT lost no time in recommending its members to abandon the industrial campaign in favour of more far-reaching and wide-ranging political objectives. At the end of 1987, teacher unions presented fresh claims for a renewed pay round in 1988. The struggle for improved teachers' pay continues.

CHRONOLOGY OF THE DISPUTE

4 September 1984	Arbitrator proposes 5.1% settlement
1 November	Government considering legislation to reform teachers' salary structure
14 November	All-Scottish teachers rally in Glasgow
29 November	NUT forces union withdrawal from talks on reform of English teachers' pay and conditions
5 December	First national 1-day strike in Scotland
4 January 1985	National teachers' unions meet to concert strategy
14 January	EIS resume snap strikes in selected areas
28 January	English employers offer 4% plus arbitration
6 February	NUT begin selective disruptive action
11 February	English employers propose 4% plus 7% = 11%, conditional on acceptance of new contract
14 February	NAS/UWT to withdraw goodwill from 26 February and apply indefinite selective action from 4 March
19 February	NUT announce 3-day stoppages from 26 February
26 February	Prime Minister rules out independent inquiry
6 March	Education Secretary criticizes Burnham machinery
17 March	Education Secretary warns no extra money, even if arbitration settles dispute
19 March	Dispute referred to ACAS
22 March	NUT announces 78% ballot in favour of disruptive strike action
25 March	AMMA announce ballot favours disruptive action in summer term
April	Education Secretary adamant on no new money without new teachers' contract
19 April	English employers and unions to make joint approach to Government
23 May	English employers improve offer to 5% plus 7% = 12% plus arbitration, unions reject offer.
21 June	Labour replace Conservatives as biggest employer group on Burnham Committee
3 July	Joint talks break down
4 July	County Councils end 'concordat'
4 July	Government to replace Burnham machinery
29 July	EIS announce plans to step up industrial action
13 September	EIS reject management offer of 18% over 3 years by 69% vote
20 September	Scottish unions back 'war of attrition'
18 October	EIS 87% vote in favour of exam boycott

5 December	10 000 Scottish teachers rally in Glasgow
January 1986	Malcolm Rifkind replaces George Younger as Secretary of State for Scotland
6 March	Rifkind offers independent Committee of Inquiry into Scottish teachers' pay and conditions
9 May	Burnham Committee agrees interim rise of 5.7%
21 May	Kenneth Baker replaced Keith Joseph as Education Secretary
23 May	Judge rules on professional obligations
18 July	Education Secretary favours replacement of Burnham machinery
29 July	ACAS talks lead to Coventry Agreement on new teacher contract for England and Wales; NAS/UWT refuse to sign deal
23 October	EIS Special General Meeting votes 7:1 against acceptance of Main proposals
November	New draft agreement signed by English unions (except NAS/UWT and NAHT)
17 November	Education Secretary hesitates to bless draft agreement
4 December	EIS mass rally in Edinburgh
11 December	Education Secretary introduces Teachers' pay and Conditions Bill into Parliament
23 December	Scottish unions agree package with Secretary of State and recommend acceptance to members
January 1987	Teachers' Pay and Conditions Act enacted

WHO'S WHO IN THE DISPUTE

Armstrong, Eric	Professor of Industrial Relations, Manchester Business School; Chairman of 1984 Teachers' Arbitration Panel
Baker, Kenneth	Secretary of State for Education and Science, 1986 to date
Jarvis, Fred	General Secretary, National Union of Teachers
Joseph, Keith (Sir)	Secretary of State for Education and Science, 1977–86
Pollock, John	General Secretary, Education Institute of Scotland
Rifkind, Malcolm	Secretary of State for Scotland, 1986 to date
Younger, George	Secretary of State for Scotland, 1977–86

REFERENCES

1 Kenneth Baker, House of Commons debate, 11 December 1986.
2 Clement Freud, House of Commons debate, 11 December 1986.
3 Talcott Parsons: 'Professions', *Encyclopedia of the Social Sciences*, 1968.

4 W. J. Reader: *Professional Men: The rise of the Professional Classes in Nineteenth Century England*, Weidenfeld and Nicholson, London, 1966, p. 23.

5 C. Wright Mills: *White Collar: The American Middle Classes*, Oxford University Press, New York, 1956, p. 113.

6 Blanche Greer: 'Teachers as professionals', *Encyclopedia of the Social Sciences*, 1968, p. 564.

7 Beatrice Webb: 'English teachers and their professional organisations', *New Statesman* (Special Supplements), 25 September and 2 October 1915.

8 G. Millerson: *The Qualifying Associations*, Routledge and Kegan Paul, London, 1964.

9 A. Flexner: *Is Social Work a Profession?* (Proceedings of the National Conference of Charities), cited by Jennifer T. Ozga and Martin A. Lawn: *Teachers, Professionalism and Class: A Study of Organised Teachers*, The Falmer Press, London, 1981, p. 12.

10 Terry J. Johnson: *Professions and Power*, Macmillan, 1972, London, p. 80.

11 Maurice Kogan: 'Education policy making: a study of interest groups and Parliament', cited by Ozga and Lawn: *Teachers, Professionalism and Class: A Study of Organised Teachers*, The Falmer Press, London, 1981, p. 12.

12 NUT Evidence to House of Commons Expenditure Committee, cited by Maurice Kogan: 'Education policy making: a study of interest groups and Parliament', 1975.

13 R. D. Coates: *The Teacher Unions and Interest Group Politics*, Cambridge University Press, Cambridge, 1972.

14 Harold Silver: 'A Class Below?', *New Society*, 17 May 1984, pp. 258–60.

15 Standing Committee on Pay Comparability (The Clegg Commission): Report on Teachers' Pay 1979.

16 David Ross: *An Unlikely Anger: Scottish Teachers in Action*, Mainstream Publishing, Edinburgh, 1986, p. 17.

17 Professor Eric Armstrong, cited by David Ross: *An Unlikely Anger: Scottish Teachers in Action*, Mainstream Publishing, Edinburgh, 1986, p. 73.

18 Professor John Hughes, cited by David Ross: *An Unlikely Anger: Scottish Teachers in Action*, Mainstream Publishing, Edinburgh, 1986, p. 73.

19 George Younger, cited in EIS Evidence to the Main Committee of Inquiry into Pay and Conditions of School Teachers in Scotland, 1985 Appendix 1, E (iii).

20 Leading article: 'More than Money', *Times Education Supplement (Scotland)*, 11 October 1985.

21 Report into Pay and Conditions of Service of School Teachers in Scotland (the Main Report), Cmnd. 9893, HMSO, Edinburgh, October 1986, Terms of Reference.

22 René Saran: 'Lessons to be learned from the teachers', *Personnel Management*, February 1987, pp. 40–41.

23 The Main Report, Cmnd. 9893, HMSO, Edinburgh, October 1986, p. 10, para 6.

24 Kathy Finn (President, EIS): *EIS Voice*, Vol. 1, No. 1, October 1986, p. 1.

25 John Pollock (General Secretary, EIS), quoted by David Ross: *An Unlikely Anger: Scottish Teachers in Action*, Mainstream Publishing, Edinburgh, 1986, p. 73.

26 John Fairhall, *The Guardian*, 26 November 1985.

27 Church Representatives' statement, cited by David Ross: *An Unlikely Anger: Scottish Teachers in Action*, Mainstream Publishing, Edinburgh, 1986, pp. 141–2.

28 John Pollock, quoted in *The Scotsman*, 20 December 1986, p. 1.

29 Leading article, 'One dispute or two?', *Times Education Supplement (Scotland)*, 10 January 1986, p. 1.

30 *Times Education Supplement (Scotland)*, 10 January 1986, p. 1.

31 EIS Evidence to the Main Committee of Inquiry, April 1986, p. 46.

32 The Main Report, Cmnd. 9893, HMSO, Edinburgh, October 1986, pp. 51–2, paras 5.3 and 5.4.

33 John Wright: 'The man who could not say no', *New Statesman*, 23 May 1986, p. 10.

34 John Wright: 'The man who could not say no', *New Statesman*, 23 May 1986, p. 10, quoting Jennie Hall from *Everyman*, 1985 (undated quote).

35 C. Baldry and C. J. Lockyer: 'Industrialising Education', *Fraser of Allander Quarterly Review*, Spring 1987.

STUDY QUESTIONS

1. Examine C. Wright Mills' contention that schoolteachers are 'the economic proletarians of the professions'.
2. Compare and contrast the Thatcher Government's handling of the teachers' dispute and the miners' strike (see Chapter 8).
3. 'Prescription or definitive contracts are unnecessary and would be counter-productive — and invite teachers to work to the letter of such prescription.' (EIS) Do you agree?
4. 'Either you go down on your knees alongside your colleagues in PAT (the Professional Association of Teachers) or you stand up and fight for the profession.' (John Pollock, General Secretary, EIS). What are the arguments for and against PAT's fundamental opposition to industrial action of any kind under any circumstances?
5. Trace the developments in the teachers' dispute with the Thatcher Government over its withdrawal of negotiating rights, since the dispute formally ended early in 1987.
6. What are the essential differences, if any, between a traditional proletarian union and a middle-class professional association?

SUGGESTIONS FOR FURTHER READING

R. D. Coates: *The Teacher Unions and Interest Group Politics*, Cambridge University Press, Cambridge, 1972.

T. J. Johnson: *Professions and Power*, Macmillan, London, 1972.

Maurice Kogan: *Education policy making: a study of interest groups and Parliament*, Hutchinson Education 1975.

Geoffrey Millerson: *The Qualifying Associations*, Routledge and Kegan Paul, London, 1964.

C. Wright Mills: *White Collar: The American Middle Classes*, Oxford University Press, New York, 1951.

Jennifer T. Ozga and Martin A. Lawn: *Teachers, Professionalism and Class: A Study of Organised Teachers*, The Falmer Press, London, 1981.

Kenneth Prandy: *Professional Employees*, Faber, London, 1965.

W. J. Reader: *Professional Men: The Rise of the Professional Classes in Nineteenth Century England*, London: Weidenfeld and Nicholson, London, 1966.

David Ross: *An Unlikely Anger: Scottish Teachers in Action*, Mainstream Publishing Company, Edinburgh, 1986.

A. Tropp: *The Schoolteachers*, Heinemann, London, 1977.

PART III

■ *LESSONS FROM EXPERIENCE*

CHAPTER 10

■ Better management of industrial conflict

The learning process involves first unlearning and then learning again.
P. K. Edwards: *Strikes in the United States, 1881–1974*

LEARNING THE LESSONS

Proverbial wisdom insists that historical experience is our only teacher. Cynics will reply that 'The only lesson to be learned from history is that there *are* no lessons to be learned from history'. [1] We reject that profoundly pessimistic view. For, as Marx taught, those who refuse to learn lessons from experience — both their own and that of others — are condemned to re-live that history, first as tragedy, then as farce. It pays us to learn the lessons of experience, wherever and whenever we can.

Reflecting on the human condition, the English playwright, Michael Frayne, notes that we are 'significance-seeking organisms'. We spend our lives making curious observations, recognizing persistent patterns, posing endless questions in a continuing attempt to find meaning and extract significance from our complex, sometimes bewildering, often ambiguous and frequently absurd world. As we slowly acquire some wisdom and understanding, we seek to preserve and transmit the painful lessons of experience to future generations in the hope that they may eventually inherit a more just and peaceful world.

What lessons can we learn about managing industrial conflict from the experience of the seven major British disputes, described and analysed in Part II? Our attention is focused here on the distinctive British experience, because experience of conflict management in other industrial societies will reflect the history, cultural institutions, laws, norms, values, social mores, folkways, customs and practices of those societies. The management of major industrial disputes in North America, for example, differs significantly from that of the UK, yet there are striking parallels, strong similarities and major distinctions that repay close study elsewhere. [2]

The first lesson to be learned is a simple one: that industrial conflict is inevitable. However much we try, it is difficult to envisage ways in which the teachers, miners, steelworkers and engineers could have avoided headlong conflict with their respective employers. The cases of the Ford Sewing Machinists, the Electrolux women and the printers at Times Newspapers are more problematic. Perhaps their disputes might have been avoided by more skilful negotiators, although it is not easy to specify on precisely what terms. For however well-designed, intelligently thought-out and diligently applied our institutions for anticipating and preventing industrial conflict, these institutions can never completely eliminate such conflict. At best, they contain it within tolerable limits.

We may therefore begin by abandoning all vain and implausible attempts to put a stop to such conflict by legislating against it or defining it out of existence; or by pretending that conflict will simply fade away, as in the classless society, predicted by Marx in the 1850s or by overoptimistic American academics in the 'Cold War' atmosphere of the 1950s. All present evidence indicates that industrial conflict is here to stay. It persists despite the most stringent laws or the most sophisticated institutions devised by man's subtlest ingenuity. We must simply learn to live with conflict and to manage it much better in the future than we have done in the past, for the quality of life in advanced industrial democracies depends very largely on how well we manage such conflict.

The second lesson to be learned is that whilst much of our industrial conflict is inevitable, it is by no means all irreconcilable. Of the seven disputes examined in Part II, only one — the miners' strike — ended without a compromise settlement (or two, if we include some unresolved elements in the teachers' dispute). For that reason, amongst others, the miners' strike was highly atypical and totally unrepresentative of recent major episodes of industrial conflict in Britain. In the six other disputes, both sides were separated by widely differing objectives and expectations, yet they succeeded in managing their conflict in ways that eventually allowed a compromise solution to emerge. In the Ford dispute, a third party, in the form of the Secretary of State, had to intervene to help to achieve a negotiated settlement. In the steel dispute, a Court of Inquiry was required to produce an acceptable solution. In the teachers' and miners' disputes, the Advisory, Conciliation and Arbitration Service (ACAS) 'ran alongside' these disputes, playing a vital role in bringing the parties together and advancing the prospects of a negotiated settlement. In the Electrolux dispute, a private consultant was called in by both sides to help to reform the company's industrial relations. By such means, the vast majority of industrial disputes are susceptible to some form of third party intervention, which assists the process of reconciliation.

The third lesson to be learned is that all industrial disputes need to be managed. That lesson derives from the observation that some episodes of conflict are distinctly better managed than others, a value judgement that clearly requires both justification and illustration. If we look back over the seven major episodes of conflict contained in Part II we may note that some disputes were shorter, some more protracted; some were more bitterly-fought than others; some were diffuse, others more sharply-focused; some involved one single major issue, others involved several major issues; some were better organized and more sensibly controlled; others seemed to lurch completely out of control and to develop an internal momentum of their own. All industrial disputes are, at best, 'semi-autonomous' in character, but some are more autonomous than others.

The engineering dispute over shorter working time, for example, was hard-fought over ten weeks, with errors made on both sides, but it was closely-targeted by the unions, who adopted a realistic and economical strategy (a selective, escalating strike), and was generally well-handled by the employers. In short, the dispute was well-controlled, well-led and well-managed on both sides and, consequently, produced a compromise solution within a matter of weeks.

By contrast, the miners' strike over pit closures soon turned into a series of bitter internal wrangles: between the miners themselves; between senior managers at the NCB; between the divided miners and a fatally-riven labour movement; and, of course, between the NUM and the NCB. The dispute was so badly organized, so badly timed, so disastrously uncontrolled that it failed to produce a compromise settlement after more than a full year's stoppage of work. No strike that lasts so long and achieves so little can be judged 'effective'. The miners' strikes of 1972 and 1974 were both brief and effective. Granted, they were fought over the cohesive issue of wages and not the divisive issue of pit closures, but these earlier disputes were patently well-managed and produced positive results. By comparison, the miners' strike of 1984–85 degenerated into a costly shambles, grossly mismanaged by both the NUM and the NCB.

The fourth lesson to be learned is that it is easier to manage a dispute where the central issues are specific, clearly-articulated and well-understood on all sides. Industrial disputes are rarely confined to one single issue. The Ford dispute was about three central issues: job grading, equal pay and the observance of procedure agreements. The Electrolux dispute was about four central issues: unacceptable pay differentials, job grading, a degenerate incentive payment system and an uncoordinated bargaining structure. The steel dispute was about three central issues: pay levels, manpower levels and the right to manage. Yet all three disputes reached negotiated settlements.

By contrast, we may question: what were the central issues in the miners' dispute? The NCB's right to manage the industry by closing 'uneconomic' pits? The NUM's right to defend jobs, pits and mining communities? The legitimacy of calling a national strike without first holding a ballot? The nation's dependence on fossil fuel in a nuclear age? The fractured solidarity of the labour movement? The validity of using a nationally coordinated police force to break

strikes? The efficacy of Mrs Thatcher's new labour laws? The personalities of Mr Scargill and Mr MacGregor? The role of the media?; or
all of these issues? Where so many issues supervene, the conflict
becomes inevitably blurred, confused and confusing. Small wonder
the miners' dispute ended in an intractable stalemate.

The fifth lesson to be learned is that the outcomes of industrial
disputes appear crucially dependent on the intelligent choice and
consistent application of relevant and realistic strategies and tactics
by both sides. In the Ford dispute, the women strikers declared a one-
day token strike, followed by an all-out work stoppage that quickly
halted all Ford production and led to an eventual compromise
resolution of the dispute. The Sewing Machinists failed to secure
the upgrading that they initially sought but they received financial
compensation far in excess of their expectations. In the national
engineering dispute, the Confed applied a selective, escalating strike,
severely damaging the employers' interests at moderate cost to the
strikers and their unions. They, too, failed to achieve their principal
declared objective — a 35-hour working week in 1979 — but nevertheless secured their longer-term objective of shorter working time.

By contrast, in the teachers' pay dispute, the unions chose to
apply intermittent selective strike action, combined with a withdrawal
of teachers' full cooperation in the schools. This failed to shut down
schools completely but caused considerable hardship to some pupils,
alienated many parents and lost the teachers the widespread public
sympathy and support that they needed to win their dispute. Had
they been able to carry their members with them in an all-out strike,
the teacher unions might well have secured a quicker, more generous
settlement for their members, without having to suffer the humiliating
imposition of new legislation, which dispossessed teachers of their
traditional negotiating rights.

But the teacher unions could no more count on the whole-
hearted support of their divided membership in an all-out strike than
the NUM in the case of the miners. In both cases, the unions' chosen
strategies were incapable of securing the desired outcomes. Both cases
resulted in long, drawn-out, badly-managed, unsatisfactory and
inconclusive disputes.

Management as well as unions make strategic errors. Management's choice of strategies is not always relevant (i.e. appropriate to
the objectives being sought) or realistic (i.e. capable of achieving the
desired objectives). In the Times Newspapers dispute, management
compounded its errors by choosing an unrealistic strategy (viz. the
delivery of an ultimatum to its highly fragmented, unionized and
militant workforce that it must negotiate an extremely complex new
deal on pay and conditions of work by a given deadline or face being
locked out of employment) and absurdly unrealistic objectives (viz.
the introduction of new technology, the abolition of many traditional
working practices, plus trouble-free production, enforced by a new

no-strike procedure agreement), which had to be negotiated and agreed by no fewer than five major unions within the space of six months. When the unions refused to negotiate under duress, the ultimatum expired and the lock-out was put into effect. At that point, management had no counter-strategy to fall back on. Negotiations dragged on for almost 12 months but, even then, management failed to secure its key objectives in the eventual compromise settlement.

The sixth lesson to be learned is that, in order to win a major industrial dispute, each side must seek to maintain discipline and united action amongst its members. In the national engineering dispute, a significant group of employers broke ranks, destroying the EEF's claim of a united resistance to the Confed's demands. In the Ford dispute, the women strikers displayed an admirable unity of purpose and action, but the management side was clearly divided between 'hawks', who sought to resist any grading concession to the Sewing Machinists, and 'doves', who sought a quick settlement and a speedy return to normal working. At Times Newspapers and at the NCB, the management sides were similarly divided, but managerial self-discipline generally prevailed.

Not so amongst the printing unions at Times Newspapers who were hopelessly fragmented in their objectives and their tactics, despite the establishment of an All-Union Liaison Committee. The miners were fatally divided into two hostile camps throughout their dispute over pit closures, a division which the NCB initially fostered and subsequently exploited to the hilt. In the teachers' pay dispute, the six unions were united on their policy objectives but were frequently and embarrassingly at loggerheads on strategy and tactics.

The seventh lesson to be learned relates to preparedness and flexibility. The classic approach to international relations — *Si vis pacem, para bellum* — appears paradoxical because it urges sovereign states to take sensible warlike precautions in time of peace against the risk of possible aggression by a hostile power. If you seek peace, you must be (moderately) armed for war. The same principle may be applied to industrial relations. Mature protagonists are rarely taken by surprise because they prepare in advance for every foreseeable contingency. Their intelligence networks provide an 'early warning system' against any sudden outbreak of conflict, but they also indicate the likelihood of a successful peace initiative. Whilst relentlessly pursuing their essential policy objectives (the 'deliberate strategy'), by whatever means seem most appropriate, mature protagonists never miss the opportunity to modify their position in order to achieve a peaceful resolution of their differences (the 'emergent strategy'), if at all possible. [3]

In both the Ford and the Electrolux disputes, management were evidently unprepared for an unprecedented all-out strike by women workers, who brought production to a complete standstill. In both cases, the women won substantial and long-lasting economic and social benefits. In the national steel dispute, the unions were first caught off-balance by the BSC's zero wage offer and then completely thrown by the BSC's announced intention to close steel plants, with thousands of job losses. Unprepared for an extended conflict against the combined forces of management and government, inexperienced in conflict management, disunited, armed with a weak, belated and ineffective counter-strategy, the steel unions were utterly routed by a determined adversary, fully-backed by government resources.

To reverse the coin: in the engineering dispute, the Confed maintained its escalating strike strategy but nevertheless continued to meet the EEF, negotiating successive improved offers until a final compromise settlement was achieved. In the teachers' dispute, despite severe internal differences, the teacher unions maintained their strategy of non-cooperation and intermittent, selective strikes, whilst regularly meeting the employers under the aegis of ACAS to negotiate an honourable peace. By contrast, in the miners' dispute, both sides appeared intransigeant neither side being ready or willing to enter purposeful negotiations, to concede an inch of ground or to reach a compromise resolution of the dispute — perhaps because in the particular circumstances of that unique dispute, no compromise solution was available to the parties.

The eighth lesson to be learned is that good timing is absolutely critical to the successful management of industrial disputes. The initiator of an industrial dispute normally controls its timing, but not always. In the engineering dispute, the Confed 'initiated' the dispute by presenting its claim for a shorter working week as part of the annual bargaining round; but the timing of the strike was finally triggered by the EEF's rejection of the claim. In the steel dispute, the unions 'initiated' the dispute by presenting their wage claim, but it was the Steel Corporation's rejection of the claim and its unilateral announcement on plant closures and redundancies which determined the timing of the strike that followed. In the Times Newspapers dispute, management unilaterally declared a negotiating deadline, but it was the unions' refusal to meet that deadline which eventually triggered the ensuing lock-out. In the miners' dispute, the NCB's carefully-timed announcement of its intention to close Cortonwood Colliery precipitated the dispute, but it was the NUM Executive's decision to endorse the Area stoppages rather than risk calling a national ballot which determined the timing of the strike. Had the NUM timed a national ballot for April 1984, many well-placed commentators believe that it might still have achieved substantial majority support for an all-out strike, which, in turn, might have produced a much shorter, better-managed dispute with a definitive outcome.*

The timing of a dispute's climax is crucial to its outcome. In

* For commentators' views, see Part II, Chapter 8, Section 3 (3).

the Ford dispute, it was by seizing the initiative and proposing equal pay legislation to the Secretary of State that management finally broke the negotiating deadlock, thereby enabling the women strikers to return to work. In the engineering dispute, it was the timing of the EEF Negotiating Committee's compromise proposal on the phased introduction of shorter working time which secured the necessary breakthrough and resolution of the dispute. In the teachers' dispute, it was the Government's timely — some would say belated — replacement of Sir Keith Joseph which allowed the new Secretary of State, Mr Kenneth Baker, to produce his revised formula for ending the dispute.

In all these disputes, the timing of the climax was crucial. The miners' dispute, by contrast, was characterized throughout by disastrously bad timing. As noted earlier, the very start of the strike, at the end of winter, with coal stocks high, was bound to prove helpful to the NCB and damaging to the NUM. Thereafter, numerous attempts were made by both sides and by third parties — from the TUC and ACAS to the Labour Party and Mr Robert Maxwell — to achieve a breakthrough. Each proved to be a false dawn. The only credit for good timing in the entire dispute goes to the South Wales miners. Shortly after Christmas 1985, they persuaded the National Delegate Conference to vote for a return to work, without a settlement, on the first anniversary of the start of the strike.

The ninth lesson to be learned is that the mature protagonist in an industrial dispute must be light on his feet, fast to react, quick to respond. Like a boxer in the ring, he fights on his toes, one foot placed firmly on the ground (the 'deliberate' or fixed strategy), the other foot continuously seeking new vantage points (the 'emergent' or flexible strategy). He fights with his left but lands good punches with his right. Regardless of his opponent's lighter weight, faster speed, greater height, longer reach, superior condition, undefeated record or improved form, the mature industrial protagonist's will-to-win is paramount. As an experienced fighter, he is rarely caught off-guard or off-balance. He sniffs the air, he learns as he goes, he listens to good advice from his own corner and tries to ignore the shouting and the tumult at the ringside.

It is this capacity to learn fast, to think on one's feet, to react swiftly and decisively which distinguishes the professional protagonist from the amateur. He may sometimes be matched against a superior opponent and he may not win every contest, but he is never caught completely unawares.

In industrial disputes, as in all other combative exchanges, experience rates very highly. Even when he finds himself up against a superior adversary, a mature industrial protagonist nearly always makes up in guile and subtlety what he lacks in speed or weight. Experienced protagonists never fight alone. They are ultimately dependent on trainers, managers and supporters. They must be fast learners, good losers and quick to recover from defeat.

The tenth and final lesson to be learned is that every industrial dispute is an exercise in risk-management. To extend the boxing metaphor: in a major industrial dispute, the stakes are high. Once the contest has begun, the adversaries often feel very isolated and exposed. From time to time, there is a quick knock-out blow (as in the steel dispute), but many contests are evenly-fought and settled only on points as in the Ford and Electrolux disputes). On rare occasions, two heavy-weights will slug it out to a standstill finish (as in the miners' dispute). Although the referee is there to see fair play and enforce the Queensbury Rules, it is not unknown for him to join in the fight or at least to appear to take sides (as perhaps in the miners' and the teachers' disputes). Those sitting outside the ring offer intermittent commentaries until it is time to deliver their final verdicts.

Ideally, the rules of the game will have been observed, but where one of the contestants is badly hurt, the cry may well go up that all such contests should be outlawed. In most industrial disputes, as in other similar contests, the defeated party lives to fight another day. There is nearly always the prospect of a return match.

These ten lessons are derived by the author from his experience and interpretation of the seven major industrial disputes analysed in Part II. It is of course an open question whether the protagonists in those disputes derived comparable lessons for themselves, from their own experience and interpretation of those disputes. To the extent that they did, their management of future episodes of industrial conflict should be more productive, long-lasting and worthwhile. The crucial lesson, perhaps, is that every major industrial dispute, like all other episodes of serious human conflict involves suffering. That suffering seems to provide the essential practical basis for all human learning. *Il faut souffrir pour être belle.* If we must suffer in order to learn, we should certainly attempt to learn as much as we can from that suffering. Otherwise, we are destined to go on endlessly repeating our mistakes and will have to endure further needless suffering.

GUIDELINES FOR CONFLICT MANAGERS

Given that most industrial conflict is inevitable but not irreconcilable, what can be done to improve the management of industrial conflict? What should be the major concerns of those responsible for public and private policy-making in this critical area of socio-economic management? And what of those with prime responsibility for the management of industrial disputes: namely, general and line managers; personnel managers and industrial relations specialists; shop stewards; full-time trade union officials; and third parties, such as representatives of ACAS — conciliators, mediators, arbitrators and tribunal members — as well as management consultants, academic advisers and others? In the light of the lessons derived from this study, the following conclusions and guidelines are proposed for consideration by each of three groups:

Policy-makers

Cynicism must be resisted. There may be a strong temptation for private and public policy-makers to succumb to the cynical and dangerous view that since conflict is so widespread, so persistent and so inevitable, there is not much to be done about it. Policy-makers and opinion-formers — whether they be in government or the civil service, company directors or executive committee members of trade unions, third parties or independent consultants — generally recognize that advanced technology has greatly increased the interdependence and therefore the fragility of all liberal democratic societies. It should not require another Chernobyl, Bhopal or Soweso to remind us of the risks that we face in the field of environmental pollution. Multinational corporations and government agencies, no less than sovereign states, must be answerable to the international community for their handling (and mishandling) of environmental safety risk.

In a similar way, some recent industrial disputes in Britain — notably, the 1979 year-long lock-out at Times Newspapers, the protracted 1984–85 miners' strike, the grievous 1985–87 teachers' dispute and the bitter printing dispute at the 'Fortress Wapping' plant of News International — all bear witness to the fact that human life soon becomes intolerable in societies where conflict is *not* better managed and brought to a swift and socially-acceptable conclusion.

This is not a cause for despair but for hope, based on the realistic assumption that most, but not all, industrial disputes are susceptible to more intelligent management and are capable of being brought to final compromise resolution with more socially-acceptable outcomes, provided that the protagonists are willing to learn and to apply the lessons of experience.

In no sense is it being argued here that such intractable conflict is inherently anti-social and therefore intolerable, or that all such conflict is susceptible to settlement by compromise. The immanent risk of social conflict is the price paid by citizens of a liberal democratic society for the right to be different, to disagree, to protest and to struggle for the promotion of ideas and values that are not always popular or acceptable to the government or other power-holders in society.

Nevertheless, industrial conflict must have its limits, if societies are to remain even moderately civilized. In the words of one veteran British trade union leader, hardened by industrial conflict:

> *The strike is a very delicate weapon. Sometimes a short, sharp strike is a good safety valve. But long strikes are of no use to union or nation.* [4]

Private and public policy-makers must address themselves more assiduously to the prevention and reconciliation of major industrial conflict.

Most major industrial disputes in Britain are now initiated by management, not unions. Policy-makers should need no reminder that, for forty post-war years, the principal initiators of major industrial disputes were employees and unions, who took the offensive in post-war conditions of full employment to secure improved real pay and working conditions for their members for the first time this century. That trend has now been largely reversed. It is now mostly employers who are on the offensive, seeking to recover the ground lost by their predecessors in the post-war decades through inadvertence or the lack of a strategic approach to the management of their labour problems. It is also worth noting that managements are generally less used to being thwarted than trade unions. Avoidance tactics, expedient compromises and fudged solutions to the fundamental problems of productivity, performance and profitability are the hallmarks of weak management. Policy-makers must urge management (and unions) to adopt radical policies for achieving fundamental, not cosmetic, changes.

Prevention is better than cure, and rewards for good industrial behaviour produce better results than punishments for bad behaviour. Policy-makers should be more concerned with preventing industrial disputes than with settling them, although ultimately they must be concerned with both preventative and remedial action. Too little attention had been given to the development of more imaginative forms of pro-active third party intervention until the arrival of Japanese corporations with their newly-discovered predeliction for single-union, 'no-strike' deals, including final-stage pendulum arbitration. Sid Kessler, a leading British academic participant–observer of third party intervention, recently pointed out that creative arbitration and other forms of pro-active third party intervention have yet to be exploited fully in the management of industrial conflict. [5]

Though conflict may be *destructive*, its *constructive* potential should always be recognized. Policy-makers must aim to curb destructive conflict, but they should also acknowledge that constructive conflict has much to contribute to a healthy economy and a dynamic society. Public policy should seek to create a supportive environment in which the parties to an industrial dispute exploit their opportunities to resolve their genuine, long-standing and unresolved differences. Long drawn-out disputes that fail to resolve such underlying differences are sterile and wasteful of human energy.

Employers and managers

An industrial dispute should be avoided wherever possible. A week's stoppage of work or a month's overtime ban usually costs more than a year spent talking about a single contentious issue. If protracted negotiations begin to seem flat, stale, tedious and unprofitable to employers, it is worth remembering that most industrial disputes are eventually settled round the negotiating table.

Everything possible should be done to contain the conflict. Employers should seek to contain the conflict within some well-defined geographical or organizational zone and not allow it to spread by contagion. Employers should immediately warn full-time union officers of the risk of a protracted, widespread work stoppage, involving even more of their members. This is a high priority exercise in damage-limitation. Other things being equal, the less extensive the conflict, the sooner it is ended.

No action should be threatened or taken that might give non-involved employees an excuse to join in the dispute. Employers often claim that many employees prefer to take no part in industrial action, but these employees may come under considerable pressure from strikers to support their cause by taking sympathetic or solidaristic action. Nothing provocative should be done by management in these circumstances, e.g. threat of subsequent disciplinary action, because it might drive these employees into the 'enemy camp'. Even when strikers succeed in involving employees who have no material interest in the outcome of the dispute, employers and managers should remain calm and remember that such involvement may serve merely to dilute the strength of the strikers' grievance and so facilitate the search for a negotiated settlement.

The legitimacy of the other side should never be questioned. Attempts by one party in an industrial dispute to throw doubt on the legitimate right of the other party to advance claims or present grievances is unhelpful to the resolution of the conflict. Most industrial action is founded on genuine, long-standing and unresolved grievances and must therefore be taken seriously by employers and managers.

The fullest use should be made of intelligence networks. Each side in an industrial dispute must seek to discover what the other side plans to do next and move swiftly to neutralize the effect of such plans. Employers and managers are nearly always better resourced to exploit intelligence networks and should feel no moral compunction in exploiting this technical advantage.

Every strategic and tactical move by the other side should be monitored and analysed. Management must learn to interpret and understand the union's past moves as the first step towards anticipating and neutralizing the effects of its future moves. Familiar patterns of behaviour will emerge, which often betray future intentions. Most individuals and groups tend to repeat strategies and tactics that have proved successful in past disputes and are reluctant to embark on more ambitious or less certain courses of action.

The media should be treated as a potential ally in harnessing public opinion. Employers and managers should be constantly ready and willing to meet the press and other media, keeping them well briefed on the management side of the dispute. The aim should be to assist the media to win and retain public opinion for management's side of the dispute.

Formal negotiations should never take place under duress. Employers must resist the temptation to meet the union side in order to end the dispute at any cost. This plays directly into the hands of the union side who will treat such negotiations under duress as a successful tactic, to be repeated on subsequent occasions. Employers have a clear, long-term interest in resisting such pressure because concessions made under duress have no moral validity. They should nevertheless be seen to be ready and willing at all times to meet the other side for informal 'talks about talks' on how to end the dispute peacefully.

No action should be taken that deliberately sets out to humiliate the other side. Attempts to make the other side look ridiculous in the eyes of its own members often backfire and are generally counter-productive. The long-term relationship between the parties needs to be cherished and assiduously cultivated. As Prime Minister Clement Attlee once advised the future Prime Minister, James Callaghan:

> *Don't insult a man today if you have to negotiate with him tomorrow.* [6]

Both sides should recognize that they will want to resume their former cooperative relationship when the dispute is over.

Disputes should be brought to an end as quickly as possible. This objective may be self-evident but employers and managers should not appear overzealous. Any premature indication of a willingness to compromise may be misinterpreted as a sign of weakness and serve merely to prolong the dispute.

Neither side should issue idle threats or make empty promises. Employers and managers should exercise self-restraint and not indulge in the temptation to threaten actions which they may not subsequently be able to implement. This simply destroys management's credibility as a dependable bargaining partner in future disputes. Strikers have long memories and do not easily forgive or forget.

One senior manager should be assigned overall responsibility for the dispute. Nothing is better calculated to weaken management's resolve than poor coordination and lack of clear leadership in an industrial dispute. The successful management of a major dispute requires the setting up of an Incident Room or Control Centre, through which all essential information on the dispute is gathered, checked, evaluated and disseminated.

A complete and accurate log of events should be kept throughout the dispute. An accurate log helps management to maintain control and plot developments whilst a protracted dispute is in progress. At the end of the dispute, the log should enable management to prepare a retrospective analysis of the dispute to ensure that its important lessons are clearly identified and thoroughly learned.

Management should never underestimate the union's will-to-win. Employers sometimes fail to give the union side sufficient credit for being able to detect or anticipate management's new moves, even when they confidently expect to be able to anticipate future union moves. The union side's will-to-win should never be underestimated by employers and managers. When you *overestimate* your opponent, you *flatter* him; when you *underestimate* your opponent, he may well *flatten* you.

Public wrangles or disagreements amongst management must be avoided if at all possible. Nothing reduces management's credibility more than divisions within its own ranks. Intra-organizational differences may be unavoidable, but they should be argued out behind firmly-closed doors. Thereafter, a united front should prevail. Any inadvertent breaches should be dealt with immediately and severely.

Any wrangles, rifts or schismatic tendencies on the union side should be exploited fully. Differences will almost inevitably arise on the union side because unions are less able to exercise hierarchical control than management. Employers may be able to exploit such divisions but should beware of creating a unified backlash. The classic tactical device of *Divide et impera* (*Divide and rule*) is as powerful and valid today as it was in Caesar's time.

Employers should never lose sight of Murphy's Law. Murphy, the legendary Irish philosopher and management consultant, propounded a series of 'laws', evidently based on his own direct experience of advising managers in industrial disputes. It may be sufficient here to remind employers and managers of just two of Murphy's Laws:

(i) Whatever it is you wish to do, you will invariably have to do something else first.
(ii) If things can go wrong, they will.

A sense of humour and proportion are the most valuable assets in the successful management of industrial disputes. During the darkest days of an industrial dispute, employers and managers would do well to remind themselves that, in the field of human and industrial conflict, outcomes are seldom as tragic or as triumphant as they might first appear. One useful psychological device is to project mentally beyond the dispute to its aftermath and to concentrate on extracting the optimum yield from the current dispute in order to prevent its possible recurrence.

Employees and unions

An industrial dispute should be avoided wherever possible. A year spent in negotiating over a single contentious issue costs the union and its members less than a single weeks' stoppage of work or a month's overtime ban. A short, sharp strike may enforce a strongly-held claim or grievance, but a sequence of short, effective negotiating steps will cost members even less.

Unions should give employers the clearest possible indication of the strength of its members' feeling behind a claim or grievance. Unions may consider mounting some token action, if necessary, to bring home to management its members' serious intent. Unions should remember that most employers would rather compromise than face an all-out strike.

A short effective strike may prove a good investment. Where the employer proves obdurate — and provided employees are sufficiently aggrieved and genuinely committed to action — the imposition of short, sharp economic sanctions may prove a worthwhile investment. These sanctions may well assist the union to secure management concessions on behalf of its members and help to ensure union control of the bargaining agenda.

The risks of becoming bogged down in a protracted stoppage should be avoided at all costs. Union officers should remind shopfloor leaders that the application of selective, intermittent or escalating economic sanctions, such as an overtime ban or work-to-rule, may prove more effective than an all-out, open-ended work stoppage and be far less expensive to rank-and-file members.

Union leaders should prefer selective action to all-out action wherever possible. A selective stoppage by a strategically-placed workgroup may cause more disruption to an integrated production or service system than an all-out stoppage by all the non-strategic workgroups taken together. Information systems personnel, key maintenance staff, internal and external transport drivers, packers and despatchers, and security personnel are all highly strategic groups. It pays the union to see them well-organized.

The conflict should not be extended prematurely. There is a strong temptation, at the outset of an industrial dispute, for aggrieved employees to try to involve other employees, who have no material interest in the outcome of the dispute. They would do well to remember that such employees may easily take over the dispute and try to bring it to a premature conclusion by voting for an early return to normal working, against the wishes and best interests of the original strikers.

External union resources should be mobilized fully. Employees about to take strike action should seek official union backing for their dispute as soon as possible. Strikers should be reminded, however, that union officers have their own interests and priorities and so may not respond as enthusiastically or as urgently as the strikers might wish. Self-reliance is a virtue, but solidarity achieves better results in the short run and helps to forge invaluable alliances in the long run.

Unions and union members should avoid becoming entangled with the law. Union members who engage in industrial conflict would do best to act always within the framework of the law that defines the rights and duties of employers and employees, unions and management, in British industrial disputes. For example, they should seek to ensure a clear majority at ballot in favour of industrial action. But this is a counsel of perfection. There may well be times when the law is knowingly broken by union members because they cannot tolerate the law's delay and need to take immediate action in defence of their collective interests. The potential costs of such unlawful action should be weighed carefully before any precipitate moves are made.

Court orders and injunctions should be complied with immediately to ensure that strikers remain within the law. If the employer invokes the law against his employees or the unions representing them, it is nearly always best for the union first to comply with the law and then to seek to remotivate its members by renewing its case against the court's pro-employer ruling. Court orders ('injunctions' in England and Wales; 'interdicts' in Scotland) that are ignored can result in 'contempt of court' proceedings, whose consequences may prove extremely painful for those required to 'purge' their contempt. Court orders should therefore be taken seriously.

If no substantial support exists, it may be better to postpone or even to abandon the idea of industrial action. Aggrieved employees and union members should remember that there is nearly always another day and another way to achieve their long-term objectives in the face of an employer's refusal to meet a claim or redress a grievance. In fact, there may be an even better opportunity to secure concessions on some other issue that is waiting in the wings to be dealt with.

Any attempt by the employer to make common cause with full-time union officers should be anticipated and forestalled. As Wright Mills reminded us: Trade union leaders are 'the managers of discontent' — they create discontent and then they sit on it [7]. In other words, bureaucrats on both sides of an industrial dispute have their own vested interests in settling the dispute, quite apart from the interests of those who initiate strike action. Three general rules of thumb in industrial disputes are:

(i)   *Employees vs. Management + Unions = Employees lose*
(ii) *Employees + Unions vs. Management = Employees win*
(iii) *Employees + Unions vs. Management + The State = Employees lose*

Unions should resist being provoked into reckless retaliation. Employees and unions should recognize from the outset that the employer is normally far better placed to endure a long strike than they are themselves. But an employer may nevertheless mount some provocative action in an attempt to bring about the sudden collapse of a dispute. Whatever the provocation, employees and unions should seek to avoid reckless retaliation. Such actions may well be read as indications of desperation. Far better for employees and unions to bide their time and take responsive action only when adequately prepared. In the words of a well-known management maxim: *Don't get mad, get even.*

Attempts by management to persuade union members to call off industrial action before they have secured their essential objectives should be resisted. Experienced shopfloor leaders know that once strikers return to work, it is much more difficult to get them out again for the same cause. Managers will understandably seek to exploit every opportunity to bring the dispute to an end before the central issues have been settled. All such attempts must be avoided and strikers should seek to obtain the required concessions from the employer in writing before they return to normal working.

Unions should go out of their way to cultivate the media. Despite their worst fears that some journalists and editors may deliberately distort the employees' case or misrepresent the union position, it may well be that, on balance, bad publicity is better than no publicity. Union members should learn to make use of the media, especially radio and television, to put their case across accurately to the widest possible audience and to keep the dispute in the public eye.

Union negotiators should always be ready (and be seen to be ready and willing) to compromise. If union leaders consider it unlikely that they can achieve all or most of their essential policy objectives, it may be better to compromise than to continue the struggle without the prospect of gaining eventual victory. Folk wisdom suggests that there are more than a dozen ways to skin a cat.

In a protracted dispute, the morale of the strikers should be maintained by regular or frequent meetings. Union negotiators should avoid offering hostages to fortune. They should pre-empt the natural tendency for disaffection to develop in any protracted dispute; head-off any premature unofficial move for a return to work without having secured essential objectives; and anticipate the presence of management spies or informers at union meetings.

Union negotiators should endeavour to maintain some unofficial lines of communication with the employer's side throughout a protracted dispute. An important maxim amongst professional negotiators is to avoid negotiating under duress. This does not mean, however, that they lose touch with the other side in a protracted dispute. Fast and effective communication links should always be maintained, if necessary through the agency of an intermediary (e.g. a representative of the Employers' Association; a member of ACAS staff; a member of the clergy). It is well to remember that in most cases, sooner or later, talks will have to take place.

Union leaders should appeal to the wider labour movement for active support. The principle of solidaristic action in the face of a flagrant injustice underpins the labour movement. It is regularly and success-fully invoked by shopfloor activists, but union leaders should not assume that such support will be forthcoming automatically. They would do well to remember that charity begins at home and should therefore beware of 'outsiders' who seek to take over the dispute for their own ends. Genuine supporters should be welcomed warmly but 'friends' who come bearing extravagant gifts should be distrusted initially.

Union leaders should not be surprised by the level of emotion that the dispute may arouse. Any industrial dispute is likely to be a highly-charged emotional event in the lives of ordinary working people. Too much emotion, like too much alcohol, may impair the intellect, leading to poor decision-making and irrational or irresponsible behav-iour. But intelligent emotion may be harnessed to good effect. Good humour and a sense of proportion are invaluable weapons in combating excessive optimism, pessimism or battle-fatigue in long, drawn-out or bitter disputes.

Union leaders should remember that Murphy's Law applies just as much to the union side of industrial conflict as it does to the manage-ment side. Whatever trade union leaders want to do, they will invariably have to do something else first. And, if things can go wrong for union leaders, they almost inevitably will.

Third parties

Third parties should seek to produce an environment in which differ-ences are openly admitted and discussed. Where conflict is suppressed, freedom is denied and resistance often goes underground where it is much more difficult to manage and resolve. The issues in dispute should therefore remain on the table and the parties should keep talking up to the very last moment, in the hope that conflict may still be averted. In industrial relations, eleventh-hour conversions are a sign of strength and should always be encouraged and welcomed.

Regular contact should be maintained with both sides throughout the dispute. Even though bilateral talks may have broken down, it is important that both sides are kept in touch through third party agencies. The significant breakthroughs in the most intractable disputes are often made indirectly, through unofficial, off-the-record contacts.

Conciliators, mediators and arbitrators should remain scrupulously even-handed. It is undesirable and even dangerous for a conciliator to be closer, or *seem* to be closer, to one side than the other. Regardless of the rights and wrongs involved, third parties should never take sides in an industrial dispute.

An arbitrator (whether public or private) should never seek to produce an arbitrated solution until all bilateral efforts to resolve the dispute have been exhausted. In the words of Sir Pat Lowry, Chairman of ACAS:

> *Arbitration will always remain the vital and indispensable instrument of last resort in dispute resolution. It can never be ignored. But there are perhaps other areas of industrial relations improvement that should be given greater priority. The need to resort to arbitration represents the failure of the collective bargaining process between employer and trade union and it is to better planning and greater consideration to improving the quality of collective bargaining itself that the greater attention should be paid.* [8]

Arbitration deliberately takes the dispute out of the hands of the principal protagonists, because they themselves can find no way of resolving their differences but still want the problem solved, one way or the other. For that reason — and with specific exceptions, such as job grading or equal value awards, where a process of 'educating' the parties is desirable — arbitrators should be discouraged from explaining the rationale for their decisions for fear of setting off a new round of the dispute.

The arbitrator's role is that of honourable peacemaker. Consistently good arbitrators are members of a rare species that should be protected and preserved. They speak with tongues of silver and are worth their weight in gold. Nothing should be done by individual arbitrators to bring the arbitration role itself into disrepute.

Third parties should conserve their role as catalytic change agents. Third party change agents require a first-class brain, the constitution of an ox, and one or two moral scruples — but no more. To devise acceptable compromise solutions to complex, intractable disputes, third party change agents need to be perceptive, creative and opportunistic. To get the support that they deserve, they should reserve their interventions to those occasions when their catalytic influence seems most likely to produce long-lasting and beneficial results.

Third parties should encourage both sides to make the clearest possible statement of their dispute objectives. It is much easier to work for a negotiated settlement where both sides understand each other — even though they may never agree — than where there is mutual misunderstanding. Third parties should therefore encourage both sides to spend as much time as necessary clarifying their respective positions at the earliest possible stage of the dispute.

Third parties should discourage precipitate action by either side, which may lead to costly errors. As in a game of chess, each side in an industrial dispute needs time to adjust to the other side's moves and decide how best to respond. Time-management is one of the least-studied dimensions of industrial conflict but one of the most valuable hidden resources available to experienced first, second or third party conflict managers.

Third parties should recognize that industrial disputes tend to develop their own internal momentum which adds to their problems of securing a resolution. Public policy requires third parties to bring disputes to an end as soon as possible. The paradox is, however, that premature attempts to initiate the peace process will usually fail because the parties are not yet ready. Third parties need to observe immaculate timing.

REFERENCES

1 Cf. Georg Wilhelm Hegel: *What experience and history teach is this — that people and governments never have learned anything from history, or acted on principles deduced from it* (Philosophy of History; Introduction). This theme was taken up by George Bernard Shaw in his *Preface* to *Heartbreak House*.
2 See the present author's *Managing Industrial Conflict: Seven Major North American Disputes 1968–88*, to be published in 1989.
3 For a more extended discussion of 'deliberate' and 'emergent' strategies, see Henry Mintzberg and James H. Waters: 'Of Strategies, Deliberate and Emergent', *Strategic Management Journal*, Vol. 6, No. 3, July–September 1985.
4 Terry Duffy, quoted in *The Financial Times*, 17 September 1979.
5 See Sid Kessler: 'Pendulum Arbitration' in *Personnel Management*, December 1987. For a more detailed examination of 'creative arbitration' and pro-active third party intervention, see the present author's *Managing Industrial Conflict: Theory, Practice and Policy*, Hutchinson, London, 1988.
6 James Callaghan: *Time and Chance*, Collins, Glasgow, 1987.
7 C. Wright Mills: *New Men of Power*, Harcourt, New York, 1949.
8 Sir Pat Lowry: *Arbitration: Past, Present and Future*, Second Strathclyde Lecture

on Industrial Relations, University of Strathclyde/The Institute of Personnel Management, April 1986, p. 13.

CHAPTER 11

■ Summary and conclusions

In his prophetic masterpiece, *Rossum's Universal Robots* (1920), the distinguished Czech dramatist, Karel Capek, created a futuristic world of benevolent industrial robots who relieve industrial workers of their toil, freeing their energies for such higher pursuits as love, art and literature. In the first act of the drama, everything goes well. The newly-created robots are obedient slaves, efficient and uncomplaining. By the second act, they begin to reveal the first signs of restlessness by questioning the orders of their masters. They soon exhibit many of the worst features of their human prototypes: vanity, greed, omniscience. By the end of the play, they have revolted against all human authority, taken complete control and enslaved their human masters in the process.

Capek makes a number of important sociological points in his pioneering science-fiction drama, acutely relevant to this study of industrial conflict management:

First — that human technical mastery is now so dazzling, we believe that we have become almost god-like in our ability to create machines that will do our bidding.

Second — that we are now so infatuated by science and technology that, far from exploiting its beneficent potential, we have become its slaves: instead of men and women having dominion over technology, technology has dominion over us!

Third — that if we persist in exploiting our fellow human beings — as if they were our robotic creations — then, like Rossum's Universal Robots, they will eventually revolt against their masters and, finally, in Marx's phrase, 'the expropriators will be expropriated'.

This study of the management of industrial conflict was written in the dawning of a new, robotic age of high technology and the ubiquitous chip. The new age promises a world of plenty, in which scarce energy resources can at last be utilized fully to satisfy more of man's limitless needs and wants. Technological imperatives will force the pace of organizational life, promoting changes in work structures, job content and employment relationships. These changes, which impact upon our expectations and satisfactions at work, will in turn produce significant long-term shifts in the balance of social power.

In short, new technology now makes it possible to conceive of a world of harmonious production, distribution and exchange that is capable of satisfying human needs and wants in ways only dreamed of on the wilder shores of science fiction. By the year 2000, that dream might be a reality. Why then does its realization seem so implausible?

Ludwig Feuerbach, the German materialist and Marx's tutor, said 'We are what we eat'. If the materialist conception of history is right, we are largely — though not entirely — the products, both physically and psychologically, of our material environment. By the twenty-first century, with its better-regulated international economy, supplying the abundant goods and services that the whole world now craves, it seems possible that man's competitive urge for material possessions and social status may have passed its zenith, to be replaced by more sociable feelings and more humanistic objectives. Robotic technology will come to serve us, instead of enslaving us as it has done hitherto.

Regrettably, the present writer sees little prospect of that dream being realized in the foreseeable future — another case, perhaps, of paradise postponed. For, as long as there are workers and managers, as long as men and women are employed in hierarchically-structured organizations, as long as there are employment relations as we presently understand them, it seems certain that there will be conflict at work over power-sharing in decision-making and over the terms that govern the economic collaboration underlying all employment relationships.

In short, industrial conflict is here to stay. Given that it is immanent, inevitable and ubiquitous in employment relations, that it is frequently destructive yet potentially constructive, how should we manage employment relations so as to avoid or at least reduce the destructive potential of industrial conflict? What more should be done, or done better or differently, to keep such conflict within reasonable bounds and to see that in future it is better managed by all concerned?

Looking back on recent major episodes of industrial conflict in Britain may help us to identify some positive and negative lessons on how conflict may be managed better in future.

In a companion study, *Managing Industrial Conflict: Theory, Practice and Policy* (Hutchinson, London, 1988), we examine the primary sources of industrial conflict and conclude that they comprise two essential demands on the part of workers — namely, a fairer deal at work in the form of a more equitable distribution of material rewards for work done or services rendered; and a more genuine voice in enterprise decision-making — and two no less important demands on the part of employers — namely, a greater commitment by employees to organizational goals; and a more open-minded and flexible attitude and cooperative approach towards change in working methods and work organization. Most of the industrial conflict that we are called upon to manage is inevitable, for the very reason that it centres on these highly emotive and contentious issues of human aspiration: social justice, organizational power-sharing, and decision-making.

We conclude this study by arguing optimistically that the human capacity for vicarious learning should enable us to extract worldwide lessons from the analysis of recent major episodes of industrial conflict. If we are then able to apply those lessons, we may avoid having to repeat our own history by re-entering 'the fire next time'.

A more sceptical view — that man is incorrigibly lazy and stupid, refusing to learn from his own past experience and that of others — implies that we are doomed to go on suffering the disruption, dislocation and distress of major industrial conflict, simply because we are incapable or unwilling to learn from our collective social history. That sceptical viewpoint is understandable but surely too cynical and ultimately wrong, for there are positive signs everywhere that, after the first two hundred turbulent years of industrialization, employers and employees in all of the advanced industrial societies — developed and developing, East and West — are seeking new and more intelligent ways of handling their inevitable differences.

This 'maturation process' — for contemporary employment relations are still far from being 'mature — has already been at work in Britain for some time. Despite several noteworthy exceptions (e.g. the miners' strike of 1984–85 and the teachers' pay dispute of 1986–87), the frequency, scale, duration and intensity of such work-related conflict has been reduced dramatically in recent years. There is now every prospect that, by the end of the century, the combined effect of new technology, new forms of work organization and new political pressures may have reduced further the level of industrial conflict. But such conflict will never completely disappear, for relative deprivation appears to be structured into human consciousness so that however skilful we may be at social engineering, we have yet to make a significant impact on the human condition of public squalor amid private affluence. There seem few prospects, in the foreseeable future, of closing the gap between man's insatiable, over-stimulated appetite and the world's finite stock of useful resources.

In Part II of this study, we offered an analysis of seven major British disputes in an attempt to discover why certain episodes of conflict appear to be managed better than others; why they develop in such different directions; and why they eventually reach such very different outcomes. The particular episodes of conflict selected for analysis covered both management and union-initiated disputes, in the private and public sectors of Britain's growing and declining industries. Without constituting a scientifically representative sample, these seven major disputes are sufficiently diverse in their origins, their subject matter, their evolutions and their outcomes to yield rich lessons for students of industrial conflict management.

In Part III, we began by extracting the lessons of experience from our analysis of these seven disputes. We identified a range of facilitating and inhibiting factors, which together contribute to the successful management of industrial conflict — from the identification of the more-obvious factors, such as physical preparedness and psychological determination (the all-important 'will-to-win'), to some less-obvious factors, such as the combined pursuit of 'deliberate' plus 'emergent' strategies and an ever-ready willingness to seek a resolution of the dispute through the process of negotiation and compromise.

No one single factor emerges as being critical in determining the eventual outcome of an industrial dispute. Six interrelated factors are of paramount importance in industrial dispute management. These factors are:

(i)   a set of realistic and clearly-articulated policy objectives;
(ii)   a 'determined' (or 'deliberate') strategy that prescribes the best means of achieving those objectives;
(iii)   the moral strength and inner resources that encapsulate the successful protagonist's 'will-to-win';
(iv)   sound intelligence networks to assist with tactical action
(v)   a 'flexible' (or 'emergent') strategy, responsive to environmental changes;
(vi)   good timing, from the initiation of the dispute to its climax.

We conclude this study on managing industrial conflict with the observation that human societies are incapable of avoiding conflict, because the individuals and collective interest groups that make up those societies have yet to evolve an equally efficient, widely-accepted alternative method of resolving legitimate differences of interest, of ideology and of values. Societies that deny the legitimacy of such conflict also deny their citizens the full measure of their human freedom.

In advanced democracies, the force of argument is still upheld as the best means of avoiding and, where necessary, of resolving those conflicts that inevitably arise in the course of employment relations. Where the force of argument fails, the argument of force may be invoked. But the resort to direct action in an industrial dispute — whether by economic sanctions, physical force, psychological pressure or other forms of coercion — can only be tolerated within certain limits, as periodically defined by the state. Strikes, lock-outs and less dramatic forms of industrial sanction cannot go unregulated, because they are capable of inflicting immense damage on individuals, on working groups, on work communities, and on local, regional and national economies.

It is therefore incumbent upon those responsible for the conduct of employment relationships to understand and accept that some measure of industrial conflict is unavoidable and perhaps even desirable. For that very reason, policies must be devised within both the private and public sectors to anticipate the possibility of such conflict and to avoid it wherever possible — but, as a last resort and above all, to manage industrial conflict more intelligently and successfully than it has been managed in the past.

The art of managing industrial conflict — for there are no sovereign remedies and, as yet, no scientific principles — can only be derived from the experience of such conflict. Yet it may be possible to learn vicariously by consulting the experience of others. The whole of human experience is available as our data-base. We may study philosophy, history, politics, psychology, economics, literature, law or sociology. Each of these academic disciplines has some distinctive light to shed, some insights to offer the student of industrial conflict management. Military history, national and international politics and sporting contests should not be overlooked, for they each share in the character of organized conflict between competing interest groups. For the most part, such groups prefer to devise and work within their own rules, to resolve their differences by means of 'the diplomatic use of force' — the restrained and most effective use of power. Where protracted or severely disruptive disputes threaten the social fabric, supplementary means must be made available — such as conciliation, mediation and arbitration — and these may sometimes have to be imposed on the parties in dispute. For, in the words of Lord Salisbury:

> *The broad distinction between a civilized and an uncivilized community is this — that in a civilized community individuals or parties of men who quarrel submit their differences to an arbitrator, while in savage states they fight it out.* [1]

It is clearly preferable if 'the parties of men who quarrel' in advanced democracies agree to submit all their unresolvable differences to the judicious arbitrament of impartial umpires. Unfortunately, recent experience with some forms of arbitration has not encouraged either management or unions to conclude agreements that provide for binding arbitration where collective bargaining fails to resolve their differences. Arbitrators have been 'leaned upon' by governments; arbitration machinery has been wound up; arbitrators' decisions have sometimes been ignored, or their findings set aside, or the implementation of their decisions delayed or phased over a lengthy period. All such actions serve to bring the arbitration process into disrepute. There is still much public education to be done in the field of arbitration, yet it must always be open to management and unions in a free society to 'battle out' their differences, provided the public interest is safeguarded by the State.

Meantime, we are surrounded on all sides by episodes of industrial conflict from which lessons may be learned. We need to learn those lessons. For, in industrial relations, as in other fields of social interaction, we need to come to terms with the past, to interpret and to understand it, in order to cope with the present and to make intelligent provision for the future. We need to develop better theories, which will enable us to understand the conduct and predict the outcomes of future episodes of industrial conflict. [2] We need to master the strategies and tactics that the parties choose to help them to achieve their objectives. Above all, we need to understand why some strategies and tactics succeed whilst others fail. This study is offered as a modest contribution towards that goal.

REFERENCES

1 Lord Salisbury, cited by Sir Pat Lowry: *Arbitration: Past, Present and Future*, Second Strathclyde Lecture on Industrial Relations, University of Strathclyde/ The Institute of Personnel Management, April 1986, p. 13.
2 For a more extended discussion, see the present author's *Managing Industrial Conflict: Theory, Practice and Policy*, Hutchinson, London, 1988.

■ Index